THE
ROCK
& ROLL
BOOK OF THE DEAD

John Lennon, on Dakota rooftop overlooking Central Park,
February 1975. (Photo by Brian Hamill/Getty Images)

THE
ROCK
& ROLL
BOOK OF THE DEAD

The Fatal Journeys of Rock's Seven Immortals
DAVID COMFORT

CITADEL PRESS
Kensington Publishing Corp.
www.Kensingtonbooks.com

CITADEL PRESS BOOKS are published by

Kensington Publishing Corp.
119 West 40th Street
New York, NY 10018

All Kensington titles, imprints, and distributed lines are available at special quantity discounts for bulk purchases for sales promotions, premiums, fund-raising, educational, or institutional use. Special book excerpts or customized printings can also be created to fit specific needs. For details, write or phone the office of the Kensington special sales manager: Kensington Publishing Corp., 119 West 40th Street, New York, NY 10018, attn: Special Sales Department; phone 1-800-221-2647.

First printing: September 2009

10 9 8 7 6 5 4 3 2 1

Printed in the United States of America

Library of Congress Control Number: 2009923871

ISBN-13: 978-0-8065-3121-2
ISBN-10: 0-8065-3121-5

To Kathy

Contents

Acknowledgments

Many thanks to my intrepid agent, Frank Scatoni; to my brilliant editor, Richard Ember; to the courageous Michaela Hamilton; as well as to all the other wonderful people at Kensington. And for their input and encouragement, my deep gratitude to Dana Isaacson, Keythe Williams, Tom Murray, Patrick and Michelle Hillman, Rob and Sherry Robinson, and Rob Comfort.

Introduction

A truck driver, a bowling alley waitress, a janitor, a paratrooper, a homeless poet, a hippie guitar teacher, a penniless art student: all had humble beginnings. But the "Seven Immortals" or "Seven" were destined to become the pioneers of modern rock and roll—cultural icons, apostles of the pop Vatican, and more.

"We're more popular than Jesus Christ," said one about his group, later declaring that he was Jesus Christ—claims that later led to his murder.

"Jesus shouldn't have died so early," said another, "and then he would have gotten twice as much across."

Four died at twenty-seven years of age. Most had premonitions of an early end. "I'm gonna be dead in two years," declared one matter-of-factly at twenty-five. "I'm not sure I will live to be twenty-eight," said a second member of Club 27. "I'm never going to make it to thirty," predicted a third.

Death had haunted the lives of most since childhood. The mothers of two perished in car accidents. Two other mothers drank themselves to oblivion. At five years of age, one watched his father drown. Another star insisted that he had "suicide genes" due to his family members who had taken their own lives.

Each had a fatal attraction. "I'm going to be a superstar musician, kill myself, and go out in a flame of glory!" exclaimed one. He called his group Nirvana, defining the term as "the total peace of death." Another star, a student of *The Tibetan Book of the Dead* like many of the others, named his band the Grateful Dead. Another called his group the Doors, a gateway to the other world, and described his music as an "invitation to dark forces." Another living legend, obsessed with the specter of "instant karma," said that when he finally met the reaper "I'll grab him by both hollow cheeks and give him a big wet kiss right on his moldy teeth because that's the only way to go—headed into the wind and laughing your ass off!" Others had an irresistible curiosity about the netherworld. Observed the step-brother of the King of Rock and Roll himself, "It was like a fantasy to see how far he could go—almost as if he wanted to die—and come back, just to see the other side."

Though each of the Seven reached the pinnacle of fame in his or her brief lifetime, it was not until they self-destructed that they became sanctified as immortals. The courtship of each with death took on a life of its own that grew to mythological proportion in a kind of martyrdom for their fans.

"Maybe my audiences can enjoy my music more if they think I'm destroying myself," said the star who overdosed scores of times before the injection that finally brought her down in an L.A. hotel room. The next day she was scheduled to record the final vocal, *Buried Alive in the Blues*, for the greatest album of her career.

"It's funny the way most people love the dead," mused another immortal. ". . . You have to die before they think you are worth anything."

All Seven, save one, had attempted suicide or threatened it. All Seven became addicts. Most died of drug abuse. Had one not been fatally gunned down, he may well have met the same end.

"Man, I'm stoned ALL the time!" declared the poet who, like most of the others, had been warned by his doctors to dry out or die. Before his stunning debut at the Whisky a Go Go in L.A., he dropped ten times the normal dose of LSD. He was fond of quoting William Blake, "The road of excess leads to the palace of wisdom." His palace of wisdom became his graffitied mausoleum in Paris's Père Lachaise cemetery beside the graves of Oscar Wilde, Chopin, and Balzac.

The favorite pastime of another star was "to smoke dope, take dope, lick dope, suck dope, fuck dope." Friends warned her to slow down. "Aw, man, I don't want to live that way," she protested. "I want to burn. I want to smolder."

She and the first member of Club 27, famous for destroying his guitars, shot heroin together before making love. His appetite was no less than hers. Recalled a famous vocalist and druggie from another supergroup, "He was the heaviest doper I ever met."

Six of the Seven were busted repeatedly. Outlaws, rebels, evangelists of freedom, they were gloriously antiestablishment. The seventh stood alone, a law unto himself—he *was* the Establishment: the King.

President Nixon deputized him as a federal narcotics agent. Never did the King deign to a street drug. In the last twenty months of his life, he was prescribed twelve thousand narcotics.

Jimi Hendrix, Janis Joplin, Jim Morrison, Elvis Presley, John Lennon, Kurt Cobain, and Jerry Garcia were the icons of the greatest youth movement in history. The Seven arose in times of tragedy. The dreams of the sixties were shattered with the assassination of its youthful heroes: the Kennedys and Martin Luther King. A half-million soldiers were lost in Vietnam; other young people went down at Kent State, the Chicago Democratic Convention, and Altamont. It all occurred in the ominous shadow of the Bomb and the Cold War.

In the midst of this, the freedom cry was taken up by a new political, cultural, and artistic voice: that of the rock star. Pioneering an art form created by and for the young, stars sang about revolution and love. Their music expressed all the idealism, innocence, and boundless energy of youth, but at the same time all the alienation, confusion, fear, and violence. In this it foreshadowed the very same struggles that beset us today.

As the times grew darker, so did the music and lives of the torchbearers. As they pushed the bounds of freedom and rebellion further and further, they found themselves in the danger zone. Janis spoke for the others when she said she performed and lived "on the outer limits of probability" where there was no speed limit or safety net. In the ultimate irony, the more famous they became, the more isolated, lonely, and self-destructive they became. The Seven began to be consumed not only by their own isolation and excesses but by the wild, near divine expectations of their worshipful audiences. Without a doubt, these musicians were geniuses and voices of generations. But they were not gods. The usual fate of earthly deities, real or imagined, is well known: martyrdom.

Like so many current artists, all Seven had been obsessed with becoming stars. But once achieved, the stardom became a gilded cage for each. Drugs alone provided a temporary escape. And, in the end, a final emancipation.

"Instant Karma's gonna knock you right on the head," sang Lennon. "You better get yourself together. Pretty soon you're gonna be dead." He had always believed he would meet an early and violent end because he had led a violent life. Still, "I'm not afraid of dying," he insisted. "It's just like getting out of one car and into another." And so it was: he got out of a limousine and, moments later, was carried into a police car where he breathed his last breath.

Others seemed equally resigned to their fate. When hearing about the death of Jimi, his former lover, Janis, just said: "I wonder if I'll get as much publicity." She joined him six weeks later. Morrison toasted her at their favorite bar: "You're drinking with Number Three," he told his companions.

Ironically, it was one of the rock god survivors, Pete Townshend, who sang the anthem of the movement: "Hope I die before I get old."

But the reality of James Dean's "living fast, dying young, and leaving a good-looking corpse," did not equal the romance. After the years of excess, most had been living posthumously. "I felt so strongly for him I cried," confessed one of Elvis's security men after another disastrous Vegas performance. "He was fat. He couldn't walk. He forgot the words to his songs. I really thought he was going to die that night."

After seeing her at a ten-year high-school reunion, one of Janis's former classmates observed: "She looked like ten miles of bad road—her face, arms, veins. I didn't expect her to live very long."

Blues guitarist Johnny Winter, said of his friend, Hendrix, near the end: "When I saw him, it gave me the chills. . . . He came in with his entourage of people and it was like he was already dead."

As the careers of the Seven prove, being a living legend can be a heaven turned hell. But due to their overpowering ambitions, none realized the toxicity of fame until it was too late and each suffocated in their superhuman images. They died for their music just as surely as they had lived for it. Though the careers of most had been brief, in the end most were exhausted, drained, and burned out, just as we see so many stars today.

The pressures of super celebrity were no less crushing than they are now. The fans demanded that their stars continually create music that was revolutionary, new, and yet cloned from the old hits. They were expected to perform night after night, year after year, with the same level of artistry, energy, and enthusiasm. In spite of their resistance, they became commercial enterprises, hundreds and even thousands of employees depending on them. Being mobbed by fans, chased by paparazzi, and harassed by the press soon lost its novelty for them. They were surrounded by hangers-on, head cases, and unscrupulous handlers. Public commodities, they had little privacy and no time to themselves. They were expected to sustain theatric, even cartoonish, images, which they had long since outgrown or which they had never wanted to begin with.

"I'm so sick of everything," Morrison told an interviewer near his end. "People keep thinking of me as a rock and roll star, and I don't want anything to do with it. I can't stand it anymore."

After a lackluster Grateful Dead performance, the longest-lived of the Seven, Jerry Garcia, complained to his last keyboardist, Bruce Hornsby, "You don't understand twenty-five years of burnout!"

Only Lennon managed to "get off the merry-go-round." He went into a five-year seclusion. But no sooner had the Beatles' founder returned to the carnival, hoping "to conquer the world again," than he had his last ride.

In spite of the unprecedented fame of these luminaries, the last days of many are still shrouded in mystery. Critical questions remain, which we will closely examine in light of the most recent investigations.

In the end, Hendrix was trying to leave his manager who had embezzled millions from the star and who had extensive mafia connections. Did Jimi take the fatal dose of barbiturates and alcohol accidentally or intentionally, or were they forced on him? Why did his mysterious fiancée take hours to call an ambulance, vanish from their hotel room before the police arrived, and, later, after a court judgment against her, commit suicide?

Janis was finishing the greatest album of her career, after countless affairs she was at last engaged to the man of her dreams, and she was kicking her heroin addiction. At least, this is the official story. Was her overdose indeed just a "tragic accident," as many have called it?

Morrison had quit the Doors and was trying to resurrect as a poet, but found himself at a creative impasse. Though otherwise an omnivorous drunk and doper, he had always avoided heroin. Did he knowingly take a fatal overdose that night in Paris? Did his junkie wife who deceived the French police and arranged for a hasty burial, kill herself two years later out of some unspeakable guilt?

Two years after the King's demise, the real cause of his death was at last revealed. Or was it? He was taking a "miracle" drug that in high doses commonly causes suicidal depression. Moreover, for years he had been ingesting the powerful narcotics found in his system—all but one to which he knew he was dangerously allergic. He secured a bottle of this drug at an emergency midnight dental appointment hours before his death. Why?

While promoting his first album in five years, Lennon refused bodyguards or security of any kind in spite of death threats and dire predictions by his wife's oracles. Since his earlier political activism, the ex-Beatle had been under close FBI surveillance. Was his hero-worshipping assassin, Mark David Chapman, a Manchurian candidate? After years of mutual antagonism and infidelity, Yoko was secretly planning to divorce John after he helped launch her own solo album. Shortly before his murder, why did she and her usually cautious psychic "directionalists" send him through the Devil's Triangle in a small sloop?

Cobain was leaving Nirvana, divorcing Courtney Love, writing her out of his will, and preparing to petition for custody of their infant daughter. His lifeless body was found above his garage, a shotgun and a suicide note beside it. Yet handwriting analysts concluded that part of the note was a forgery. Moreover, according to the autopsy, three times the maximum lethal dose of heroin was present in the blood. How could Cobain have possibly pulled the trigger of the shotgun himself?

Much has been written about the legendary pioneers of rock music. But never before has a book been written which is a condensation of every extant biography, weaving diverse points of view of insiders—as well as the words and music of the stars themselves—into a single, dramatic tapestry.

We no longer live in an age of kings and queens. Our new aristocrats are celebrities. The kings and queens of our populist royalty are the superstars. Portraits of stars are often distorted to prevent any impact on royalties and survivors who depend on them. Or in spite of First Amendment protections, they are self-censored due to the threat of lawsuits intended to deny the public's right to know.

Generally, star biographies come in two varieties: the hagiography or the exposé. The first kind, often "authorized" by family, eulogizes its subject, enlarging on legend while euphemizing or ignoring critical information. The second kind, often denounced by insiders, pierces the façade, diminishing its subject, while overlooking the positives. Like kings and queens of old, stars have their subjects on one side and their enemies on the other—and both know that the pen can be mightier than the sword.

The greater truth of a historic personality is found in a judicious inclusion of faithful and critical perspectives—not in a rigid adherence to one or the other. So here, for the first time, these legendary personalities will be portrayed from an impartial point of view committed not to adulation or defamation, but to the truth. "Just gimme some truth now," sang John Lennon, on *Imagine*. "All I want is the truth." This work is dedicated to that call.

In both major and minor keys, the seven stars are revealed as brilliant and charismatic but complicated and conflicted human beings—very different from the legends we thought we knew. Yet, in the end, it is their very humanity and struggle that inspire our compassion and love, not their legend.

Each of the seven chapters that follow is a larger-than-life story of isolation and excess that led inexorably to an early end. The chapters are ordered chronologically, following the sequence of these deaths during what was the golden age of rock and roll. The interludes between these living stories trace the fatal undercurrents common to these historic artists—the lonely childhoods, the drug addictions, the mental instability, the disastrous relationships, and the consumptive celebrity.

Wrote the psychologist Carl Jung, "Great talents are the most lovely and often the most dangerous fruits on the tree of humanity. They hang upon the most slender twigs that are easily snapped off."

Extremism and destructiveness afflict many creative personalities, particularly the young. This is especially true in a performance art of explosive spectacle and sound that return us to our ancient, ceremonial, ecstatic roots. Rock and roll has always been about youth, freedom, the storming of the Bastille. In a word: revolution—not just political revolution, but living revolution.

"Elvis freed the body," declared Bruce Springsteen at his own induction into the Rock and Roll Hall of Fame, "Dylan freed the mind."

Performers are modern shamans, grand wizards, who deliver us into a new world of intoxicating energy and release. Real rock is dangerous: the "crossfire hurricane" of Jumpin' Jack Flash. At its peak, it is the Zen art of controlling the uncontrollable, of dancing the high wire without a net. And some pay the price.

By way of contrast, legendary survivors of rock will be examined: Mick Jagger and Keith Richards, the Narcissus and Lazarus of "The Greatest Rock and Roll Band in the World"; Eric Clapton, the Cream guitarist once known as "God"; Paul McCartney, the most prolific and successful composer of the twentieth century; Dylan, the greatest lyric poet of our time. Though they have seen many of the same life and career hardships, they have persevered where the others have not. Why?

Said Richards: "The legend part is easy. It's the living that's hard."
Said Jagger: "Either you're dead, or you move along."
Added Dylan: "Every day above ground is a good day."

As for the Seven, each lived under the brilliance of an eclipsing sun, which gave an otherworldly intensity and passion to their art and which, in the end, made each immortal.

1

JIMI HENDRIX

November 7, 1942–September 18, 1970

AFTER THE SALVATION

I died a thousand times in this group and was born again.
—Jimi Hendrix, speaking of the Experience

Hendrix is getting some much-needed rest after Woodstock. He recently closed the historic love and peace festival, playing his "Star-Spangled Banner" to what was left of a wasted, rain-soaked crowd. After his act, he collapsed offstage and was choppered back to his nearby estate, Shokan House, where he slept for three days.

The Experience had disbanded a month earlier. Jimi's bassist, Noel Redding, had left the group, exhausted from the last tour. "We stopped making music and started doing time," he later wrote. ". . . We got through it by constantly telling ourselves, 'This is our last American tour. We can do it. We'll survive, we'll survive'—when we felt like death warmed up."[1]

Which is how Jimi himself felt after Woodstock.

The spring and summer of '69 had been punishing. At the end of the American tour, he was busted in Toronto for heroin possession. Then

---

1. Noel Redding and Carol Appleby, *Are You Experienced?: The Inside Story of the Jimi Hendrix Experience* (New York: De Capo, 1990).

his friend and champion, Rolling Stone, Brian Jones, was drowned in his swimming pool. And, the Experience imploded. But that wasn't the worst. After three revolutionary albums and more than two years of relentless touring, he feared that he was washed up. "The pressure from the public to create something even more brilliant each time, while basically expecting us to stay the same," wrote Redding, "was crushing." Besides, a fundamental rift had developed in the group. "Jimi wanted to be a star, I wanted to be a musician," Redding went on. "My most wonderful dream was becoming the most nightmarish imposition."

Jimi replaced the bassist with Billy Cox. Even before Woodstock, he confessed to his old army buddy that his creativity had run dry. Though he hoped to resurrect from the Experience with the Band of Gypsys, he confessed the same fears to the new drummer, Buddy Miles, another old friend. "Jimi was not happy," confided Buddy. "He felt powerless. He couldn't do what he wanted to do. So he missed meetings, he missed gigs. He could be a real bastard. Sometimes, when he didn't want to rehearse, one of the things he'd do was to get real stoned, really high; didn't want to talk to anyone. He used the drugs to put up a barrier."

Though Jimi insisted that the heroin had been planted on him in Toronto, he dreaded the upcoming trial, certain that he would be convicted and his career ruined.

But for now he's trying to forget all this at Shokan House. He spends his day here at his favorite distractions: fixing, entertaining his female admirers, and driving around in his silver Corvette, trying not to total it as he has all the others.

His Woodstock vacation has hardly begun before it is interrupted when a black limousine speeds up to the mansion. His manager, Mike Jeffery, a nattily dressed, mustachioed little Brit in shades, jumps out, flanked by two stocky bodyguards in dark suits. The assistants take up positions at the house exits as Jeffery hurries upstairs to his star's bedroom. He's tried to phone, but Jimi always seems to be unavailable. It's early afternoon now, about the time the guitarist usually gets up.

Upstairs, Jeffery offers his client some wake-up blow. The two used to drop acid together and discuss the zodiac; now they just share business pharmaceuticals and talk shop. Downstairs, Cox, Miles, and other houseguests have their eye on the two suits covering the front and back door. Though they look like feds, nobody's headed to the bathroom to flush their stash.

After powdering his nose, Jeffery breaks more bad news to his star: Electric Ladyland is high and dry again. They've poured $300,000 into Jimi's dream project, the state-of-the-art recording studio in New York, but it's already exhausted. They need another three. Hendrix knows he's grossing $100,000 per gig now, he's done over four hundred shows in the last two years, and he's got three gold albums. So another three hundred grand seems a modest figure. He tells Jeffery to cut a check, but is suddenly interrupted.

Outside, his manager's men are blasting a tree with their Berettas.

"We don't have the bloody bread right now," confesses Jeffery who packs his own piece in a custom, kidskin shoulder holster under his double-breasted blazer. He mentions rising tour overheads, getting shorted by local promoters, paying the exorbitant legal tab for Toronto, not to mention the mounting expenses for Stingrays, Stratocasters, and Bolivian imports.

Jimi spaces, thinking of Redding again. The bassist made no secret of why he was splitting the Experience. More than just being burned out from touring, he was fed up collecting a pittance for being "treated like shit." "It would be nice to know what they did with the money," Redding—who would become a penniless woodcutter—later wrote, estimating that the Experience had earned $30 to $40 million.

Jimi is wondering the same thing himself now, and not for the first time. He's heard the rumors from his other handlers: that Jeffery's secretary has been taking regular flights to Majorca and the Grand Caymans, stockings stuffed with money, and that he's had to take out some high-interest loans to cover the losses of his British and Spanish nightclubs. And that, only a few days ago, one of Jeffery's creditors promised him a bullet in the head if he didn't cover his balance.

But Jimi doesn't like confrontations, business or personal. He tried to fire Jeffery only months ago, but wound up backing down, reasoning, "The devil you know is better than the one you don't."

"All we need's a couple more gigs, mate," Jeffery assures him in his Cockney drawl as the target practice continues outside. "Just for the studio."

This is exactly what the exhausted star doesn't want to hear. But he says he'll think about it. Just as long as he can have a little more time to get his head together. His doctor tells him he's got ulcers and his liver's about gone too.

Leaving, Jeffery adds one last thing. The owners of the Electric Ladyland real estate on East 8th in the Village refuse to sell the studio space, only offering a five-year lease. But they might reconsider if Jimi agrees to play an establishment of theirs in the area, The Salvation Club. The proprietor, Bobby Woods, is a friend of Hendrix's. He's also his coke dealer.

"What the fuck," says Jimi wearily, glancing out the window at the shooting gallery again and reaching for the last of his blow. "For Bobby—cool."

Two weeks later, Hendrix does The Salvation. The show is billed as "The Black Roman Orgy." The sound system sucks, the audience begins walking out after only a few numbers, and the members of his makeshift band, Gypsy Sons and Rainbows—mostly refugees from the Buddy Miles Express—are threatening to kill each other. Also, behind the bar, there seems to be some heavy shit going down between Woods and his manager, Johnny Riccobono, of the Gambino family. Besides that, Jimi can't get his guitar tuned, and Riccobono's goons keep yelling "Foxy Lady!"

He snatches the mike. "Just leave me the fuck alone and make all the goddamn money you want!"

During the break he has another row with his manager. Jeffery begs him to get Redding and the Experience back together for a ten-gig tour in the northeast; Jimi tells him no, he's fried, the Experience is dead anyway, and Jeffery storms out. His friend, Eric Burdon of the Animals, Jeffery's former client, had warned him about Jeffery, and now Hendrix is starting to wish he'd listened.

After the Salvation gig, Jimi takes a ride with Bobby to score some much-needed medication. The next morning, the NYPD shovels the dealer's bullet-ridden body off 8th Avenue. That night, the composer of "Machine Gun," unaware of the news, is thrown into a car outside of another club. Soon he finds himself in an abandoned warehouse, blindfolded and gagged, with a .38 to his head. He is told that he'll be joining Woods unless he signs his contract over to new Gambino-friendly management.

The guitarist is experiencing déjà vu all over again. Last year when trying to collect his fee after the Underground Pop Festival in Miami, he was backed out of the CFO's office with a .12 gauge to his chest. "I think you'll wait, Mr. Hendrix," said the treasurer. Months later, when he refused to let his Gambino opening act, The Vanilla Fudge, use his gear, another businessman pulled a revolver and asked him to reconsider. Jimi reconsidered.

"I pick up my axe and fight like a bomber now," he sang, "but you still blast me down to the ground."

Two days after the abduction, he is back upstate at his Woodstock compound under what his captors call "house arrest." Suddenly, a black sedan screams up, three suits jump out, they smash through the back door, then empty their clips in the wake of the captors' getaway car. It's almost like Hollywood. Hendrix later confides to his friend, musician Curtis Knight: "I was taken to some deserted building and made to believe that they really intended to hurt me. They never did tell me why they abducted me. The whole thing seemed very mysterious when I was rescued."[2]

Soon, Jimi confesses a paranoid fantasy to his best friend, Billy Cox: what if his very own manager is behind the kidnap and rescue? And what if Jeffery masterminded the Toronto bust too—planting the smack on him? Jeffery often boasts of his premanagement career as a covert op for British Intelligence—of murder, mayhem, and mind games in Cold War cities. He is fluent in Russian, and to discourage frivolous audits, keeps all his business records in that language.

After Hendrix confides his suspicions of Jeffery to his bass player, Cox quits the group. "There's too much bullshit going on all around Jimi," he explains.

Hendrix is ready to cash it in too. "I don't want to be a clown anymore. I don't want to be a rock and roll star," he tells Rolling Stone magazine after his kidnap.

But after laying low and chilling for a few weeks, Hendrix changes his mind and forms the Band of Gypsys. He pleads with Billy to come aboard. The bassist, against his better judgment, does so, completing the trio with Buddy Miles.

The all-black Band of Gypsys is short-lived. At Jeffery's urging, it is replaced by a new Experience with Mitchell back on drums and Cox on bass. Late the following summer, 1970, Cox is slipped some bad acid at a performance in Sweden. Unaccustomed to psychedelics, the bassist is hospitalized and administered Thorazine, a powerful antipsychotic sedative. After his release, Cox remains acutely paranoid. Jimi flies his old friend to London and nurses him in a hotel.

---

2. Alex Constantine, *The Covert War Against Rock: What You Don't Know About the Deaths of Jim Morrison, Tupac Shakur, Michael Hutchence, Brian Jones, Jimi Hendrix, Phil Ochs, Bob Marley, Peter Tosh, John Lennon* (Venice, CA: Feral House, 2000).

"We're gonna die!" Billy keeps babbling. "We're not gonna get outta this place alive! It's a frame-up. We're gonna die!"

"NOBODY is going to die!" Jimi keeps telling him.

Days later, Cox arrives in the States alive, but barely. Jimi is in the back of a London ambulance, soaked with vomit and red wine, soiled bedsheets wrapped around him mummy-like. The paramedics have tried to revive him, but it's only a formality. They know he's been dead for some time. Having never seen a body in this condition, they can't imagine what has happened.

But the truth is far worse than their imagination.

ELECTRIC RELIGION

> When I get up on stage—well, that's my whole life. That's my religion. My music is electric church music. I am electric religion.
> —Jimi Hendrix

In the fall of 1961, Private Billy Cox was walking past the service club one day at Fort Campbell, Kentucky, when he heard some explosive riffs inside. Entering, he introduced himself to Private James Marshall Hendrix and told him he was a bass player. Jimi was a Screamin' Eagle paratrooper with the 101st Airborne. He was playing "Betty Jean," his red electric Danelectro guitar named after his sweetheart back home in Seattle, Washington. He told Billy he was just fooling with Betty Jean, trying to get the sounds of jump school out of her: the thundering plane bass and parachute vibrato.

Cox had never heard shit like this before. He borrowed a bass and the future Band of Gypsys jammed. Soon they did their first gig at the Pink Poodle Club in Memphis, Tennessee. They called themselves the King Kasuals.

Jimi had started his first band, the Velvetones, in high school. At YMCA and Polish Hall gigs, he played an acoustic guitar that got drowned out on Coaster and Ray Charles tunes. Then his father bought him a Supro Ozark electric, and he defected to the Rocking Kings who earned thirty-five cents apiece for their debut at Seattle's National Guard Armory. In 1960, the Kings placed second at the All-State Battle of the Bands. By this time, Jimi was playing his Ozark ambidextrous, behind his back, and with his teeth. Due to his catlike stealth on stage, he was called The Creeper.

Music was in Hendrix's genes. His father, Al, formerly a Golden Gloves fighter and a dancer with traveling vaudeville shows, met the vivacious sixteen-year-old Lucille at a Seattle jitterbug competition in 1941. Lucille got pregnant, they tied the knot, and Al got drafted. His commanding officer in Alabama locked him in the brig so that he wouldn't go AWOL to see his firstborn, Johnny Allen Hendrix. Discharged four years later, Al returned west and retrieved his son from foster care in California. Suspecting that Lucille had named the boy after her new lover and pimp, John Page, Al renamed his son James Marshall Hendrix in honor of his own recently deceased brother.

"My dad was very religious and level headed," Jimi would later remember, "but my mother used to like having a good time, dressing up. She used to drink a lot and didn't take care of herself. She died when I was ten, but she was a real groovy mother."

In fact, due to her serial infidelities, Al divorced Lucille when Jimi was ten, taking custody of him as well as his two younger brothers and fostering out his three little sisters whose paternity was unknown.[3] After many affairs as well as a second marriage, Lucille passed away five years later at age 32. Jimi was fifteen. Found unconscious and brutally beaten in an alley, she died in the hospital from a ruptured spleen and cirrhosis of the liver. She had been hospitalized earlier for severe beatings by boyfriends and by Al himself in drunken rages. Later, her beloved son would write "Angel, Little Wing," and "The Wind Cries Mary" for her.

By age sixteen, Jimi had lived in fourteen different places and had been pulled in and out of as many schools. His father took what odd jobs he could, but would quickly exhaust his meager pay drinking and gambling. The malnourished Jimi and his brother, Leon, stole food from grocery stores. At last, the welfare department stepped in, demanding that Al put them up for adoption, which is the only time his sons saw him weep. A church friend, Dorothy Harding, took Jimi in. Though she already had nine children of her own, she supported her extended family by working two full-time jobs.

One day, Jimi began crying inconsolably. "Aunty Dorothy," he

---

3. The part-time janitor, gas station attendant, and landscaper had wanted the divorce for years but had been unable to afford the $25 legal fee.

sobbed, "when I get big, I'm going far, far away. And I'm never comin' back. Never."

Following the death of Lucille, Al had begrudgingly bought Jimi his first real guitar for $5 from a drunk. When the boy saw from a hilltop above the Seattle stadium a performance by Elvis and Little Richard, he became obsessed with the instrument, playing it constantly and taking it to bed with him.

He was still sleeping with his beloved guitar as a paratrooper with the 101st Airborne in Kentucky and taking flack for this from his fellow Screamin' Eagles in the barracks. Only one recruit found it natural: Billy Cox.

Jimi served ten months of a three-year stint. He was, according to the official story, discharged from the Airborne after breaking an ankle on a skyhook during his 26th jump. Biographer Charles Cross[4] asserted that he was discharged for "homosexual tendencies," having told the base doctor that he was fantasizing about his bunkmates.

Private Hendrix had joined the Army to avoid prison. He'd been arrested for riding in a stolen vehicle and the prosecutor had agreed to a two-year suspended sentence if he enlisted. He knew he'd be drafted anyway. Besides, his prospects in Seattle didn't look good. A high school dropout, Jimi was rejected for a grocery bagger job and was reduced to working for a dollar a day in his father's landscaping business. His musical career at home didn't seem any more promising: his last steady gig was with Thomas and the Tom Cats, and he couldn't afford the $5 jacket rental for shows.

In July of 1962, he found himself outside the gates of Fort Campbell with Betty Jean, the clothes on his back, and $400 severance pay in his pocket. He blew it in twenty-four hours. "I get foolishly good-natured sometimes," he remembered. "I must have been handing out bills to anyone who asked me."

Having spent his bus fare for Seattle, he and Cox headed to Nashville. Here the King Kasuals became the house band at the Del Morocco while living upstairs at its sister club, the House of Glamour. "That's where I learned to play really—Nashville," said Jimi. He played tirelessly: at the Morocco, at the House of Glamour, and on the streets to and from. He soon gained the nickname "Marbles" because every-

---

4. Charles R. Cross, *Room Full of Mirrors: A Biography of Jimi Hendrix* (New York: Hyperion, 2005).

body thought he'd lost the few he had, even the musicians. He took a break from practice only once a week.

"Every Sunday afternoon we used to go downtown and watch the race riots," he recalled. "Take a picnic basket because they wouldn't serve us in the restaurants."

In 1964, tiring of the Southern "chitlins circuit," Jimi left Billy and headed to Harlem to try for the big time. He won the $25 first place at the Apollo amateur contest. But this seemed like beginner's luck. "I'd get a gig every twelfth of never," he would recall of his first days in New York. "Sleeping outside between them tall tenements was hell. Rats runnin' all over your chest; cockroaches stealing your last candy bar."

Overcome by the manic depression that would plague him the rest of his life, he attempted suicide.[5] "He fluctuated so fast from great joy to intense unhappiness," said one of his lovers. "I mean suicidal, not interested in life, completely disinterested in his body."

Hendrix may not have survived New York had it not been for his new love, the beautiful, streetwise, and well-connected Faye Pridgeon. Faye introduced Jimi to her ex-boyfriend, Sam Cooke,[6] as well as to other movers and shakers on the scene. But things didn't turn around overnight for the couple. "We were down to our last dollar debating whether we should buy cat food or share a hot dog," recalled Faye. "The ASPCA made the decision for us."

Jimi's big break finally came when he successfully auditioned for the Isley Brothers. After the tour, he played backup for his idol Little Richard, who later said of him, "He loved the way I wore these head-bands around my hair and how wild I dressed. . . . He began to dress like me and he even grew a little mustache like mine." But soon the "Tutti Frutti" showman decided his Seattle homeboy was trying to upstage him. "I'm Little Richard and I'm the King of Rock and Rhythm and I'm the only one who's going to look PRETTY on stage!"

He threatened to fine Jimi unless he turned over his pretty shirts. Though the guitarist begrudgingly surrendered the threads, the rhythm

---

5. According to Noel Redding, Jimi made a second attempt after the 1968 Experience tour. "He slashed his wrists," wrote the bassist in his memoir. "This was kept very quiet, but we all felt horrified." Later, the star's autopsy report revealed a scar on his left wrist.

6. Not long after the meeting, Cooke was shot and clubbed to death in a Hollywood hotel.

king soon fired him for flirting with girls and missing the tour bus once too often.

The Creeper landed on his feet, joining the tours of Ike and Tina Turner, then Sam and Dave, then King Curtis.[7]

Although, by the summer of 1966, Jimi had backed up the biggest names in R & B, he had grown frustrated with the rigid routine that allowed little room for improvisation. He longed "to do his own thing." Not black music, not white music, but a kind of "universal" sound that had never been heard before except in his head. The only thing close to it for him was Dylan. Hendrix was crazy about Dylan.

One night at a Harlem club, he pulled Wilson Pickett from the platter and queued up "Blowin' in the Wind." Suddenly, he found himself cornered by his brothers. "I'm going to cut your throat!" said one.

"People in Harlem have a lot to learn," he declared dejectedly afterward.

Jimi retreated to Greenwich Village. Here he started his own band, Jimmy James and the Blue Flames, which played for $3 a gig when one was available.

One night Linda Keith, Keith Richards' girlfriend, spotted him at the Cheetah Club. The British Invasion was underway then; the Stones, the Beatles, and others were on American tours. According to Richards' "No Ol' Ladies on Tour Rule," the Stones' guitarist had left Linda in New York to seek her own musical entertainment. What the beautiful twenty-year-old British sophisticate saw at the Cheetah blew her away: Hendrix assaulting his amps, chewing out savage riffs, and playing killer shit behind his back and inside somersaults.

"Back in those days," said Rolling Stone Ronnie Wood, "all of us skinny white British kids were trying to look cool and sound black. And there was Hendrix, the ultimate in black cool. Everything he did was natural and perfect."

What really blew Linda away was that this cat was unknown. Smitten by the Creeper, she made it her business to change this. But star making proved dicier than she'd imagined. She first contacted the Stones' flamboyant producer, Andrew Oldham. "Andrew was absolutely turned off," she recalled. "He thought Hendrix was a wild man." Linda approached other producer friends, but their reactions were no

---

7. The saxophonist fired Jimi for refusing to wear his band's "KC" cufflinks. Curtis would be stabbed to death in New York in 1971.

more enthusiastic. Finally, she persuaded the Animals' bassist, Chas Chandler, to check Jimi out at the Café Wha? Chas was just winding up his own American tour with the Animals and thinking about producing.

Chandler was floored. He told Jimi he wanted to take him to London and make him a star. He promised to introduce him to his mates, the British guitar god trinity—Clapton, Beck, and Townshend. Jimi thought that sounded groovy, but considering all his career Hindenburgs since leaving the Airborne, he wasn't holding his breath.

On September 24, 1966, he and Chandler touched down at Heathrow. His New York landlord had taken all his clothes as payment for back rent. So Jimi was traveling light: He had his white Stratocaster, and, in the case was one satin shirt, a jar of Noxzema, a toothbrush, and his hair rollers.

Waiting to meet him was Chas's own manager Mike Jeffery. He'd just returned from the Grand Cayman Islands where he deposited all the Animals' earnings in a numbered account accessible only to him. Always on the lookout for fresh talent, the pop Svengali was anxious to meet this black guitarist from the states who Chas had told him could become as big as Elvis and the Beatles.

RUMOR TO LEGEND

If I'm God, who the fuck is HE?
—Eric Clapton, after seeing Hendrix perform

Chas took Jimi out clubbing and introduced him to the Beatles, the Stones, Cream, the Who, the Yardbirds, and the other stalwarts of the British Invasion. Meanwhile, he held auditions for the Jimi Hendrix Experience, a name that popped into his head after witnessing his client's "Hey, Joe" epiphany at the Café Wha? in New York.

The power trio was born overnight: The Seattle homeboy plus two diminutive Englishmen, Mitch Mitchell on drums and Noel Redding a guitarist who had never played bass before—both refugees from minor bands. They signed on for fifteen pounds a week. Redding got an advance for train fare home. And Chas treated them to Afros like Jimi's.

The Experience had hardly begun to rehearse before the "French Elvis," Johnny Hallyday, spotted the trio at a club jam and asked them to open for his new European tour. When they returned from ravaging the Continent, Chandler knew the Experience was ready for its official British debut. "I had six guitars and I sold five of them to pay for the reception at the Bag O'Nails," he remembered. He invited the rock royalty and the press to the club, as well as his manager, Mike Jeffery. After the premiere shows, even the English guitar gods became converts.

"Jimi got up and just blew everybody away," said Traffic's Dave Mason. "I remember thinking I might as well take up another instrument."

"He gets up, all soft-spoken," recalled Terry Reid, "and all of a sudden, WHOOOOR-RRAAWWWRR!!! I could see everyone's fillings falling out."

American Mike Bloomfield knew the feeling too. "I was the hotshot guitarist on the block," he said after Jimi's gig at the Café au Go Go in New York. "Hendrix knew who I was and, that day, in front of my eyes, he burned me to death . . . H-bombs were going off, guided missiles were flying . . . I didn't want to pick up a guitar for the next year."

But the Hendrix phenomenon wasn't just his axemanship—it was his look. The British press dubbed him "The Wild Man of Borneo" and "The Black Elvis." Chas advertised him as "Dylan, Clapton, and James Brown all in one!" Jimi reveled in it all, refining his image carefully with Chandler. They went to Granny Takes a Trip boutique in Piccadilly and bought up royal Veterinary Corps dress jackets, charmeuse and crushed velvet pants, and kaleidoscopic vests. After gigs, they would stay up all night at Chas's flat, playing Risk and Monopoly (at which Jimi was invincible), discussing the next career move.

Joining them in their efforts was the pop Svengali himself, Mike Jeffery. No sooner had Chas signed Jimi than Mike had made his move. "Strictly speaking, you are still signed to me and anything you do, I've got a commission on it," Mike told Chas. Not one to quibble with the redoubtable Jeffery, Chandler turned 50 percent of the Experience over to him and let him take over its management. Pulling strings with his cronies in immigration, Jeffery secured a visa and working permit for Jimi. Then, he landed a Polydor record deal with Kit Lambert and Chris Stamp, managers of the Who. Finally, Jeffery locked Hendrix into a contract with his, Lambert's and Stamp's company, Yameta Productions, awarding himself 40 percent of all future earnings.

Hendrix signed without hesitation. Though the toast of the town, he was still penniless. Recalled his flatmate, "For breakfast we ate dog biscuits. That was the only food in the house at the time, because I had a beagle."

Chas and Mike had yet to show him the money, but Jimi was confident it would come soon enough. He trusted the forthright, dedicated Chas implicitly. As for Jeffery, he found him "a loveable rogue."

Jeffery's other major client, Eric Burdon, agreed with this assessment of the flamboyant manager—more or less. "Like most people of felonious intent," the Animals' singer wrote in his memoir,[8] "he was charming, attractive, and sometimes a riot to be around." Mike had amused Eric and the Animals over Guineses and black bombers with his 007 stories about his British CIA days: blowing up Russian/Egyptian bases in the Suez, playing decoy in Greek assassinations, escaping medieval torture in the dungeon of a Balkan castle. Eric thought it was the ale talking until Mike invited him to his Majorca villa overlooking the harbor where the U.S. Seventh Fleet happened to be trolling for lost nukes. Early one morning, his manager emerged from the water in scuba gear, holding a black box. Grinning, pointing to the Yank armada, the ex-spy pulled a switch: suddenly the harbor was rocked with underwater explosions. "Jeffery was thrilled with his pyrotechnic display on the beach that led to a huge riot," wrote Eric, who now realized that Mike hadn't been exaggerating when telling him that his specialty in the MI6 had been "creating civil unrest."

Jeffery had made the transition from demolition and espionage to show business by studying under "The Al Capone of Pop" himself, Don Arden. Also known as "The English Godfather" and "Mr. Big," Arden had imported Little Richard, Sam Cooke, and Gene Vincent to Britain. He went on to manage the Small Faces, Electric Light Orchestra, and Black Sabbath.[9] Known for his old-fashioned business methods—bribery, blackmail, assault, kidnapping—the diminutive Jewish businessman and his muscle had dangled rivals from windows, rearranged their kneecaps, and extinguished cigars in their faces.[10] Jeffery proved

---

8. Eric Burdon, *I Used to Be an Animal (But I'm Alright Now)* (London, UK: Faber & Faber, 1986).

9. Arden's daughter, Sharon, went on to manage and marry Sabbath's Ozzy Osbourne.

10. See Don Arden, *Mr. Big: Ozzy, Sharon and My Life as the Godfather of Rock* (London, UK: Robson Books, 2004).

his own mettle against his mentor when he stole the Animals from him without losing life or limb.

The retired spy parlayed his MI6 and Arden experience to become a rock-and-roll Dr. No. "His own mob sprang up around him like morning mushrooms," wrote Burdon. ". . . His main enforcer was The Turk, a nasty bastard whose tools of choice were an ax and two highly trained German shepherds." Civilians, including his clients, learned not to mess with Jeffery. He moved in the business world, Burdon went on, "like a great white shark, devouring everything in its path." Though, according to Redding, he "looked the perennial bookworm type" and read metaphysics, he also collected guns, threw knives, bugged rooms, and razed restaurants. When he burned down his Club Marimba and built his premiere Club A Go Go with the insurance money, nobody investigated. When, later, the Animals discovered all their money had disappeared into their manager's Grand Cayman tax shelter account, they hardly protested.

But Burdon, who soon became fast friends with Hendrix in those early days, did share with him a few cautionary tales about his new representative. To Jimi, the stories made Jeffery seem all the more colorful. Besides, knowing rock and roll to be a rough-and-tumble business, it seemed to him that this dynamo—James Bond, the Godfather, Timothy Leary, and the Maharishi all rolled into one—was just the sort of man he wanted in his corner. Because, in spite of differing opinions, everyone agreed on one thing about Jeffery: when it came to the war of star making, he took no prisoners and defeat was not in his vocabulary. And Jimi Hendrix, after his long struggle, wanted above all else to become a star—at any cost.

By the end of '66, though the sensation of the British rock scene, Hendrix was still an unknown in his own country. Jeffery and Chandler changed all that the following spring at the greatest pop festival in history: Monterey.

To get Jimi on the bill, they needed a little help from their friends: Paul McCartney and Brian Jones. The Beatle and the Stone contacted the event's organizer, John Phillips of the Mamas and Papas, pointing out that a festival of the world's greatest bands wouldn't amount to a thing without the world's greatest guitar player.

No sooner did Jimi arrive at Monterey than he ran afoul of the Who, managed by Jeffery's partner, Kit Lambert. Months before, he'd opened for the *My Generation* powerhouse at a London gig, after which Peter Townshend confessed, "I'm not ashamed to say he blew us away." Determined not to face the same embarrassment at Monterey, Townshend refused to perform after Hendrix. But Hendrix refused to go after the Who. So they flipped a coin. Jimi came up tails.

"Okay," he told Townshend, "if I'm gonna follow you, I'm gonna pull out all the stops."

The Who knew about Hendrix's pyrotechnics. But the best defense being an offense, "they blew the entire stage up with bombs and fireballs," said Phillips. Striding offstage, Keith Moon, the Who's drummer destined to OD in ten years, crowed at Jimi, "You're on, mate!" "Moon the Loon" had never counted himself among the Hendrix genuflectors: on first seeing him months before in the recording studio, he'd said, "Who let that savage in here?"

Peaking on a double hit of Monterey Purple now, Jimi smiled his timid smile, then strapped on his Stratocaster while Brian Jones introduced him to the crowd of 90,000 as "the most exciting performer I've ever heard!"

Jimi took the stage with the Experience. What followed was perhaps one of the greatest apotheoses of rock, climaxing with "Wild Thing" and the burning of his guitar.

"The Jimi Hendrix Experience owns the future!" proclaimed the *Los Angeles Times* the next day. "When Jimi left the stage, he had graduated from rumor to legend."

By the time of the Monterey performance, Jimi's debut album, *Are You Experienced*, topped the charts, second only to the Beatles' *Sgt. Pepper's*.

The guitarist traveled from Monterey to L.A. where he became the toast of the musical elite. He opened for the Jefferson Airplane as well as for Big Brother and the Holding Company, earning $500 per night. Shortly, he became the headliner and his fee rose accordingly.

The Experience toured tirelessly in 1967, doing 255 shows. That fall, *Melody Maker* named Hendrix Top Musician of the Year. The next spring, *Life* magazine hailed him as "The Most Spectacular Electric Guitarist in the World." Returning to Seattle in early 1968, the mayor gave the native son the keys to the city.

"The only keys I expected to see in that town were of the jailhouse," the convicted felon told reporters.

By 1969, Hendrix was voted Performer of the Year by *Rolling Stone* magazine. The Experience now commanded $100,000 for a fifty-minute set. Though the Rolling Stones slightly exceeded this, the Experience was the highest grossing international act thanks to Jeffery who cut out the middlemen and took in eighty-five cents on the dollar.

A musician's musician, Hendrix was as popular with his peers as with the public. Dylan called him "incredible." Neil Young considered him "absolutely the best guitar player that ever lived." He was a seminal influence on future stars as well. "He was like a Venusian, like someone from another planet," said Sting. "His act was almost too awesome to deal with. You felt like you were on the edge of a precipice. 'Hey Joe' was what decided me to become a musician."

About the only professional criticism of Jimi came from Frank Zappa.[11] After seeing him at a Café au Go Go gig in New York, the Mother called him "great" except ". . . I was physically ill. . . . I didn't see how anybody could inflict that kind of volume on himself. He ended by taking the guitar and impaling it in the low ceiling of the club. Just walked away and left it squealing."

Another Hendrix fan was Jim Morrison. "Hey, Jimi! Jimi! Lemme come up and sing, man, and we'll do this shit together," pleaded the Doors' front man from the audience at an Experience gig.

"That's okay, fella. I can handle it myself," said Hendrix.

"Hey, do you know who I am?" cried the Lizard King. "I'm Jim Morrison of the Doors!"

"Yeah, I know who you are," shot back the Voodoo Child, "and I'm Jimi Hendrix."

A month earlier at L.A.'s Scene Club, Jim had interrupted Jimi again by crawling on stage and trying to give head to his Stratocaster. Later, an interviewer asked the guitarist if his act had ever been obscene. "Maybe somewhat vulgar," he allowed, "but 'obscene'? You confuse me with Jim Morrison."

Proving Hendrix's popularity and influence, President Nixon's press secretary, Ron Ziegler, invited him to the White House for a Fireside Chat in April 1969. Jeffery turned the invitation down without informing him.

The Feds soon placed Jimi on their "Security Index," a list of celebrity "subversives" to be rounded up and placed in detainment camps in the event of a national emergency. The Establishment considered his

---

11. His only other detractor was Petula Clark. "Jimi Hendrix is a great big hoax," said the " 'Don't Sleep in the Subway' star."

"Star-Spangled Banner" an aural flag burning. And, by the peak of his popularity, he was associating with a group that the feds considered one of the most dangerous in the country: The Black Panthers.

ELECTRIC LADYLAND

He was the most sexual man I ever saw on stage. Even Mick Jagger said so.
—Nico, Velvet Underground vocalist

If Jimi Hendrix was a legendary guitarist, he was no less a legendary lothario.

"He came to bed with the same grace a Mississippi pulpwood driver attacks a plate of collard greens and corn bread," recalled his first New York girlfriend, Faye Pridgeon. "He was creative in bed too: there would be encore after encore, hard driving and steamy like his music. There were times when he almost busted me in two the way he did a guitar on stage."

Women were no less infatuated by his gentlemanliness. He helped them with their chair, graced them with presents, whispered sweet nothings in their ear. When meeting his first white girlfriend, Carol Shiroky, at New York's Cheetah Club, he said, "I wanna tell you something, but you're gonna laugh." He was a penniless backup guitar player. The beautiful blonde, who had heard every come-on in the Big Apple, promised not to laugh. "I wanna kiss you on your knee," whispered Jimi. Then he told her he was a Venusian.

Soon they were living together and Shiroky was cooking him his favorite breakfast: spaghetti and garlic without sauce. She bought him his first new Stratocaster. Then he started missing dinner and not coming home till dawn. "I knew he was in someone else's bed and I would never question him," she said, "because if I did he'd be gone."

His next girlfriend was another blonde, Kathy Etchingham. Meeting the former lover of his champion, Brian Jones, just after his arrival in London, his first words to her were, "I want to tell you something." He kissed her ear and whispered, "I think you're beautiful."

One of the few ingenues who got away was Marianne Faithfull. After performing at London's Speakeasy Club, Jimi "began whispering in my ear . . . all the things he wanted to do to me sexually. Telling me he'd written 'The Wind Cries Mary' for me."[12] Ignoring her boyfriend, Mick Jagger, sitting beside her, Hendrix continued, "Come with me now, baby. What are you doing with this jerk anyway?"[13]

"I wanted more than anything to go with him," said Marianne, "but I couldn't do it. Mick would never have forgiven me." The "As Tears Go By" singer later confessed that her life's "greatest regret" was not having an affair with Hendrix.

If the woman whisperer had a way with foxey ladies before his star rose, when the Experience started touring, he was spellbinding. "Jimi was the most charming, polite person in the entire world," recalled booking agent, Melissa Chassay. "He took off your coat, that kind of thing . . . Backstage, there'd be a queue of girls. One by one, they'd go in and Jimi would fuck them, and after an hour he'd go onstage and tear the place apart."

"He had hot and cold running girlfriends," confirmed his drummer, Mitch Mitchell. "But nothing came between Jimi and his guitar."

In order to keep track of the notches on it, Jimi put together an 8mm romantic comedy starring all his groupies. Complete with commentary, he called his tour diary *The Goodbye Films.*

On another whim, he allowed the Cynthia Plastercaster team to immortalize his "Penis de Milo" and enshrine it with those of other rock legends. "We needed to plunge him through the entire depth of the vase," reported Cynthia. "It's fairly huge, very thick and rather long. He got stuck . . . but didn't panic. I believe the reason we couldn't get his rig out was that it wouldn't get soft!"

The Voodoo Child enjoyed groups. He once invited his friend, Jerry Morrison, over for R & R at his Woodstock mansion. "Jimi had a huge bed and there he was in the middle of it, covered by six or seven girls who were sucking on every orifice and protuberance," recalled Jerry.

But, the guitarist never let anybody, especially a woman, get too close. He couldn't chance it. The loss of his mother, his one love supreme, had almost been more than he could bear. "All those people who say they knew Jimi—well, that's ridiculous," said his bassist, Noel Redding. "He was very close to a chick he dug in Sweden [Kirsten Nefer]

---

12. Marianne Faithfull, *Faithfull: An Autobiography,* with David Dalton (Boston: Little Brown, 1994).

13. Chandler had recently asked Jagger to co-sponsor the Experience: the Monkey Man refused.

but the chick he met in Dusseldorf [Monika Dannemann] . . . well, he spent three days with her. They say they knew him, but they don't."

Another Nordic beauty, Eva Sundquist, became the mother of Hendrix's second child, James. Jimi Jr. was conceived in a Stockholm hotel, only days after Hendrix had told the reporters that his British love, Kathy Etchingham, was his "Yoko Ono." Diane Carpenter, a 16-year-old New York hooker, was the mother of Hendrix's first child, Tamika, a daughter. Both Eva and Diane were to file paternity suits. Eva was coerced to do so by welfare officers, though she told them she "didn't want Jimi to have the trouble fatherhood would bring." Later her son, who never met Jimi, would protest, "Don't tell me any more, I don't want to know about my father."

By this time, Hendrix's reputation as a chivalrous gentleman was tattered. "Jimi was shy," said another ex-lover, Pat Hartley, "but that doesn't mean he wasn't going to beat you up if you took too much liberty with him. . . . some of it was an absolute horror." "On occasion," wrote his biographers, Shapiro and Glebbeek,[14] "Jimi dangerously blurred the distinction between guitar and woman."

But, in this, he was no an exception: woman beating is a rock and roll tradition. Chuck Berry, James Brown, Jerry Lee Lewis, Brian Jones, Jim Morrison, Eric Clapton, Jimmy Page, John Lennon—to name only a few—were impassioned disciplinarians of the fair sex.

"Jimi Hendrix was a genius," declared his friend, Eric Burdon. "But one minute he's on stage singing about the mass of underdogs in America and the next he's kicking the hell out of some poor chick in a back alley."

One of these chicks happened to be the Animals' ex-wife, Angie. Hendrix did a three-way with her and a friend one night but, come morning, the girls were in no hurry to leave his London hotel suite. "Jimi suddenly went bananas," claimed Angie, "and started banging our heads together." Then he hurled them into the sitting room. The girls were ready to take leave now, but their clothes were locked in the bedroom. Angie (fatally shot by a boyfriend two years later) placed a 999 to Kathy Etchingham. Jimi's Yoko taxied over and negotiated the release of the girls' clothes.

No stranger to Jimi's wrath herself, Kathy recalled how "he locked

14. Harry Shapiro and Caesar Glebbeek, *Jimi Hendrix: Electric Gypsy* (New York: St. Martin's Griffin, 1995).

me in the bathroom for absolutely ages." One time, at the Bag O'Nails Club, he'd caught her on the telephone and, thinking she was arranging a tryst with another lover, pummeled her with the phone until she was rescued by Lennon and McCartney. Another time, he kicked her in the face, breaking her nose in three places.

Booze made Jimi forget his manners, as it had with his father, Al. "He just couldn't drink," said his friend, Herbie Worthington. "He simply turned into a bastard." Noel Redding, agreeing that Jimi "couldn't handle booze" like "a seasoned English pub crawler," recalled one besotted night in Sweden's Gothenburg Hotel. Here Noel, Mitch, and Jimi—along with a gay Swedish journalist—were chilling, trying to anesthetize themselves after an enervating performance earlier that evening. Soon the flirtatious Swede suggested a four-way, and Jimi, three sheets to the wind, started hitting on Noel who wanted no part of it.[15] Suddenly, "Jimi started dashing about smashing everything in the room," recalled the bassist. When the police arrived, Hendrix decked two, then tried to jump out the broken window. He was arrested, fined and, in the future, had difficulty booking a suite in Stockholm. "Man, I was just drunk," Jimi admitted after the incident. "Usually I can drink a lot of booze. Someone must have put some kind of tablet in my glass." But he added, "You can't expect artists to be goody-goodies all the time."

He got in another scrape while in L.A. for his *Life* magazine photo shoot. "He attacked a few young ladies with bricks," recalled Noel. "One of them was because she came to my room, not his. . . . We used girls to get back at each other." The ladies filed suit and Electric Ladyland, Inc. chivalrously cut them a check for their troubles.

After Jimi's demise, when Eric Burdon was asked to sum up his feelings for his old friend, he said, "He was a cunt! He was great, but he was a cunt. That's why I loved him."

If there was one woman who could give as much she could take, it was Devon Wilson, aka "Dolly Dagger."

"The Cleopatra of groupies" was rumored to be into black magic, a covert Black Panther, an undercover narc, or a mole for Jeffery. Nobody fucked with her—including Jimi. She met him in 1965 during the Isley

---

15. The "official" story was that Jimi lost his temper with several tenacious groupies. Little else has been written about his bisexual leanings, though rumors about his relationship with his friend, Love's Arthur Lee, persist.

Brothers' tour. Though a teenage runaway then, Devon had already bedded most everybody who was anybody in rock.

"I was attracted to Jimi's flamboyance, even though at the time he wasn't an established star," she recalled. "I introduced Jimi to his first acid trip, and he liked it a lot," she went on. "He tried various pills with me and our relationship became one of excitement and exhilaration."

Hendrix later wrote "Dolly Dagger," singing, "She drinks her blood from a jagged edge." And in honor of Devon's taste for S & M, "She's got a whip as long as your life."

A contender for Wilson's affections was Sir Mick himself, whose blood she sampled after he cut himself on a wineglass at a party. She was the subject of the Stones' "Brown Sugar" on *Let It Bleed* and in "Can't Always Get What You Want": "I met her today at the reception . . . in her glass was a bleeding man."

The Voodoo Child and Dolly Dagger taunted each other with their serial flings. "I'm not the only one accused of hit-and-run," sang Jimi in "Crosstown Traffic." "Tire tracks all across your back, baby, I can see you've had your fun."

But an unbreakable bond existed between the two. Devon was not only Jimi's lover, but also his big sister and his mother. She advised him about his career, protected and defended him, yet scolded him when his performances were lackluster—a liberty he allowed no other woman.

Devon might have been a healthier influence on Hendrix had she not been a smack freak. On first meeting, she admitted that they did coke together, "but he had no desire to get into heroin at the time, because he knew that this was a one-way street that led to nowhere." Faye Pridgeon, Jimi's significant other during his Harlem days, saved Devon from fatally OD'ing three times. Devon's appetite for junk rivaled that of Janis Joplin herself who shot up with Jimi at Monterey. Hendrix's habit never equaled theirs, but its effect on his music and career was significant.

"He suffered from the drugs he was taking," said his drummer Buddy Miles, "because he was doing heroin, and after a while that will hurt anybody."

"He was inclined toward the temporary escape of heroin," wrote Noel Redding. "Headwise, that was a huge barrier between us."

Jimi at last fell for a woman who might have been a wholesome and revitalizing influence. Monika Dannemann was a German skating champion, drug free, allegedly a virgin, and wanted nothing more than marriage and a family. In her biography,[16] Ms. Dannemann identified herself as Jimi's only true fiancée. True, the guitarist was a serial proposer: after allegedly proposing to Monika, he had popped the question to Danish model, Kirsten Nefer, as he had done with others—but this time he'd finally met his true love. Monika insisted on it.

According to Ms. Dannemann, she met Jimi in January 1969 after attending the Experience's Düsseldorf concert. A German baron friend offered to introduce her to Hendrix at a bar that night, but she refused due to his reputation as "a wild man" and a "raw, uncivilized person." "I certainly didn't want to meet a man like this," the proper fräulein insisted. But when the baron persisted, she agreed to a meeting the next day at Hendrix's hotel. After speaking with him briefly, "I realized I had fallen in love with Jimi," she wrote. Feelings were supposedly mutual. "The moment he had seen me, he had fallen in love," she went on. The next month, she recalled rendezvousing with her lover in London, though other biographers agree that the guitarist was living with Kathy Etchingham then. In March, Dannemann claimed they exchanged "engagement rings," each embossed with a golden snake that Hendrix told her was "a magical symbol of wisdom and enlightenment used to ward off evil." At the Speakeasy Club, he showed friends the rings "from table to table," she wrote, "announcing that they had just become engaged."

Again, others had no recollection of this. They had seen Jimi at the Speakeasy only with Kathy Etchingham. Though Ms. Dannemann insisted she had a history with the star, she was all but invisible to others until the last days of his life in London. No one else had seen her with the snake ring until September 16, 1970, two days before his death. No one identified this as an "engagement" ring, except the mysterious groupie herself.

In fact, only days before, a Dutch tabloid had run this headline: WORLD STAR GETS ENGAGED TO DANISH MODEL! This was the beautiful Kristen Nefer who had accompanied Jimi to the Isle of Wight Festival a short time before. Meanwhile, Dannemann had moved into a secluded flat in London and was lying in wait for *her* "fiancé."

When Devon heard the news of the Nefer engagement—not Dannemann's fantasy engagement—she flew to London to get to the bottom of things. She had heard through the grapevine that Jimi's be-

---

16. Monika Dannemann, *The Inner World of Jimi Hendrix* (New York: St. Martin's, 1995).

havior was wildly erratic. His friend and biographer, Sharon Lawrence,[17] had been told by another friend of his, Jack Meehan, "Somebody needs to keep a protective eye on Jimi. He's walking around in the middle of a nervous breakdown." In spite of her own deceits, Devon had always considered herself, if nothing else, Jimi's protector.

Just before traveling to London, the composer of "Love or Confusion" consulted a German psychic who told him several times: "Be careful of women. They mean you no good."

Devon was not the only one who arrived in London for Jimi Hendrix's swan song. In a harmonic conversion of bad karma, all the major players in his chaotic life descended on him for what would become a violent tragedy of Shakespearean proportion.

BROKEN GLASS

> I used to live in a room full of mirrors, all I could see was me . . .
> Broken glass was all in my brain . . .
> it used to fall on my dreams and cut me in my bed.
> —Jimi Hendrix, "Room Full of Mirrors"

> He started to hate his image.
> He would sit at the end of the bed almost in tears.
> —Kathy Etchingham

Jimi's honeymoon after Monterey was short-lived. After the tour de force performance, he was opening for the Monkees. Without consulting him, Mike Jeffery had signed the deal with Dick Clark Productions. "Are you out of your fucking mind?" raged Jimi's producer, Chas Chandler, on hearing the news.

Jeffery insisted that the sacrifice in "musical integrity" was worth the media exposure. Bubblegum heartthrobs, the lip-synching Monkees starred in their own TV comedy that made the Partridge Family look like Tennessee Williams. "The Monkees were in the derriere-garde of music," leader Peter Tork allowed, "and Jimi was in the avant-garde."

It didn't take too many boos and cries for "Daveyyy!" before Hen-

---

17. Sharon Lawrence, *Jimi Hendrix: The Man, the Magic, the Truth* (New York: Harper Entertainment, 2005).

drix turned his back on the crowd and refused to sing. After a few gigs, Chandler rescued the Experience from the tour by kiting a story that the Daughters of the American Revolution were up in arms over his star's corrosive influence on young girls.

Hardly had Jimi been extricated from this fiasco when he found himself at odds with Chas too. Ever the perfectionist, the guitarist demanded endless retakes while recording the Experience's second album, Axis: Bold As Love, ignoring his producer's input. Though Chandler was a musician himself, Jimi refused to tolerate any creative interference. "He just wasn't listening anymore, I felt like an alien," complained Chandler who, like Jimi, was losing his hair due to alopecia, a stress-related condition.

The other members of the Experience were bummed too. "We'd be in the studio for days," wrote Redding, "but we'd just never get any work done 'cos Hendrix would arrive with 1,400 hangers-on." Sometimes the bassist would refuse to show up at the studio at all "because I couldn't face the Jimi entourage. . . . Jimi's ego fed off his celebrity, but in the end he was forced to become 'Jimi Hendrix' round-the-clock host to parasites."

Mike Jeffery wasted no time exploiting the dissention. He ingratiated himself to Jimi by dropping acid with him often, talking about mysticism, and denouncing the Establishment. "Incredible as it seems," wrote Noel Redding, "Jeffery became a real groovy-hipman-babe-far-out-flowerchild-acidhead." It hadn't yet occurred to Jimi that his manager was taking placebos while dosing him with powerful hallucinogens. "Jeffery always made sure Jimi was not short of drugs," continued Redding.

For his part, Chandler had never done heavier drugs and didn't like their effect on Hendrix. "Acid got in the way of his brain," he said. "It was fucking madness. It had to stop." At first, Chas hadn't realized Jimi's appetite for psychedelics, much less whom he'd been tripping with: Lennon and McCartney. "They were all pouring acid down their throats!" he declared. "I was living in the same flat as Jimi and I had no idea!"

Finding the rift irreparable, Chandler turned Hendrix over to Jeffery exclusively. But, knowing his duplicitous ex-partner all too well, he did not abandon the star without reservation. "The window of opportunity was there for Jeffery to scoop it all up," he said. "I knew that something dodgy was gonna happen. But I never dreamed it would lead to his [Jimi's] death."

Chandler had clothed and sheltered Hendrix, introduced him to all his friends, and when the money dried up, sold all his guitars to bankroll his debut. More than a producer, he had been a true benefactor and friend. So when he returned to London two years after launching Hendrix's career, it was not without a bitter sadness. But he forbade his lawyers from including anything in the dissolution agreement that would "hurt or interfere with Jimi." Only a month after the dissolution was complete, the Electric Ladyland album was released and Chas received no credit.

The day before Jimi died, he implored Chas to come back. But it was already too late.

The departure of Chas Chandler and the ascension of Mike Jeffery was the beginning of the end for Hendrix, professionally and personally. Jeffery kept him on an exhausting tour schedule. Jimi gained the reputation for being a volatile and unpredictable performer: one night he was brilliant, the next withdrawn and lifeless. After many gigs, Redding would say, "We died the death. Jimi pulled another moody."

"Ever since I can remember I've been moody," Hendrix confided to *Fab* magazine. "I'm sorry. I can't help it." His manic depression had returned. He became hostile toward the fans when they called for a hit he didn't want to play or got impatient with his interminable guitar tuning. "While you're picking your noses and your asses," he shouted at Newport, "you can all just choke yourselves. Fuck it!"

He was a musician, he insisted, not a "clown." He became sick and tired of the theatrics the fans expected: playing behind his back, between his legs and with his teeth, burning and smashing up his guitars. "Most nights it took forty-five minutes just to convince Hendrix to go on," recalled his road manager, Gerry Stickells. "Give them their money back!" he yelled.

Jimi desperately wanted to evolve musically, to escape the room full of mirrors reflecting an image that suffocated him. "The pop business is much harder than people think," he said. "The people who dig ditches for a living don't know how lucky they are."

Hendrix's despondency and frustration soon infected the Experience. Redding noted how shocked he was "to discover how easily and effectively you can be destroyed by getting what you want." Then he revealed, "The band actually broke up in the summer of 1968. But no one knew about it."

Cream, Traffic, the Byrds, Animals, Hollies, Lovin' Spoonful, Spencer Davis, Big Brother, and Blood, Sweat & Tears—1968 was the year of the Big Breakup. The Experience might have suffered the same fate then had Mike Jeffery not put his cash cow on life support. The band played posthumously for another year as resentments escalated. "It got to the point once in New York when I told Hendrix he was a stupid cunt," said Redding. ". . . To get back at him, I would purposely play out of tune. I wanted to scream: 'Stop being a star and play the guitar!' "

Earlier, onstage, they had improvised brilliantly with each other and loved performing; offstage, they were great buddies and enjoyed ribbing each other—Jimi calling Noel "Bob Dylan's grandma," and Mitch "Julie Andrews," Noel and Mitch calling him "The Bat" due to his vampire love of dark hotel suites. But in the end all the playfulness, the enthusiasm, and the love seemed to have vanished.

The trio endured the last year of the Experience the way other groups did when strapped to a dying animal: they drugged themselves to oblivion. Mitch was the tour pharmacist. Recalled a roadie, "He had an airline bag with three compartments for sleepers (barbiturates), leapers (speed), and creepers (hypnotics)." Said a guitarist who jammed with the Experience at the Record Plant, "On Mitch's floor tom-tom was a substantial pile of Peruvian Flake . . . The size of that pile is something that I won't ever forget."

When journalist Jane de Mendelssohn interviewed Hendrix, she reported that he was naked in bed and that "on the bedside table was the biggest collection of alcohol and drugs . . . three different types of hash, grass, amyl nitrates, and lots of different kinds of bourbon and whisky. We just helped ourselves. He was constantly smoking joints and we were both drinking . . . At one point he offered me some amyl nitrate and we both went out of our skulls."

In the earlier days, the Experience's drug of choice was, according to Noel, "acid, acid, acid. We were spaced constantly." But nobody could keep up with Jimi. "He took out this little candy tin, popped the lid, and offered me some acid," recalled Quicksilver's Gary Duncan. "He had about twenty hits in there; I took about five and he took the rest."

Hendrix hit the wall at the end of the Experience's last tour: he was busted for heroin in Toronto.

Though Jimi was chipping junk by this time, he insisted that he'd been set up. Before crossing the border, the band had been forewarned, according to Mitch, "that there were going to be problems in Toronto. The roadies came round and said, 'Just check all your baggage and make sure that there's nothing that could possibly be planted.' "[18] Not only did he ditch his creepers, leapers, and sleepers, Mitch even took off his underpants and wore a suit without pockets. Jimi too took precautions, but customs uncovered smack in his carry-on bag.

Jimi freaked. Was he suffering from paranoid fantasies? At last, he became convinced of the incredible: his own manager, his acid buddy, had set him up. He'd recently told Jeffery he intended to disband the Experience after their latest tour. Desperate that he would lose his cash cow, Jeffery engineered the bust so Hendrix would be forced to keep the Experience alive to foot his legal expenses. Moreover, heroin was draining Jimi of all his performance and creative energy, leaving him nearly immobilized; Jeffery wanted to see him clean and back on coke and acid.

Convinced of his manager's subterfuge, Jimi took the offensive. He told his lawyer, Henry Steingarten, he wanted to pull the plug on the Experience and on Jeffery too. Steingarten asked why. Not mentioning his conspiracy theory lest counsel think him delusional, Jimi claimed Jeffery was ripping him off. Steingarten insisted he would need proof—documents, receipts, tapes, anything—in order to terminate the management contract.

Jeffery, tight with Steingarten's partner, Steve Weiss, was soon busy with a paper shredder and more heavy commuting to Spain, and the Grand Caymans.

Though Hendrix dissolved the Experience, he abandoned his efforts to terminate Jeffery, and went into seclusion at Shokan House after his friend, Brian Jones, was drowned in his own swimming pool. Later, when asked what he'd been doing since the last tour, the guitarist replied, "I've been doing like Yogi Bear. I've been hibernating, hibernating."

He was awakened from hibernation when Jeffery and his muscle arrived at the Woodstock retreat, demanding that he play The Salvation Club not only to rescue Electric Ladyland from financial collapse, but to pay for his legal defense in Toronto. So Hendrix did "The Black Roman Orgy," his coke dealer buddy was gunned down gangland style, he was kidnapped, and Jeffery "rescued" him. Now Jimi didn't dare try to fire the ex-MI6 agent.

Jeffery was starting to scare him. Shitless.

---

18. Mitch Mitchell, *Jimi Hendrix: Inside the Experience*, with John Platt (New York: St. Martin's, 1990).

VOODOO CHILD

If I don't meet you no more in this world then I'll meet you in
the next one and don't be late, don't be late, 'cause I'm a voodoo
child.
—Jimi Hendrix, "Voodoo Child"

The Panthers, ever short on cash and role models, had been watching
Jimi with interest for some time now. Near the end of the Experience's
last tour, they cornered him for a brother-to-brother talk.

They called the Voodoo Child a "coconut," and an Uncle Tom. They
wanted to know why he kept fucking blondes. They asked him why
he played with two crackers, worked as a white man's nigger, and performed for honkies.

In the past, Jimi had tried to make himself clear on these questions.
"The only colors I see are in my music," he'd told the press. "Music is
stronger than politics," he went on. "I feel sorry for the minorities, but
I don't feel a part of one . . . Every man is an island and music is about
the only way we can really communicate." As for activism, he'd said,
"I want to show black kids that music is universal—that there is no
white rock or black rock."

The Panthers had no patience with such hippie bullshit. They told
Jimi he needed to put his money where his mouth was, for the cause.
Jimi told them he was short at the moment. The Panthers were puzzled;
he'd just finished a fifty-gig tour at a hundred grand a pop—and he was
broke? They offered to have a chat with his CFO. Jimi declined. Okay,
they continued, instead of the bread, how about a benefit concert? Jimi
confessed he didn't have control over his gigs at the moment, either.
Besides, his band was history and he didn't have a new one yet.

The Panthers left their brother bodyguards, saying they'd be watching his back and hoping he'd soon be clearing up his professional problems with a mind to affirmative action.

Jimi drafted his old friends, Billy Cox and Buddy Miles, and started
the all-black Band of Gypsys. His manager was not pleased, especially
when he heard "The Power of Soul." And when, at one of their first
gigs, Jimi introduced "Voodoo Child" with a fist: "It's a black militant
song and don't you ever forget it!" Afterward, he told the press: "You
are either a rebel or like Frank Sinatra."

Now, Mike Jeffery had never been a political animal. Money was
his gig. But his financial partners happened to like Frank Sinatra very

much. In fact, the Chairman of the Board was a personal friend of some. Besides, the Panthers were horning in on their pharmaceutical monopoly uptown and queering their other investments there too. So when Jeffery sat down to lunch with them after the Salvation, they came directly to the point:

"Either you chill your nigger, or we do."

He'd certainly been trying his best. The Toronto bust and the Salvation kidnap succeeded in keeping his artist on the ropes, but now Mike—who used moles and routinely bugged his clients' offices—had learned he was about to defect to Miles Davis's manager, Alan Douglas. In fact, rumor had it that Douglas—who'd also represented Duke Ellington, Charles Mingus, John Coltrane, and other jazz greats—was now trying to put together a Miles-Jimi collaboration.[19] Meantime, he'd been doing everything he could for Hendrix's black band.

Before dealing with this interloper, Jeffery knew his first order of business was to kill the Gypsys and revive his golden goose, the Experience. The Gypsys had only been touring a few months before he saw his opportunity: the 1970 Winter Festival for Peace in Vietnam, at Madison Square Garden.

Jimi's new band had started performing after he was acquitted of drug charges in Toronto, leaving him "happy as a newborn baby" as he said. "I'm really, really trying to get off of this [drugs], because it's controlling my mind," he told reporters.

But before the Gypsys' Garden gig, he downed a toxic cocktail. His drummer, Buddy Miles, later insisted that he saw Jeffery slip Hendrix two tabs of bad acid. But Hendrix would later claim Devon dosed him. Anyway, according to his friend and jamming partner, Johnny Winter, Jimi was in a frightening condition even on arrival for the gig. "When I saw him it gave me the chills," recalled the albino blues guitarist, a smack freak and not the picture of health himself.[20] "It was the most horrible thing I'd ever seen . . . It was like he was already dead."

The Gypsys took the stage at 3 A.M. Jimi collapsed after two songs. "That's what happens when earth fucks with space, never forget that!" he shouted to the 20,000 fans before staggering offstage for what was to be the Gypsys' swan song. While Jimi freaked in his dressing room,

---

19. The collaboration never materialized since the ever-pragmatic Miles refused to participate without a $50,000 advance.

20. The guitarist would finally manage to kick his addiction five years later and return to popularity with his hit, "Still Alive and Well."

Jeffery fired Miles, saying, "The trip's over!" The drummer later declared, "He didn't want Jimi playing in an all black band. I told Jeffery he was an out-and-out complete idiot and a fucking asshole to boot. And he was. One of the biggest reasons why Jimi is dead is because of that guy."

Days later, with a beaming Jeffery standing by, Jimi told a *Rolling Stone* interviewer that the Experience was re-forming. Jeffery hastily summoned Redding and Mitchell from England. But when Redding arrived for rehearsals, he was told that Jimi had rehired Billy Cox instead and that his services on bass wouldn't be required after all. So Redding started work on a solo album, *Nervous Breakdown*.

"Most people would like to retire and just disappear from the scene which I'd *love* to do," admitted Jimi at the time, "but then there's still things I'd like to say. I wish it wasn't so important to me." So he rose from the ashes again—this time with the revived Experience, sans Redding. But the seventeen-gig Cry of Love tour, projected to gross $1.3 million, was a disaster too.

That summer Electric Ladyland Studio had its gala opening attended by the biggest names in rock. But having cut down on social engagements since his kidnapping, Jimi refused to go. According to insiders, he was now totally freaked and consuming drugs nonstop.

Fueling his paranoia, he'd recently had another run-in with his manager's stateside business associates. "This particular gangster was a serious terror in Harlem," recalled Arthur Allen, a friend who was with Jimi. "He ran several big-time disc jockeys, had a few bodies under his belt and *nobody* fucked with him . . . Lo and behold, there was this guy with three of his henchmen. It was confrontation time." The businessman was advertising that Jimi would be playing at his club. "You have no right to do this!" Jimi screamed at him. "My lawyer will be talking to you guys!"

"He was lucky he wasn't killed," said Allen.

Even so, Jimi finally agreed to attend the Electric Ladyland party after being promised an NYPD escort afterward to the airport for his European tour, starting with the Isle of Wight festival.

As arranged. New York's finest delivered him to Kennedy. Soon, three thousand miles from his manager and the rest of the madness, the Voodoo Child was relieved to safely touch down at his home-away-from-home where it had all begun for him four years before: London. "New York's killing me at the moment," he told a journalist on arrival.

But Hendrix found that his feeling of security abroad was illusory.

He arrived at the *Love and Peace Festival* on the German Isle of Fehm-arn for what was to be his last performance. It was raining torrentially, the fans were in a foul mood, and the Hell's Angels security men—two-fisting booze, leapers, and creepers a la Altamont—were not feeling the love either. Which got worse when Jimi refused to perform as sched-uled for fear of being electrocuted on the wet stage. When he finally emerged—drunker than he'd ever seen him, said Noel—it was to the chorus of "boos" and "Go homes!"

"I don't give a fuck if you boo—so long as you boo in key," shouted the guitarist, not a stranger to disgruntled fans by now. He did a quick set, kicking it off with "Killin' Floor" then managed a getaway in a taxi before the Angels torched the stage, shot one of his roadies, and shanked his tour manager, Gerry Stickells, with a nail-studded plank.

Jimi's old friend, Billy, became hysterical, convinced that they would return home in body bags. Doctors attributed his "acute para-noia" to the bad acid he'd been slipped days before. But Jimi's kidnap-ping, the threats against his life, and the Fehmarn carnage were not acid delusions. "We're gonna die!" Billy kept sobbing on the plane from Hamburg back to London.

Jimi tried to chill him. But the star hadn't forgotten drawing the Death card when the chief clairvoyant of the King of Morocco had read his Tarot the summer before. "I'm going to die!" he'd cried to his traveling companion and lover, Colette Mimram. After that, "he kept repeating that he was going to die before he was thirty," said Colette. The king's psychic wouldn't confirm or deny it, only telling Colette, "You will not be friends with this man in a year's time."

According to biographer David Henderson, in Morocco Jimi and Colette were "followed by several strange men wherever they went."[21]

ITINERARY OF A GHOST

> I've been dead a long time.
> —Jimi Hendrix, at a Denmark concert, September 1970

Hendrix had once said, "If I'm free, it's because I'm always running."

What was he running from? Whatever it was, after his kidnap, he

---

21. David Henderson, *'Scuse Me While I Kiss the Sky: The Life of Jimi Hendrix* (New York: Atria, 1978).

began to run faster. He loved Dylan and followed Dylan's survival motto: Don't look back. But on arriving in London for the last time, he glanced over his shoulder as a fleeing man will do, sensing he is being gained on.

"Lately I've been thinking that I'm circled by wolves," Jimi tells Sharon Lawrence. Looking behind him, he has discovered that everyone he'd wanted to escape in New York has tracked him here in London. But he can't run anywhere else or any faster.

Mike Jeffery is the first to arrive. His management contract expires in a few months and he fears Jimi will defect to Alan Douglas, Colette's brother-in-law. He'd recently confronted his rival in New York and accused the jazz producer of "trying to steal my artist!" Hendrix, who hasn't seen Jeffery since the Electric Ladyland party, is not returning his phone calls and is dodging from one place to another in London so he can't be found.

But his manager isn't the only one he's hiding from. Before he contracted with Jeffery three years before, the star had signed with a small-time producer, Ed Chalpin. Chalpin has filed suit and is now on his scent in London too. "Jimi really did not want to face Ed Chalpin," recalled Daniel Secunda, his British record label rep. "He was doing all sorts of drugs to escape from the reality of things like these legal actions." Chalpin, however, saw things differently. "Jimi was having problems with his career. He wanted to pull out of the music business and called me in New York, begging me to join him in London."

Rounding out the roster of business stalkers is the guitarist's lawyer, Henry Steingarten. He, too, has just arrived to serve paternity papers on Jimi, filed by his former lover, Diane Carpenter. So he's doing his best to avoid Steingarten as well.[22]

Hoping for help, he calls on his old friend, Chas Chandler. He unloads all the shit that's gone down with Jeffery, confides that he is about to defect to Douglas, and begs Chas to produce his music again. His benefactor agrees and promises to begin work as soon as he gets back from a family outing to the country.[23]

---

22. At a recent concert in Sweden, he had dedicated "Foxey Lady" to all the girls who were throwing panties on the stage, saying "It's close to Mother's Day, anybody that wants to be a mother, come backstage." Even so, the paternity suit freaked him out.

23. According to several accounts, Jimi later called Chas, leaving a frantic message on his answering machine, "I need help bad, man!" But Chandler had no answering machine.

Next, Hendrix secretly visits Douglas who has also just arrived in London. During an all-night heart-to-heart, the two hatch a scheme whereby Jeffery will be sacked, Douglas will take his place, and Jimi will do only four concerts a year that will be marketed as films.

Jimi sees his music becoming more free form and jazz influenced, and this is Douglas's forte. Jimi also wants a classical angle. "I dig Strauss and Wagner—those cats are good—and I think they are going to form the background of my music," he said. "Floating in the sky above it will be the blues . . . and then there will be Western sky music, and sweet opium music and these will be mixed together to form one." But he doesn't foresee this musical transition to be an easy one for his fans to follow. "The trouble is, I'm schizophrenic in at least twelve different ways," he admits, "and people can't get used to it."

The trouble isn't so much his schizophrenic music but his conflicting moods: a part of him is exhilarated at the prospect of this new direction with Douglas; another part is pessimistic. He confessed to Billy Cox that he's "dried up creatively." He's just told an interviewer, Anne Bjorndal, he won't make it to twenty-eight, adding:

"The moment that I feel that I don't have anything more to give musically, that's when I won't be found on this planet unless I have a wife and children."

While he hides from the wolves of London, Hendrix seeks solace from his new Danish fiancée.

Kristen Nefer accompanied him from Germany to London. The actress has only known him for several days, but has spent most of her time trying to chill him out. He's just learned that a member of the Mafia-controlled Vanilla Fudge, with whom he toured a few years ago, has just been gunned down in the English countryside. He's also freaked about the sudden death of Canned Heat's Alan Wilson. The singer was to join the Experience's European tour, but his body has just been found in California, OD'd on gin and Seconal.

Alarmed by Jimi's manically paranoid behavior, Ms. Nefer, without an engagement ring or a good-bye from him, flees London and returns to the movie she's making with the current James Bond, George Lazenby. Hardly is she gone when the mysterious Ms. Dannemann suddenly shows up at his hotel.

On his second-to-last night, Monika accompanies a wasted Jimi to a Soho club where Burdon is playing with his new group, War. Devon Wilson is already there with friends, waiting to have a serious talk with her ex-lover. He eludes her, disappearing backstage, hoping to arrange a jam with Eric. The singer turns him away. "I was devastated," he later wrote. "Jimi was a mess—dirty, out of control like I'd never seen him . . . He had a head full of something—heroin, ludes, or the German sleeping pills."

While Jimi is backstage with Eric, Ms. Dannemann shows off her gold snake ring to Devon, telling her Jimi has given it to her for their "engagement." Devon has seen more than a few of Jimi's one-night stands over the years. But this one is even more wigged out than the others. She kicks Monika out of her chair and onto the floor.

Jimi reemerges from backstage. "I'm almost gone," he mutters as he stumbles from the club, his battered new companion hurrying after him.

The next day Hendrix is, according to friends, "out of his mind," looking for drugs. At one connection house, after witnessing a customer jump down a stairwell, breaking both legs, Jimi dashes out, screaming.

But in her book, Monika Dannemann insists that her husband-to-be spends his last day joyously. "He was very happy, making plans in regard to us getting married, having children," she recalls. Though he already has two illegitimate children whom he has no interest in meeting, Monika writes that he wants her to have his baby and that he already even has a name for their love child: "Wasformi," Cherokee for Thunder.

The couple rises at about noon that day. Monika, an aspiring photographer and painter, takes snapshots of her trophy boyfriend in the Samarkand Hotel gardens. Then they go out shopping in Chelsea. Here they again run into Devon and her girlfriends. Ignoring Monika today, Devon invites Jimi to a party that night. To Monika's dismay, Jimi accepts.

Early that evening, Ms. Dannemann drives Jimi to dinner at the flat of a new friend of his, Phillip Harvey, hippie son of conservative Parliamentarian Lord Harvey of Prestbury. Phillip's starstuck houseguests—Penny, a sixteen-year-old English schoolgirl, and "Sunshine," a nineteen-year-old Canadian folksinger—serve Jimi wine, joints, and a vegetarian dinner. Phillip, according to his 1993 affidavit to the police, finds Jimi "remarkably pleasant," but Monika increasingly "out of sorts" as the evening progresses. Finally, the skater cries, "I'm leaving now! I've had enough!" She storms outside, Hendrix following. Sir Phillip and the girls hear Monika outside "verbally assaulting him in the most offensive possible way." Fearing commotion at this hour might raise the police, Jimi's host ventures outside to intervene, and recalls, "As I approached them, I remember hearing her shout at him, *'You fucking pig!'*" Perhaps Monika has become jealous of Penny's and Sunshine's attentions toward her man. More likely, she is furious with him for now wanting to go to the party with Devon who publicly humiliated and assaulted her at Tony Scott's club only last night.

With profuse apologies to Sir Phillip, Jimi departs with Ms. Dannemann. According to her own 1993 affidavit, she now drives him back to the Samarkand. "At this time," she would assure authorities, "there was no stress or argument; it was a happy atmosphere." She goes on to testify that she serves Jimi a midnight dinner and, afterward, enjoys a bath while he writes a poem, "The Story of Life." "The story of Jesus so easy to explain . . ." it begins. ". . . The story of life is quicker than a wink of an eye. The story of love is hello and good-bye until we meet again," it ends. According to Monika, Jimi gives her the poem, saying "I want you to keep this forever . . . It's a story about you and me and don't give it to anybody else."

Now Monika drives Jimi to Devon's party, dropping him off at 1:45 A.M. and picking him up a half hour later. He attends the party, she continues, for only one reason: "To warn her [Devon] to leave me alone."

Those at the party, however, have a different version of events. They say Jimi arrives at 11 P.M., meaning he'd come directly from Harvey's flat, and not returned to the hotel with Monika at all. Which seems a more likely scenario than Jimi enjoying a candle-lit dinner, then writing a love poem to a woman who had just publicly assailed him as a "fucking pig."

According to those at the party, Devon serves Jimi Chinese take-out. Then they do some speed and grass. Others say Jimi, Devon, and Stella Douglas (producer Alan's wife) snort Owsley acid.[24] Angie Burdon recalls that Jimi is very "jumpy."

At about 2:30 A.M., the telephone starts ringing. Monika is calling from a phone booth just outside, frantic for Jimi to leave the party. He refuses to take her call. But she keeps ringing him over and over. Finally, partygoers throw open the window and shout, "Fuck off and leave him alone!"

At around 3 A.M., Jimi leaves the party.

---

24. This seems unlikely. Toward the end, Hendrix no longer took LSD because, as he explained to an interviewer, "It is naked. I need oxygen."

This is the last time anyone identifiable, except Monika Dannemann, sees him alive.

Earlier in the day, Hendrix had made plans to jam with Sly Stone and Noel Redding at the Speakeasy. Noel and Sly wait for him till 4 A.M., but Jimi never shows. Noel finds this very "odd," later writing that Jimi was looking forward to the gig and would never have missed it.

According to Ms. Dannemann, she drives Jimi back to her hotel, they talk until 7 in the morning when she takes a sedative and falls asleep "in Jimi's arms." Her Harlequin romance goes on: "He was very happy before I went to sleep. He had no personal troubles. Business problems never worried him." Everyone else, though, agreed that he was on the brink of collapse over these matters. Monika adds two other notable details to her fantasy. Jimi hung a crucifix around his neck before falling asleep. Then he asked her for a favor: in case he should "die," would she watch over him for three days "to make sure he was really dead" and not "on astral travel"?

Monika recalls awakening at about 11 that morning. Finding Jimi unconscious, she goes to the corner store for cigarettes. Returning, she finds him still asleep and discovers an empty packet of her prescription pills on the floor—Vesperax, a powerful German brand of Seconal.[25] She had been prescribed the drug after a painful skating injury. The pills come in packets of ten. Since she has taken one, she assumes that after she had fallen asleep Jimi had taken the remaining nine. But later the police discover one under the bed.

After stumbling on the empty pill packet, Monika looks more closely at the unconscious Jimi. She now notices vomit around his mouth. She shakes him, but he still doesn't stir. Could he be astral traveling? At last, she phones her friend, Judy Wong, who in turn gives her Eric Burdon's number. She awakens the singer with her call, and he tells her "there was no need to worry and that I should wait and see if Jimi woke up on his own." I said I thought I should call an ambulance at once, and Eric replied, "Then call the fucking ambulance!"

According to official records recovered years later, an ambulance is called at 11:18 A.M., but the caller neglects to identify him or herself. It reaches the Samarkand Hotel at 11:27 A.M. Monika says the atten-

---

25. In addition to Canned Heat's Alan Wilson, other celebrities have fatally overdosed on Seconal, including Judy Garland and Marilyn Monroe. Another Seconal-based barbiturate Somulose, is commonly used to euthanize horses and cattle.

dants assure her that Jimi will be fine, and she rides with them to St. Mary Abbots Hospital. Here she gives the on-duty doctor the sleeping pills, but according to her affidavit: "This man just didn't bloody give a damn . . . I said to him, 'Listen, it is Jimi Hendrix . . . he's a very famous musician' . . . They could have saved him in the hospital. They could have just cut the air pipe and it's the easiest thing."

Soon, the doctor emerges from the ER to inform Ms. Dannemann that the patient is dead.

Again, others provide a different version of events.

Eric Burdon insists that he received a phone call from Monika Dannemann not at 11 A.M., but "at first light of dawn." At about 7 A.M. Groggy himself and assuming that Jimi had overdone it at the party, he tells Monika to let him "sleep it off." Burdon goes back to bed, but he soon gets up and calls her back demanding that she call an ambulance immediately. He then taxis to the Samarkand. His girlfriend, Alvinia Bridges, in a separate car, arrives first.

"I didn't want to look at the mess," Eric later tells Kathy Etchingham, Jimi's first fiancée, who investigated his death. "We got the guitars out, and . . . I left Alvinia to take care of the distraught girl."

When ambulance men, Reginald Jones and John Saua, arrive at 11:27 A.M., "the door was flung open, nobody about, just the body on the bed," Jones later swore in an official statement. "We called out for someone, loads of times, so we walked in. . . . The bedroom was dark because the curtains were still pulled. He was covered in vomit, there was tons of it all over the pillow, black and brown it was. His airway was completely blocked all the way down, his tongue had fallen back. I knew he was dead as soon as I walked in the room."

Added Jones's partner, Saua, "His mother wouldn't have recognized him . . . His bowels and bladder, all that goes when you're dead."

Dr. John Bannister, the physician who worked on Hendrix at the St. Mary Abbots, concurred with the paramedics, saying he neither saw nor spoke with any woman attending the patient.

"Jimi Hendrix had been dead for some time, without a doubt," read his official statement submitted years later. He had no pulse, had turned blue, and wine was flowing from his nose and mouth. Bannister attempted to clear his airway with an 18-inch metal sucker, but to no avail due to the quantity of wine in his stomach. However, finding only traces of alcohol in the blood, the doctor hypothesized, "Someone apparently poured red wine down Jimi's throat to intentionally cause asphyxiation." His report concluded that Jimi had literally been "drowned" in the wine because he had first been "slipped a large quantity of barbiturates" which induced a coma.

But, at the time, coroner Dr. Gavin Thurslon listed the immediate cause of death as "inhalation of vomit following barbiturate intoxication."

As for the cause of this fatal condition itself, the pathologist left an "open verdict."

He didn't know and didn't venture to speculate.

THE WAKE

Will the wind ever remember the names it has blown in
the past, and with this crutch, its old age and its wisdom it
whispers, "no, this will be the last."
—Jimi Hendrix, "The Wind Cries Mary"

In late 1993, Hendrix biographers, Kathy Etchingham and Tony Brown, petitioned the London attorney general's office to reopen the case. As a result, the statements of Jones, Saua, Dr. Bannister, and others, were taken. But in February 1994, Scotland Yard advised the attorney general that it was "no longer in the public interest to re-open the original inquest." Investigators reached this conclusion in spite of a key additional bit of evidence that came to light then as well.

The original autopsy revealed that Hendrix's stomach contained undigested rice kernels, likely from the Chinese dinner he'd eaten at the party around 11 P.M. Rice takes three to four hours to digest. Therefore, Hendrix must have died soon after leaving the party with Monika at 3 A.M. The critical question then becomes: what happened immediately after Jimi left?

Did Monika overdose him with the Vesparax and "drown" him in red wine as soon as they returned to the Samarkand? If so—what motive? Tony Brown suggests jealousy toward Devon and Jimi's other girlfriends.

When Sharon Lawrence questioned Monika on that day, she found his "fiancée" remarkably placid—"no tears, no sense of grief." In fact, Monika seemed upbeat about the prospect of launching a career as a painter and "exhibiting my work for him all over the world." "Bye-bye, Jimi; hello, Monika, the great artiste!" wrote Sharon. Insisting that

Jimi no longer ever drank red wine, she demanded of Monika, "When he was choking, gasping for breath, did you pour red wine down his throat? I KNOW you did!"

"It was all untidy," Monika tried to explain. "He was messy. I thought it would help."

"You are a cruel and terrible person," cried Sharon. "And a goddamned liar!"

Even so, Ms. Lawrence concluded that Hendrix committed suicide. Her conclusion was based on two bits of evidence: the pills and the poem. She thought Jimi took nine pills though, in fact, he took eight. Jimi, a student of numerology, had told Lawrence nine was either "very good or very bad" and mentioned his depressed "number nine days" in the last year. She concluded, "I was certain that he *deliberately* confronted fate, made a conscious decision. If the Vesperax pills—*nine* of them—didn't do it, then he wasn't meant to die. Finally, Jimi Hendrix had found peace of mind." Lawrence's second bit of suicide evidence was equally unreliable. He composed his poem "The Story of Life," "in the gloomy early hours of September 18," she wrote. But this was based on the chronology of Dannemann whom she herself dismissed as a liar. According to everyone else's timetable, Jimi wasn't writing poetry that night, but partying with Devon. He kept all his writing in a notebook that he carried around with him. No one could know for certain when he composed this poem—it could have been days or even months before.

But Eric Burdon also interpreted "The Story of Life" as a suicide note. He told a BBC interviewer days after the tragedy that "his death was deliberate. He was happy dying." The singer, however, soon recanted the statement, confessing in his autobiography that "in defiance . . . of all that Jimi stood for, I got stoned before the interview." Later, he changed his view entirely.[26] In a second autobiography, Burdon described Ms. Dannemann as a "stalker"[27] who had "followed Jimi around Europe." He concluded, "Once she had him in her flat, she didn't want to let him go."

---

26. Eric Burdon, *Don't Let Me Be Misunderstood*, with J. Marshall Craig (New York: Thunder's Mouth, 2001). The former Animals' front man also revealed in this second autobiography that after the Hendrix investigation was reopened in 1994, Kathy Etchingham phoned him and warned, "You better get your story straight . . . or you could be looking at doing time."

27. In his Hendrix biography, *Room Full of Mirrors*, Charles Cross wrote that Dannemann, on arriving in London, "tracked him down at his hotel."

Chas Chandler spoke for most other insiders when he flatly stated, "I don't believe for one minute that he killed himself. That was out of the question." Practically speaking, for Jimi eight barbiturates was a modest dose, particularly considering his drug tolerances and desperately wired condition in the end. Had he intended to kill himself, he surely would have taken the extra thirty Monika said she had in the cabinet. Or he would have slit his wrists as he'd done in the past.

So, did Dannemann indeed kill Hendrix as Tony Brown believes? Pouring liters of wine down the throat of a choking, overdose victim, thinking this might "help," was surely not the act of a sane person. But why might Danneman want to kill her lover? She was surely aware of his prolific romantic history. Under the circumstances, jealous she may have been, but homicidally so?[28] If yes, then why didn't *she* dose him with her remaining thirty pills?

But if Monika did *not* indeed murder him, why the elaborate lies and cover-up? Could she have been an accomplice of some sort? If so, whose? Likely, whoever had the most to gain from Jimi's death.

On the morning of September 17, Alan Douglas told Hendrix's lawyers that he would be relieving Jeffery of his management duties. Meaning, not only was Jeffery losing his cash cow, but his nemesis Douglas would, in taking over the books, discover his embezzlement and mismanagement over the years. Thus, the end of Jeffery's career, if not imprisonment. With Jimi gone, however, Jeffery's contract would be renewed by default (which it did), and he would reap the immense profits of posthumous record sales (which he did). Moreover, he had recently taken a million-dollar insurance policy out on the star.

The day before Hendrix's death, Jeffery flew to his villa in Spain without leaving any forwarding number. Before the fatal news was publicized, Jeffery called Jim Marron a colleague, and canceled their dinner date in Majorca, saying, "I've just got word from London. Jimi's dead." Then he added, "I always knew that sonuvabitch would pull a quickie," he added. "He's up and done it!"

Jeffery was already trying to pass the death off as a suicide, at least privately.

Hendrix's New York office was unable to reach the manager for a week since it was his habit never to reveal his whereabouts. When he finally called from Spain and was told arrangements for the funeral

---

28. The MO is not unprecedented. In 1972, New York Dolls' drummer, Billy Murcia, died after his girlfriend poured coffee down his throat while he slept.

were overdue, Jeffery, pretending he hadn't even heard the news, stammered in astonishment, "What funeral?"

Jeffery's motto had always been "Sheer confusion is best." To further cover his tracks, the manager flew back to London to "personally investigate" his client's death. More likely, it was to make sure that no evidence remained. Within hours of Jimi's death, all his hotel rooms and crash pads in London, as well as New York, were turned over: clothes, instruments, writings, drugs—everything vanished.

Soon Alan Douglas announced that Hendrix was murdered and, astonishingly, that Jeffery had confessed involvement to him. Adding another dimension to the motive, Douglas stated, "In my opinion, Jeffery hated Hendrix because Jimi had slept with Lynn Bailey [Jeffery's girlfriend]."

Others agreed with the assassination theory. "I believe the circumstances surrounding his death are suspicious," declared Ed Chalpin. "I think he was murdered." In his memoir, Noel Redding wrote that murder was "a distinct possibility." Later, an informant told the bassist that a French hit man had been responsible. In 1981 the French newspaper *Le Monde* interviewed a contract killer who, though he denied personal involvement, stated that he knew who arranged Hendrix's assassination. Jimi's musician friend, Buzzy Linhart, told *Metronome* magazine that Jeffery had conspired with Monika Dannemann.

Dannemann, however, continued to profess innocence. Implicating Jeffery, she stated in her 1995 memoir that he had actually tried to silence her by offering "to pay me a large sum every month and to make me famous through my paintings—with him as my manager!" She also noted that Jimi had felt "people around him could no longer be trusted . . . having been bought or promised advantages by Jeffery." In fact, it was well known that the ex-spy employed many moles to keep him apprised of Jimi's whereabouts and activities. The question is: Could Dannemann have been one of them? If so, it would have been a brilliant stroke on Jeffery's part. Who could be a more passionately dedicated mole than a star-obsessed, infatuated stalker?

But insisting that she was dedicated to exposing the truth, not her own celebrity, she immediately set to work writing a book. Hardly had she done so, though, when Jeffery told her to "forget about the idea, or something nasty could happen to me." Next, she was called by "the manager of a famous English rock band" who warned her that "my life was in danger" and "I should get some bodyguards." She took the precaution of giving her manuscript to a lawyer. But she said it was soon

stolen by an English businessman connected to Jeffery. Didn't the lawyer still have a copy? Hadn't she made other copies? Apparently not. A
rational person might conclude that this manuscript was yet another
figment of Ms. Dannemann's prolific imagination.

In any case, she did at last take up her pen more than twenty-five
years later—when Jeffery and everybody else seemed to be dead—to
clear up any misunderstandings once and for all. "I myself feel that
there is a slight possibility Jimi was murdered," she wrote timidly,
"especially when I remember the unidentified compound found in his
body." In fact, no such compound was reported in the autopsy.

Clearly the retired skater had a casual relationship with the truth or
lived in a reality all her own. Her memoir—with *by his fiancée, Monika
Dannemann,* in bold on the cover—was filled with her otherworldly
paintings of her soul mate: Jimi engulfed by cosmic fire and doves; Jimi
crowned by lightning from God's hand; Jimi, under a flying saucer, jamming on the White House roof; and most revealing of all, Monika peering into mystical waters, beholding not her face, but Jimi's.

Considering the many conflicting stories—hers and everyone
else's—Dannemann's real involvement in an assassination remains
a matter of speculation. If Jeffery had indeed employed her as an in-
former—what were the details? Knowing Jimi's weakness for Nordic
blondes, had he arranged Monika's original meeting with Jimi in Düsseldorf? Did he hire her to seduce his client and, in the end, to set
him up? Or did Jeffery draw her into the conspiracy later? If so, how?
Providing her with Jimi's touring schedule, did he ask her to keep him
abreast of Jimi's activities on the pretense that he, Jeffery, was concerned about Jimi's deteriorating, drugged-out condition? If so, might
things have gone much further than she ever anticipated?

As for how things actually went down that fateful night, this is
an even greater matter of conjecture. Possibly, as Redding was told,
an assassin infiltrated the Devon party and dosed Hendrix there. Or
maybe the hit man had the party staked out, captured him when he
left for the Speakeasy jam or for his own hotel, killed him, and then
dropped the body at the Samarkand. Or perhaps Monika promised to
drive him to the Speakeasy, detoured to the Samarkand instead, and,
as prearranged, was followed there by the assassin.

In 1975, *Crawdaddy* magazine concluded that a death squad had
targeted the star. The 2004 docudrama, *Hendrix: Last 24 Hours,* suggests such a scenario, with three assassins: one to hold Hendrix, the
other to pour the wine, the third to handle Monika.

In any case, one thing is certain: hours elapsed between the time of the murder—shortly after 3 A.M.—and Monika's phone call to Eric Burdon between 7 and 8 A.M. What happened during these hours? If there was indeed a conspiracy, likely the assassin or assassins rehearsed an OD alibi with Monika, perhaps threatening her life lest she not stick to it.

After a lengthy interview with Dannemann in 1995, Hendrix screenwriter, Alan Greenberg, concluded that she did in fact stick to an alibi—though ever changing—to the bitter end. He told the *New York Press* in 2000 that while questioning her he set several "traps which she fell into." Convinced that "she was a liar," he sent the interview transcripts to Tony Brown of the UK's Jimi Hendrix Archives. After hearing them, Hendrix's sleuth biographer told Greenberg, "You broke the case." The following spring, Greenberg sent his just-completed Hendrix screenplay[29] to Monika portraying her as, in his words, "guilty of murder or manslaughter." At the very same time, Scotland Yard and the courts threw out Dannemann's libel suit against Kathy Etchingham, Tony Brown, and Noel Redding, confirming the trio's allegations that she was a conspirator. On April 5, 1996—days after this court ruling against her and after receiving Greenberg's damning screenplay—Monika Dannemann asphyxiated herself or was asphyxiated.

Though it seemed like a suicide, Dannemann's last lover, guitarist Uli Jon Roth of the Scorpions, denied the possibility. While admitting that she was "very upset" by the court ruling against her, he insisted that "she didn't believe in the concept of suicide." He added that she had received numerous death threats since Hendrix's demise, leaving open the possibility that the original assassins or their associates were involved in her sudden end too. In fact, on the morning of Monika's demise, a London radio station announced that she was scheduled to give a lengthy radio interview in which she would at last reveal exactly what happened on that predawn morning of September 18, 1970, twenty-six years before, thus exposing the conspirators at last. She did not appear for the interview, but was found dead in her monoxide-filled Mercedes.

Adding to the casualty list, Monika's rival, Devon Wilson, jumped or was pushed from a Chelsea Hotel window in 1971. She had just com-

---

29. The screenplay remains unproduced due to disagreements between Hendrix estate executrix, Janie Hendrix, and Hollywood financiers.

pleted an interview for Warner's *Film About Jimi Hendrix* in which she stated that her lover had been assassinated. The footage of the interview was destroyed.

Compounding and completing the Hendrix mystery, Mike Jeffery died in a 1973 airplane crash over France. Or did he? He was listed as a passenger on an Iberian DC-9 from Majorca, Spain, to London during a French air traffic controllers' strike. The DC-9 collided with a smaller Spantax Coronado, killing all 68 passengers. Hendrix biographer, David Henderson, considered the disaster "fuel for paranoia" since flight patterns were being closely monitored and directed by the French military. He believed Jeffery was "the target of assassination" and "merely a tool, a mouthpiece, for the real villains."

Eric Burdon, however, asserted that the ex-spy manager may have faked his own death. ". . . At the last moment," he theorized, "he decided not to board the aircraft, as he'd done dozens and dozens of other times at the last minute." But, still on the fatality list in the crash, "he was a free man with a briefcase full of money." Admitting it might be his "hard-won paranoia," Burdon wondered if his ex-manager might be "on a beach somewhere sipping a fruit drink . . . Jeffery was exactly the kind of person who could pull off a scam like that."

The Experience's Noel Redding agreed. "Everything considered," he wrote, "I don't entirely believe he is dead." The body parts of the former demolition expert were never recovered from the ten-mile radius of debris, a span usually the result of a mid-air explosion, not a collision. Only the jewelry in his checked luggage was identified. Redding explained that Jeffery was due in London court within days to defend himself in several huge lawsuits—one of them the bassist's own—relating to his embezzlement, money laundering, and fraud. According to Eric Burdon, in the end his former manager was trying to extort "serious cash" from investors for unreleased Hendrix tapes which he was palming off as the work of "an undiscovered genius" successor to Jimi. "The last time he [Jeffery] left New York," Burdon went on, "he was carrying a briefcase filled with tapes—and several million dollars in cash."[30]

---

30. After years of legal wrangling for compensation from the multimillion dollar Hendrix estate, Redding was finally paid $100,000, which evaporated in fees. The famous bassist went on to become a chimney sweep. He died in 1996.

POSTMORTEM

"The next time I go to Seattle will be in a pine box," prophesied Hendrix.

Months later, he did so, dressed by the undertaker in a flannel logger's shirt. Sharon Lawrence had called his father, begging that Jimi, according to his wishes, be buried in London. Ignoring her plea, Al had a more pressing concern. "Would you be knowing how much money there is?"

Two years before, returning triumphantly to Seattle for the first time since high school, Jimi told Sharon about his reunion with his father: "He came right out and asked me what I was doing about a will and about him being the beneficiary . . . He's twice my age, and he wants to be beneficiary . . . I guess they all want me to die."

"Rich didn't happen soon enough for Al," concluded Sharon.

Jimi Hendrix's open-casket funeral was held on October 1, 1970, at Seattle's Dunlap Baptist Church. In attendance were his father and several other family members and friends, including Devon Wilson. Also present were Mitch Mitchell, Noel Redding, Buddy Miles, Johnny Winter, John Hammond Jr., and Miles Davis. Devon, hysterical, tried to throw herself into the open grave. Sitting in a limousine outside, Mike Jeffery "paid his respects," but refused to participate in services. He donated a guitar-shaped floral display. Hendrix's favorite white Stratocaster, which was to be buried with him, was stolen.

The star's will left everything to his father, Al. But he had not signed the document. Just before his passing, Aunt Freddie Mae who had cared for him as an infant, asked why. "Oh," protested Jimi, "that's like signing a death certificate. That's an omen."[31]

Jimi had one final prophesy: "If anything happens to me, the lawyers will be fighting it out for the next twenty years."[32]

And so it was. Al Hendrix, with the help of Microsoft co-founder, Paul Allen, battled in court for twenty-six years before receiving the full inheritance. After a successful paternity suit, Eva Sundquist received $1 million from the estate for her and Jimi's son, James. Losing her own paternity suit, Diane Carpenter received nothing for her daughter, Tamika.

---

31. Harry Shapiro and Caesar Blebbeek, *Jimi Hendrix: Electric Gypsy.*
32. Sharon Lawrence, *Jimi Hendrix: The Man, the Magic, the Truth.*

Al Hendrix died of heart failure in 2002. He was buried beside his son in Seattle's Greenwood Cemetery. Several months later, the two bodies were disinterred and moved a short distance away into a million-dollar, thirty-foot-high, three-pillared granite dome. The body of Jimi's beloved mother, Lucille, remained nearby in a pauper's grave with no headstone but only a welfare brick marked MITCHELL, her second husband's name.

Jimi Hendrix's most recent biographer, Charles Cross, expressed the persistent popular but myopic view of his death. "The circumstances and choices that had led Jimi to this hotel room, and this fate," he wrote, "were solely of his own making." Noel Redding, one of the star's few and true friends, concluded his own memoir in a very different manner. "If it is impossible to maintain consciousness after death," he wrote, "then Jimi must be in agony."

But, in spite of it all, surely not. Jimi once said, "My goal is to be one with the music. I just dedicate my whole life to this art." Few doubt that he achieved this in his all-too-brief life. It is generally acknowledged, too, that he was one of the most powerfully original guitarists in history and had an unprecedented influence on the way the instrument was played. In his hands, it became like a magical, voracious creature endowed with a life all its own. Yet his music went far beyond the guitar. It was in a category all its own—not white or black music, as he said, but "universal" music rising like a cathedral of soaring chords. In this, he taught us that "with the power of soul" anything is indeed possible.

"The eagle . . . took me past the outskirts of infinity," sang the Voodoo Child. ". . . And if I don't meet you no more in this world, then I'll, I'll meet you in the next one, and don't be late."

Interlude: Orphans

I used to say to my auntie, "You throw my fuckin' poetry out, and you'll regret it when I'm famous," and she threw the bastard stuff out. I never forgave her for not treating me like a fuckin' genius or whatever I was when I was a child.
—John Lennon

What always worried me, John, was that you wouldn't be so much famous as notorious. You were certainly that as a child . . . If the Beatles hadn't come along, you could have ended up on the scrap heap.
—Aunt Mimi, to John after he became a Beatle

Jimi Hendrix's parents regularly abandoned him. When Al and Lucille returned home from their drunken escapades and tried to reunite, brutal fights broke out. "Mama and Daddy are always fighting," young Jimi would cry to his guardian of the day.

The worst trauma occurred when he was only four. His mother had again vanished and his father, back from the War, snatched him from his California caretaker and put him on a train back to Seattle. "No one could ever know how I felt going off with this strange guy," Hendrix would later recall. "I cried and cried. It was the worst thing that ever happened to me."

His father's return might have turned things around had he been more liberal with love than the back of his hand. "Al hit his son when he was in a rage," said Pernell Alexander, a member of Jimi's first group, the Velvetones. "He was a brutal man . . . It was a rough scene, man. It was straight up ugly."[1]

---

1. Charles R. Cross, *Room Full of Mirrors*.

The only joy in the boy's life was when his mother came back. But, at last, after another severe beating by Al, she fled for good, crying, "Jimmy baby, I have to escape this!" The boy, who had constant night-mares about his mother dying, became moody, withdrawn, and de-veloped a stutter. He escaped in Hans Christian Anderson fairy tales, in Flash Gordon comics, and in his drawing books. Thinking he was from outer space, he drew Martian sunsets, flying saucers, and ETs. He jumped from his roof, thinking he could fly.

His favorite toy was his broom guitar. When Al was down and out again, Jimi found sanctuary with his Aunt Dorothy and her nine kids. Every night, Cousin Shirley would tell him the story of "Roy the sweeping boy . . . who made it big as a guitar player, became rich and famous because of his broom guitar."

Lucille died in the hospital where she had given birth to Jimi. The 15-year-old was devastated. Al gave him and his kid brother, Leon, a shot of Seagram's 7, but he forbade them to attend their mother's fu-neral. "He never really forgave our dad for that," Leon would remember. And he never truly recovered from the death of his mother, whom he called his "angel" and his "goddess in the sky." "Instead of long-term planning," wrote Charles Cross, "he lived every day as if it were his last." In "The Wind Cries Mary" he sang, "A broom is drearily sweep-ing up the broken pieces of yesterday's life . . . Somewhere a queen is weeping, somewhere a king has no wife."

Real intimacy became impossible for Jimi. Just before the end, he would confess to Sharon Lawrence, ". . . Once in a while I may say 'love' to a girl, but I don't mean it . . . I've never truly been in love, the kind of love that lasts. The only person who ever really loved me was my mother. And she's long dead." As for his father, Jimi said he had only seen him twice since leaving Seattle, ". . . . and the only time I hear from him is when he'd like me to send him a check."

During his brief career, he would have thousands of women and propose to at least four. But as one of the first, Linda Keith, observed, "There was no depth to any of his relationships." He was known for surrounding himself with hundreds of groupies but, as Mitch Mitchell observed, he was "a loner and a recluse."

One dreary Liverpool afternoon, the fifteen-year-old Quarryman, John Lennon, was sitting down with his mates, Paul and George, enjoying tea and toast served by George's mum in the Harrisons' row house. He'd known McCartney for a year, but from the very first had had a burning question that he suddenly blurted out as soon as Mrs. Harrison left the room.

"How you can sit there and act normal with your mother *dead?*" he demanded of the ever-cheerful Paul, who had recently lost her to cancer. "If anything like that happened to me, I'd go off me head!"

Less than a year later, John's mother, Julia, was run over by a drunk, off-duty policeman outside the house of his guardian, Aunt Mimi. "The copper came to the door to tell us about the accident," recalled the Beatles' founder. "It was the worst thing that ever happened to me. I thought, I've got no responsibilities to anyone now." He later wrote "Mother, Julia, and My Mummy's Dead" for her. "I can't get it through my head," he sang. "It's hard to explain. So much pain."

Recalled Paul, "Now we were both in this, both losing our mothers. This was a bond for us, something of ours, a special thing." Similarly, John's first wife, Cynthia, had, at 16 years old, lost her father to cancer. "The loss of a parent," she wrote, "was one of the things we had in common and proved a powerful bond."[2]

Lennon's own father, Freddie, who himself had grown up in Liverpool's Blewcoat Orphanage, had abandoned him at the age of five. "Father, you left me but I never left you," he sang. "I needed you but you didn't need me." He later told an interviewer: "I soon forgot my father. It was like he was dead." He called him a "drunk and almost a Bowery bum."

No sooner had Freddie, in the merchant marine, shipped out than Julia took up with other lovers, bearing a daughter to one and then marrying another. Like Hendrix's mother, Lucille, the beautiful Julia Lennon was a flirtatious, fun-loving jitterbug queen. John adored her, just as Jimi had Lucille. The two had a "girlfriend-boyfriend relationship," said John's boyhood pal, Pete Shotton. "Julia was his mate, not his mother."

After Freddie's desertion, Julia's straitlaced elder sister, Mimi—considering her "frivolous and unreliable," and "not fit to have a child"—insisted she turn John over to her for a proper upbringing. John would later bitterly recall that he had lost his mother twice: first at 5 years old when moving in with his Aunt Mimi and then at 16 when she was killed. When Julia turned her son over to her sister, the boy was crushed. "The worst pain is that of not being wanted," he later said.

Even so, Lennon, wanting no pity, bristled at the David Copperfield

---

2. Cynthia Lennon, *John* (New York: Crown, 2005).

rubbish about his childhood. "I never had that fear and adulation of parents. Well, that's the gift of being a so-called orphan—which I never was at all," he declared in his last interview. ". . . This image of me being an orphan is garbage because I was well protected by my auntie and my uncle."

Protected, yes; loved, no—at least not demonstrably by Mimi. "All she cares about is fucking money and cats," he told his wife Cynthia. Friction with his implacable aunt was ever growing due to his trouble-making in and out of school. "We are born in a prison, raised in a prison, sent to a prison called school," he sang. "We live with no reason, kicked around for no reason." His headmaster often called Mimi about John's poor grades, hostile insubordination, and cruel pranks. His teachers, after caning him repeatedly to no avail, dismissed him as a "class clown," and a "wasted intelligence." Parents forbade their children to play with him. "The parents instinctively recognized I was a troublemaker," admitted John. "I did my best to disrupt every friend's home there was, partly out of envy that I didn't have this so-called home."

At her wit's end, Mimi nearly gave up on the boy. "No doubt the impossibility of pleasing her was at least part of John's drive toward success," observed Beatles' biographer, Bob Spitz.

But on the face of it, young John had always been "very arrogant and very self-assured," recalled one of his neighbors. "I'm JOHN LENNON!" he would announce to strangers. "We were all a little frightened of him," said one of his schoolmates. His favorite prank was lying in the street playing dead. Otherwise, he amused himself by shoplifting, setting fires, and blowing up mailboxes. He gained the reputation as a bully, and his Aunt Mimi would walk him to school to avoid "scraps."

His only solace and refuge in Mimi's house was her henpecked husband, George. Doting on the boy, the jovial retired dairyman and bookie was like a second father to John. But this relationship, too, was tragically short-lived: the year before Julia was killed, George died suddenly of a liver hemorrhage.

Now the only father figure in John's matriarchal family of "Amazonian Aunties," as he called them, was his mother's common-law husband, John Dykins, a bon vivant, bisexual wine steward in the habit of beating Julia when drunk. Due to his excitable disposition and facial tic, John called him "Twitchy." On one occasion, the boy stumbled on Twitchy being pleasured by his mother; on another, he watched the waiter drive her out into the yard, stripped naked and weeping. Such episodes soured young John's maternal affections. "He reviled his mother in the most obscene language I have ever heard," his stepmother, Pauline, later wrote,[3] "referring to her repeatedly as a 'fucking, cocksucking whore!' " John's fondness for his stepfather, however, remained to the end. In 1966, a drunk Twitchy was killed in the Riley roadster his now famous stepson had given him.

Like Jimi Hendrix, John Lennon grew up a lonely child who found only one true love in his life: rock-and-roll music. Jimi's father gave him his first guitar after the death of his mother; John's mother gave him his first guitar the year before she was killed. As boys, both idolized the King of Rock and Roll himself.

"Before Elvis there was nothing," John declared.

In the King, the founder of the Beatles saw a pioneer and kindred spirit. Wrote Albert Goldman, the biographer of both legends: "They were the same human being . . . lonely only children reared by overprotective matrons. . . . Both escaped from their throttling families by striking rebellious poses."

Elvis Aron Presley's identical twin, Jessie Garon, was stillborn. His superstitious, God-fearing mother, Gladys—who herself almost died in the delivery—believed he had inherited the soul of his dead brother and was "the One." Years later, Gladys would suffer a miscarriage, making her all the more protective of her only surviving child. "My mama never let me out of her sight," said Elvis. Recalled his father, Vernon, "He never spent a night away from home until he was seventeen. The three of us formed our own private world."

The security of that world was shattered when Vernon was convicted of check fraud and was sent to Parchman, the most medieval of the Mississippi penitentiaries. Elvis, though only three at the time, never forgot the loss and humiliation. "He felt crippled by his father's prison record, his family's poverty, and his mother's need to be cared for," wrote his stepbrother, Rick Stanley.[4]

Vernon's imprisonment galvanized Gladys's obsessive fear that loved ones could, without warning, be taken from her or senselessly stricken down. When she was 18, her father, Bob, died suddenly of pneu-

---

3. Pauline Lennon, *Daddy Come Home: The True Story of John Lennon and his Father* (UK: Angus & Robertson, 1990).

4. Rick Stanley, *Caught in a Trap: Elvis Presley's Tragic Lifelong Search for Love*, with Paul Harold (Dallas, Tx: World Publishing Group, 1992).

monia. Months after the birth of Elvis, tuberculosis claimed her sickly mother, Doll. Her parents had been first cousins. Many of her other siblings were stricken with mental and physical disabilities. Gladys, Vernon, and Elvis were sleepwalkers and all suffered from terrifying nightmares of impending doom.

Like Lucille Hendrix and Julia Lennon, Gladys Presley had once been a vivacious and fun-loving party girl and "buck" dancer. But after all the family losses, protecting her only son became Gladys's life. She slept with Elvis until he was thirteen.[5] She also walked her boy to and from school every day. For his eleventh birthday, Elvis wanted a bicycle, but, fearing that he might get run over on the way to school, Gladys gave him a guitar instead.[6]

"Elvis saw his parents as his 'babies,' " said his friend and employee Lamar Fike. "He called his mother his baby." Just as Gladys protected her baby, he protected his. "Hit her again and I'll kill ya!" he'd threatened his father more than once.[7] The normally mild-mannered Vernon would occasionally get frisky on sour mash when his overbearing wife would berate him as a "dullard" and a "donkey." But Elvis's mother could give as good as she got; she once nearly killed Vernon with an iron skillet.

In 1948, the penniless Presleys fled little Tupelo for public housing in the metropolis of Memphis. When his parents dropped Elvis off for his first day at the 1,600-student Hume High School, their 13-year-old "was so nervous he was bug-eyed," recalled Vernon. The delicate, long-lashed hillbilly boy in the flashy clothes and with the guitar strapped over his shoulder was bullied for two years. One of his classmates recalled that the other boys threw rotten fruit at him "because he was different . . . quiet . . . shuttered and was a mama's boy." The Hume High toughs also stole his guitar, cut the strings, and cornered him in the boy's room once and tried to cut his magnificent hair.

Red West, the varsity football jock who rescued him, would later become the King's bodyguard. By this time the once-bullied mama's

---

5. Years later, Elvis's stepmother, Dee Stanley, whom he deeply resented, would not only claim that they had intercourse, but that Elvis had "a secret gay life."

6. Others recalled that Elvis asked for a gun, but that Gladys refused him, insisting "you're liable to kill all your little playmates."

7. Years later, in 1967, Elvis had a fistfight with Graceland gardener Troy Ivy. Afterwards Ivy accused Elvis of being crazy and trying to kill Vernon while Elvis accused Ivy of being drunk. No charges were filed.

boy—now obsessed with karate, guns, and law enforcement—told his movie directors that he wanted to be "the baddest motherfucker around." His hero was Dirty Harry. He bought Shaft's limousine. On-stage he donned Captain Marvel's white thunderbolt capes.

In 1953, Elvis, now a truck driver for Crown Electric, gave Satnin a special birthday gift: his first recording, "My Happiness." The next year, "That's Alright, Mama" put him on the charts, and soon he was rich beyond his wildest dreams. Long before, he and Gladys had mar-veled at a Memphis mansion on one of their walks to school. "Mama," he told her, "some day I'm gonna buy you a house just like that!" In 1957, he gave her Graceland, plus a pink Cadillac, though she couldn't drive.

"A man who has been the indisputable favorite of his mother keeps for life the feeling of a conqueror," wrote Freud.

Gladys had never known anything but shotgun shacks, jalopies, and public housing; when her father died, her family couldn't afford a marker or a winding sheet; and when Elvis was born, welfare paid the doctor's $15 delivery fee. Now, to be under the same magnificent roof at Graceland with her boy was like a dream come true. But the dream soon became one of her nightmares. "After Elvis became famous, Gladys was never happy another day," remembered her best friend, Lil-lian. "She never had peace no more."

When her son was touring, as he always seemed to be now, the fans mobbed and tore at him. She forbade him to fly in airplanes after his chartered prop lost an engine over the Ozarks and crash-landed. So he drove to all his gigs, but she feared he'd have a fatal accident. "If you don't slow down, you won't live to 30!" she warned him. One night she suddenly bolted out of bed and cried to Vernon, "I see our boy—he's in a blazing car!" The next day, Elvis called her from Texarkana and said his rented Cadillac had burst into flames and he'd narrowly escaped.

The overwrought, alcoholic Gladys started popping pills to sleep, took speed to wake up, and consumed increasing quantities of vodka to cope. When Elvis returned to Graceland, he would shower her with gifts, but even the most extravagant now left her cold.

"Mama, what do you *want?*" pleaded Elvis.

"For you to say HOME, baby!" Gladys would cry.

Soon after moving to Graceland, her son got a draft notice from the Army. Remembering how her cousin, Junior, had lost his mind in Korea and massacred innocents, she begged Elvis not to go. But he felt it his duty. No sooner was he in uniform than she suddenly died of cirrhosis of the liver. Like Lucille Hendrix, Gladys Presley drank herself to death.

"Please don't take my baby away!" Elvis sobbed, throwing himself over her coffin and refusing to let go. "She's not dead. She's just sleeping." Then as she was lowered to her resting place, "Good-bye, darling. I love you so much. I lived my whole life just for you."

Later, the King of Rock and Roll would say of his mother, much as both Lennon and Hendrix had of theirs, "I lost the only person I ever loved." Her death was the greatest tragedy in his life, and from that day on, he became an utterly different person.

"Basically, Elvis's personality was that of Gladys's," Fike later wrote. "There wasn't a dime's worth of difference between them."

In 1975, Vernon Presley was hospitalized after a near fatal heart attack. Elvis occupied the next bed, detoxing from another near fatal narcotic overdose. He and his father had grown apart since Gladys's death, largely due to Vernon's brief mourning and hasty remarriage. For Vernon's part, something had been burning in his chest all these years, and that day in hospital, he suddenly spit it out. "You worried your mama right into the grave!"

"Elvis broke down and cried," remembered his cousin, Billy. "It about killed him."

Two years later, the King of Rock and Roll fatally overdosed himself on the very same day he had buried his mother nineteen years before.

Calling his childhood "an open sore," Jim Morrison told his band, the Doors, that he was an "orphan." Later they discovered he had a mother after all. The officer's wife who had raised the boy almost single-handedly was sitting in a front-row seat her son, "the Lizard King," had reserved for her in the Washington, DC, auditorium. During the show's climactic number, "The End," he sang about fucking his prim mother and killing his autocratic father.

The Oedipal anthem, a departure from Elvis's "That's Alright Mama," which had seemed so revolutionary only a decade before, established its composer as one of the most savagely original rock performers, linking the ancient to the adolescent. He was "a thousand years old . . . though he acted like an adolescent," observed his record label rep Daniel Fields.

Like his idol Elvis, James Douglas Morrison was an Adonis, a Narcissus, a Dionysus. Frank Sinatra had condemned the King's music as a "rancid-smelling aphrodisiac." Ed Sullivan, though he would only televise Elvis "the Pelvis" above the waist, called him "a good wholesome boy." But the enfant terrible, Jim Morrison, was another matter. Jackie Gleason and Anita Bryant mobilized a national protest against the self-described "Erotic Politician" after he allegedly exposed himself at a Miami concert. Morrison called his exhibitionism in his home state of Florida "a fitting tribute to my parents." As for "The End," when a journalist once asked the Lizard King if he really wanted to fuck his mother, he replied, "No, I want to fuck yours."

Morrison did, however, seem serious about wanting to murder his father. Elvis had threatened to kill Vernon for beating his mother; Lennon threatened to bury Freddie at sea for abandoning him as a boy. Where both the King and the Clever One were inclined to sword rattling, Morrison was, according to his acquaintances, a "psychotic" and a "sociopath."

If the singer's violent destructiveness was rooted in patricidal fantasies, what had his father done to provoke them? James M. Morrison was the youngest admiral in the Navy. In disciplining his eldest son, he used a military "dressing down" approach: he would humiliate the boy to submission and apology. When psychological terrorism became less effective with his precocious, increasingly rebellious son, Admiral Morrison got old-fashioned. He beat him with a baseball bat. Jim also confided to his lawyer that his father had sexually assaulted him and that he never forgave his mother for allowing it. His mother dismissed the charge as one of her son's malicious lies. "In spite of his medals," said Jim of his father, "he's a weakling who let her [his wife] castrate him."

Unlike the others, Morrison had had a seemingly secure upper middle-class upbringing; his parents weren't boozers or deadbeats; he was a class president and an honor student; and his mother and father didn't divorce or die on him. The closest he came to death as a boy was when, at 5 years old, while driving with his parents through the New Mexico desert, he witnessed the crash of a truckload of Indians. He would later call this "the greatest event of my life," believing that one of the dying Indians "leapt into my soul" much as Elvis believed his dead twin possessed his own soul. As for any earlier recollection, the star later confessed, "Actually I don't remember being born, it must have happened during one of my blackouts."

The fact that Jim Morrison called himself an "orphan" had more to do with his self-mythology than alienation. A fabulist intellectual and a voracious reader, he gave birth to himself as Frederich Nietzsche's Superman. Every time he performed "The End," he became the Superman "breaking on through to the other side" by violating man's most sacred laws against incest and murder. Rock and roll was the vehicle for this since, of all art forms, it was the wildest and most primal. "When I was just a little boy, 'bout the age of five I went to sleep, I heard my mama and papa talking," he sang in "Rock Is Dead." "She said, 'We got to stop that boy, he's gettin' too far out, he's goin' wild, we gotta stop that child.' "

If Elvis brought sexuality to rock, at least to white audiences, Morrison brought it feral rage. In this he laid the groundwork for a new form fueled by adolescent angst and anger: Punk. A *New York Times* columnist once observed that Punk was "what happens when children of divorce get their hands on guitars." And it gave its heroes an alternative to prison or a mental hospital.

The Lizard King escaped prison by taking asylum in Paris, and he may have seen the rubber room had he not packed stadiums as rock's wild child savior. "All right, wild child full of grace, savior of the human race," he sang in "Wild Child". ". . . Natural child, terrible child, not your mother's or your father's child: Your wild child full of grace, savior of the human race."

As for Morrison's successor, Kurt Donald Cobain was a regular in the Seattle County jail. Then this child of divorce got his hands on a guitar and became the Father of Grunge.

Kurt called himself "happy" until the age of nine; then his parents broke up, and he said he became "a seriously depressed kid." Soon after the divorce, his mother, Wendy Cobain—a promiscuous beauty like Lucille Hendrix and Julia Lennon—married an alcoholic longshoreman who beat her, terrorized Kurt, and called him a faggot. The boy, who called his stepfather "a mean, huge wife beater," started back talking and throwing tantrums. His mother tossed him out of her doublewide when he was 14. He slept on the floors and couches of friends' houses, but they all kicked him out because "it was like living with the devil," as one adoptive parent put it. On his own now, Kurt lived under bridges, in abandoned cars, and in county jails for the next five years. But wherever he went, he took his guitar with him just as Elvis, Jimi, and John had done.

Like his idol and fellow Washington left-hander, Hendrix, Cobain thought he was an extraterrestrial. "I wanted to be from another planet really bad," he said. "Every night I used to talk to my real parents and my real family in the skies." In another interview, he confessed, "Subconsciously, maybe I thought I was adopted. . . . I really related to *The Partridge Family* episode about Danny being adopted."

Like Jimi, Kurt had an imaginary playmate too: His name was Boddah; Jimi's was Sessa. "I'm so happy 'cause today I found my friends— they're in my head," he sang in "Lithium." After Boddah disappeared, Kurt began adopting stray and wounded animals. His menagerie would stay with him for the rest of his brief life.

Besides caring for his pets and playing his guitar, Kurt's other favorite pastime was drawing. Jimi, Jim, Janis, John, and Jerry were all gifted artists too. But Kurt's work was in a league all its own. By kindergarten, he was drawing Donald and Daisy Ducks with enormous dicks, vaginas, and assholes. Young Jimmy Morrison's erotica was comparable, but with less attention to detail. Soon Kurt was taking his subjects not from nature but from his prolific nightmares: dead fetuses, deformed "flipper babies," and dolls with shot-out eyes hanging from umbilical nooses. His art matured during the launch of his first group, Fecal Matter: mixed-media compositions with gynecology journal photos of diseased vulvas beside deli special clippings from supermarket fliers. He varnished these collages with what he called his "secret ingredient.": his cum. A Renaissance man, Kurt was also a graffiti artist, decorating buildings and shop fronts with guerilla haiku such as God Is Gay! Abort Christ! and Nixon Killed Hendrix!

Shock and awe became the Sturm und Drang of Punk. In this Kurt was the maestro. Upping Morrison's ante, he gobbed and pissed on fans; he smashed up guitars, tour buses, and hotel suites; he paraded on stage in women's lingerie and hospital gowns; and he did Manson-eyed photo ops with revolvers in his mouth. With such stagecraft enlivening Grunge anthems such as "Smells like Teen Spirit" (a vaginal deodorant), he became the pied piper of the once voiceless Generation X.

Kurt Cobain dreamed of "going out in a flame of glory like Hendrix." And instead of trying to outgrow his painful childhood, he sought to embrace it. His only tattoo was a *K* inside a shield on his forearm. The *K* was for KAOS, his local punk radio station, which played the songs of the child-friendly K Records. Explaining the significance of the tattoo, Kurt said, "It was just a nice reminder of innocence . . . to try to remind me to stay a child."

* * *

The boyhood of Jerry Garcia, the longest-lived of the Seven, hadn't been a walk in the park, either. At 5 years old he watched his father drown. His mother, Ruth, remarried and turned the boy over to her parents to raise, just as Julia Lennon had turned the 5-year-old John over to her elder sister, and just as Clara Morrison had turned the adolescent Jimmy over to her own parents. Free spirited and promiscuous like Julia and Lucille Hendrix too, Ruth Garcia was not the doting Gladys Presley–type matron.

After moving in with his grandparents, "Jerry was bereft . . . feeling that he was not loved and that he was not worthy. These scars would never fade," wrote the Grateful Dead's biographer and archivist Dennis McNally.[8] The boy hated his stepfather, an alcoholic carpenter whom Ruth had met at the bar she owned and managed. "Jerry had never entirely forgiven his mother for the death of his father, nor for remarrying," McNally went on, adding that he—like Lennon and Cobain too—disparaged his mother's morals and that his "trust in women had been permanently damaged."

Ruth divorced her carpenter after two years, then married a sailor who became her bartender. Meanwhile, according to a school friend, Jerry became lost "in his own world." The boy's two favorite pastimes were, like many of the others, drawing and consuming comic books (his estate later included his $30,000 collection). In spite of recurrent nightmares, the Dead's future leader especially loved J. C.'s *Tales from the Crypt*, with Frankenstein, Dracula, and Wolfman. His drawings reflected these literary interests: he doodled skulls, crossbones, and monsters.

As teenagers, he and his older brother, Tiff, set fire to the San Francisco hills and threw rocks through police station windows. From street gangs, he scored "candy." At 15, he discovered his favorite brand. "Wow! Marijuana," he exclaimed. "It was great, it was just what I wanted . . . that wine thing was so awful, and this marijuana was so perfect!"

For Jerry, only one other thing rivaled the high: rock and roll. For his 15th birthday, Ruth gave him an accordion that he pawned for an electric guitar. At the same time, Ruth reunited the family, moving with Jerry and Tiff to a little coastal town north of San Francisco. Here,

---

8. Dennis McNally, *A Long Strange Trip: The Inside History of the Grateful Dead* (New York: Broadway Books, 2002).

away from city distractions, Jerry spent all his time practicing his guitar. After graduating from high school, Jerry stole his mother's car, got busted, and was given the same ultimatum by the courts as Hendrix in Seattle for the same crime: jail or the Army.

Jerry, like Jimi, was deemed "psychologically unfit for military service" and discharged. After his release, he was nearly killed in a car accident that claimed the life of his best friend, a talented painter. At around the same time, John Lennon's best friend, Stu Sutcliff, "the fifth Beatle" and also a talented painter, suffered a fatal brain hemorrhage. Jerry, calling the tragedy "the slingshot for the rest of my life," founded the Grateful Dead months later.

In 1973 the Dead's keyboardist, Pigpen McKernan, died at age 27. Several years earlier, Jerry's mother, Ruth, suffered a fatal auto crash. He and his brother appeared unmoved. After their father's death, "We were all cried out," Tiff Garcia explained.

Jerry seemed equally stoical when hearing about his friend, Janis. "She was on a real hard path," he said. "She picked it, she chose it, it's okay. She did what she had to do and closed her books."

In the year before her death, Janis suffered six heroin overdoses, two nearly fatal. Her manager had sent her to endocrinologist Dr. Ed Rothschild. Rothschild put her on methadone and diagnosed her as "intellectually bordering on brilliant. She really could think circles around most people . . . but her emotions were childlike and uncontrollable."

Her parents knew this all too well. Their eldest daughter had seemed happy in her early years but then in high school, "She just changed totally, overnight," recalled her mother. The once pretty little girl was now fat and had acne. Wounded by her classmates' mockery, she became, to her parents' dismay, a fighter, a foul mouth, and a hell-raiser. "You're ruining your life!" was her mother's constant refrain. After becoming a star, Janis would tell reporters, "My mother kicked me out of the house when I was 14."[9]

"Pearl" as she called her rowdy, party-hearty self, soon ran away from home and adopted rock-and-roll relatives. "They're like my family," she said of Big Brother and the Holding Company. "I've balled 'em all." Wrote her psychologist sister, Laura, she "was creating a new core family for herself."

---

9. In her biography, *Love, Janis* (New York: Harper Collins, 2005), Laura Joplin wrote that this was one of her famous sister's fabrications, and that, on hearing it, "our parents were crushed. . . . They felt powerless and wronged."

And so it was with the other stars as well: Jimi Hendrix adopted the Experience and his legendary entourage; Jim Morrison called the Doors "my only brothers"; Elvis became the godfather of his Memphis Mafia brotherhood; Lennon became the alpha quadruplet in the Fab Four; Garcia became the father of the Dead; and Cobain at last found family in Nirvana.

"Well, that's my life to the present date," wrote Buddy Holly in a high school essay, "and even though it may seem awful and full of calamities, I'd sure be in bad shape without it." In this, the pop pioneer, whose plane would crash in a Kansas cornfield, spoke for the Seven.

Each star had endured early traumas and a kind of virtual orphanhood that fed their later fatal isolation and distrust. Like so many other artists, most were raised by overshadowing mothers with whom they shared a love-hate relationship, thus undermining the maternal nurturing role. And most had weak or absent fathers whom they resented, feared, or held in bitter contempt, thus undermining the paternal authority role. Parents are a child's paradigm of human relationships. In the case of divorce, infidelity, and estrangement, the hypersensitive child is often inclined not only to feel abandoned and betrayed but to distrust all future relationships. In the wake of parental death, the child can grow up under a kind of emotional sword of Damocles. In either case, these early misfortunes were certainly at the center of the later consumptive solitudes of the Seven.

It is said that a ghost is born from a horrific final event and is fated to the purgatory of reliving this until it is resolved and the soul freed. Some exceptional children remain children even as adults because exorcising their early pains, or forgiving those who inflicted them, is as impossible as escaping their own shadow. Some don't even try to escape, cradling their hurt as a kind of holy offspring and only friend.

Most of the Seven remained children to the end. As if aging were synonymous with death itself, all had a morbid fear of growing old.[10]

This was particularly true of Elvis and Morrison who, in their own eyes and those of their fans, were the eternal golden youths, the Adonises, the Narcissuses, of rock and roll. Each was possessed of an androg-

---

10. The Who's Pete Townshend, composer of "My Generation" with it's famous line "I hope I die before I get old," was to declare later on: "I haven't been able to achieve that one great ambition I had when I was nineteen. But I've tried to compensate by actually making myself happy."

ynous beauty which seemed godlike and ageless. Ironically, the drugs they were taking—in part to endure such an impossible charade—aged both prematurely and turned them into portraits of Oscar Wilde's debauched Dorian Gray. The others, with the exception of Hendrix, far from suffering such youthful vanity, were neurotically insecure about their looks. Janis felt "ugly and old"; Lennon felt fat and resented Paul "The Cute One"; Cobain wore many layers of clothes to disguise his skeletal, bent frame. Only Garcia, the most mature of the lot, didn't seem to give a shit.

Even so, "I don't think of myself as an adult," said Jerry who reached the ripe old age of fifty-three. "An adult is someone who has made up their mind. . . . I feel like someone who is constantly on the verge of losing it, or blowing it. I feel tremendously insecure."

John Lennon didn't think of himself as an adult, either. "Grow up means: Shut up, clean up, dress up, and die," he told biographer, Sandra Shevey. "Then you are allowed to live half dead, which is what most people do. That is the difference between a real artist and people going through the motions. I refuse to be half dead."

Nature trumped nurture. The Seven were indeed born artists. In their cases, artist stereotypes are not without truth: their highs were higher, their lows lower, and their actions often more compulsive than reasonable. But these childhood loners and misfits sought to reinvent and glorify themselves in a profession of exhilarating power and freedom: rock and roll, the only true art form created for and by the young—children.

In spite of the most humble and troubled beginnings, Roy the Sweeping Boy with his broom guitar became the Voodoo Child; the admiral's prodigal son became the Lizard King; the seaman's orphan became the Walrus; the mama's boy from Memphis became the King himself; the fatherless delinquent became Captain Trips; and the "pig girl" from the little Texas backwater became the Queen of the Blues.

2

JANIS JOPLIN
January 19, 1943–October 4, 1970

THE LAND MINE

The phone in Room 105 is ringing again. The curtains are open to the sliding glass doors overlooking Hollywood's Franklin Park. As dusk falls, the working girls and junkies can already be seen lining up their action for the evening. When the phone goes dead, all that can be heard in the motel room are the TVs in adjoining rooms with the evening news covering Vietnam, Kent State, and the assassination attempt on Pope Paul VI in the Philippines.

Now, a knock on the door. "Janis?"

It's John Cooke, her road manager who is also staying at the Land-mark Hotel, otherwise known to the resident shooters as "The Land Mine." "Janis, what the fuck are you doin'? You're late!"

Cooke opens the door with the passkey from the manager. The room has been "Janisfied": walls festooned with Persian bedspreads, tables arranged with lace, jasmine candles, incense burners, and galleries of lover snapshots. He looks from the kitchenette, to the empty bathroom, to the unmade double bed to the vacant balcony overlooking Franklin Park.

Still no Janis.

Maybe she hitched a ride and is already at the studio, thinks Cooke. They've been working on *Pearl* for more than a month now; she just finished Kristofferson's "Bobby McGee" yesterday, and all she has to do now is lay down the vocals for "Buried Alive in the Blues" and "I'm Going to Rock and Roll Heaven." Last night at Barney's Beanery, Janis as usual was the life of the party, knocking back tequilas and already enthusing about her next album.

"If any of you guys ever leave me, I'll kill ya!" she announced to her band, Full Tilt Boogie, before staggering out.

Cooke turns away from the empty bathroom and makes for the telephone to call the studio and see if she's arrived yet. He's only gone a few steps before he stops short. He stares at a purple brocade sash on the floor. Just beyond, he fixes on a leg protruding from between the bed and the bedside chair. Moving around the chair, he can't believe what's in front of him.

THE DUES

She showed me the air and taught me how to fill it.
She's the reason I started singing.
—Janis, of Bessie Smith

As a girl growing up in the Bible belt town of Port Arthur, Texas, Janis Joplin's idol and role model was the legendary black singer, Bessie Smith. The "Empress of the Blues," renowned for her onstage tirades and offstage brawls, sang with a gut-wrenching intensity never before heard. At the peak of her career prior to the Depression, Bessie commanded $2,000 per performance and traveled in a private railcar with a forty-five person entourage. In the end, drink got the best of her, her career declined, and she bled out in a hospital after her boyfriend, Richard Morgan, Al Capone's bootlegger, rear-ended a truck and she flew out the windshield into Memphis's Route 61.

Bessie was laid to rest in an unmarked Pennsylvania grave until Janis, just before her own passing, bought her a headstone that read: "The Greatest Blues Singer in the World Will Never Stop Singing." This, too, would have been a fitting epitaph for Janis herself who took the Empress's life and voice to the next level.

Like Bessie, Janis began singing in her local church choir.[1] Though the Empress started touring at the age of twelve, Janis's own solo abilities were not recognized until age sixteen when she performed an impromptu recital for an audience of three.

The year was 1959. The venue: an abandoned Coast Guard shack on a bluff overlooking the Gulf of Mexico. The audience: her buddies from Thomas Jefferson High School: Jim Langdon, a trombone player; Grant Lyons, varsity football; and Dave Moriaty, school newspaper editor. The four were Port Arthur's resident beatniks: they read Kerouac, played Leadbelly and Bessie Smith records, and had a precocious taste for Jim Beam.

They were passing the courage around that evening by candlelight when Grant pointed out that the only thing they were missing was a phonograph and some blues. At that, Janis belted out her best Bessie rendition of an Odetta tune. After her explosive finish, she snatched back the bottle while the boys starred, slack-jawed.

"That was fucking *amazing*, Janis!" Grant finally stammered. The guys had never heard anything like it, even on their records. They begged her for an encore.

"Hey, fuck you!" snapped Janis, thinking they were just busting her balls like everybody else at school.

Her nickname at Jefferson High was "pig." As a little girl, recalled one of her classmates, "she'd been cute, then all of a sudden she got ugly. Her total self-respect took a broadside." But her nickname was not just due to her acne, her pudginess, her casual hygiene, or her mannish features. She had the reputation of being a foul mouth and a slut. The guys would flip coins to see who would hit on her after church choir practice. She pulled her top during a football pep rally, and the rumor soon grew into a Port Arthur urban legend: she had taken on the entire football team.

Her mother called her a "harlot." Dorothy Joplin hadn't forgotten sewing her own wild oats as a flapper who had danced on tabletops and worked at a progressive Amarillo radio station, but her eldest daughter's behavior was becoming a social embarrassment. In his bachelor days, her husband, Seth, now a Texaco engineer, had been a playboy,

---

1. Her mother, a Sunday school teacher with a music degree from Texas Christian University in Fort Worth, also sang in the choir but had lost her voice after a surgeon accidentally severed a vocal cord nerve during a thyroid operation.

a dope smoker, and a bathtub gin brewer. But he, too, was concerned about his wild child.

Janis appeased her bookish parents—both loved Tolstoy and Dostoyevsky—with her straight A's and her voracious reading. "I was a misfit," she recalled. "I read, I painted, I didn't hate niggers." But she had no interest in becoming Jefferson's Posture Queen, Miss Ideal Secretary, or Football Sweetheart. Joining the Future Nurses of America in her senior year was as far as she went. But instead of becoming a nurse after graduation, she had a nervous breakdown, and the family hospitalized her for alcoholism.

Her father was known to pound a few himself while tinkering with his tools in the garage. Unlike the devout Dorothy, Seth was an overworked Sisyphus and a firm nonbeliever, viewing life as "the Great Saturday Night Swindle." Man toils and labors all week for a good time on Saturday night that never happens. He had taught his eldest daughter the lesson well.

"He was very important to me because he made me think," Janis would later admit. "He's the reason I am like I am, I guess."

After her hospital dry out, Janis, a talented painter, considered a career in art.[2] But she abandoned the idea after deciding that others did it better. "If she couldn't be the best in the world, she wasn't gonna do it," wrote her confidant and friend, Myra Friedman.[3]

So Janis turned to folk music. She briefly abandoned this, too, after hearing a vocalist in Austin who she felt did a better Joan Baez than she could.

The 18-year-old now hitched to L.A. and became a keypunch operator while living with her aunt. Still trying to play it straight, she returned to Port Arthur and enrolled in Lamar College as a sociology major. Here a local fraternity voted her "ugliest man on campus." Off-hours she waitressed at a bowling alley in Nacogdoches. She quit when her ex-high school drinking buddy, Jim Langdon, the trombone player, got her a paying gig to sing a savings bank jingle he'd composed.

Returning to her brushes, Janis transferred to the University of

---

2. Many of the other greats were artists and art-school dropouts themselves: Lennon, McCartney, Richards, Ronnie Wood, Jeff Beck, Jimmy Page, Ray Davies, Pete Townshend, Eric Clapton, David Bowie, Jerry Garcia, Kurt Cobain, and others.

3. Myra Friedman, *Buried Alive: The Biography of Janis Joplin* (New York: William Morrow, 1973).

Texas as an art major. Off-hours she sang for beer on open-mike nights at Austin bars. Soon she was spotted by a beatnik folkie, Chet Helms. "Listen, Janis," he told her, "if people on the West Coast could hear you, it would knock them on their ass. They've never heard anything this raw, and that's what they're looking for."

So Janis and her Bobby McGee, formerly a preacher from Missouri, hitched to San Francisco in the summer of 1962. Helms landed many gigs for her in the city of love—from coffeehouses, to biker bars, to dike dives. Accompanied by future Jefferson Airplane guitarist, Jorma Kaukonen, or accompanying herself on autoharp, she wowed fellow struggling folkies from David Crosby, to Jerry Garcia, to Tim Hardin. At about this time, Janis wrote to her parents, "I'm awfully sorry to be such a disappointment to you . . . Please believe that you can't possibly want for me to be a winner more than I do."

But soon, rather than sing, she preferred to "smoke dope, take dope, lick dope, suck dope, and fuck dope." Developing an appetite for shooting meth and cheap Mexican smack, the future Queen of the Blues supported her habit by shoplifting, panhandling, and pulling the odd trick. She finally showed up at San Francisco General Hospital as an eighty-seven-pound skeleton, but was turned away as a derelict.[4] Chet Helms passed the hat among her speed freak friends and bought her a bus ticket back to Port Arthur before she killed herself.

Meantime, she had gotten engaged to a beguiling grifter, doper, and space cadet by the name of Peter de Blanc. Before returning to Texas, she'd checked Peter into a sanatorium. Her fiancé had been getting messages from the moon that he was to be attacked by spacemen, so he had fitted his VW with machine guns. In spite of his quirks, Janis hoped her folks would appreciate his manners and his fertile, if quirky, mind.

In a last ditch effort to become what her mother wanted her to be—a wife, a stenographer, and alive—she reenrolled at Lamar College and prepared for her wedding. While her fiancé's extraterrestrials were being exorcised on the coast, she busied herself learning shorthand, sewing a wedding dress, and embroidering a Texas Lone Star quilt for the nuptial bed. Then de Blanc beamed out. At last Janis located her fiancé in New York, not having been abducted by aliens, but designing hard-

---

4. Similarly, blues myth tells us that after her car accident Bessie Smith was denied admission to an all-white hospital in Tennessee and bled to death on the way to another ER. In fact, Thomas Hospital in Clarksdale was black and the singer was admitted, but too late.

ware for IBM. He kept pondering a wedding date until Janis discovered
he was already married and had two kids.

This was the Queen of the Blues' first, but not last, taste of her
father's Saturday Night Swindle.

Dropping out of secretarial school, Janis resumed her singing career
in Austin. Her old school buddy, Jim Langdon, now a staffer for the
Austin Statesman, wrote a feature on her, calling her "the greatest
white blues female singer in America." When Janis's mother read this,
she called Langdon, fit to be tied. "Stop encouraging her!" she cried.

But, by now, Langdon was not Janis's only admirer. A freak buddy
of hers from U of Texas, Travis Rivers, was crazy about her too. He'd
heard through the grapevine that her original benefactor, Chet Helms,
now a San Francisco rock promoter, was looking for a "chick singer"
for his new band, Big Brother and the Holding Company—an antiestablishment, tripping band Helms had named after the totalitarian over-
seer of George Orwell's *1984* dystopia. The group had a strong local
following, but their guitar-heavy style of "progressive-regressive hurricane blues," as they called it, cried out for an equally earth-shattering
voice. So Travis begged Janis to audition. Since she'd nearly drowned
in the City of Love drug scene, she was hesitant to return. But Travis,
a rustic but charming rogue, soon allayed her fears.

"I'd been conned into being in the rock business by this guy that
was such a good ball," she later confided. "I was fucked into being in
Big Brother."

Having at last paid her dues, Janis was truly ready to play the blues.
She just hoped it wouldn't turn her to roadkill, like it had Bessie.

THE OUTER LIMITS OF PROBABILITY

We have a report of a woman screaming in here.
—San Francisco police, on arriving at the Henry Street
    Firehouse, where Janis did her audition for Big Brother

Oh, no. That was no woman.
That was Janis Joplin!
—Audience member Stanley Mouse

Janis, who had never sung for a rock-and-roll band, took the edge off
her nerves before the audition with Southern Comfort. Then, donning

Salvation Army Levis, a ragged sweatshirt, and Tijuana huaraches, she took the stage and was soon hitting decibels that rivaled the wailing guitars and thunderous drums of Big Brother. Afterward, everybody stood speechless, not sure what they had just heard.

"She's either great or really awful," ventured the Grateful Dead poster artist, Stanley Mouse. Recalled Big Brother's manager, Chet Helms, "She was strange and weird and off the wall and she raised the hair on the back of your neck."

In short, she was hired.

During the summer of 1966, the new singer for Big Brother earned $50 a week and crashed in their Victorian flophouse on the Haight. She wrote home, "Dear Mother—From all indications I'm going to become rich & famous. Incredible! . . . Wow, I'm so lucky—I just fumbled around being a mixed up kid & then fell into this." Her other letters to her parents were filled with incredulous exclamation: *Gasp! Egad! Groovy. Arrgghhh! Isn't that too much?*

After Janis signed with Big Brother, her second Svengali, Travis Rivers, divorced his wife and proposed to the singer. When she refused, Travis nodded with resignation. Which pissed Janis off. "Don't you wanna know *why?*" she demanded.

Travis shrugged. He could see her mind was made up and only a masochist would need an explanation. But she insisted on giving one since he'd been the one who had fucked her into Big Brother.

"I know I'm going to be really big. Really, *really* big!" she told him. "This will be the only time in my life I'll be able to have any boy over the age of 14 I want and I don't intend to miss the opportunity." When Travis absorbed this with equal resignation, she cried, "After I've said something like that to you, you'd have to beat me up if you really loved me!"

Janis Joplin's sexual appetite was as omnivorous as it was insatiable—for young "pretty boys," fellow rockers, bikers, and other women. More than compensating for what she lacked hormonally in a testosterone business, she would later guesstimate she'd "gotten it on with a couple thousand cats and a few hundred chicks." At the same time she continued to "lick dope, suck dope, and fuck dope."

She, Hendrix, and Morrison were the first performers who made what Janis called "sexdrugsandrocknroll" a single orgasmic act and way of life.

One of her first relationships during that Summer of Love was with Big Brother guitarist, James Gurley. Having worked with his stunt car driver father as a "human hood ornament"—plowing through flaming walls, and once knocking out his front teeth—the lanky, golden-haired axeman from Motown had the perfect rock pedigree. And blessed with a sensitive side too (he'd studied to be a Franciscan monk) Gurley was irresistible to the rapacious Janis. No matter that he was already married.

The singer and the guitarist hadn't been getting it on long before his wife, Nancy, walked in on the couple while they were in the throes. Though upset at the time, Nancy, an Aquarian astrologer and bead-maker, became a close friend and shooting partner of Janis's.

Janis became fond of triangles, particularly with married couples. Her favorite partners were the Gravenites: Linda, a dressmaker, and Nick "the Greek" Gravanites, aka Gravy, a Chicago folkie who would later compose "Buried Alive in the Blues" for her. Linda masterminded Janis's image shift from Salvation Army freak to the bangled-and-beaded hippie siren.

Like Janis, Linda was "an up-front, no bullshit lady who was at once earthy, witty, and sexual," according to Ellis Amburn.[5] While her old man, Nick, was touring in Chicago, she became Janis's roommate and bedmate. The ménage a trios evolved when Nick returned to the West Coast. Nick recalled that Janis tripped out when alone. So he and Linda "would flip a coin to see who'd fuck her." After one steamy evening with the inexhaustible Nick, Janis asked for his hand in matrimony.

"I can't," Nick told her, "I'm married to your roommate."

While doing the Gravenites, Janis multitasked with fellow stars. Her affair with the "I-Feel-Like-I'm-Fixin'-to-Die" revolutionary, Country Joe McDonald, was brief but tempestuous. She and Jimi Hendrix became bed and heroin-shooting partners at Monterey and Fillmore West. Her fling with Rhodes scholar, chopper pilot, and fellow Texan, Kris Kristofferson was legendary, and she credited him as the only man who could drink her under the table. She would later help launch the songwriter's career with her cover of his "Me and Bobby McGee" that would become, posthumously, her only number one hit single. Finally there was Joe Namath. After working out the Jet quarterback on the floor of his Manhattan loft, she asked for his white shag rug as a memento. Broadway Joe begrudgingly handed it over, and she laid it on her chauffeur. Then she ordered her manager to drop a dime on publisher

---

5. Ellis Amburn, *Pearl: The Obsessions and Passions of Janis Joplin.* (New York: Warner Books, 1992).

Jann Wenner and "tell him Janis fucked Namath, and I want it in the next *Rolling Stone!*"[6]

Recalled Bob Seidemann, the photographer who took the famous nude poster shot of Janis and who also shared her bed, "There wasn't any aspect of outrageous that she left uncovered." Janis didn't disagree. "I never hold back, man. I'm always on the outer limits of probability."

In the blossom of her career, Janis—who, according to another conquest, *"really* knew her way around a mattress"—got what she wanted. With a few exceptions. When she met George Harrison, she told him in front of his wife, Patti, "Hey, man, I've been wanting to make it with you for years!"

"I don't think I'd be big enough for you," replied the quiet Beatle who had heard about "Gabriel," the three-foot penis in her front yard.

As over the top as Janis was in private, she pulled the stops on stage. "I only live to perform," she declared. "That's the only time I really feel." Only then could she go beyond the limits of a one-on-one, or ménage, and consummate with a stadium. "No guy ever made me feel as good as an audience," she said. She compared performing to "an orgasm," to "falling in love twenty times," and to "having a baby."

Both she and her audience fell in love twenty times at Monterey Pop in the spring of 1967—the gig that turned her, as it did Hendrix, from a local cult figure into an international sensation. No one had heard a human being—man, woman, or child—sing like this before. Riveting, almost harrowing in its intensity, her "Ball and Chain" was something beyond song. She used her voice like Hendrix used his guitar, but with greater emotional range—tenderness, tears, and desperate longing beneath the raw power. Hers was a song from the heart, the soul, and every fiber of her being, which left the audience of 70,000 breathless and awestruck. Its collective reaction was expressed in the openmouthed, dazzled look of Mama Cass in the front row. Janis's "Ball and Chain" was no Mamas and Papas' "Monday, Monday" or "California Dreamin'."

Touring with Big Brother, Janis went on to take the world by storm with her electrifying performances. Whether playing stadiums, festivals, or clubs, she always gave her all and demanded full attention. She became the Hell's Angels' favorite chick rocker, and once while doing an Angel funeral concert, she upstaged the leathered, technicolor

---

6. Alice Echols, *Scars of Sweet Paradise: The Life and Times of Janis Joplin* (New York: Henry Holt, 1999).

corpse by tearing off her top. She incited near riots and she cursed the cops who tried to control them. Of working her audiences, she said, "All you gotta do is give'm a big fucking kick in the ass, man . . . A riot. Groovy! . . . Then the promoters get goony, turn the lights on, pull the power, but by then it's all over. I dig it! I dig it so much, man!"

The only mortal who rivaled Janis, both on- and offstage, "in the outer limits of probability" was Jim Morrison of the Doors. Though this seemed to be a boundless area, each star believed that it had room for only one occupant or at least for only one with an ego the size that theirs had grown to.

The Queen of the Blues and the Lizard King had exchanged bodily fluids as a professional matter of course; but, fiercely competitive, there was little love lost between them. "Janis and Jim were two big egos clashing in the night," recalled James Gurley. "She didn't like Morrison and he didn't like her. They were too much alike—two monstrous egos."

The enfants terribles of rock had several public clashes. When the other triumvirate member, Jimi Hendrix, performed at The Scene in New York, Morrison, three sheets to the wind and floored by Jimi's fretwork, staggered onto the stage and tried to fellate the guitar god. Janis, pissed at him for spilling drinks on her during his exit, tackled the singer and landed a few punches to his pretty face while Jimi laid into "The Wind Cries Mary."

The couple had a return bout at the Beverly Hills mansion of *Hollywood Square* regular and variety show host, John Davidson. After the Lizard had drained the TV star's liquor cabinet and puked all over his cowhide rug, Janis proceeded to give him a Miss Manners tongue lashing. Jim, never one to abide authority much less propriety, started jackhammering her head into a coffee table until she fled and locked herself in the bathroom. When Morrison finally left the party, she followed him out; coldcocked him with a whiskey bottle; boogalooed around his body, cackling; and then returned to the festivities for another round.

Though she'd overextended herself a few times by going toe-to-toe with Hells Angels, Janis, a true-blue Texas girl, had never taken shit from men. Especially the likes of Jerry Lee Lewis. As with Morrison, Janis and Jerry Lee took an instant and visceral dislike to each other. "The Killer"—the Pentecostal junkie who married his thirteen-year-old cousin, who shot his bass player, and who was later suspected of offing his fourth and fifth wives—disapproved of Janis's godless lifestyle.

Though Janis was a "Great Balls of Fire" and "Whole Lotta Shakin' " fan, Jerry Lee was exactly the kind of six-fingered bayou boy who had run her out of Port Arthur. Even so, one night at the Austin Channel Club, she went backstage to pay her professional respects to the Killer. Ignoring her, Jerry Lee told her pretty younger sister, Laura, that she shouldn't try to dress like her—a slut. Janis hauled off and clocked him. The Killer, no stranger to haymakers, shook it off and snarled, "Oh, if you're gonna act like a man, I'll treat ya like one." Then he slugged her right back.

Janis, like her colleagues, had few sober moments from the onset of her fame to her demise three and a half years later. If there was one irresistible undercurrent that carried her and the others to an early grave, it was insatiability. As far out as she went, it was never far out enough for her. Her unquenchable appetites were hardwired, as they are for many artists, but she also was like a once starved person who gorges, fearing that the food will again be taken away. For sensitive, wounded souls, drugs can become the essential food group, providing both anesthesia and release. For Janis, toward the end of her career, drugs filled and electrified the emotional void briefly, then made it a black hole all the wider, deeper, and more inescapable.

It was hard to know which of her favorite fixes were more damaging to her: whiskey or junk. Booze was her staple, like dinner; smack was her treat, like dessert.

Heroin offers a voluptuously warm, womblike embrace. Initially it can be seductively titillating. Take your best orgasm, junkies have said, multiply it by a thousand, and you're still not close to the magnitude of the first rush. One feels swallowed up, every nerve aglow, as if floating in a velvet underground. Lou Reed, the founder of the group of this name, sang in his famous song "Heroin," "When I put a spike into my vein . . . things aren't quite the same. When I'm rushing on my run, I feel just like Jesus's son."

The purest and most potent rush from junk can only be had by shooting intravenously or "skin popping." When asked why she preferred shooting to snorting, Janis replied, "Why jack off when you can fuck?"

"Janis was a maniac with needles," recalled Big Brother drummer, Dave Getz. "She loved to do other people up, loved the thrill of hitting somebody . . . And she wanted you to really get off." When Dave agreed to try heroin for the first time, Janis and Nancy Gurley bickered about who was going to shoot him up.

"The possibility of death made using even more exciting to her," explained another friend. "She didn't hesitate to go too far, always. She liked to push it. She liked to see how high she could get. She liked playing Russian roulette." If Janis liked to play roulette with herself, she also played it with others. She once shot Terence Hallinan, the boyfriend of her favorite girlfriend, Peggy Caserta, with so much junk that he blacked out. While Hallinan was dying on the floor, Janis made passionate love to Peggy. When they finished, Peggy fellated her boyfriend back to life. Caserta, too, had experience with Janis's game of Russian Roulette, later writing in her memoir, *Going Down with Janis*, that the star used "the needle on me not only as a surrogate cock, but also as a deadly, destructive weapon."

The star nearly killed another first-timer and lover of hers Milan Melvin, the statuesque hippie actor. While she topped off the syringe, Milan begged, "Janis, LESS! I'm clean!" But the Queen of the Blues loved nothing more than breaking a virgin. She gave the actor a full hit of killer smack and he collapsed. Then she OD'd Peggy. When the couple miraculously came to the next morning, she berated them for being lightweights. Besides, they'd ruined her plans for a three-way.

Her favorite shooting partner, Nancy Gurley, fatally OD'd in 1968, and her husband, James, was tried for murder. Janis was bummed but undeterred. "Nothing will ever happen to me," she declared, "because I come from good pioneer stock and I'm strong." In her friend's memory, she scored more junk and shot herself up. Then she dedicated her 1969 *Kozmic Blues* to Nancy G. She would later tell an interviewer, "Kozmic Blues just means that no matter what you do, man, you get shot down anyway. . . . The Kozmic Blues doesn't exist, unless you have nothing."

Janis's addiction dated back to Monterey Pop. "She attributed her heroin use to the fear that would accompany her growing fame," wrote her assistant and first biographer, Myra Friedman. "Chronic suicide was what she was involved with her entire life."

KOZMIC BLUES

The more you live, the less you die.
—Janis Joplin

By her own admission, onstage Janis experienced the purest and most intense expression of living. Watching her perform was like watching both an agonizingly wonderful birth and a self-immolation. As far beyond the limits of life and probability the Queen of Blues went, she never lost sight of who she was doing it for: her ever-expanding audience, which, like an insatiable but passive suitor, demanded more and more. Yet, just as the fans couldn't get enough of her bursting heart, she couldn't get enough of their adoration.

Janis's ambition became ruthless. Though Big Brother was an established band when they hired her and she a virtual unknown, she soon eclipsed the group and it became little more than a backup band. The resulting resentment escalated when she fired their manager, Chet Helms, who was responsible for launching her career in the first place. Chet refused to be her yes-man or to agree that Big Brother was nothing without her, and for this she handed him his head declaring, "I'll kill anybody who gets in my way!" The only Big Brother member she retained was Sam Andrews, but she soon fired him too, allegedly for stealing her smack. But the guitarist knew better, complaining to Peggy Caserta: "Ain't my music good enough for that egotistical cunt? . . . Travis, Chet and me, we MADE that bitch!"

To reach the next level, she needed a manager who shared this attitude, not Chet's fuck-the-bread, we're-all-family, hippie love-child trip. No, she needed a real take-no-prisoners moneyman. And that man was Albert Grossman, Dylan's manager. "He was kind of like a Colonel Tom Parker figure," observed Dylan. ". . . You could smell him coming." The songwriter's biographer Michael Gray added, "He was a pudgy man with derisive eyes . . . and many people loathed him. In a milieu of . . . folkie idealists, Grossman was a breadhead, seen to move serenely and with deadly purpose like a barracuda circling shoals of fish." But he could be disarmingly straightforward with his clients. "Don't ever trust me," he told Dylan, on signing him. As for Janis, after seeing her at Monterey, Grossman simply said, "Tell me what you want." To be the biggest blues singer in the world, she told him. To which he simply replied, "Okay."

After Big Brother's second album, *Cheap Thrills*, Janis dumped Helms and hired her "Uncle Albert." Having already heard about Janis's appetites, Uncle Albert had only one condition for managing her: "No schmeeze," he told her. His first wife had died of a heroin overdose. Janis promised to avoid the same fate and stay clean. But her promise was an addict's promise: it came with a strict statute of limitations: a few weeks. After that, she was back on the schmeeze.[7]

She needed more antistress medication now because, no sooner did she sign with Grossman and hire her vanity band, Kozmic Blues, than she suffered critical blowback for abandoning the popular Big Brother and Chet. "Her new band is a drag," wrote *San Francisco Chronicle* critic, Ralph Gleason. He suggested she go back to them, "If they'll have her." But no such reunion occurred and Big Brother fell into obscurity within a few years.

Meanwhile, her well-connected Uncle Albert launched a formidable Janis publicity machine: he got her on the cover of national magazines, he scored her major interviews, he put her on TV. Finally, to maximize her audiences and receipts he partnered with his equally driven friend, rock producer extraordinaire, Bill Graham. Like Grossman, Graham was the anti-Chet. And like Grossman, Graham was of Russian Jewish stock and no stranger to hardship: when he was two days old, his father had died; later his mother was exterminated at Auschwitz. As a young man, Bill, born Wolfgang Grajonca, worked as a croupier and maitre d' at a Catskills resort—perfect training for rock-and-roll management, he later noted. He went on to open the legendary Fillmore East in New York, plus the Fillmore West and Winterland, both in San Francisco. Tyrannical, fiercely efficient, but a tireless champion of his artists, he was called "part Al Capone and part Mother Teresa." If his artists saw his second side, his major competitor—Chet Helms—saw only his first. Chet's Family Dog Productions staged stoned-out hippie rock shows at the rundown Longshoreman's dancehall, Haight Street's hole-in-the-wall Straight Theatre, and at the funky Avalon Ballroom where Janis had premiered with Big Brother in the fall of 1966. Here Chet ran benefits for the homeless, peace in Vietnam, and Zen centers, often losing track of the gate money. Meanwhile, nearby at the

---

7. Though Grossman officially discouraged heroin use by his clients, Helms would later insist that he encouraged Janis's Billie Holiday inclinations and maintained a don't-ask-don't-tell drug policy with her.

Fillmore, Bill gave out apples, counted every penny, and parlayed his profits into increasingly large venues.

With the help of Graham and Grossman, Janis was soon on the fast track to wealth and international fame. And taking the country by storm with her supercharged performances, Janis's ego exploded. She was scheduled to be on *Newsweek*'s April 7, 1969, cover, but former president Dwight D. Eisenhower replaced her. "Motherfucker!" she spat. "Fourteen fuckin' heart attacks and the son of a bitch has to croak in my week. MY week!" Another time, after doing Nashville, she called the Man in Black. "This is Janis JOPLIN!" she exclaimed from her hotel phone. "I wanna speak to Johnny Cash! I'm the biggest singer in America, you stupid nut and he'll know who I am!"

But the Port Arthur pig girl was never far below the surface. Before dining with actor Rip Torn and his wife, Geraldine Page, she fretted to her assistant. "What'll I wear? She's a star. She's a LADY. Christ, I'm just a weirdo freak!" She managed to put something together and later admitted that she might have had a good time with the actors "if I just wasn't so ugly!"

Though Janis became one of the great sex symbols of the decade, she never stopped racking herself with how unattractive she felt, especially as she got older and the fast lane began to take its toll. "Nobody wants an old chick like me," complained the 26-year old to Myra Friedman, pulling at the skin under her arm viciously. "They want young girls!"

"Nobody really loves me, NOBODY," was her constant lament. "The only people who love me are the junkies I used to know . . . and the people on my payroll."

To make matters worse, reviews for *Old Kozmic Blues*, were brutal. "Her melodrama, overstatement and coarseness are not virtues," wrote Jon Landau. "She doesn't much sing a song as strangle it to death," added another *Rolling Stone* reviewer. "A major talent she is not," pronounced *The New York Times*.

Her producer for *Cheap Thrills*, John Simon, abandoned her latest project and was no more charitable in his assessment. Her popularity, he insisted, was based on her "liberation of all the plain-looking, overweight, loud young women." He concluded, "That's how Janis Joplin could happen in the first place. Everyone's mind was fried."

Crushed, Janis reverted to self-flagellation. Speaking of her fans to journalist David Dalton,[8] she confessed, "If they know anything about anything, they know I'm not a star. They know I'm a middle-age chick with a drinking problem, man, and a loud voice . . . I'll never be a star like Jimi Hendrix or Bob Dylan."

At the bottom of it all was her hypersensitivity. "Her nerves were nearer the skin," explained Milan Melvin after leaving her to marry Mimi Farina, Joan Baez's kid sister. "And nobody broke like Janis; nobody seemed to reach the depths of disappointment or to take hurt so heavy." Another friend went further. "When Janis is happy," he said, "she *still* isn't happy."

Finally, at the insistence of Uncle Albert, she went through a successful heroin withdrawal under the care of endocrinologist Dr. Ed Rothschild. Afterward she promised her roommate, Linda Gravenites, she would learn horseback riding, practice yoga, become a pianist, and lead a wholesome life. Trying to turn over the new leaf, she and Linda went to carnival in Rio. "The idea was that Janis could stay so busy having fun that she wouldn't have any time to think about heroin," explained Linda.

And the idea almost worked. Janis did indeed have fun in Rio, as only Janis could. Though she fell into some terrible lows toward the end, she had a boundless enthusiasm for life's little pleasures and often enjoyed dizzying natural highs. This was especially true when she was in love. In Rio, Janis fell for "a big bear of a beatnik," as she called him, David Niehaus. A teacher and Peace Corps volunteer, her new beau was fun loving, adventurous, and junk free. Soon the couple was discussing marriage, but each had a different future in mind: David wanted Janis to bum around the world with him; she wanted him to become her boy toy in California. "This is getting intense," she told Linda when he followed her home from Rio. "David's determined to turn me into a school teacher's wife. Why can't he see that my way's better?"

"Because he's a *real* person," Linda pointed out.

That scared Janis. It drove her back to her lover, Peggy Caserta, and back to the needle. Peggy hadn't a clue what Janis had seen in David to begin with, calling him "a big gangly boy with slightly-bucked teeth who was constantly intellectualizing. . . . and in love with *being* in love." Soon David split for the Himalayas after catching the girls

---

8. David Dalton, *Piece of My Heart: The Life, Times and Legend of Janis Joplin* (New York: St. Martin's, 1986).

shooting up together in bed. As for Linda, as soon as she discovered Janis was off the wagon again, she moved out of her house in disgust.

Devastated by the loss of her two loves, Janis poured her heart out in "Ball and Chain," "A Woman Left Lonely," "All Is Loneliness," and "Cry Baby." "You might find out later . . . Honey, the road'll even end in Katmandu," she sang to her wanderlust David. "You can go all around the world. . . . I know you got more tears to share, babe, So come on, come on, come on, come on, come on, And cry, cry baby, cry baby, cry baby."

Hoping to bring her motherly Linda back, Janis went to a dry-out retreat in Mexico. This treatment, however, turned out to be more short-lived than the first. No sooner was she discharged than she joined the "Festival Train" Canadian tour with the Grateful Dead, Bonnie & Delaney, and others. She whiled away the six-day junket getting it on with strangers (sixty-five, by her count), shooting smack, and "puking out the window of the train the whole trip."

By the end of the tour, Toby Ben, her roadie, told Myra Friedman: "You better talk to Albert, because that girl is going to *die!*"

BETWEEN ROCK AND A HARD PLACE

Pearl was destined to become the title of Janis's final and posthumously released album. It was, as Myra explained it, Janis's "hard drinking swearing always partying fuck anybody get it on get it off stay stoned keep on rocking floozy" nickname. Janis said she might use it for the bar she intended to buy after retiring, where she'd stay drunk and play piano for the *Casablanca* regulars.

In spite of the "rocking floozy" Pearl alter ego, a part of Janis longed for the quiet domestic life which her mother had always championed. "Just give me an old man that comes home," she told Myra near the end. "Like when he splits at nine I know he's gonna be back at six for me and only me and I'll take that shit with the two garages and the two TVs."

Pearl had rejected David Niehaus's proposal for the same reason she had Travis Rivers' years before. She not only wanted to become "the greatest blues singer in the world," as she told her new producer, Paul Rothchild, but she wanted to enjoy the garden of earthly delights.

After the Niehaus breakup and just before the *Pearl* recording sessions, she decided to do something that appealed to both Janis, the hometown girl, and Pearl, the world-famous rocker. She announced her intentions on *The Dick Cavett Show* in July 1970. "They laughed me out of class, out of town, and out of state," she told the talk show host. "So I'm going back!"

For Janis, attending her tenth high school reunion in Port Arthur was like going into the belly of the beast and hoping for closure; for Pearl it would be a dragon-slaying mission. "We're going to raise hell at my high school reunion," she pledged. "I've always had this fantasy of getting even with them some day. . . . I'm going to show up with bells and feathers and I'm gonna say, 'Remember me, man? What are you doing? Still pumping gas?' "

Preferring not to do this gig solo, the Queen of the Blues brought her consort. Like her original Langdon-Lyons-Moriaty high school support group, this one also consisted of three worthies: John Cooke, Bobby Neuwirth, and John Fisher. The dashing Cooke and Neuwirth, aka the "Harvard Hillbillies," were her on-again off-again road managers; the party boy, Fisher, was her sometime chauffeur and Sancho Panza. She described the trio as "crazies," like herself.

Reporters flocked to Port Arthur for her arrival. "What have you been up to since 1960?" they wanted to know.

"Tryin' to get laid. Stay stoned!" exclaimed the hometown girl.

On the evening of her high school reunion, she struck poses for photographers, drained the wet bar, and wisecracked about her cameo appearance for "the Last Supper." Sitting down for this, she told her classmates, "Everybody lay whoever you're sitting next to!" When her suggestion was greeted by Stepford wife stares from the former Miss Posture Queen and Miss Ideal Secretary, she cackled to the reporters, "We're freaking out the farmers, aren't we?"

Though Port Arthur's prodigal daughter was pulling down half a million a year now, she and her boys crashed at her parents' house. Her mother made up a cot for her while Cooke, Fisher, and Neuwirth passed out on whatever furniture was available. Accustomed to five-star suites, Janis was unhappy with the accommodations and told the reporters so.

Her complaints and scandalous behavior precipitated a violent fight with her tightly wound and usually reticent mother who at last blurted out something that she had thought before but hadn't dared to utter to her own child:

"I wish you'd never been born!"

Leaving Port Arthur, Janis told reporters, "Well, you can't go home again, right?"

Her bandmates called her "Little Miss Reader." Among her favorite novels were Thomas Wolfe's *Look Homeward, Angel* and *You Can't Go Home Again.*

TOMORROW NEVER HAPPENS

If you got it today, you don't want it tomorrow, man.
'Cos you don't need it. So as a matter of fact,
as we discover all the time, tomorrow never happens, man.
It's all the same fuckin' day, man!
—Janis, to her Calgary audience, July 4, 1970

Janis flew from Texas to L.A. where she began recording *Pearl.* She was excited about the new album. She considered Full Tilt Boogie the best band she'd ever had. Not only that, but her new producer, Paul Rothchild had done the Doors' *Light My Fire* album and other rock milestones.

But there was a downside. Due to everyone's high expectations for *Pearl,* Janis felt under an enormous pressure to deliver the goods like never before. Since her Mexican detox, she had been seesawing, but now the strain of the recording session turned her back to the needle. She'd assured her road manager, John Cooke, that she was only "chipping"—shooting a couple times a week—and that she would go cold turkey as soon as the album was finished.

As much as Cooke had wanted to believe this, he couldn't help but feel skeptical. While recording *Pearl,* she'd insisted on lodging in her old Hollywood haunt, the Landmark Hotel, a shooting gallery not conducive to moderation, much less sobriety. But ever the diplomat and devoted employee, Cooke had not objected to the idea and had taken a room upstairs to get her to and from the studio straight enough to sing.

They'd only been recording for a few days, when Jimi Hendrix died in London. "There but for the grace of God," said Janis on hearing the news of her former lover's death. "I can't say I was shocked, I wasn't!" She dismissed the tragedy in the same way she had the overdose of Nancy Gurley the year before. She even managed to find something positive in it. "It just decreases my chances," she insisted. "Two rock stars can't die in the same year."

Soon after Hendrix's passing, Janis went out for a drink with her old sparring partner, Jim Morrison. The Doors' front man—deathly pale, bloated, and unsure of foot—told Janis his rock-and-roll days were over and that he was moving to Paris to write poetry. Trying to go on the wagon, he drank wine, she drank stomach-soothing vodka and milk. The rock legends parted with a hug, never to see one another again.

Unlike Morrison, Janis still had every reason to be optimistic about the future now. Not only did she have the great new band, the great new producer, the million-dollar contract—most importantly, she had a great new man whom she wanted to marry.

Seth Morgan was from a well-to-do New York family and an heir to their soap fortune. His father, Frederick, gentleman poet and founder of the *Hudson Review*, included the boy in his salon dinner parties with the likes of Dylan Thomas and e. e. cummings. A brilliant but unruly boy, Seth was booted from a string of elite prep schools, then he had come west to attend Berkeley. A dead ringer for Janis's old flame, Joe Namath, Morgan was ruggedly handsome and, according to Janis's kid sister, Laura, "a silver-tongued devil." Even better, "he had his own bread," boasted the penny-pinching Janis, shamed by her own modest upbringing in the Texas sticks. While supplementing his $30,000-a-year trust, Morgan made ends meet by selling coke.

Pearl met the preppie pusher that summer of 1970 when he had dropped by her house in Larkspur to collect on a $400 coke tab run up by Peggy. Though he'd threatened to beat the shit out of her roommate, Janis just took it for dealer bluster. Besides, she had always had a thing for outlaws and said he "looked good enough to eat."

Two days after meeting, she and Seth became engaged. While she was working on *Pearl* in L.A., he flew down from San Francisco on weekends, attending recording sessions and crashing with her at the Landmark. Most of Janis's friends considered Morgan "a sleazy motherfucker."

Soon after the engagement, she confided to her keyboard player, Richard Bell, "We're supposed to get married, but I don't know. He's got all these emotional problems, and, well, we're just not getting along." She'd asked Seth to "lean" on her and help her kick heroin, but he'd laughed in her face and blamed her for the monkey on his own back.

The couple had recently had a public blowout. Seth had spotted a shirt in a Strip boutique window, which he suggested his fiancée buy for him. The ever-frugal Janis told him to put his soap money where his mouth was. Seth called her a "cheap cunt." Janis called him a "fucking leach." Seth stormed back to San Francisco.

Prophetically, Janis feared that she'd never see her fiancé again.

When John Cooke's phone rang at the Landmark, it was about 7 P.M. He was running a little late that evening, was on his way out the door, and he figured it was the studio wondering where he was. But it wasn't the studio, it was Seth. The dealer said he was at the San Francisco airport, waiting to board his flight to L.A.

"Where the fuck's Janis?" demanded Frederick Morgan's prodigal son.

"The studio," replied the proper son of British intellectual and *Masterpiece Theater* host, Alistair Cooke.

At the Beanery last night over drinks, Janis had told everybody to make sure they were on time—6 sharp. She was anxious to put the wraps on *Pearl*.

"I just called the fucking studio," Morgan snapped. "They said call you. I been trying her all fucking day!"

Cooke knew that Janis had been calling Seth all day yesterday from the studio and couldn't get *him* on the phone. Seth hadn't seen her since their blowout over the shirt; he'd promised to fly down yesterday, but had stood her up. So Seth had been mindfucking Janis yesterday by not answering his phone, and she seemed to be returning the favor today.

"I'll check her room," offered Cooke wearily.

"Have somebody pick me up in Burbank," ordered Morgan. "Be there in an hour!"

Cooke hung up. He'd been with Janis longer than anybody and he was getting tired of this gig. Especially the babysitting and the boyfriends' part. After the RFK assassination, he'd come close to getting into politics and making a real difference—but Janis had begged him back. She'd always fondly called him "the road Nazi."

He made his way downstairs to Room 105. After knocking several times, he looked out into the parking lot and saw that Janis's Porsche was still there. Well, okay, maybe she was napping or showering, he thought. Or maybe she picked up another fiancé last night after leaving the Beanery and was busy with him inside now. It wouldn't be a first. Or, worse, maybe she was out on foot buying Seth's shirt as a kiss and make up.

Cooke trudged downstairs, got the passkey from the manager, came back up, and when there was still no answer to his knock, he let himself in.

After glancing into the empty bathroom, he turned toward the bed and found himself staring at what appeared to be a length of bloody gauze on the floor. Which got the adrenaline running. Suddenly he froze in his spot, eyes on a blue leg protruding from between the bed and the bedside chair.

Moving around the chair, he found Janis Joplin in panties, wedged between the bed and the night table. The hair of the Queen of Blues was tousled all around her livid face, her nose was smashed, her mouth filled with dried blood, and a rigid, heavily ringed hand clutched four, one dollar bills.

The body was already eighteen hours in rigor mortis.

She leaves Barney's Beanery at about 1 A.M. She's pounded more than a few screwdrivers and chased two Valium. But they haven't helped her forget that Seth had promised to be with her tonight. That he's stood her up—him and Peggy, too. Actually, they had a three-way engagement party planned back at the Land Mine.

Another Saturday Night Swindle!

On the way back to the hotel, now in her technicolor Porsche, she curses Seth. She wonders if she'll ever see him again. Another fiancé DOA. Over a fucking shirt!

Or maybe it's the prenup. She'd mentioned it, he seemed cool with it, so she'd had her lawyer draw it up yesterday. She'd told Seth over the phone it would be ready to sign when he got back to L.A. While she was at it, she'd drawn up a new will too. She hadn't told him yet he wasn't in it; but he had his own bread, right? So why should he care?

She screeches into the Landmark parking lot, staggers out of her car and weaves her way to her room. She gropes in her dresser drawer and pulls out a brown paper bag her man, George, dropped by earlier, promising it was "primo shit." He hadn't mentioned that his "taster" was out of town for the weekend, so he didn't know exactly how primo it was, but he'd never had a disappointed customer.

Janis pulls out her hype kit and slumps into the bedside chair. Opening the bag, she scoops some scag into a Pepsi screwtop, and cooks it over her Bic. "Fuck you, Seth," she keeps muttering to herself. She draws the hot syrup into an eyedropper through a Number 25 needle. She tourniquets her purple sash around her arm and pulls it tight between her clenched teeth, needle poised. Then she hits herself.

Her hand goes slack and the needle falls to the floor. Her eyes float up under her lids as she draws in a breath; then her head collapses against her chest, mouth ajar, saliva collecting at the corner. She is draped in the chair like a rag doll. With a twitch, her eyes crack open. She peers around the room between heavy lids, her head moving in slow motion. Then she suddenly heaves forward, pukes in the wastebasket, and clears the corner of her mouth with the back of her hand.

She sits there for another minute or two as if in suspended animation. Then she gropes for her cigarettes on the bedside table. She crumples the empty pack and lets it fall to the floor. Gripping the sides of her chair, she tries to get up, but teeters and falls back. Finally, gaining her feet, she weaves toward the door.

She navigates her way down the hotel corridor dimly lit by sulphurous yellow sconces and a scarlet EXIT sign. She dreamily hums "Happy Trails" to herself as she goes, the song she sang last night with the band at the Beanery, along with an early Happy Birthday ditty to John Lennon. She's forgotten all about Seth. She's forgotten all about Peggy. She's forgotten all about *Pearl*. She giggles to herself.

Entering the abandoned lobby of the Landmark, she drifts toward the check-in desk. The night clerk, George Sandoz, is sitting behind it reading yesterday's paper.

"Hey, man," she drawls, "got change for a five? Need so'more smokes."

She tosses a crumpled five across the counter. Sandoz punches the register and hands her back four fours, plus quarters for the machine. The Land Mine is a rocker crash pad, and he doesn't pay too much attention about who's who or their coordination, especially at this time of evening.

She shuffles over to the cigarette machine, drops two quarters, pulls a pack of Marlboros and twenty cents change. Lighting up, she meanders back over to the counter and shoots a little shit with Sandoz. She goes into a rambling rap about her record, her fiancé, this and that. Finally, she bids the night clerk a good night and returns to her room still humming "Happy Trails."

As she enters her room, she teeters against the wall. Shoving off it, she makes her way over to the bedside, tosses down her cigarettes, and begins to undress.

Suddenly hit by an overwhelming vertigo, her legs buckle and she collapses, smashing her nose and her lip against the edge of the bedside table. As blood gushes from her face, her body twitches spasmodically on the floor for an instant, then suddenly becomes still.

Still clutched in her right hand are the four fours.

POSTMORTEM

John Cooke phoned Janis's manager, Albert Grossman, as well as her attorney. The attorney and his brother-in-law, a doctor, soon arrived at The Landmark's room 105. By the time the LAPD and the medical examiner's team arrived, they found no drugs or paraphernalia in the room.

Janis Joplin was pronounced dead at 9:10 P.M. Had she been alive, she would have been at the studio recording the last song on *Pearl:* "Buried Alive in the Blues."[9]

On the morning of the following day, October 5, the drugs and paraphernalia rematerialized in the room. Chief medical examiner Dr. Thomas T. Noguchi,[10] investigating the possibility of murder, discovered them in the dresser, on the bed, and on the floor. Testing the powder, he found it to be 50 percent pure, or at least five times as potent as the average street variety. That weekend in L.A. ten other people fatally overdosed on the same batch. Ruling out murder and suicide, Noguchi listed the cause of death as "accidental overdose of heroin."[11]

Janis was cremated. A private memorial service for the Joplin family was held on October 7, 1970, at the Westwood Village Mortuary. When the Joplins returned to Port Arthur, they were barraged with hate calls from residents.

According to Janis's new will, drawn up days before her demise, half her estate was left to her parents, the other half to her brother and sister, Michael and Laura.

---

9. The cut was included on the album as an instrumental.

10. Known as "the coroner to the stars," between 1967 and 1982 Noguchi performed autopsies on Marilyn Monroe, Robert F. Kennedy, and many other notables.

11. Manager Albert Grossman collected his $100,000 life insurance policy on Janis. In 1974, the policy carrier filed a civil action, challenging the payout, claiming the singer's death was suicide. The claim was denied by the court.

Janis's will set aside $2,500 for a wake. The invitation read "Drinks are on Pearl." The party was held at the Lion's Share nightclub in San Anselmo. Recalled her former lover James Gurley, "Everybody just got as drunk and as fucked up as they could."

Seth Morgan arrived at Burbank Airport at about the same time the police arrived at the Landmark. After hearing the news, he retired to a bar with her girlfriend Peggy Caserta and tried unsuccessfully to seduce her. The next day, he avenged himself on Janis's dealer by shorting him $1,000 on a cocaine transaction.

Morgan later became a porno theater proprietor, then a hawker at a strip joint, then a pimp. He was convicted of armed robbery in 1977, did thirty months in Vacaville, and, while there, wrote a novel called *Homeboy* about the L.A. criminal and S & M sex underworld.

Janis had once dreamed that she would be killed with her fiancé on his motorcycle, telling him in the morning about "the short and happy life of Janis Joplin ending crashed on a motorcycle!" Twenty years after her death, in October, Morgan drove his Harley-Davidson into a bridge piling, instantly killing himself and his girlfriend Diane Levine. Seconds before impact, she was seen pounding on his back, screaming. The autopsy revealed that he was drunk, and his tattooed arms bore fresh needle marks.

Janis once said, "People . . . like their blues singers miserable. They like their blues singers to die afterwards." Perhaps she was a martyr to her profession. But, in a more profound way, having an unquenchable lust for life in all its joys and sorrows, she had done more living in her brief but tempestuous twenty-seven years than many would ever know regardless of longevity.

Janis never betrayed the vow she had made to herself early on and before embarking on her legendary career. In spite of "the whole success thing," as she called it, she remained true to herself, never straying from "the person I was on the inside," never failing "to be righteous to myself . . . to be real." Or as she told others even more succinctly, "Don't compromise yourself. It's all you've got."

Despite all the pain, despite all the pressures, despite all the temptation, Janis never did compromise herself. Her determination, her integrity, her openness allowed her to "feel as much as I can, it's what 'soul' is all about." Few artists, before or since, have dug deeper into their feeling and into their soul and turned it into sublime music. Hers was a song of such power and of such breadth that even fellow musicians couldn't define it, but only pay tribute to it.

A few years after her passing, her friend, Jerry Garcia, wrote "Birdsong" for her. "All I know is something like a bird within her sang," it went. "All I know, she sang a little while and then flew on. Tell me all that you know, I'll show you snow and rain."

Interlude: Stoned

Let me tell you about heartache and the loss of God
Wandering, wandering in hopeless night
Out here in the perimeter there are no stars
Out here we is stoned—Immaculate.
　—Jim Morrison, "Stoned Immaculate"

"Everybody must get stoned!" sang Dylan, in 1966.

The times were "a-changin'," and everybody was indeed getting stoned now, especially the stars. The 60s were all about freedom, and the soundtrack of the revolution was rock and roll. The voice of his generation, Dylan began with songs about societal freedom—"protest" songs—but soon sang more about individual freedom. Freedom of the mind. The transition was reflected in his switch from acoustic to electric at Newport. It was also reflected in his everybody-must-get-stoned anthem. Dope was the elixir for personal and creative freedom.

Freedom is an evolutionary, four-step ladder: political, to cultural, to creative, to existential. The first two steps are social or external freedoms; the second two, individual, internal freedoms. The 60s was a decade of unprecedented struggle for liberation on all fronts. Whereas, at the start, folk and rock music championed the antiwar, civil rights, free speech, and free love movements; toward the end, it was more about freeing the mind and soul from the stifling conformity of the postwar 50s.

In part this was a result of the political tragedies and disillusionments of the decade: the assassinations of the great liberators—JFK, RFK, and Martin Luther King—Kent State, Chicago, Mi Lai. If violence, suppression, and corruption seemed impossible to overcome, if real social change was unreachable, at least a person could liberate himself and perhaps this was prerequisite to collective change.

Sit-ins gave way to "be-ins." Protesters united in a single cause gave way to "do your own thing" hippies. Where the cry had once been "Take to the Streets," now it was Timothy Leary's "Tune in, Turn on, Drop out." The seeming innocuous mantra had seismic impact on the children of the 60s and on their rock rebel idols.

Observed drug historian, Stuart Walton:[1] "The sudden introduction of a powerful deconditioning agent such as LSD had the effect of creating a mass defection from community values, especially values based on a denominator hierarchy accustomed to suppressing consciousness and awareness."

For all its prosperity, the 50s had been a decade of almost Orwellian conformity. Everyone seemed to be a character who had stepped out of a Norman Rockwell painting, a vacancy behind their canned smiles and scrubbed faces. The Emancipation Proclamation had long ago been signed and people weren't sold anymore, they were just rented or leased. You had your happy carpenter, your happy policeman, your happy teacher—all forty-hour slaves with weekends, vacations, and retirement packages. Americans considered themselves the democratic leaders of the "free" world, yet they were robots of social expectation, their personal perceptions and experiences restricted by what was allowed and what wasn't. They lived their lives to the accompaniment of Bing Crosby, the Beaver, and *Bonanza*.

LSD, Leary, and the Beatles dropped into this windup world like Little Boy over Nagasaki. "The greatest conspiracy ever mounted against the mass of humanity—greatest because so enormously ambitious in its reach," continued Walton, "is the effort to close off access to alternative mental states completely."

The fascism of consciousness dominated the Victorians and peaked in Prohibition. But of course Homo sapiens have been consuming psychoactive drugs since their arrival. The interdictions by the religious right and other activists in society's thought police have been blessedly brief. "The ubiquity of drug use is so striking that it must represent a basic human appetite," noted Andrew Weil in *The Natural Mind*.

---

1. Stuart Walton, *Out of It: A Cultural History of Intoxication*. (New York: Harmony Books, 2001).

"If you can get a whole room full of drunk, stoned people to actually wake up and think, you're doing something," said Jim Morrison.

His heroes, the romantic and symbolist poets of the nineteenth century, were experimenters too. Inspired by Blake, Coleridge, and others, Aldous Huxley wrote his *The Doors of Perception* (1954), relating his experiences with mescaline. This in turn inspired Timothy Leary to write *The Psychedelic Experience* (1964), based on the ancient *The Tibetan Book of the Dead*. By the time these works came out, the Beatniks and Beat writers—Allen Ginsberg, Jack Kerouac, William S. Burroughs, Jr., and others—were already studying Eastern religions and experimenting with psychedelics themselves. Then Ken Kesey and his Merry Pranksters boarded the magic bus.

Ironically, it was the Establishment, the military that introduced acid to rock's premiere space cadet: Jim Morrison. While attending University of California in 1964, Morrison, the son of a Navy admiral, signed up for a CIA-financed, experimental drug program at the UCLA Neuropsychiatric Center.[2] Here, wired up and supervised by technicians, he ingested pure clinical LSD (legal until 1966). In order to guinea pig more often, he used the alias of Frederick Nietzsche. Later, he hitchhiked to Mexico to take peyote with Indians. He returned bloodied and bruised, having run into no shamans,[3] but only a gang of drunken Mexicans who didn't cotton to gringo hippies. After graduat-

---

2. Military researchers believed psychedelics had Cold War potential for interrogations, assassinations, etc. The first federally funded LSD tests were performed on Manhattan Project workers in the forties. Later, the CIA's MK-ULTRA program conducted psychotomimetic research at prisons and mental hospitals. During MK-ULTRA's "Operation Midnight" in San Francisco, junkie prostitutes were paid to dose johns with Sandoz acid, their reactions monitored through two-way hotel mirrors. Soon superpotent compounds were synthesized: STP (Serenity, Tranquility, Peace—developed in 1964 by Dow Chemical), DMT, and BZ ("a monster acid" lasting a week and causing psychosis). By the late sixties, the Army had stockpiled fifty tons of BZ, "enough to turn the whole world into raving lunatics," according to *One Flew Over the Cuckoo's Nest* author, Ken Kesey, who also guinea-pigged for the feds.

3. Morrison had recently met with UCLA graduate student Carlos Castaneda, who had just written a thesis about his Yaqui shaman teacher Don Juan. Morrison wanted to do a movie about *The Teachings of Don Juan* in which Castaneda detailed his experiences with sacred medicinal plants, including psilocybin mushrooms and Jimsonweed. Castaneda went on to write a series of best-selling books about the Yaqui sorcerer.

ing from UCLA, Morrison moved to a rooftop and, here, dropped acid every day and composed his first poems, which would soon become Doors' lyrics.

"Have you ever been experienced? . . . Not necessarily stoned, but beautiful," sang Jimi Hendrix on his debut Experience album. Jimi had been very beautiful. "It was acid, acid, acid. We were spaced constantly," recalled Noel Redding. ". . . If I took two tabs, Jimi took four." A Buffalo Springfield member remembered that the guitarist "popped acid like aspirin . . . enough to kill a horse."

The guitarist's occasional tripping partner was John Lennon. In 1968, tipped off that the narcs were on their way to bust him, the Beatle feverishly set to work vacuuming his London flat, cursing, "Fucking *Jimi Hendrix* used to live here. Christ knows what the *fuck* is in *these* carpets!" By his own estimation, Lennon tripped over a thousand times. Observed his bandmate, George Harrison, "The fact that we [the ex-Beatles] do have some brain cells left and a sense of humor is quite remarkable."

Jerry Garcia called his life "a long, strange trip." "Captain Trips"—like Hendrix, Morrison, Lennon, and Cobain—started out as a pothead and acid evangelist. If pot was an acoustic buzz, acid was electric, with Marshall stacks. "Psychedelics were probably the single most significant experience in my life," said Jerry. He and the Dead dosed themselves before every performance in the 60s. LSD was a communion wafer for the band because the purpose of the group was "for getting high" and "forgetting yourself," he explained. "And to forget yourself is to see everything else. And to see everything else is to become an understanding molecule in evolution, a conscious tool of the universe."

Everybody seemed to be getting beautiful in the 60s, even the Beach Boys. "You'll never listen to surf music again!" Jimi sang before climaxing with his mind-bending feedback. At that time, Mr. Surfin' USA, Brian Wilson, was tripping daily in an 8-ton sandbox he had built under his piano at his Malibu mansion. The Beach Boy opened a freak shop, The Radiant Radish, and would be diagnosed with tardive dyskinesia, a debilitating nervous condition resulting from acid saturation.

Even Cary Grant was a tripper. After dropping LSD sixty times under the supervision of his doctor, the *North by Northwest* star declared, "I have been born again." Interest piqued, the King of Rock and Roll himself picked up a copy of *The Psychedelic Experience*. Even more fascinated now, the ever-curious but cautious Elvis had his two bravest bodyguards, Red and Sonny West,[4] guinea pig White Lightning. When they survived without straitjackets, the King dropped with his wife, Priscilla, and his other two worthies, Lamar Fike and Jerry Schilling. The four giggled for hours in Graceland's Jungle Room and Meditation Garden, then, over take-out pizza, they watched H. G. Wells's *The Time Machine* on the big screen TV. Afterward, Lamar wandered into the front yard and made out with a maple tree, telling it: "I love you."[4]

But not everybody had a groovy trip. After dropping, Sonny repaired to the bathroom and in the mirror saw "the ugliest wolf man I'd ever seen . . . [Then] I fled back to the bedroom and felt the walls closing in on me." Going out for fresh air, he started playing in an ivy patch. "My own skin suddenly became transparent, and I could see my veins, muscles, tendons. They were all green, like the ivy's." "We are all from God," he whispered to himself. Though the trip ended on this positive note, "It was an exhausting, emotional roller coaster, and something I never cared to try again."

Acid was not Janis's cup of tea either. On her first and last trip, she told her partner, after throwing up, "We're at the bottom end of a microscope, man. And that's God's bloodshot eye up there lookin' down at us." She didn't even like grass because it "makes me think too much."

Though Hendrix's appetite for psychedelics was legendary, he wasn't immune to the occasional freak-out himself. After eating acid-laced birthday cake in New York, he staggered out into Park Avenue traffic, wailing, "I can't see! I'm blind!"

Even Captain Trips was shaken on his maiden voyage. Instead of seeing "the face of God and all that good shit," as his lyricist, Robert Hunter, had told him he might, Garcia was plunged into one of his worst nightmares until Hunter chilled him out with excerpts from *The Tibetan Book of the Dead*.

Lennon hadn't been quite prepared for his virgin experience, either. The Beatles' dentist dosed him, George, and their wives, Cynthia and Patti, at a nightclub. After escaping a carnivorous club elevator, the Clever One and the Mystical One fled to the latter's Bentley and, en route back to the security of their mansions, nearly lost their minds in the phantasmagoria of the London streets. Infatuated with the mind-eating Lucy in the Sky with Diamonds, Lennon later insisted Cyn-

---

4. Sonny West, *Elvis: Still Taking Care of Business*, with Marshall Terrill (Chicago, IL: Triumph Books, 2007).

thia join him for a "bonding" experience. When she at last agreed, she nearly jumped out a window. Similarly, when Morrison persuaded his wife, Pamela, to try the rabbit hole, her first flash was, "Blood! I'm seeing blood everywhere!"

The stars soon learned that LSD could be a double-edged sword: while taking it in search of heaven, one could just as easily find hell. And when they arrived there, they discovered hell wasn't a place, but a feeling. An inexpressible and inescapable horror.

Still, five of the Seven often decided to take their chances, for professional reasons if nothing else. Acid tuned their radios to supernatural bandwidths, stimulating the creative juices. A day-tripper may wake up the next morning to find that what he thought was a masterpiece was in fact rubbish, but not always. The lion's share of rock, needless to say, has been created and performed under the influence. Would "Voodoo Child," "Light My Fire," "Lucy in the Sky," "St. Stephens," "Downer," or any of the stars' other immortal songs, have been created straight? Unlikely.

Was Lennon on milk and cookies when he wrote, "Yellow matter custard, dripping from a dead dog's eye. Crabalocker fishwife, pornographic priestess, I am the eggman . . . I am the walrus, goo goo g'joob?"

Or Cobain: "Sickening pessimists. Despicable masses. Asseverated commumists. Apocalyptic bastards?"

Or Hendrix: "Well, mountain lions found me there waitin', And set me on an eagle's back. He took me past to the outskirts of infinity?"

Garcia called the Dead's second album, *Anthem of the Sun*, "a metaphorical acid trip . . . mixed for the hallucinations."

Yoko Ono declared: "We were taking it [drugs] in celebration. We were artists. It was beautiful to be on a high."

Cobain said: "I never took drugs as an escape. I always took drugs for learning."

The songs of the stars inspired many civilians to try the surrealistic pillow themselves. Did a listener need to be experienced to fully appreciate the music? Not necessarily, but it helped. Those who didn't indulge could get a contact high just listening to the albums. In a real sense, the stars were drugs for their fans.

Each of the Seven spent most of his or her professional life getting stoned or recovering from a stone. If psychedelic consumption could be creatively and spiritually liberating, most stars agreed that doing other kinds of dope—speed, booze, and smack in all varieties—could be just plain fun. No one denied the simple hedonism of it. Life can be a drag. Why not get high?

"Feelin' good, feelin' good. All the money in the world spent on feelin' good," goes an old blues song, "Medley: Fool for a Cigarette/Feelin' Good." More sensitive and depressive than others, the stars spent many millions on feel-goods. They squandered many more millions on detoxes, busts, and substance-abuse health problems. Still, the politically incorrect truth remains: if drugs are so terrible, why do so many do them?

The problem is simple: at first, dope tends to give more than it takes away; but, with overconsumption, it takes far more than it gives. Too often there is a balloon payment after an all too short honeymoon. This is not a problem intrinsic to the dope itself, but to the user. The overuser, the insatiable, the addictive personality. The person, often an artist, for whom a high is never quite high enough. The person who regularly crosses the line from getting high to getting blitzed, blottoed, wasted, wrecked, totaled.

The Seven were the proverbial candle burners at both ends: they rocked and fixed almost all the time and the double helped kill most. But, for them, life without the high was life lite, life unplugged—no life at all. And rock without dope was rock unplugged—it wasn't rock at all.

Doping among the stars progressed through the usual three overlapping stages. First came the sensitizers: pot, acid, mushrooms. Then, energizers: crank and coke. Finally, the de-energizers/de-sensitizers: booze and smack. The last two stages were the most damaging, both to the sword swallower and everyone in the vicinity.

The fundamental ingredient of rock and roll is energy: so, not surprisingly, the stars took supplements to jack up their already extraordinary natural energy. Speed was the steroid of rock. "If acid wrote the lyrics, speed played the music," noted Noel Redding. "Cocaine, Seconal, Quaaludes, and heroin became part of the landscape," he added.

After taking the Pepsi challenge of the 70s, the stars were unanimous: the original Coke was the winner. Coke was crank deluxe: it not only delivered the kilowatts but a sense of euphoric invulnerability. Morrison said his idea of paradise was a desert island with a mountain of coke. Janis did enough to conquer her weight problem and become an 87-pound skeleton. Lennon got down to 135 on "the devil's dandruff," as he called it, and deviated his septum. The perennial dieter

Elvis stuffed his nostrils with coke-soaked cotton balls and suffered "nosebleeds that lasted an eternity," according to Lamar Fike. "We took so many uppers," he continued, "our teeth chattered like Xavier Cugat's rhythm section . . . I should be dead, really."

Garcia, too, soon caught the devil's dandruff. Although his own Colombian weight-watchers regimen did little to reduce his bulk, it helped him get to and through 2,314 Dead gigs over three decades. His friend, acid king Merry Prankster, Ken Kesey, called coke the "Nazi drug" since Hitler developed it for his troops. His wife, Carolyn, said, "If anything ruined our lives, it was cocaine."

"The irony was undeniable," wrote the Dead's Phil Lesh,[5] who had also defected from acid to coke. "Drugs had helped us to create our group mind and fuse our music together, and now drugs were isolating us from one another and our own feelings, and started killing us off."

"Drivin' that train, high on cocaine, Casey Jones you better watch your speed!" sang Jerry. Finding that coke was a runaway locomotive, he soon turned to the only thing that could slow it down: smack. Knowing the danger of shooting China White like Janis, he smoked "Persian"—95 percent black tar heroin. "It's the thing of being removed from desire," he told an interviewer. By the time he fell into a near fatal coma in 1986, Jerry had a $700-a-day Middle Eastern monkey on his back. Though he miraculously resurrected and enjoyed what Deadheads called his "Second Coming," he jumped back on the Horse, and it soon rode him down to join Jimi, Jim, Janis, Elvis, and so many others.

There has always been romanticism about the poppy, especially among musicians. John Coltrane, Charlie Parker, Thelonius Monk, Miles Davis, and many of the other jazz immortals had been junkies. "If God made anything better, He kept it to himself," said Charles Mingus. According to Frederick J. Spencer (Jazz and Death), "Heroin use had become almost a rite of passage among young jazz musicians . . . and one reason was the example of Charlie Parker. The fact that Parker—whose genius had become a beacon to everyone in jazz—was a hard-core heroin addict reinforced the musicians' urge to use the drug." In rock, the Lennon-Clapton-Richards triumvirate became a comparable beacon.

Gen X rockers paid tribute to their forebears. "The tradition of the

---

5. Phil Lesh, *Searching for the Sound: My Life in the Grateful Dead* (New York: Little Brown, 2005).

musician on dope was part of the myth," admitted Kurt Cobain. "Everyone from Leadbelly to Iggy to Sid Vicious—these were my heroes." The Father of Grunge also found "my heroine," as he called it, to be the only remedy for "the burning, nauseous pain in the upper part of my stomach lining." He added: "I feel like a junkie as it is, I may as well be one."

Another addict, Marianne Faithfull, wrote: "The other drugs had been taken in a quest of sensation. Heroin was the cessation of all sensation. What is so seductive about it is that there is an absolute absence of any kind of pain—physical or otherwise." In other words, a junk high was as close as you could get to death without actually being dead.

The Lennons went on the same pain management regimen. John and Yoko had "a special place in their hearts for heroin," wrote Robert Rosen.[6] ". . . Nothing killed their pain better." By the seventies, the couple had a $1,000-a-week habit. Lennon had developed his early on. It had helped kill not only the Beatles but his marriage to Cynthia. Of the launch party for *Sgt. Pepper's*, she recalled, "He did indeed look terrible. I feared he might kill himself. John had always had the potential to self-destruct and now he seemed hell-bent on fulfilling it."[7] The Beatle himself admitted, "Togetherness had gone. . . . Round about *Sgt. Pepper's* it was wearing off. . . . I was stoned all the time . . . on H . . . and just didn't give a shit."[8] Only a few years before, the Fab Four, before receiving their MBE awards from the queen, had been giggling and blowing joints in the Buckingham Palace bathrooms.

John's idol, Elvis, turned to narcotics in the later 60s, too. But ever the law-abiding citizen, the King never deigned to a street drug; in the last twenty months of his life, he was prescribed nearly 12,000 Schedule 1 substances and injectables: Dilaudid (synthetic morphine), Demerol, Seconal, Tuinol, Placidyl, and Valmid, to name a few. His "medicine," as he called it, was not just for his glaucoma, inverted bowel, hypertension, and many other ills. "E loved the shit out of pills," Lamar explained.

Though the King employed Dr. Feelgoods from coast to coast, his Rexall appetite was so insatiable that sometimes his stash would evap-

6. Robert Rosen, *Nowhere Man: The Final Days of John Lennon* (Oakland, CA: Quick American Archives, 2002).

7. Cynthia Lennon, *John*.

8. Bob Spitz, *The Beatles* (New York: Little Brown, 2005).

orate and he'd hit the wall. One time, jumping up on his pool table and air-conditioning the Graceland ceiling with his Beretta, he raged, "I'll buy a whole goddamn drugstore, if I have to!" He sent his guys out to do so, but his ever-sober manager, the Colonel, put the kibosh on the idea. In other times of need, the King would get another "ingrown toenail": he would dig holes in a foot until infection set in, then tell Lamar, "Bet I get some good stuff now!"

Though Elvis had threatened to hunt down and shoot all the pushers in Memphis, in 1974 he accidentally shot his own, Dr. George Nichopoulos, aka "Needle Nick," after a performance in North Carolina. When Dr. Nick threatened to cut back on his chemo, the King pulled his piece and sprayed his hotel suite. One slug ricocheted off the TV and wound up in Nick's chest. "Son, good God almighty!" cried his father, Vernon, "What in the world made you do a thing like that?" The King snickered, "Aw, hell, daddy, so I shot the doc. No big deal. He's not dead." But he gave Nick a gold Mercedes for the inconvenience.

Soon, rumors that he was a junkie started circulating. In an attempt to nip them in the bud, he staggered onstage one night and announced: "I never been strung out in my life—except on music!" Another time, in Vegas, he informed his fans that if he seemed a little under the weather, he was battling the flu and that if he found the junkie rumormongers, he would "pull their goddamn tongues out BY THE ROOTS!"

Two years later, the King's bloated 300-pound corpse was found on his bathroom floor in Graceland. The coroner discovered eleven major narcotics in his system.

Elvis was a teetotaler in a family of fundamentalist moonshiners.[9] He'd seen the blight of booze firsthand: his kin—prone to knife and gunplay when lubricated—had nearly killed themselves and others too. His excitable mother, Gladys, called whiskey "my medicine for my nerves." Wrote his stepbrother, Rick Stanley, "Elvis was an adult child of an alcoholic. As such, he was schooled in the patterns of avoidance and dishonesty." Though Elvis mostly avoided the hair of the dog, early on he came to rely on a pill to sleep, another to get him up, then fistfuls in between. Like his mother, he called these his "helpers" and chose them from the *Physicians' Desk Reference*. "The PDR was like a Bible," said Lamar. "Elvis read the PDR like I do a damn motor magazine."

---

9. On the few occasions when the King indulged, he tended to get more ornery than usual: he once speared a groupie with a pool cue. On another occasion, he threatened to attack Sonny West with a bottle.

Many fans of the King still ask why. "He just liked to get fucked up," explained Lamar. "He loved it! It wasn't to escape any kind of reality, either. Shit, there was no reality in that group in the first place, so how can you escape it? Jesus Christ!"

Whenever substance abuse is discussed, "escaping reality" invariably comes up. The phrase of course begs the question: What is "reality"? With psychedelics, the argument can be made that one is escaping not from, but to, reality. That one is escaping the self-deceptions, atrophied senses, and robotic routines of one's daily life.

Tom Rapp of Pearls Before Swine, offered another perspective when he sang, "I don't want to escape reality, I want reality to escape from me."

Another take on the question comes on T-shirts: REALITY IS FOR PEOPLE WHO CAN'T HANDLE DRUGS.

Anyway, as far as Elvis and the other stars were concerned, Lamar was right: the worlds they all lived in were a far cry from what the rest of us call reality. In the end they all wanted to escape from the unreality of fame.

In *Buried Alive,* Myra Friedman wrote, "Janis attributed her heroin use to the fear that would accompany her growing fame." Janis said she "lived" for her performances, but "I make love to 25,000 people, then I go home. Alone." The Queen of the Blues shot smack after gigs as a way, explained biographer Alice Echols, "of prolonging the onstage high by fending off the inevitable post-performance depression."

Not long before her fatal overdose, Janis told her old lover Kris Kristofferson that she was thinking about suicide. "Man, you got everything going for you," he told her. "You got a man you love; you got a producer you love!"

"What's it all worth?" muttered Janis.

She poured her heart out to her friend, Myra Friedman, about the hardship and torment of her career. "Then QUIT!" Myra begged her. "This is killing you!"

Janis began crying uncontrollably. "I don't have anything else!"

So she ended it all with the only medication that made her forget the profession she couldn't quit. "There's a lot of people using junk in the rock scene, and they're on death row," said Nick Gravenites, "the rest of them are on Tier C."

In this sense fame can be the most insidious drug of all, since very few can detox from it. Observed Eric Burdon: "Entertaining thousands of people is an incredible narcotic, and applause junkies are easily made. You feel like a god as you leave the stage . . . You're uncomfortable being alone for anything more than an hour or two."

After Janis was gone, others were resigned much as she had been on hearing of Hendrix's demise. They seemed blind to its parallel in their own lives. "It was the best possible time for her death," said the pre-heroin Jerry Garcia, still in his hallucinogenic period. Offered his Grateful Dead bandmate, Bob Weir, "I can't bring myself to be in abject misery about it because, like I say . . . she lived up to her image."

Linda Gravenites provided the most realistic epitaph: "It would have gotten ugly for her had it continued."

However, the simple chemical fact is that Janis didn't just die from heroin but from mixing it with booze. Cobain knew about the deadly combination. "You just don't mix alcohol with heroin at all or you'll die," he said. ". . . . Everyone I know of who's OD'd has gotten drunk. And it's been late at night too."

Just as Janis had died late at night, after combining the two, so did Morrison nine months later. Of the Seven, Janis and Jim were the two alcoholics.

"I think I think too much. That's why I drink," said Janis, who readily admitted she was a "juicer." Toward the end, Southern Comfort gave her a $2,500 honorarium for being their unofficial spokesperson and product mannequin. "Can you imagine getting paid for passing out for two years?" Janis cackled.

In his prime, Morrison was draining three bottles of Scotch a day. Once in a Honolulu bar, he pounded thirty-two mai tais. "I'm not a musician, I'm a poet, and I'm Irish," he told an interviewer. "The drug of Irish poetry is alcohol. Booze beats dope for me any day." He compared his benders to craps: "You go out for a night of drinking and you don't know where you're going to end up the next day. It could work out good or it could be disastrous. It's like the throw of the dice."

Late at night, July 5, 1972, the singer threw snake eyes after scoring smack at a Paris bar. Until now, the star had been like Malcolm Lowry's hero in *Under the Volcano:* "A drunk of gargantuan proportions," wrote Ronald Siegel,[10] "yet a man who seems never to have let go of an almost preternatural degree of self-awareness, even when facedown on the floor of a pub or a cantina."

10. Ronald K. Siegel, *Intoxication: Life in Pursuit of Artificial Paradise* (New York: Pocket Books, 1989).

As physicians know, alcohol has caused far more death and damage than all the other drugs combined. And yet it is the only legal intoxicant. In excess, alcohol eats the brain, the liver, the heart, the GI tract, the pancreas, and the central nervous system. Heroin, on the other hand, even in comparable excess, causes little organic damage except with contaminated needles. Withdrawal is far less severe and dangerous than with booze.

Both Janis and Jim knew this. Their doctors had told them they had only a short time left. But they found it impossible to dry out.

Janis successfully detoxed from heroin twice and considered this her "greatest accomplishment." She fell off the wagon on both occasions, but she'd been unable to wean herself from booze even briefly.

Morrison was the same. He didn't necessarily have to quit altogether, just back off. Way off. But moderation was not in his temperament, nor in Janis's, nor the other five. They all had monster habits. Habits that would have killed ordinary mortals long before it did them, thus proving that they were indeed strong, but not quite so strong as they thought.

Stuart Walton observed: "It is as though there were some critically ambivalent quality in the creative gift that may dispense exemplary talent, but at the cost of an inability to live proportionally and with restraint. In some the self-annihilating urge leads to quiet, meticulous suicides. In others, it is a drawn-out sequence of collapses, arrests, and detoxing, ending in the final Coleridgean ignominy of death in a hotel bathroom, in blood and vomit and diarrhea."

Five of the Seven suffered the second fate. Most of the people surrounded them—family, friends, bandmates, managers—saw it coming and tried to throw out the lifesavers.

"Everybody tried to stop him," claimed Morrison's producer, Paul Rothchild. "He was unstoppable!" Ray Manzarek tried too, but at last gave up in futility. "What could you say to him?" he wrote.[11] "Jim, don't have too many drinks. You're killing yourself." The most the Doors' keyboardist got out of his singer was the sheepish concession, "I know I drink too much, Ray. I'm trying to quit."

"Janis, you're drinkin' too much. You're dopin' too much," Nick Gravenites told her. But this admonition, too, fell on deaf ears.

"Everything you did, Kurt had to do six of," said his friend, David

---

11. Ray Manzarek, *Light My Fire: My Life with the Doors* (New York: Putnam, 1998).

Haig. Remembered Nirvana's bassist, Krist Novoselic, "He looked like shit. He looked like a ghoul . . . You can't change anybody or preach some kind of morals or anything. What am I going to do? Nothing."

Noel Redding wrote of his rivalry with Hendrix: "Getting high had become a new competition: a game of Russian roulette. Only, instead of holding a gun to your head, you boasted, 'I can take more than you.' " Jimi invariably won. At least in the short run.

When Garcia's manager, Sat Khalsa, asked him why he was killing himself with dope, the guitarist simply replied, "Why live?" At their wit's end, the Dead finally pulled an intervention on him in '89; Jerry was beyond pissed. "These things always feel like a lynching to me," he argued. "If a good friend wants to come to my house and die on drugs, that's okay."

As in everything else, where his own addiction was concerned, Elvis again proved himself to be the King. "You're doing too much dope, pal," Red West told him. Elvis ignored him. So Red ramped it up a notch. "You sonuvabitch, get a grip!" His boss ignored this too. So Red went to one of his suppliers and told him he would break his legs. When Elvis found this out, he told his protector to "stay out of my personal life. I'm going to do whatever it is the fuck I wanna do!" But Red didn't want to see him die—he couldn't stay out of it. So Elvis fired him. In his place, he hired his kid brother, David Stanley. Soon David, though already a junkie himself, told Elvis he was confiscating his stash. The King put a gun to his head and said, "No, you're not."

"There's only two choices you can make, man," Morrison told a friend early on. "We've each made our own: I'm on the side of life; she's on the side of death." She was his common-law wife, Pamela Courson. Pam had been a junkie for years. Later, he became ambivalent. "You favor life, he sides with death," he sang in "Adolf Hitler." "I straddle the fence and my balls hurt."

By the time Jim moved to Paris, the booze had taken its toll: his liver was shot, his stomach ulcer riddled, and he was puking 80 proof blood. Days before he drew his last rasping breath from a collapsed lung, he fell off the fence and onto Adolf Hitler's side.

"The poppy rules the world," he wrote in his journal, floating on his first snort of smack. He'd scored from his wife's ex-boyfriend, Count Jean de Breteuil, the infamous "dealer to the stars," who, not long before, had provided Janis with her own last fix.

Exactly two years before Jim took his own final dose from the count, his friend, the Rolling Stone Brian Jones, drowned in his swimming pool. Jim had composed a memorial poem "Ode to L.A. While Thinking of Brian Jones, Deceased," which ended:

> *I hope you went out smiling like a child*
> *into the cool remnant of a dream.*

After taking a final taste of the White Lady, Morrison was soon found in his bathtub, smiling like a child as if he had indeed descended into the cool remnant of a dream, joining Brian at the bottom of his pool.

"He had such a serene expression," his addict wife, Pamela, later said.

So, in the end, Morrison came to rest in the arms of Morpheus, as did so many of the other stars. But what is it that brought him there so late?

3

JIM MORRISON

December 8, 1943–July 3, 1971

THE END: PRELUDE

This is the end, my only friend . . .
No safety or surprise the end.
—Jim Morrison, "The End"

"I don't want to die of old age or OD or drift off in my sleep," he once said. "I want to feel what it's like. I want to taste it, hear it, smell it. Death is only going to happen once. I don't want to miss it."

He lies motionless in the bathtub now, eyes closed, mouth ajar. His U.S. Army combat jacket and his prize French riding boots are scattered across the floor. A thread of blood streams from his nose down his bloated chest into the pink bathwater. All that can be heard is the metronome drip of the faucet.

Paris still sleeps: the July dawn will not break for an hour, traffic has yet to begin on the Rue Beautrellis.

She gently dabs the blood from his nose and the foam at the corner of his mouth. "Jim?" she whispers. "Baby? Wake up, Jim baby. I'm here."

Only yesterday he was afraid to be alone. He had been walking the streets of Paris with Alain Ronay when he collapsed on a bench, coughing up blood. He begged his old friend not to leave him. Alain implored him to stop drinking or "end up like Oscar." While visiting the Père Lachaise cemetery together only weeks before, Jim had told Alain he wanted to lay with Chopin, Balzac, Molière, Oscar Wilde, and the others.

His wife brushes back the hair from his cool forehead and gently kisses him again, tears welling in her eyes. "I'm here, Jimmy," she whispers. "I'm here, baby. I'll never leave you."

Pamela reaches over to the hand mirror, cuts another line, and inhales. Her eyes roll back. Suddenly she sees the dark highway that he has told her about so many times before and where it all began.

EGGSHELL MIND

Indians scattered on dawn's highway bleeding.
Ghosts crowd the young child's fragile eggshell mind
—Jim Morrison, "Dawn's Highway"

The four-year-old boy was sitting in the idling family car with his mother and grandmother. He watched his father and grandfather dash toward the smoking, overturned truck and the bodies strewn over the broken asphalt. Dawn was breaking over the New Mexico desert, orange and black thunderheads were stacked over the eastern horizon. Some of the bodies were still and contorted; others heaved and tried to crawl, an unearthly song came from them. The boy's mother hugged him, trying to cover his eyes and ears.

By the time his father ran back to the car, the child was sobbing. "It's just a dream, Jimmy!" said his father.

"It was the most important event in my life . . . The first time I discovered death," he would later recall. "The souls or ghosts of those dead Indians were just running around, freaking out, and just leapt into my soul."[1]

He later claimed that he was possessed by one of the victims. He believed the Indian was a shaman who gave him supernatural powers—the power to visit the spirit world and to return with healing visions. He believed that he had been chosen for an extraordinary fate.

---

1. Jim's sister, Ann, said, "He enjoyed telling that story and exaggerating it. He said he saw a dead Indian by the side of the road, and I don't even know if that's true."

Otherwise, James Douglas Morrison seemed at first to be an ordinary boy, if somewhat solitary and withdrawn.

His father, George, the only son of a Methodist laundry owner in Georgia, was a career naval officer. He had named Jimmy after General Douglas MacArthur and expected his son to follow in his footsteps. Jimmy's mother, Clara, was the daughter of a Wisconsin lawyer and Communist Party activist. Pretty, outgoing, and gracious, she made the perfect captain's wife.

The ambitious Captain Morrison rose quickly through the military ranks. Soon after Jimmy was born in the middle of World War II, his father shipped out to fly Hellcat fighters in the South Pacific. When Jimmy saw the dying Pueblos in the desert, his father commanded the nuclear weapons systems in New Mexico. By the time Jim was a teenager, his father had become the youngest admiral in the history of the Navy.

Due to the admiral's career, the Morrisons were always on the move. By age four, Jimmy had already lived in five different places, coast to coast. Since his father was gone for long periods, his mother, Clara, became the disciplinarian. Jimmy grew rebellious. Returning home from duty, his father, accustomed to thousands of men obeying his command promptly and without question, had no patience with his first son's insubordination and backtalk. He spared no effort trying to get the boy on the straight and narrow.

But his parents' efforts seemed only to make Jim Morrison all the more incorrigible. A verbal boy, he, like Janis, soon developed a dirty mouth. And Jimmy was a cutup and a daredevil; one time he packed his little brother and sister onto the front of a toboggan and jettisoned them to the bottom of a hill where they would have collided with a tree had their father not intercepted them.

Moving from town to town and school to school, the admiral's son never grew close to anyone, but made friends quickly. His classmates found him funny, if scary at times, and elected him president of his fifth-grade class. In his school photo that year, clean cut and beaming, in a pressed white shirt, he looked like Jerry Mathers, the Beaver.

At George Washington High in Alexandria, Virginia, Jim made the honor roll with little effort. He had an IQ of 149. He appeared to be smart by stupefying people. Disdaining teachers who taught him nothing but facts, he loved laying head trips on them. Often late to class, he would tell them he had been kidnapped by gypsies. One time he cut school saying he had to have a brain tumor removed; the principal later called his mother, anxious to know how the operation went.

Jim was a precocious performer too. He often collapsed and played dead, much as John Lennon had as a boy. His twitching paraplegic impersonation was another favorite bit of his, as it was for the future Beatle. But when running into a cute girl, Jim played the Southern gentleman: he would bow, recite a Shakespearean sonnet, then bow again and take his leave.

His first steady girlfriend at George Washington High, outside the nation's capital, was Tandy Martin. The pretty and straitlaced brunette had never met anybody quite like Jimmy Morrison. At first, she found him smart, funny, and cool. Then he started getting weird on her. One time they were walking home from school in their upper middle-class neighborhood of congressmen, diplomats, and generals when Jim unzipped his fly and announced, "Ah'm gonna take a piss on that there fireplug!" Another time he dropped to the floor of a crowded commuter train, yanked off one of her saddle shoes, and drawled, "All ah wanna dooo is kiss yore presh-usss feet!" But Tandy was never so mortified as when he challenged her to kiss the behind of a marble nude outside the Corcoran Gallery on the Washington Mall. "Go on, Tandy," he taunted, "put your orbicular muscle to work. Kiss the gluteus maximus!" Tandy's mother had warned her about Jimmy from the start. "He seems unclean, like a leper," she'd told her daughter.

The couple broke up senior year after Tandy had accused Jim of "wearing a mask" all the time. Jim broke down in tears, saying he truly loved her. Then he twisted her arm behind her back and threatened to razor her face "so no one else will look at you but me."

Jim in Virginia, like Janis in Texas, became the nucleus of an elite high school clique that included jocks, the school paper editor, and the class president. Soon his favorite time was not spent with his peers but with visionaries and madmen. While Commander Morrison was busy at the Pentagon, Cape Canaveral, or on the Navy golf course and Clara at officers' wives' club meetings, Jim was holed up in his basement room devouring Kerouac, Blake, Baudelaire, Rimbaud, de Sade, and Burroughs. He quoted these literary outlaws to his classmates and, in response to their befuddled looks, burst out with Dean Moriarty's hyena hee-hee-hee! from *On the Road*.

By seventeen, Jim Morrison's favorite philosophers were Arthur Schopenhauer and his devotee, Frederick Nietzsche. A man whose ideas shared some elements with Buddhism and a defender of suicide, Schopenhauer asserted that man is driven by desire and, thus, predestined to misery and disillusionment unless he cultivates willful intellect. Nietzsche advanced this argument, asserting that "God is dead" and replaced by the willful Superman who supersedes morality and becomes a law unto himself. The idea of the Superman grew to be the cornerstone of Morrison's adolescent identity. The fact that the manic depressive, bisexual philosophers lived their thoughts to their solipsist climax—Schopenhauer dying wretched and alone with his dogs, Nietzsche in a glorious syphilitic madness—canonized them in the young man's mind.

Jim graduated from George Washington High in 1961.[2] To his parents' dismay, he didn't condescend to collect his diploma. Celebrating his own graduation, George Morrison had just been named commander of the USS *Bonnie Dick*, the largest aircraft carrier in the world, based in San Diego. The admiral and Clara moved to California with their two younger children. The prodigal son was left behind in Florida to live with his grandparents while attending St. Petersburg Junior College.

"He hated conformity," recalled Grandmother Morrison, a devout Methodist. "He'd try to shock us. He loved to do that. He'd tell us things he knew would make us feel queer." He often threatened to bring a "nigger girl" home from college. His room was littered with empty wine bottles. He refused to cut his hair or clean his clothes. And he wouldn't speak to his grandparents for days.

He started hanging out at The Contemporary Arts Coffeehouse and Gallery run by gay intellectual Tom Reece. Jim first appeared onstage here on open-mike night; he performed bourbon-fueled stream-of-consciousness poetry while accompanying himself on the ukulele. The infatuated Reece encouraged him. Years later, Jim confided to his lawyer (for his Miami obscenity trial) that while in junior college he had had an affair with an older man who was a nightclub owner.

In 1962, Morrison transferred to Florida State University. Free of adult supervision at last, he was determined to "try everything" now. He started experimenting with drugs at FSU. He lost his virginity to Mary Werbelow, a Sun 'n' Fun beauty queen and aspiring dancer who had once wanted to become a nun. Meanwhile, he excelled academi-

---

2. Mama Cass Elliot graduated from GW the year before and was destined to die only a year after him.

cally, writing scholarly papers on everything from the surrealist paintings of Hieronymus Bosch to "The Sexual Neuroses of Crowds," an analysis of the collective eroticism aroused by popular music. He also took to the stage for the first time in a student production of Harold Pinter's *The Dumbwaiter.*

After his junior year, Jim saw his father for the last time. His mother insisted he wear new clothes and get a haircut so as not to look like a "beatnik" on arrival in San Diego. Jim begrudgingly consented. But no sooner did he board the USS *Bonnie Dick*, than Admiral Morrison sent him to the ship barber for a regulation Navy haircut. Then for R & R he let his shorn son shoot dummies in the ocean with a machine gun.

Thinking he had fulfilled his duty, Jim asked the commander permission to transfer from FSU to the UCLA Film School, among the most radical liberal arts programs anywhere. Permission was denied. Jim, now 21, cashed in a trust fund and enrolled anyway.

His parents disinherited him. Or, as he Jim preferred it, he disinherited his parents.

From now on, he would refer to himself as an "orphan," just as his heroes had been—Schopenhauer's father having committed suicide, Nietzsche's having suffered a fatal brain tumor.

The UCLA film school was enjoying its "Golden Age" in 1964. The program boasted an avant-garde faculty of famous filmmakers including Jean Renoir, Stanley Kramer, and Josef von Sternberg. It attracted "film poets" such as Jim Morrison and a new classmate of his, Francis Ford Coppola.

Jim soon fell in with a clique of the best, brightest, and weirdest auteurs at UCLA: the eccentric Frenchman, Alain Ronay, who would later bury Morrison; Dennis "the Weasel" Jakob, who shared Jim's obsession with existentialist philosophers; Felix Venable, who in two years would fatally overdose, and who introduced Jim to LSD; and finally, the fourth, Ray Manzarek, who called Venable "an evil-minded fuck," was an aspiring musician and filmmaker.

Though Jim excelled at UCLA, his final project—a surrealistic film noire—was a disaster. It featured Daliesque dream imagery: a hooker in spike heels dancing on a TV showing goose-stepping Nazis; wasted space cadets making finger shadows on the wall while watching porno; the dancer licking off the camerman's eyeball. Jim called the untitled project "a film about film." His faculty advisor gave him a D, calling it the worst thing he'd ever seen. Jim cried. But in 1965 he graduated with a BS in cinematography.

Disillusioned with the failure of his first artistic endeavor, Morrison moved to the rooftop of Jakob the Weasel's apartment in Venice and, here, weighed his postgrad options. Penniless, he ate little except LSD. Meanwhile, he composed poetry and pumped iron on Venice beach.

One day Ray Manzarek ran into his classmate on the beach. Four years Morrison's senior, Manzarek had studied classical piano as a child in Chicago, held a degree in economics as well as in cinematography, but hadn't decided whether he wanted to be a filmmaker or a pop keyboardist. On this sunny afternoon in Venice, he hardly recognized his former classmate. Jim had lost about forty pounds since graduation—he was lean, ripped, and sported a beautifully unruly mane halfway down his back. With his Byronic lips and azure eyes, he looked like his hero Alexander the Great, the precocious student of Aristotle and son of a general like himself.

Ray asked Jim what he'd been up to lately. Jim said he'd been writing some songs and poetry. Ray asked for a sample. "Aw, Ray, I don't have much of a voice," protested Jim. Ray said Dylan didn't either and urged him to take a shot. Jim knelt down into the beach sand, looked into the cloudless California sky, and closed his eyes.

"Let's swim to the moon . . . / Let's climb through the tide," he sang quietly. *"Penetrate the evenin' / that the city sleeps to hide."*

"Those are the greatest fuckin' song lyrics I've ever heard!" exclaimed Ray who had a bar band of his own. "Let's start a rock 'n' roll band and make a million dollars!"

"That's exactly what I had in mind," replied Jim.

"What'll we call ourselves?" asked Ray.

"The Doors," said Jim without skipping a beat.[3]

---

3. He and Jakob the Weasel had joked about starting an underground duo called "The Doors: Open and Closed." The name was based on the William Blake line, "If the doors of perception were cleansed everything would appear as it is, infinite." Aldous Huxley had recently written a book about psychedelic drugs, *The Doors of Perception,* based on the same excerpt.

A BEAUTY THAT TERRIFIES

The Doors music . . . speaks of madness that dwells within us
all, of depravity and dreams. . . . That is its strength and its
beauty—a beauty that terrifies.
—Jim Morrison

Ronnie Haran was the booking agent for L.A.'s Whiskey a Go Go—the
venue for the Turtles, the Byrds, Van Morrison's Them, and the other
top acts. She spotted the Doors at the London Fog, a biker bar run by
the great grandson of Jesse James. As the house band, the Doors were
paid $5 apiece on weeknights, $10 on weekends—plus free food and
beer. They played "Moonlight Drive" and a few other originals, plus
"Gloria," "Louie Louie," "Little Red Rooster," and other standards.

"I knew Jim had star quality the minute I saw him," recalled Ronnie. But "He didn't have a pot to piss in . . . I had to dress him, get him
some T-shirts and turtlenecks at the Army-Navy store."

She got the Doors into the musicians' union and persuaded Elmer
Valentine, the Whisky's owner, to take a chance on the band as an
opener for $135 per week. Then she invited the homeless Jim—crash-
ing under the Venice pier by this time—to move in with her. Ronnie
helped introduce Morrison to the movers and shakers of the L.A. rock
scene. Soon Frank Zappa, Dylan, and Arthur Lee of Love became sup-
porters. Finally, she persuaded Jac Holzman of Elektra Records in New
York to catch the Doors at the Whisky.

To date, the group had shopped their demo around to every recording executive in L.A. and been shot down by all. A mix of blues, classical, and European "art" rock, their sound was dismissed as overly
eclectic; Morrison's lyrics were called esoteric and pompous; and their
performances were thought contrived and self-consciously theatrical.
And there seemed to be no chemistry between the performers.

The oldest of the Doors, Manzarek, was "Screamin' Ray Daniels,
the bearded blues shouter" of Rick and the Ravens, a jukebox band with
his brothers, which played the likes of "Hoochie Coochie Man" and
"I'm Your Doctor" for wasted UCLA film students in a funky watering
hole by the name of The Turkey Joint West. John Densmore, a sociology dropout from community college, played drums for weddings, and
was into Coltrane. Robby Krieger, the son of a well-to-do aeronautical
engineer, was a UCLA physics major into flamenco fingerpicking and

Indian sitar, and he played trippy bottleneck for a garage band called The Psychedelic Rangers.

The three instrumentalists had only one common denominator: they were all students at the Maharishi Meditation center in Santa Monica. And then there was the indefinable pagan free spirit, Jim, who all agreed couldn't sing but showed promise.

Observed the group's manager, Bill Siddons, "Ray was the controller and Jim was the wild artist and Robby was the space cadet and John was the little old lady."

When Elektra Records' Jac Holzman saw the Doors at the Whisky for the first time, like so many L.A. producers before him, he was underwhelmed. As he left, Ronnie Haran chased after him and begged him to return for the second set. Doing so, he was somehow taken by "The Alabama Song"—a pop operetta originally penned in the Twenties by communist playwright Bertolt Brecht—and offered the Doors a three-album contract for $5,000.

Still unsure of the band's potential and how to package them, Holzman soon returned to the Whisky with his producer, Paul Rothchild, to check out their new material. By this time, the Doors were being called "The American Rolling Stones." Hoping he hadn't flushed five grand, Holzman wanted to see if there was any merit to this. Haran told him he still hadn't seen Morrison at his best. Most of all, the executive wanted to find out why everybody on Sunset Strip was now calling his singer "that crazy motherfucker."

"Jim! Come on, man," Ray yells. "Second set's in ten minutes. Elmer says we're not getting paid if you don't show!"

It's a hot August night on the Strip, 1966. Manzarek is pounding on a door at the Tropicana Hotel.

For the last few months, the Doors have been the house band at the Whisky, opening for Love, the Byrds, and the Buffalo Springfield. This is the first night they're the headliners. They've been told that everybody who is anybody will be there, including their label rep and his producer.

John Densmore, the usually laid-back drummer, shoves Ray aside and uses his fist on the door. "Get your ass out here, Morrison! You're not the only one in this band!"

The Doors have only been performing for five months, but there is already friction, particularly between the singer and the drummer. As usual Ray, the diplomat of the group, smoothes things over. "Open up, Jim—please! Elmer's shitting bricks. Everybody's waiting!"

At last the door swings open to reveal Jim in cowboy boots and Skivvies. "Ten *thousand* mikes," he grins, eyes lit up. Three hundred micrograms of LSD is the usual dose for civilians.

Ever since Jim signed the contract with Holzman, he's been dropping ungodly quantities of acid. And, in the embrace of infinity, he's become less than punctual about showing up for gigs. He invites his bandmates to join him in a round of windowpane. They decline, get him dressed, and toss him in Densmore's VW bus. "He was humming like a generator," Ray later recalled.

Backstage at the Whisky, they clear Jim's head with a couple brews. He asks the waitress for a blow job to help him focus, but Ray is already dragging him toward the stage. Outside, the crowd is growing restless. On premiere nights, it includes the likes of Brian Jones, Steve McQueen, Natalie Wood, and Warren Beatty.

The singer stumbles out onto the stage, stabilized by his bandmates. Catching Holzman's eye in the front row, he turns his back and begins twirling dreamily like a dervish, arms swimming and sculpting the air. He mumbles through three tunes, then signals to Ray for "The End." This puzzles Ray because the band reserves this tune for the finale. But, accustomed to the unaccustomed from Jim on ten thousand mikes of acid or not, he breaks into the keyboard intro, just thankful the singer is still vertical.

Perched birdlike on one foot and clinging to the mike stand, Morrison throws his head back, closes his eyes, and tremulously sings the first verses of the song about breaking up with his first love, Mary Werbelow, Miss Sun'n'Fun, over his drug habit. Then he suddenly falls silent, cutting the last lyrics short. As the band continues hopefully with the hypnotic melody, a weird vibe overtakes the Whisky. All eyes are on Morrison—Haran's, Holzman's, Rothchild's, and the rest of the SRO crowd—as if he is in a dream and everyone is about to become a part of it.

"The killer awoke before dawn. He put his boots onnnn," he booms ominously.

Manzarek eyes Densmore, Densmore eyes Krieger. The Doors have never heard this before. Jim seems to be improvising with the acid. "He took a face from the ancient gallery, and he walked on down the hallll."

This is adding a new dimension to the Werbelow breakup song, thinks Ray, who studied Greek tragedy with Jim at UCLA. "At this point, I *saw* it," he would later recall. "The whole room did. I thought, My God! He's doing *Oedipus Rex!*"

"Mother?" shouts Morrison, "I want to . . ." He suddenly drops to his knees and wails into the phantasmagoric floods: "FUCK YOU MAMA! FUCK YOU MAMA ALL NIGHT LONG!"

By the time the singer segues into a Kill-Fuck-Kill-Fuck mantra, the Whisky manager, Phil Tanzini, is on a 911 to the owner, Elmer Valentine. "We've got this crazy fucking Morrison here and he's singing about FUCKING HIS GODDAMN MOTHER!" he yells to his boss. "What are we gonna do?"

"Pull him off the fuckin' stage and break one of his fuckin' legs," orders Elmer.

But it's too late. The Doors are already climaxing as the singer gasps, "This . . . is . . . the . . . ENDDD."

The band jumps off the stage, leaving Holzman, Rothchild, and the rest of the audience in stupefied silence. No sooner are the Doors in the dressing room than Tanzini bursts in, bellowing—"You *filthy* motherfuckers! Morrison—you can't say that shit about your *mother!* Are you shitting me? What kind of fuckin' *pervert* are you? You're fucking fired as of right NOW."

Peaking on the ten thousand mikes, the motherfucker seems to realize that his band's career has broken through to the other side. And with the Elektra contract under his belt, job security is not an issue. Not that it ever was. "Okay, Phil," belches Jim, after draining another beer. "But can we still have a bar tab?"

Back out in the front row, Holzman, the straitlaced Park Avenue executive, is still speechless and on the brink of Tourrette's. He doesn't seem to appreciate the irony that his label, Elektra, is named after the Greek virgin who murdered her mother and loved her father. "What the fuck did I just see?" he finally stammers to his producer.

A classically trained musician whose mother once sang for the Metropolitan opera, Paul Rothchild is not a stranger to the Oedipus myth either. Nor to dope—he'd just finished a six-month stretch for pot possession in Jersey.

"I don't know," he tells his boss. "But I think I just saw the fucking future of rock and roll."

"The End" was rock opera. It may not have been Rothchild's mother's kind, but he'd just seen *Oedipus* upstage *Aida*. If rock and roll had always been about pushing the freedom envelope, Morrison had just performed the Emancipation Proclamation.

"Kill the father," Rothchild later explained to *Crawdaddy* magazine, "means kill all of those things in yourself which are instilled in you and not of yourself. . . . Those things must die. . . . 'Fuck the mother' means get back to the essence . . . the reality."

After "The End" tour de force at the Whisky, Morrison was often heard muttering what he called his "magic formula mantra" to break into the unconscious: "fuckthemotherkillthefather." For the poet, this was a marriage of his two favorite myths, ancient and modern: Sophocles' Oedipus and Nietzsche's Superman. Only by committing the ultimate sin, Oedipus became Superman—free and above man's laws. And by singing about incest and patricide, the admiral's son declared his own Superman freedom. When these subtleties eluded the fans, Jim became more succinct in explaining "The End":

"It's about three things: sex, death, travel."

Indeed, it was a synthesis of the theories of his mentors—Schopenhauer and Nietzsche—in Freud's philosophy of Eros and Thanatos. The two fundamental and opposing drives of man, asserted the father of psychotherapy in his *Beyond the Pleasure Principle*, are the love/life/libido drive on the one hand and the death drive on the other. If anyone exemplified this existential conflict, it was Jim Morrison himself.

The Doors recorded their revolutionary debut album for Elektra in six days. After the taping of "The End," a tripped-out Jim broke into the studio at midnight and blasted it with a fire extinguisher. "He wanted to cool it down," Ray explained. That seemed reasonable to Rothchild, the producer, so he sent the repair bill to Elektra.

Released in January 1967, *The Doors* quickly climbed the charts thanks to the single "Light My Fire" and an uncensored version of "The End." Also spurring sales, Elektra sent each major music critic a complimentary copy of the album along with a gift box of hashish.

"The Beatles and Stones are for blowing your mind," wrote Gene Youngblood for the *Los Angeles Times*, "the Doors are for afterward when your mind is already gone."

"Jim Morrison is an electrifying combination of angel in grace and dog in heat," enthused Tom Robbins who got a gift box too. "The Doors are musical carnivores in a land of musical vegetarians."

The *Village Voice* voted the Doors "Best Newcomer" of 1967. The next year it voted Morrison "Top Vocalist."

Soon the group had three platinum albums: *The Doors, Strange*

Days, and *Waiting for the Sun.* The last recording, which Morrison originally wanted to call "Celebration of the Lizard," established him as the Lizard King. "I am the Lizard King . . . the Changeling," he declared. "I can do *anything.*"

As usual, few knew what the poet was talking about. "The lizard and the snake are identified with the unconscious and with the forces of evil," he explained. "The snake embodies everything we fear. The 'Celebration of the Lizard' is a kind of an invitation to dark forces." In short, this was not hippie flower-power music. It was, as Morrison went on to explain, an incantation "from the primeval swamp."

The Doors, now a top-grossing act, went on national tour. Fans flocked to their concerts as much for the Lizard King's riveting "no one here gets out alive" performances as for the music. He whirled like a dervish, he popped amyl nitrates under his bandmates' noses during solos, he gave Krieger's guitar head, he shrieked like a dying animal, he invented the mosh pit dive, he leapt, collapsed, and resurrected.[4]

Then there was his signature finale: the kill-your-father, fuck-your-mother thing. During the Doors' 1968 tour, before their Fillmore gig in New York, the Lizard King received an unexpected phone call.

From his mother.

Having not seen or spoken to him for more than three years, Mrs. Morrison told Jimmy over the phone how relieved she was to have found him at last. Then she told him how she'd managed to track him down. She had wanted to hire a private detective, she explained, but his father wouldn't allow it. Finally, Jim's brother, Andy, brought *The Doors* home one day, saying "You're not gonna believe it, Mom—it's Jimmy!" He put the LP on and the family sat down for a listen. Admiral Morrison stayed buried behind the daily news. The sports section began shaking when "The End" began and more violently during its climax. As for Mrs. Morrison, she immediately called Elektra and was given Jim's hotel phone number in New York.

After telling her son how good it was to find him alive and well, she pleaded with him to come home "for an old-fashioned Thanksgiving dinner." "Will you do your mother a big favor?" she added over the phone. "You know how your father is, will you get a haircut before you come home?" Since leaving home, her son had developed a shamanis-

---

4. Jim had been passing out and falling since his youth, leading some to speculate that he suffered from petit mal epilepsy, or the "falling sickness," which afflicted many luminaries including his hero, Alexander the Great.

tic Samson attachment to his hair: when Ray himself suggested a trim recently, he was startled by the violence of his bandmate's protest. But, ever diplomatic with Delilah, his philistine mother, he told her he had a previous engagement at the Fillmore, but would try to get her tickets to his Washington, DC, concert.

Days later, there was Mrs. Morrison in the front row of the Hilton concert hall to see her son, the Lizard King. When "The End" rolled around, Jim turned to the front row, raked a hand through his gloriously unruly locks and bellowed, "Mother, I want to . . ." then bared his teeth and snarled "FUCK YOU!"

After the concert, a shaken but still determined Mrs. Morrison was escorted to her son's hotel suite where she had been promised he would be waiting for her. Instead, he left for the *Ed Sullivan Show*, telling his road manager that he never wanted to see her again.

Jim Morrison was to die three years later and, true to his word, never saw his mother or any other member of his family again.

THE ROAD OF EXCESS

The road of excess leads to the palace of wisdom.
—William Blake

If rock legends are, by nature, extremists, Jim Morrison was the most extreme of the lot. Everything he did, he overdid. He seemed to know the price of this and be prepared to pay it. "You know how I see myself?" he said to Ray early on. "As a great shooting star, a huge fiery comet. Everyone stops and gasps, 'Oh look!' Then whoosh—I'm gone!"

His companion on the trip was Pamela Courson who would bury him and come to her own abrupt end soon afterward. A nineteen-year-old art student whom Jim had met at the London Fog, Pamela had an equal appetite for destruction. "She was Jim's other half," recalled Ray. "I never knew another person who could so complement his bizarreness. . . . They were the same person."

Pamela, whose father was a naval officer too, called herself, "Jim's creation." Jim called Pamela "my cosmic mate."

The pretty, petite redhead collected German Lugers and loved fast cars. She also proved to be a helpmate in the studio. When the Doors recorded their second album, *Strange Days*, Paul Rothchild called in a hooker to inspire the "You're Lost Little Girl" vocal. The producer was shooting for a laid-back Sinatra sound and hoped the hooker could help Jim into this groove. But after repeated takes—no mojo. And no Sinatra. So Pam was asked to pinch hit. The resulting "Lost Little Girl" was so silken that Sinatra, on hearing the love song later, said: "We oughta let that guy have an accident."

Jim and Pam might have been a perfect pair had Jim, the self-proclaimed Erotic Politician, not felt professionally obliged to fuck half of L.A. on an equal opportunity basis. When returning to Pam's bed, Jim—according to his predilection for all things Greek—insisted on being her backdoor man. She Magic Markered his favorite vest with FAGGOT. Granted, he did enjoy gay parties with his poet buddy, Michael McClure, and got so lubricated he no longer recognized gender. Then, there were his pickups on the Strip. One of his favorite street-corner satisfiers, Freddie, had threatened blackmail until a Doors' enforcer sorted him out.

Privately, Jim had never made any bones about being bi. All his heroes had been gay: Alexander the Great, Nietzsche, Rimbaud, Wilde. And, after all, he was "the Changling who could do anything"—so what was a little switch-hitting for somebody who sang about fucking his mother and killing his father? Not only did his sacrilege deliver him from all taboos, but it helped liberate his forbidden instincts, including his bisexuality.

Pam tried to ignore her cosmic mate's libertinism until he came home from one of his lost weekends and gave her the clap. She threatened to out him as Freddie had. He laughed in her face. (Having a historically romantic view of STDs, he'd once joked to Manzarek that he'd like to die of syphilitic madness.) So, giving him a taste of his own medicine, Pam became Neil Young's Cinnamon Girl; she took up with *Barbarella*'s John Phillip Law, and other actors, and she maintained an on again, off again thing with Comte Jean de Breteuil, the jet-set junkie count.

When none of this seemed to faze Jim either, she once tried grabbing the steering wheel of his "Super Snake"—a Ford Shelby Cobra 500, which he called The Blue Lady[5]—and pulling them into Benedict

---

5. The Blue Lady was the ghost of a beautiful but neglected young wife said to have been killed in a car crash en route to meet her lover at an isolated café above Half Moon bay on the California coast. Soon afterward, her lover, a philandering piano player, was decapitated and thrown into the sea nearby. She is said to haunt the café and to walk the windy bluffs above in her blood-spattered blue gown. The tale fascinated Morrison who visited the haunt.

Canyon. Another time, she succeeded in stabbing him with a fork. This was nothing new. A New Orleans lesbian had recently stabbed him with a penknife when he tried to hit on her girlfriend, impressing him with "the intensity of lesbian love." His and Pam's love was equally intense: he confiscated her fork, started a fire in the closet, and threw her inside.

In their more harmonious domestic moments, Pam would cook Jim his favorite dinner: rare beef heart. And Jim would again assure Pam that he intended to make an honest woman of her, but that it wouldn't be good for his "image" just now. Hedonism aside, his image was all about freedom from, if not contempt for, society's most sacred institutions. "To marry means to halve one's rights and double one's duties," wrote his mentor Schopenhauer, adding: "The true man wants two things: danger and play. For that reason he wants woman, the most dangerous plaything." And, above all, Ms. Courson was dangerous, which, ironically, was the basis of the Erotic Politician's attraction to her. "I found an island in your arms, country in your eyes," he sang. "Arms that chain, eyes that lie."

Finally, the singer's "creation" became impatient. Rather than risk another episode with the silverware or the Blue Lady, Jim proved himself to be a normal man after all: instead of a diamond, he bought her an XKE. When the Jaguar exhausted its romance, he built her a $300,000 designer clothes store, complete with a peacock feather ceiling. She fancied calling the boutique Fucking Great, but—deferring to Jim's classicism—changed the name to Themis, in honor of the Greek earth goddess.[6] After Jim's funeral, Pam would close Themis down by driving her VW bug—bought with her inheritance—through the display window.

Though Morrison had countless lovers, Ms. Courson finally learned to content herself with the fact that she was always his destination on the rebound. Which in rock and roll is as good as sickness and health, if not till death do you part. So Pam began wearing a wedding ring and calling herself Mrs. Morrison. And Jim didn't object.

But, later on, it didn't prevent him from marrying Patricia Kennealy, the editor of *Jazz & Pop* magazine, in a Celtic witch ceremony at her Manhattan apartment. After a purification bath, bride and groom

---

6. Themis became Jim's supplier for leathers, lizard skin jackets, and a $2,200 suit made from the hide of an unborn pony (which he later tossed into an airport disposal).

donned black robes, and exchanged blood and vows inside a magic circle. The groom relieved the bride of her diaphragm and they consummated. Then the groom, on acid, passed out.

The next time Mrs. Morrison II saw her husband, it was a year later. She'd just had an abortion. He'd promised to be there for her, but the date had slipped his mind. After the procedure, she showed up at his L.A. motel unannounced and introduced herself to Mrs. Morrison I: Pam. When Jim arrived, Pam retired for another fix. The next morning she found him in bed with Pat. Too tired to make an issue of it, she just said: "Oh, Jim, you always ruin my birthday."

If by this time Jim's cosmic mate seemed resigned to his excesses, the same was not true of his band and his managers. They didn't see the path of excess leading to wisdom—just to arrests, concert riots, aborted recording sessions, and disappearances.

As he became more infamous, Morrison had gotten into the habit of vanishing for days and even weeks on end. After coke and bourbon-fueled benders, he would black out behind bars, in bathrooms, and under boardwalks; or he would wake up in the desert, in a ravine in the Blue Lady; or he would find himself in bed with strangers. Meanwhile, the press buzzed with "Jim is Dead!" rumors. And the Doors' managers panicked. It wasn't that they thought Jim was suicidal. It was worse: they knew he thought he was immortal. Unbreakable. And he took every opportunity to prove it with crazy escapades and superman stunts.

He jumped from speeding cars "for the experience." Once he leapt from a 15th-floor hotel window in Seattle, using the windowsill as a trapeze. Another time he climbed the 150-foot Yale bell tower and swung stark naked from a shutter. During the filming of the Doors' *Feast of Friends*, he danced on a 17th-story ledge above Sunset then golden showered the crowd below.

Then there were the busts. Morrison was the first rock performer to be arrested on stage. In December 1967, after inviting a New Haven cop to "eat" him, he got maced, incited a riot, and was charged with "breach of peace, resisting arrest, and indecent exhibition." A month later in Vegas, he earned another Drunk and Disorderly for calling cops "chickenshit pigs and assholes." He racked up other D & D's and DUI's in L.A., plus Lewd & Lacivious behaviors.

"Some people are sweet drunks, but Jim was gross, obnoxious, and rude . . . a complete sociopath," said Steve Harris, Elektra's vice-president, after an award ceremony at the Atlanta Regency Hyatt where his star pissed in all the empty wine bottles and put them back on the bar. Few in the Doors' circle disagreed that, on Jack Daniels, the singer could go from zero to asshole faster than his Blue Lady.

In '69, Jim and his sidekick, Tom Baker, an alcoholic ex-porn star and Pam's ex-lover, were busted by the FBI for profanity, public intoxication, and assault. Bound on a Continental flight for a Stones' concert in Phoenix, the boys got to spilling drinks, chucking peanuts, and groping the stewardess. Under a new Air Piracy anti-hijacking law that protected against any and all in-flight shenanigans, they were subject to a ten-year prison term. But Jim's ever-resourceful lawyer, Max Fink, saved the day. Not that Max didn't have his hands full on other fronts.[7]

Worse, the FBI was amassing a Morrison file. The cross-dressing J. Edgar Hoover, a stickler for convention, had opened it after the New Haven riot.

Finally, the Doors managers decided to find a babysitter or "minder" for their star. A kindred poetic soul who could "out party" Jim yet keep him out of jail, or from killing himself or others. This was no small order. But as luck would have it, they found him. Bobby Neuwirth had unimpeachable credentials: a Harvard-educated poet, painter, and rock filmmaker, he could drink his friends and legendary juicers, Janis and Kristofferson, under the table, and had allegedly pleasured Warhol's Edie Sedgewick for forty-eight hours without respite. It was said that Dylan wrote "Like a Rolling Stone" about him and had been his lover.

But the minder gig was short-lived. Jim drank more to keep up with Bobby. The last straw was when the babysitter started nailing his groupies after the Lizard passed out. By this time it had become clear to Morrison's handlers that his excesses were less of a road to truth than an escape from it: that he was dying creatively and becoming a parody of himself.

Morrison disagreed: the problem, he believed, was not that he had pushed the envelope too far, but that he hadn't yet pushed it far enough onstage. The author of "The Sexual Neuroses of Crowds" always strove to "break on through to the other side" with Doors' fans, so he felt it

---

7. Fink, whom Jim called "the only father I've ever known," was defending Jim in no fewer than twenty paternity suits at the time. For Max's trouble, Jim gave him a set of golf clubs for Christmas.

was time to go to the next and final level in a true "no one gets out of here alive" show.

Such performances had been staged by the Dionysiac cult of ancient Greece, the Bacchae, and were later systematized by another Morrison mentor, Antonin Artaud, in his revolutionary work *The Theatre and Its Double* (1939). The French dramatist espoused the "Theater of Cruelty" that employed violent melodramatics and physical confrontations with the spectator to shock him into "his dreams, his taste for crime, his erotic obsessions, his savagery."[8] These ideas had sprung from his study of the ecstatic peyote ceremonies of the Tarahumara shamans of Central Mexico.

As Morrison biographers, James Riordan and Jerry Prochnicky, observed, "Shamanism crystallized" Nietzsche, Blake, and Artaud for him and "focused the passion behind his rebellion and the power behind his persona." As a result, "His performances often contained elements of symbolic death."[9] In this sense, Morrison viewed himself as a psychopomp, an intoxicated shaman who led the living to the land of the dead.

The singer explained the significance of this in a late interview with *Creem* magazine. "I see the role of the artist as shaman and scapegoat," he said. "People project their fantasies on him . . . and can destroy their fantasies by destroying him. I obey the impulses everyone else has but won't admit to—erotic and destructive impulses in particular."

In spite of its primitive roots, a theater of ritualistic life and death—of eros and thanatos—had never before been seen on a rock-and-roll stage.

And in Miami, in the spring of 1970, the Lizard King psychopomp, climaxing all his former excesses and intoxications, decided to change all that and sacrifice himself in the process.

---

8. To Morrison's further fascination, Artaud's own dramatis persona mirrored his ideas: a drug addict, a manic depressive, and a psychotic, the playwright spent more than a decade in asylums where he was regularly administered electroshock treatments until he committed suicide. In life, the cadaverous, raven-haired Frenchman walked with a cane of gnarled burlwood, which he asserted had belonged to St. Patrick and formerly to Jesus Christ and Lucifer themselves.

9. *Break on Through: The Life and Death of Jim Morrison* (New York: William Morrow, 1991). James Riordan and Jerry Prochnicky.

ONE GLORIOUS EVENING

> I was just fed up with the image. . . . I just wanted to put an end
> to it in one glorious evening.
> —Morrison, on exposing himself in Miami

> Honey, I just wanted to see how it looked in the spotlight.
> —Morrison, explaining it to Pam

"Hey, how 'bout fifty or sixty of you people come up here and love
my ass!" shouts Jim, the rest of the Doors jamming behind him on
"Backdoor Man." The audience of 13,000 roars and presses the stage
at Dinner Key Auditorium. It's a dilapidated seaplane hangar. "You
know, I was born right here in this state. You know that?" continues
the native son.

The band breaks into "Love Me Two Times," trying to get Jim off
his rap and back into the music. He mumbles a verse, his voice trails
off again, and Robby fills in with an impromptu solo.

The Doors' 20-year-old manager, Bill Siddons, watches nervously
from the wings as Jim collapses to his knees and pretends to blow his
guitarist. Siddons knows he should have cancelled the gig. Morrison is
even more wasted than usual tonight, just as Janis had been in honor of
her own homecoming. Besides, he's on the outs with Pam again, having just sent her back to L.A. after another knock-down-drag-out with
her about his screwing around.

In shades and black leathers, under his skull and crossbones hat, he
meanders across stage then suddenly shouts into the floods and above
the din of the crowd, "I wanna change the world . . . Let's see some action out there! Now c'mon, get on up here. No limits. No LAWS!"

The cops tighten their formation around the wobbling makeshift
stage, pushing the roaring fans back again. A roadie lays a lamb on Jim.
It's a present from a supermarket heir on tour with the Doors to promote vegan pacifism. Jim fondles the lamb. A thousand cameras flash.
"I'd fuck her," Jim tells Miami, "but she's too young."

A cup of champagne flies from the mosh pit and drenches him.
Ditching the lamb, he tears off his jacket and throws it into the audience. "Let's see a little skin, let's get NAKED!"

The crowd explodes again as Ray breaks into "The End" intro and
Jim stalks the stage, glowering out at the sea of flailing arms and pumping fists. He tears the mike from the stand and improvises a new lyric.

"I'm lost in my own mind's pain . . . Loss of oxygen, I'm going insane!"

More bottles, joints, bras hit the stage.

"I'm going down to the ground," he shouts, still riffing drunkenly, "to see my funeral and watch my casket be buried. I wanna hide behind a gravestone and watch them cry over me." Densmore skips a beat, glaring over a Ray. Robby turns his back, huddling next to his amp. They all look offstage toward Siddons helplessly. Morrison lunges toward the heaving mosh pit, screaming, "I'm not NORMAL, can't you fuckers see? You're all a buncha fuckin' idiots!"

The band launches into "Touch Me," trying to rein him back. He slurs a few lines before turning on the crowd again. "You're all a bunch of slaves, man!" he roars. "You didn't come here only for the *music* did you? You came for something else—WHAT IS IT?"

Déjà vu all over again, think Ray, Robby, John. He pulled the same trip on L.A. a couple weeks back. "You came for something *more* than the music, something greater than you've ever seen, right?" he shouted at the Forum crowd. He ordered the band to take five, recited all 133 lines of the "Celebration of the Lizard," then stalked out.

Ray, Robby, and John don't know if they're in for a poetry curtain call in Miami tonight. In a way they don't even care. They're no longer the Doors anyway: they're just a backup band, not for a Dionysius drama or a guerilla theater, but for a traveling Lizard King motherfucker freak show.

And they hate him for it.

Densmore hated Morrison's guts almost from the start. "I'm in a band with a psychotic!" the drummer complained to Manzarek. He quit the group regularly for his physical well-being[10] no less than his sanity. But Ray or Robby always managed to talk him back. As far as Morrison was concerned, feelings were mutual.

"I can't stand John as a human being," Jim told Ray. "He's a downer, man. A fuckin' whiner. We gotta fire him." Again, Ray, the diplomat, had to straighten this out to keep the crystal ship afloat.

Then, the last nail in the coffin. It was the fall of '68, a few months before the Forum and Miami concerts. Jim was in London trying to patch things up with a pissed-off, spaced-out Pam. In his absence, Gen-

---

10. Soon after joining the group, the drummer contracted a serious skin rash that didn't go away until Morrison died.

eral Motors had contacted the Doors offices in L.A., offering a hundred grand to use "Light My Fire" for a Buick ad. Unable to reach Jim abroad, Ray, Robby, and John, okayed the deal. After all, Robby wrote the song. "Fuck this," raged Jim on return. "I thought we were supposed to be *brothers!*" He accused his bandmates of "selling out to corporate America."

"That was it—the end of the dream," recalled Bill Siddons. "That was the end of Jim's relationships with the other members of the band. That was the day Jim said, 'I don't have partners anymore. I have associates.' "

His only other so-called friend, Tom Baker, had recently told him after touring the swanky new Doors' headquarters on Sunset, "You hypocrite, Morrison. . . . You're a fucking corporation. You're financing the very authority you claim interest in overthrowing." At that, the singer lost it—he trashed the place, top to bottom.

Then he threatened to trash the Doors and retire. But everyone knew this was just a ploy to find out how they felt about him. By this time, he was getting a lot more hate than love from everybody—including critics. John Mendelsohn of the *Los Angeles Times* called Morrison's performances "overmannered, murky and dull . . . an exploration of how bored he can sound as he recites singularly simple, overly elaborate psychedelic non sequiturs and fallacies." His future biographer, Albert Goldman, described his stage presence as "goofy, awkward, extremely gauche . . . You get embarrassed for him." Sir Mick dismissed Morrison's '68 Hollywood Bowl performance as "a bore." In her feature for the *Saturday Evening Post*, Joan Didion, author of the acclaimed *White Album*, called him a "narcissistic asshole."

Jim tried to appear amused. "We're universally despised and I kinda relish the whole situation. Why? I don't know. I think that we're on a monstrous ego trip, and people resent it . . . They hate us because we're so good." Like most egomaniacs, Jim tended to use "I" and "me" in the face of adulation, and "we" and "us" in the shitstorm. Which didn't endear Ray, Robby, or John. After all, they weren't the ones who sabotaged recording sessions, didn't show for gigs, incited mayhem.

But now and then Jim would face the music. "The whole world hates me!" he cried in New Haven after being maced by the cops and before starting another riot.

So Jim is not feeling a strong love vibe tonight from Miami, much less from his band "brothers." Miami wants a freak show, his cosmic mate wants fidelity, and the Doors want music. Everybody keeps *wanting* something from him—and he intends to give them more than what they want now. Set the night on fire. Burn the whole thing down on this glorious evening.

"You didn't come here only for the *music* did you?" he shouts again, stalking across stage to the wilting chords of "Love Me Two Times." He grins savagely at the expectant audience. "You want to see my cock, don't you? That's what you came for, isn't it? YEAH!" The crowd roars. He tears off his shirt and starts fluttering it in front of his groin like a bullfighter's cape. 'Okay, watch now . . . here it comes!' " he taunts, playing peekaboo. "Did you see it? Did you see my cock?"

He grabs his crotch. Ray yells to the offstage roadies. Vince Treanor rushes out and hurdles Densmore's drums. He grabs the singer from behind, picking him up by his belt loops so he can't get his leathers down.

"No limits, no laws!" Morrison keeps bellowing. "C'mon, anything you want goes. LET'S DO IT!"

The crowd charges the stage and bursts through security as the band breaks into a deafening "Light My Fire." Suddenly more than a hundred screaming fans pile on the buckling stage, tearing their clothes off.

The auditorium lights flash on. Security pulls the stage plugs and kick in Densmore's drums. They wrestle Morrison for the mike. Tearing it from him at last, they heave him into the crowd.

Morrison springs to his feet, leading the mob in a snake dance back for the stage. He is tackled by his roadies and dragged to the dressing room.

The Erotic Politician was arrested and charged with Lewd and Lascivious Behavior, Indecent Exposure, Open Profanity, and Drunkenness. Together they comprised a good deal more than his misdemeanors of the past. He did not contest the last charge, conceding that he was "too drunk to remember" if he exposed himself. The Doors themselves insisted that the crowd had suffered a "mass hallucination," as if in the face of a UFO. Anyway, Jim had a simple explanation for the entire episode in his home state. "I tried to reduce the myth to absurdity." Then he added, "It was a good way to pay homage to my parents."

The *Miami Herald* and its readers didn't see it that way. GROSSED OUT BY THE DOORS! ran the headlines. GET RICH QUICK: BE OBSCENE! The chief of police even weighed in, calling Morrison "the dirtiest, most foulmouthed person we ever had in Miami's history."

Bill Siddons had a more practical take on the debacle. "It cost us at least a half million dollars and almost caused the group to break up."

The Doors' tour was canceled. Their music was banned on many radio stations. In Miami's Orange Bowl, Anita Bryant, Jackie Gleason, and Pat Boone staged a "Rally for Decency" against the group, backed by President Nixon. The Concert Hall Managers Association banned the Doors from future performances unless they signed "The Fuck Clause"—a bond for Obscenity.

Found guilty of Profanity and Indecent Exposure in Miami, Morrison was fined $500 and sentenced to six months hard labor. His lawyer, Max Fink, filed for appeal, and the singer was released on $50,000 bail. "Dionysius had been defeated by the forces of righteousness," wrote Jim's Apollo, Ray. The prosecution submitted 150 photos of evidence, "but not a single one of Jim's schlong."[11]

A few weeks later, on the day after his 26th birthday, Jim announced to everybody in the Doors' offices: "I think I'm having a nervous breakdown. I want to quit. I can't take it anymore."

Ray tried to convince him that he just needed to cut down on the booze and take a rest. But everyone knew there was more to it than that. The year 1969 had been a killer for Jim. Days after his friend, Brian Jones, was drowned, his UCLA acid buddy, Felix Venable, died of alcohol poisoning. Then came Jim's self-immolation in Miami. Two days after his conviction, he was arrested for air piracy in Phoenix. And now Pam had the clap and, already on the rebound from their Miami blowout, had run off with Count Jean again. The future didn't look any brighter: he was facing hard jail time in Florida.

Morrison avoided a true breakdown until the Doors played New Orleans a year later, December 1970. Halfway through the set, during the "Light My Fire" solo break, Morrison collapsed. When it was time for the last verse and he still seemed catatonic, Densmore kicked him in the back. Struggling to his feet, a wildly drunken and frustrated Morrison jackhammered the mike stand into the stage floor until splinters flew; then he heaved it into the audience and stormed offstage. Densmore threw down his sticks in disgust and did the same.

New Orleans was the Doors' last performance.

"It seemed that Jim's life force was gone," Densmore would later recall.

---

11. Ray Manzarek, *Light My Fire*.

Ray claimed to have seen his "psychic energy go out the top of his head."

Had the dying shaman who he believed had possessed him years before on the desert highway abandoned him?

In the limousine on the way back to the Pontchartrain Hotel, the Doors hardly spoke a word to one another. When the car stopped and Jim stumbled out, Ray simply said, "Okay. It's finished."

"GOD HELP ME"

Cancel my subscription to the resurrection.
—Jim Morrison

France was the motherland of Jim's historic heroes, Antonin Artaud and Arthur Rimbaud. He had always wanted to be a fleur de mal poet like them. Before leaving the City of Night for the City of Light, he declared as Hendrix had not long before, "I'm so sick of everything. People keep thinking of me as a rock 'n' roll star, and I don't want anything to do with it. I can't stand it anymore."

"Life is the farce which everyone has to perform," the nineteen-year-old Rimbaud had said before abandoning his masterpieces—"Drunken Boat" and "A Season in Hell"—and vanishing in North Africa. "The poet makes himself a visionary through a long, prodigious, and rational derangement of all the senses," he had said, achieving this with great quantities of absinthe and hashish that had delivered him, like Morrison, not to heaven but to hell. "I have wept too much!" he wrote. "The dawns are heartbreaking. Every moon is atrocious and every sun bitter." Rimbaud, however, had made good his escape to Cyprus and Ethiopia, at least temporarily.[12] Could Morrison do the same in France?

"The purpose of the Paris vacation," his old friend the Frenchman, Alain Ronay, would later write, "was to detoxify Jim of alcohol and for him to forget the anguish that his fame as a rock star had caused."

So the former Erotic Politician shed his leathers, cut his hair, and be-

---

12. The poet—who became a coffee merchant and gunrunner—would return to his motherland twenty years later to have his leg amputated and to be consumed by cancer and tertiary syphilis.

came Monsieur James Douglas, expatriate poet of Paris. New Orleans seemed like a lifetime ago, though it had only been seven months. The Lizard King expired on that night as suddenly and spectacularly as he had been born three years before at the Whisky and two decades before that on a New Mexico highway.

But, abandoned by his muse, Monsieur Douglas soon realized that there would be no resurrection at all—that he was living posthumously, in limbo.

Before escaping to the continent, he was visited in L.A. by his second wife, Patricia. On seeing his ghostly pallor and alcoholic bloat, she said, "By now I was absolutely convinced he was going to die." The next morning she found him in bed with a teenager. The former Lizard King drew a knife on himself and revealed his will.

"One of you gets my cock," he declared, "the other my body."

"Who gets your soul, Jim?" asked Patricia.

"Oh," he replied, "I'm going to keep that if you don't mind."

"I knew it was the last time I'd see him," his Druid wife later remembered. She had done everything in her power to help, but "People can't be saved unless they want to be saved, and Jim didn't," she wrote. "I think he had this idea that once he was saved he wouldn't be an artist anymore."[13]

After saying good-bye to Patricia, he dropped by his favorite watering hole on the Strip, Barney's Beanery, where Janis had had her own last drink nine months before. He proposed a toast to her and to Jimi. "You're drinking with Number Three," he told his companions matter-of-factly.

Jim had been anticipating The End for years. The regular rumors of his demise amused him. "How did I go this time?" he would ask on seeing another UPI headline:

JIM MORRISON DIES! . . . MORE LATER!

When asked for his reaction, using almost the same words that Hendrix had, he replied: "I don't mind. I'm dead already."

A tombstone tourist, Jim had visited many of his predecessors. During the "Light My Fire" summer, he danced around Valentino's crypt in the Hollywood Cemetery. He and Pamela made a pilgrimage to Chol-

---

13. Patricia Kennealy-Morrison, *Strange Days*.

ame Road where James Dean, in his silver Porsche Spyder, collided at 90 miles per hour with Donald Turnipseed's Ford. He drank six-packs outside Sheila Graham's L.A. apartment where F. Scott Fitzgerald had his last heart attack while listening to Beethoven's *Eroica* and consuming Hershey bars to alleviate his craving for Scotch.

Morrison's escape to Paris violated his bail restrictions for the Florida obscenity conviction, but France was unlikely to extradite him. His lawyer, Max Fink, had urged the flight before his passport could be confiscated. Max had also heard of a plot to murder him in prison.[14] Before leaving L.A., he simply said to Ray and the other Doors, then mixing the group's sixth and last album, *L.A. Woman*, "Don't count on me, good-bye."

Already in Paris herself with Count Jean, Pam secured an apartment for Jim in the Beaux Arts Building, Apartment 17, complete with sky blue salon ceilings, classical wall reliefs, and travertine fireplaces. The little mailbox in the lobby four floors below was soon marked "James Douglas"—his nom de plume.

He was under contract with Elektra to produce a solo poetry album. But the writing in Paris did not come easily. Hoping for inspiration, he traveled with Pamela to Spain and Morocco, retracing Rimbaud's own footsteps to Africa a century before. But Marrakech and Casablanca failed to reawaken the muse. On return to Paris, he drank more and wrote less. His notebooks were filled with aborted poems, fragmentary lyrics, and scatological haiku: "Jerkbait scrotum, inc" and "Fuck shit piss cunt." One of his few completed pieces was an elegy: "Lament for the Death of my Cock . . . sore and crucified."

Finally, he scrawled a journal page with GOD HELP ME.

Then he took the fall. It happened at L'Hotel where, seventy-one years before, Oscar Wilde[15] uttered his famous last words, "Either that

---

14. A well-connected friend of Max's had persuaded California governor, Ronald Reagan, to arrange a pardon from the Florida governor. "It's enough to make me a Republican," said Jim. But, due to the public outcry among conservatives, Reagan reneged on his promise.

15. The two artists had much in common. Like Morrison, Wilde was an expatriate, having escaped Britain after serving two years in prison for homosexual offenses. He, too, suffered a near fatal fall (in the prison chapel). Finally, the playwright also took a French nom de plume (Sebastian Melmoth) and hoped for a literary rebirth in Paris.

wallpaper goes, or I do," before slipping into a syphilitic coma. Jim was standing on his balcony beholding the rainy Paris dawn, when he suddenly jumped over the iron railing and landed on the roof of a parked car below. Pamela tried to get him to a doctor. But, spitting blood, he sought medical attention at the nearest whisky bar just as he had for his last fall.[16]

Days after the L'Hotel accident, Monsieur Douglas finally consulted a doctor about his chronic chest pains, profuse nosebleeds, and racking cough. Diagnosed with bleeding ulcers and a punctured lung, he was told to control his three-pack-a-day cigarette habit, not to mention his alcohol and cocaine dependency.

So he turned to the only painkiller left—heroin.

His wife, Pamela, had been an addict for years. Her supplier was her paramour, Comte Jean de Breteuil, whom she had met in 1966 when he had attended UCLA. Count Jean, whose family owned all the French-language newspapers in North Africa, graduated to become a self-described "dealer to the stars": Janis Joplin, Jimi Hendrix, Keith Richards, and others. He had recently moved out of Richards' London house and was now living in Paris with Mick Jagger's ex, Marianne Faithfull.

The Morrisons regularly socialized with the count. They had been houseguests of his mother, the Comtesse, at her villa in Marrakech. On their trip south, they had also stayed at the mansion of oil heir Paul Getty and his wife, Talitha, a Dutch actress. A good friend and customer of the count's too, Talitha would fatally overdose a year later.

Though Jim was a drug omnivore, until now he'd never gotten into heroin like Pamela. She'd turned him on to opium years ago, but he insisted he was "on the side of life," and she "on the side of death." She had often threatened suicide. "Me and the devil, walking side by side," he had sung in "Woman is a Devil," "Well she feel like dying, but she's only twenty-one." Then in "Five to One," his *Strange Days* anthem—a double entendre about a heroin-cutting formula and Russian roulette with revolvers—he sang, "Five to one, baby. One in five. No one here gets out alive!"

But now, in Paris, he converted to Pamela's side. "The Chinese junkies will get you in the end," he wrote in his Paris journal. Junk made

---

16. He was swinging from a rain gutter into his second-floor suite at Hollywood's Chateau Marmot when the gutter broke, and he fell to the concrete on his back.

him forget everything: the pain of his wasted body, the excesses of the past, the vacancy of the future, and most of all, the loss of his muse.

It was as if his French forefather, Antonin Artaud, had composed his epitaph when the artist wrote: "No one has ever written, painted, or sculpted . . . except literally to get out of hell. Hell is of this world and there are men who are unhappy escapees from hell, escapees destined eternally to reenact their escape."

The final page of James Douglas Morrison's Paris notebook read: "Last words, last words—out."

Monsieur James usually arrives at the Rock and Roll Circus not long after midnight. Tonight is no exception. The hip Left Bank nightclub is a favorite hangout for the Rolling Stones, Pink Floyd, and other stars, as well as for Count Jean himself. The Circus's twenty-six-year-old manager, Sam Bernett, greets Jim, his friend and regular customer, and notes that tonight he doesn't look "in great form."[17]

After ordering his usual, vodka and beer, Jim briefly chats with the count's salesmen, then disappears into the bathroom, locking the door behind him. When he doesn't return, Bernett and an assistant force the door and find themselves "mesmerized by a baffling spectacle": Morrison motionless on the floor, head between his knees, mouth frothing.

A doctor is located in the bar and, after a quick examination, tells Bernett his customer has suffered a fatal overdose. The manager wants to call the paramedics but Count Jean's assistants, insisting Morrison has just "fainted," carry him out the club's rear entrance, drive him back to his apartment, and deposit the body in the tub.

The count's dealers are assisted by another of Jim's bar friends, 19-year-old photographer, Patrick Chauvel, just back from Vietnam and adept with corpse transport. "We carried him in a blanket and got him the hell out of there," Chauvel told *Time* magazine in 2007, confirming Bernett's account. "I guess if you have a nightclub and Jim Morrison dies in your toilet, it is not good PR." Paul Pacini, a representative for the Circus owner, tells Bernett, "The club has no responsibility for

---

17. Sam Bernett, *The End: Les Derniers Jours de Jim Morrison* (Chez les Editions Privé, Juin 2007.) Bernett, who went on to become a vice president of Disney Paris, told the UK's *Daily Mail* that he had delayed coming forward with his story until 2007 for fear of legal repercussions and professional disaster. "Today, I'm past 60," he said, "and want to get rid of my heavy load."

what happens here. So we saw nothing, we heard nothing, we shut up! Okay? It's what we better do to avoid a scandal." Others present that night, including Count Jean's girlfriend, Marianne Faithfull, swear themselves to secrecy.[18]

Early the next morning, Alain Ronay is awakened by a phone call from Pamela Courson. "Jim's unconscious and bleeding," she sobs. "Call an ambulance! You know I don't speak French. Hurry up. I think he's dying!"[19] After Ronay's filmmaker girlfriend, Agnès Varda, calls an ambulance, the couple speeds across town to Jim's apartment in the Marais district off Montparnasse.

When they arrive, Pam is standing in front of the bedroom door, delirious. The ambulance men are already inside, having moved the body from the bath to the bed. Pam's clothes are soaking wet. "My Jim is dead, Alain," she tells Ronay. "He left us. He's dead. I want to be alone now, please leave me alone." Ronay freezes in his spot, unable to move. "My Jim, man, he's so beautiful," she goes on in a singsong voice. "Go see."

Sickened, mind racing, Ronay refuses to enter but glances through the door and confirms for himself that his friend is indeed gone. He'd been with Jim only yesterday. Overtaken by another coughing fit, Jim had collapsed on a street bench and begged Alain not to leave him. No sooner did the coughing subside than Jim was overtaken by uncontrollable hiccups. Ronay had heard the superstition that violent hiccups can be a sign of imminent death but had never paid it any heed until his own father had been plagued by them and perished in the hospital hours later. Jim was also carrying a current French copy of *Newsweek*, which he asked Alain to translate for him. The title on the cover: The Plague of Heroin. What to Do About It. Alain suddenly looked at Jim and was horrified. What he saw, he later told his girlfriend, Agnes, "was not a face—what I saw was a death mask."

As he stands with Agnes and Pamela outside the bedroom where Jim's corpse lies now, Alain is overwhelmed. He feels that he has been overtaken by a dream, an impossible nightmare. When the police inspector arrives, Ronay does his best to collect himself.

"My friend's name was Douglas James Morrison, an American," he tells the detective. "He was a poet. He was an alcoholic, but no, he didn't use drugs." Though Ronay later confesses that this was "deceit-

---

18. To date, Faithfull still refuses to discuss the incident.
19. *Paris Match*, April, 1991. "La Derniere Ballade de Jim," by Alain Ronay.

fulness on the lowest level," he instinctively knows that he can't possibly tell the truth, not that he even knows the half of it yet.

After the inspector leaves, Pamela flushes her stash and burns Jim's papers in the fireplace, though Ronay protests, telling her this might arouse suspicion on such a hot Parisian morning. Finally, she tells Ronay her story. After a movie and dinner last night, she and Jim returned and started snorting heroin, she tells him. Later, Jim awakened in the middle of the night gasping for breath and vomiting blood. After helping him into the bath and nursing him there, she went back to bed. Then, hours later, she returned to find him dead. Knowing Pam and Jim to be users, Ronay has no reason to question this alibi. Indeed, she had recently told him she wanted to "fill the apartment to the ceiling" with heroin.

Soon after Pam finishes her account, Count Jean himself arrives, telling Ronay that Pam has called him and that he already knows "everything." Which of course is a good deal more than Alain knows: the OD at the Rock and Roll Circus, the transport of the body back to the apartment, then the creation of the alibi in which Pam agrees to conspire to protect her lover and supplier, Count Jean, from prosecution. Unaware of the collusion, Alain begs the dealer to leave before the medical examiner arrives, telling him that otherwise "terrible trouble could happen." Jean is of course in full agreement and, as he takes his hasty leave, informs the widow that he on his way to his estate in Morocco now and that he has made arrangements for her to join him there. No sooner is he gone than Pamela tells Alain: "I want Xanax. Give them to me now! I have to calm down, you see? It's so simple."

That afternoon, while her dealer is safely landing in Marrakech, Pam, with Alain's assistance, files a statement at police headquarters. In order to avoid an investigation and publicity, they still conceal the true identity of the deceased. But the captain insists that a death certificate and burial permit will not be issued until the medical examiner inspects Monsieur Douglas's remains.

That evening, Dr. Max Vassille completes a cursory examination. Seeing no evidence of foul play, he records the cause of death as heart failure. A mortician is called in to ice the body until the death certificate is issued and the burial arrangements made. "The heat is against us," he tells the widow.

Pamela proposes cremation, saying she wants "to disperse the ashes in a wonderful place." But Alain admonishes, "Don't even think of it. Here in France, it [cremation] is like admitting you know something about a crime . . . They would request an autopsy." He explains that shipping the body back to the U.S. is also out of the question since, by law, "the casket must be opened for inspection."

But Pamela remains hesitant, telling Alain, "I think perceptions remain in the body after death." So, if they should bury him, "Jim would feel the earth falling on top of him," she goes on. "He would even be able to hear what people were saying around his tomb." Assuring her that no one would say anything to upset him, Alain recommends Père Lachaise cemetery where Jim might rest with Chopin, Balzac, Proust, Wilde, Modigliani, Molière, and other kindred spirits. Though disappointed that Rimbaud is not in residence as well, the widow at last agrees.

So that hot August night and the next, Pamela sleeps with the corpse. She tells Ronay she feels secure lying beside her Jim. She tells him she could "live like this forever." Jim Morrison is all her own now—her faithful lover at last.

Ronay hires an undertaker and succeeds, with the help of Agnes's press contacts, in keeping his friend's death unpublicized. On the third day, the mortician relieves the widow of the star's decomposing body, dresses it in a black suit, and lays it in a veneer coffin. Pam arranges all her photos around her "beautiful man."

The next morning, they bury James Douglas Morrison in the Poet's Corner of the Père Lachaise cemetery. Besides Pamela and Ronay, only three friends attend. They include Jim's secretary, Robin Wertle, and the Doors' manager, Bill Siddons. None of the Doors are present. Nor is there a priest. "The whole scene was piteous and miserable," said a witness.

The service lasts only minutes. As the casket of the star disappears in the earth, Pamela recites the final lines of "The Celebration of the Lizard."

Now night arrives with her purple legion
Retire now to your tents and to your dreams
Tomorrow we enter the town of my birth
I want to be ready.

POSTMORTEM

Pamela Courson returned to L.A. after the funeral. In the next days, she sat by the phone, waiting for "my old man to call." She believed Jim's spirit had possessed their German shepherd, Sage. When the dog whined, she would kneel down beside him, whispering, "Yes, Jim? What are you trying to tell me?"

Morrison bequeathed everything to Pamela. But the surviving members of the Doors petitioned the will and sued the estate for outstanding bills, leaving her penniless.

She had brief affairs. She prostituted herself for drugs. She attempted suicide several times.

In 1974 Pamela was finally declared Morrison's legal heir. With her initial cash disbursement of $20,000, she bought a VW, a monogrammed Saks mink stole, and an ounce of China White heroin.

On April 25, 1974, Pamela went out for dinner with her boyfriend, Randy Ralston, and others. Leaving, she told them, "It's time for me to go be with Jim now." Hours later, she was found dead of a heroin overdose. Like her husband, she was 27 years old.

A week after her passing, Pamela was posthumously awarded half a million dollars, plus a quarter of the Doors' future royalties. The award was transferred to her parents.

In 1975, Jim's father, Admiral Morrison, retired from the Navy and petitioned the court for a share of his son's estate. He received half. He died in 2008.

Jim's best friend, Tom Baker, fatally OD'ed in a New York smack-shooting parlor in 1982.

Count Jean de Breteuil died of an overdose months after Morrison himself. "Had he lived, he might have turned into a human being," wrote Marianne Faithfull who miraculously survived her own prolonged addiction as well as numerous suicide attempts.

Among the survivors of Jim Morrison's life is his second "wife," Patricia Kennealy-Morrison. At the end of her book, *Strange Days*, she writes: "Question to self: What do you think killed Jim? . . . Miami and Pamela, not necessarily in that order."

But, in the end, Kennealy concludes, "Jim Morrison killed himself . . . The deadly weapon that Jim used on himself wasn't heroin, though, but the fatal dichotomy—self-created, self-inflicted, self-perpetuated—between Jim Morrison the stage madman and James Douglas Morrison the inner vulnerable, loving soul."

But, if there is a method to a man's madness, is he indeed mad? And if he is so vulnerable as to armor himself from real and lasting intimacy, can he be loving?

What killed Morrison was living life beyond the speed limit: his consuming passion and thirst for a freedom that in its outer reaches became what fearful men call madness and chaos. "One must still have chaos in oneself to be able to give birth to a dancing star," said Morrison's Superman mentor, Nietzsche. But after becoming this, he found himself in a cage of popular stardom that he could only escape by burning it up on one glorious evening and sacrificing himself.

But in the process, he gave birth to theater, to philosophy, and to poetry in rock music—one of the last vestiges in the mechanistic modern world of primitivism, of magic, and of soul.

Interlude: Crazy

Once I had a little game: I liked to crawl back in my brain.
I think you know the game I mean: I mean the game of going
insane. . . .
Just close your eyes, forget your name, forget the world,
Forget the people, and you'll erect a different steeple.
—Jim Morrison, "Go Insane"

The Lizard King held madness and its famous role models—Nietzsche, Artaud, Rimbaud—in very high regard. Following in their footsteps, he cultivated a "derangement of the senses" to turn dementia into his church and steeple. "Craziness is like heaven," he declared. "The Doors speaks of madness that dwells within us all." But the madness of which he spoke was not lunacy, per se, but something quite different. As Artaud pointed out, "In every madman is a misunderstood genius."

John Lennon was of the same mind, even in his youth. "I used to think, well, I can't be mad because nobody's put me away, therefore, I'm a genius," he reasoned. "Genius is a form of madness . . . Genius is pain."

Each of the other suffering geniuses cultivated their craziness no less than Morrison or Lennon. Crazy was a drug for each—the natural high of their magical circuitry. "You have to go on and be crazy," said Hendrix. Janis told her biographer, "You're supposed to be doing an article on me, man. Fuck reality!" Cobain called himself "a sicko," "desperate," "the pathological type." As for Jerry Garcia, the more things got "good and weird" the better.

The hero and original inspiration of all the stars went by many names: E, Boss, Mr. Tiger (his karate handle), Aron Silve (his detox

moniker), the King of Rock and Roll. But the one engraved on Elvis's
ID bracelet was CRAZY.

Elvis and his successors were no strangers to psychiatrists. But,
without exception, none of the Seven had gone to shrinks willingly,
but had been driven by concerned family, friends, and/or managers. All
had made their escapes from the couch before being shrunk. Had any
encountered a therapist as enlightened as Carl Jung, they might have
returned for a follow-up. "Show me a sane man and I will cure him for
you," proclaimed Freud's rebel student.

Jung saw the synergistic intimacy of genius and what "sane" men
have called madness. Both are unstable, explosive elements. Like ura-
nium.

As children, the stars had the building blocks for implosion: manic
energy, differentness, and an inordinate need for attention. "Why
didn't anyone notice me?" Lennon wondered as a boy. "So you scream
it: Look at me, a genius, for fuck's sake! What do I have to do to prove
to you son-of-a-bitches what I can do and who I am?"

All children thrive on attention, but the appetites of the stars-to-be
were insatiable. "He was always the center of attention," recalled one
of Lennon's boyhood friends. An Elvis insider observed, "Unless he is
the center of attention, he just isn't interested." Said a Morrison school
classmate, "When someone actually did these nervy things, things
we wanted to do, we felt gratified. . . . He was the center for us." The
Queen of the Blues told a promoter, "Honey, this Janis's tour so . . . you
better pay attention to me, motherfucker!"

As kids, the stars were shock-jocks and hell-raisers. The alpha lunatic was Morrison. "Jim was . . . a bizarrist," said a school friend.
"He liked to shock people and cause controversy." While attending
Florida State, the Lizard King yelled "Nigger!" at the top of his lungs
from class windows. Janis "freaked the farmers" as both a student and
alumna of Port Arthur High. Cobain grafffitied buildings with HOMO
SEX RULES! Lennon bullied and insulted his classmates, once heckling
"a creepy Jewboy," "They should've stuck you in the ovens with the
rest of—'em!" And, like Morrison, the Beatle-to-be loved doing imper-
sonations of slobbering, twitching cripples.

Lennon later confessed, "I was just a weird, psychotic kid covering up my insecurity with a macho façade." But even as an adult, the
psycho kid inside often got the best of the Clever One, especially when
he was under the influence of the devil's dandruff and brandy Alex-
anders. During his "lost weekend" in L.A., he heckled the Smothers

Brothers onstage, crowing "Fuck a cow!" He called Yoko "a slant-eyed bitch," and his in-laws "gooks." When performing in Hamburg, wearing a toilet seat around his neck, he cackled, "Hey, remember the war? We fuckin' won!" then grabbed his crotch and goose-stepped the stage, crowing 'Siege Heil THIS!' "

Adulthood didn't diminish Morrison's taste for in-your-face shock and awe, either. He regularly reminded his audiences that they were "a buncha slaves" and "fuckin' idiots." He taunted the cops as "pigs," he mind fucked everybody from Andy Warhol to Ed Sullivan, and he joked about killing Simon and Garfunkel.

Cobain upped Lennon's and Morrison's ante. In drag onstage, he chanted "Fuck the Pope!" to his Rome audience. He once checked into a Holland hotel naked and covered in blood. Another time, he told reporters he looked forward to touring Japan "to repay the cunts for Pearl Harbor."

Manic energy fueled this exhibitionism. As children and adults, the Seven were hyper. If your average kid draws fifty amps, each star drew five times that. The ADD/OCD Cobain was on Ritalin at four and, if the drug had been around in the 50s, he would have had famous company.

"I'm a very nervous person, really," said Lennon. "I'm so nervous," said Elvis. "I've always been nervous, ever since I was a kid." A boyhood friend described him as "squirrelier than a yard dog." Cobain called himself "neurasthenic" and "twitchy." Morrison regularly told his band members he was having "a nervous breakdown." Janis had hers when she was seventeen, and Lennon, his after the Beatles' breakup. As children, most had suffered insomnia, anxiety attacks, and terrifying nightmares. Later, as much as they loved the spotlight, all but a few had major stage fright.

If the stars' amperage and diffferentness led to manic attention seeking early on, it too had an opposite effect. It isolated and divided them. They were all extro-introverts. When they weren't commanding an audience, they were off by themselves in their own worlds. Hendrix and Cobain thought they were ETs. Most were comic book junkies like Elvis. "When I was a child I was a dreamer," said the King. "I read comic books, and I was the hero of every comic book I ever read." Elvis's greatest hero was the alter ego of twelve-year-old Billy Batson who cried "Shazam!" and turned himself into "the most powerful boy in the world"—Captain Marvel. Possessing the power of Zeus, the strength of Hercules, the stamina of Atlas, the speed of Mercury, the courage of Achilles, and the wisdom of Solomon, Marvel defeated Black Adam, Captain Nazi, and the fiendish Mister Mind and his Monster Society of Evil.

Like Elvis—the original sun around whom the others orbited—all sought to recreate themselves as stars. During this reinvention, their childhood specialness and egocentrism became megalomania; their extrovert-introvert split developed into a kind of schizophrenia; their high spiritedness evolved into violence and paranoia.

And it was at the point when their dreams of stardom were realized that things truly got crazy for the Seven.

Not long after John Lennon announced to the world that the Beatles were "more popular than Jesus"—the Vatican officially forgiving him for the claim in 2008—he told his bandmates that he *was* Jesus and demanded an Apple press release.[1] He'd discovered his identity while on acid the night before. The revelation came as no surprise to the other Beatles. "We felt like fucking gods!" said McCartney after Albert Hall. Paul had recently tripped with John and flashed on him as "the absolute Emperor of Eternity . . . It was a very freaky experience."

Even before John's Jesus incarnation, "He talked gibberish about buying an island in the sun, switching the sun on and off and controlling the weather," his first wife, Cynthia, recalled. In the spring of 1967, Lennon bought Dornish, an island off the coast of Ireland. Months later, on the heels of the Beatles' single release, "Baby, You're a Rich Man," he acquired the sixteen-acre Greek island, Leslo, but sold it back to the government before finding out if the weather there was manageable.[2]

Lennon's friend, Keith Richards, once observed: "You think you're semidivine when you're in the limo and semidivine at the hotel, until you're semidivine for the whole goddamn tour." He went on to explain how this brought down his bandmate, Brian Jones: "He really got off on the trip of being a pop star. And it killed him. Suddenly, from being

---

1. Even so, a few years later, Lennon turned down the part of Christ in Andrew Lloyd Webber's production of *Jesus Christ Superstar* staged at St. Paul's Cathedral. By this time the Vatican had accepted his apology for his "more popular than Jesus" remark, and he had said, "I always remember to thank Jesus for the end of my touring days."

2. In the end, he tried to establish "Nutopia," a sovereign state with, as he explained, "no land, no boundaries, no passports, only people."

very serious about what he wanted to do, he was willing to take the cheap trip. And it's a very short trip."

In a rare harmonic conversion, both Presley and Lennon discovered that they were messiahs at the same time. It was the spring of 1968: Elvis had just done his comeback TV special, watched by more than a billion people; John had just finished levitation training in India with the Maharishi. While John, on acid, was now buying islands where he would orchestrate the weather, Elvis, on prescriptions, was at Graceland moving clouds with his mind and watching the leaves of the trees "tremble with my vibes." John, who had many incarnations—the Elvis-outlaw-skiffler, the meet-the-Beatles mophead, the-Sgt.-Pepper's-acid-magician—was now the bearded guru in white. Elvis, also a believer in costume magic, donned a jeweled turban before laying hands on his cousin Billy's boy and curing him of pneumonia. "Elvis looked like Ali Baba," said one of his disciples. As for Lennon, never a natural healer like the King, he had always fled the cripples who had mobbed him at the peak of Beatlemania.

The King also overshadowed the Beatle when it came to epiphany. His performances became deus ex machina extravaganzas. "He sort of had this superman complex," said Red West. In his Marvel capes and gem-studded divine jumpsuits—the Egyptian Pharaoh ensemble, the Conquistador, the Aztec "Teocuicatl"—he materialized onstage to the apocalyptic strains of 2001's *Zarathustra*. He dazzled his worshippers with supernatural song and dance. He tossed tens of thousands of dollars' worth of jewelry into the crowd. Then he dematerialized, leaving a single Wizard of Oz voice resounding in the darkness, "Elvis has left the building!"

In 1965, the King begrudgingly agreed to give an audience to the Beatles, then on their second U.S. tour and stealing his throne. When his manager, Colonel Parker, had suggested a get-together during their first tour, Elvis snapped, "Hell, I don't wanna meet them sons o' bitches!" So the Colonel sent the Fab Four cowboy outfits, ten-gallon hats, and six-shooters—"with Elvis's best wishes." When he changed his mind two years later, the Fab Four braced themselves for the burning bush. "Nothing really affected me until Elvis," John had once said. Added Paul: "Elvis was the guru we'd been waiting for. The Messiah had arrived." So that day the Fab Four were saucer-eyed in front of the King.

"Well, look," Elvis finally growled, "if you damn guys are gonna sit there and stare at me all night, I'm gonna go to bed! I didn't mean for this to be like a thing—the subjects call on the king!"

Elvis had never cottoned to wannabe's in the business. Whenever Mel Torme, Robert Goulet, or Jim Nabors came on his TV, he would shoot his competitors with one of his Patton pearl-handled .45s. When super guitarist, Eric Clapton, dropped by the Memphis Vatican to kiss the papal ring, the King disinterestedly inquired, "And what do you do?" Replied the Cream superstar, "I play guitar." "Well," Elvis told God, "my guitar player's name is James Burton, and maybe he can show you a few things."

Lennon was equally contemptuous of minor celebrity. When an ailing Judy Garland returned to the stage after a nervous breakdown, he crowed from the crowd, "Aw, fuck off, Sophie!" Afterward, he introduced her to his starstruck manager, Brian Epstein, as "Judy Garbage." As for his historic meeting with the King himself, the Clever One would later recall, "It was like meeting Englebert Humperdinck." He didn't think much more of Dylan or his skill as a lyricist. "Dylan got away with murder," he said. "I can write this crap too."

Regarding the fans themselves, even during his Messiah period, Lennon had never liked being gawked at, much less mobbed. But the only thing he hated more than being recognized was not being recognized—even when he was three sheets to the wind and, expecting his mental period, wearing a sanitary napkin as a yarmulke. When he asked a waitress at L.A.'s Troubadour club, "Don't you know who I fucking am?" "Yeah," she said, "you're the asshole with a tampon on his head."

The descent from divinity to asshole with a tampon on his head was steep, so, in his last years, John dropped his crown of thorns for something less uncomfortable. "I'm the king, and every encounter with pawns weakens me," he told his assistant, Fred Seamans. "You're my knight, and it's your job to protect me from such encounters . . . The less I'm seen, the more power I have." He was now in what he called his "househusband" period in New York with Yoko and his son, Sean. Having converted to his wife's new age metaphysics, he now believed that he was the reincarnation of Napoleon, and Yoko of Josephine.

After the Beatles' breakup in early 1970, Lennon suffered his first nervous breakdown. On his own now and "divorced," as he called it, from his adopted family and three alter egos—Paul the Politician, George the Mystic, Ringo the Clown—he unraveled. Bedridden for weeks and refusing to see anyone but Yoko, he later recalled, "I felt like a hollow temple filled with many spirits . . . each inhabiting me for a little time and then leaving to be replaced by another."

Surrendering to fan worship, others fell into the same head trip of self-deification. The Lizard King never called himself Jesus, but crucifixion was ever on his mind. During the Doors promo video for *The Unknown Soldier*, Morrison, posing as the Love Generation savior, was shot on the cross. Before his obscenity trial in Miami, he sent his bandmates a Sacrifice of the Divine Lamb postcard from St. Louis: "Don't worry, the end is near," it read. "Ha ha."

Janis reached a more modest rung of megalomania. She called herself "the greatest blues singer in the world," and lived on the outer limits of probability. Morrison and the others lived here too, and fans got a contact high from orbiting their madness, if at a safe distance. But, revealing the sexism of deification, Janis was never worshipped like her male counterparts.

Her lover, Jimi Hendrix, when he was playing backup for the Chambers Brothers, predicted "I'm going to be the greatest." After he went solo and was recognized as such, Chambers Brother Rae Warner observed, "Jimi was a changed man. He wanted everyone's attention in the whole world." Stardom had transformed the guitarist. "We were so overwhelmed by the money and the glamour of being so-called pop stars, we all forgot we were people," admitted bassist, Noel Redding.

Later, Pete Townshend called Hendrix "a psychological mess of a man." Jimi called himself "schizophrenic in twelve different ways." He was a partier and an extrovert; but he complained "I never get any time to myself" and "I just want to be left alone." He was a peacenik and championed the downtrodden; but he became uncontrollably violent and beat women badly. One acquaintance called him "the most charming, polite person in the entire world"; others called him a "bastard" and a "cunt." One night he would tell the crowd he loved them; on another he would shout, "You can all choke yourselves. Fuck it!"

John Lennon was schizo in just as many ways. In 1974, L.A. psychiatrist, Milton Weiss, attempted to analyze the former Beatle gratis, but "gave up in despair," declaring, "If I was doing this as a job I'd have to send him two bills—one for each personality!" The doctor had only to compare the patient's lyrics to his life. The "all you need is love, give peace a chance" evangelist had not lived a loving or a peaceful life: like Morrison, he spewed hate-filled harangues; he'd assaulted and hospitalized a London deejay and a German sailor, among others; and he'd threatened to kill others. "I was a hitter," he confessed. "I couldn't express myself and I hit. I fought men and beat women." He traced his dark side to the loss he had suffered as a boy. "After my mother was killed I felt betrayed by all womankind," he confessed. "I used to have fantasies about torturing women to death. I still have violent fantasies."[3] He once confided to a friend: "I've always wondered what it would be like to kill a woman, many women! It was only becoming a Beatle that saved me from actually doing it. Can you imagine, a Beatle serial killer?" His murderous tendencies were not unique: Elvis very nearly killed four people; Cobain one; Janis had almost fatally overdosed several. Morrison fantasized about homicide no less than Lennon. "If I had an ax . . . man, I'd kill everybody," he said.

"John was filled with rage that was with him every moment that he lived," said his producer, John Brower. To vent, the ex-Beatle tried Primal Scream therapy. Its founder, Dr. Arthur Janov, showed him how to release his rage in a less harmful manner than in attacking people. The result of the therapy can be heard on The Lennon/Plastic Ono Band album which, with the Ono duets, sounded like a soundtrack from an asylum or a delivery room.

Ahead of its time, the world's first punk album bombed. Meanwhile, the popsicle debut from McCartney, whom Lennon now called "McAsshole, was climbing the charts, which made Clever One really want to scream. While the Cute One's solo album was praised, and his own panned, Lennon snorted more smack. Soon he hit the wall, tied himself to a chair, and went cold turkey, "Can't see no future, can't see no sky," he sang. ". . . . I wish I was a baby, I wish I was dead."

For his second solo effort, Lennon released "Imagine" with its sweet McCartney-like piano. "Imagine all the people living a life in peace . . . a brotherhood of man." But John must have had trouble imagining this himself, feeling that "all people are basically shit . . . and deserve abuse." The misanthropy of megalomaniacs often feeds on self-loathing, and this seemed to be the case with the schizoid John. He'd written "Nowhere Man" about himself long before. "Part of me suspects I'm a loser and part of me thinks I'm God Almighty," he told *Playboy* magazine.

---

3. According to his biographer, Geoffrey Giuliano, he kept a collection of whips and S & M mannequins in the Dakota storerooms.

Dr. Janov had shown the Beatle that all his identity crises, his conflicting emotions, and his anger were rooted in his childhood. After leaving Primal Scream, John invited his father and infant half-brother out to his estate in the English countryside. Hardly had Freddie Lennon arrived when John went ballistic, blaming him for abandoning him as a boy and turning him into "a raving lunatic."

Jim Morrison had the reputation of a loose cannon schizo too. "You just never knew," said his producer, Paul Rothchild, after the singer destroyed the studio with a fire extinguisher. "Was he going to be Dr. Jekyll, or was he going to be Mr. Hyde?"

Ray Manzarek had a name for Morrison's Mr. Hyde. "Jimbo," he wrote in his memoir, was "Jim's evil doppelganger . . . on a quest for domination, power, and kicks . . . a Frankenstein monster, the destructive golem." The star's doppelganger, Ray went on, set out to kill the Doors and, in the end, succeeded not only in this but in killing Jim too. The same can be said of other stars' alter-egos: Pearl killed Janis and the King killed Elvis.

After the Lizard King was arrested in Miami, his lawyer, hoping for an insanity defense, had convinced him to seek psychiatric help. At his first appointment, Jim challenged the shrink to a game of chess. The next day he told his lawyer he wouldn't be returning to the doctor because "she had a fat ass." Besides, he added, "how can I take advice from someone who can't even win a chess game?"

Kurt Cobain was no shrink fan or love child, either. Confessing that he had "this terrible Johnny Rotten complex," he later added, "Ninety-nine percent of humanity could be shot if it was up to me." "We're all the same—just flies on a turd," he pointed out another time, echoing Lennon. "He hated everything, everybody. Hated, hated, *hated*," said his wife, Courtney Love, no stranger to the emotion herself. "Kurt doesn't necessarily know what he wants, but he's *pissed*," observed his producer, Butch Vig. Apparently, though, the grunge star, unlike Lennon and the King, wasn't after deification. "People are treating him like God, and that pisses him off," said his publicist, Nils Bernstein.

Cobain's attitude grew from a naturally excitable disposition and a less-than-idyllic upbringing. "When I grow up I want to be a faggot, nigger, cunt, whore, jew," he wrote in his journal, climaxing with a Morrisoneque mantra: "Kill yourself kill yourself kill kill kill kill kill kill rape rape rape rape rape is good, rape is good, rape kill rape greed greed good greed good rape yell kill." For his photo on the *Roll-*

ing Stone cover, he wore a custom-made KILL THE GRATEFUL DEAD tee. Years before, he had nearly beaten a school bully to death with a stick. "It was a scary reminder of how violent I can be. . . . It actually felt good," he later recalled.

A born primal screamer, the homeless boy from the Washington backwater didn't need to go into therapy like John, or drain bottles of scotch like Jim, to bring out his inner Chuckie onstage. In his most riveting performances, nobody knew whether he might go Columbine on them or on himself. "I always thought I'd be voted Most Likely to Kill Everybody at High School," he once said, "but I'd probably opt for killing myself first."

But like Lennon, Morrison, Hendrix, and Joplin too, Cobain had his Jekyll side: introspective, self-deprecating, shy. This Kurt would discuss and write about his music and his life thoughtfully and articulately. In what is called his "suicide" letter, he wrote, "I must be one of those narcissists who only appreciate things when they're gone. . . . Since the age of seven, I've become hateful towards all human beings in general. . . . I have a daughter who reminds me too much of what I used to be, full of love and joy . . . I can't stand the thought of her becoming the miserable, self-destructive death rocker that I have become."

Many of the stars buried themselves in their frenetic touring schedules since, in their quieter moments of self-reflection, they often tended to surrender to depression, self-loathing, and suicidal thoughts. Occasionally, they succeeded in drugging themselves out of these valleys but, as time passed, more often they drugged themselves deeper in.

Jimi Hendrix, the composer of "Manic Depression," was well known for his "moodies," as his band called them. Janis fell into crying fits, feeling ugly, alone, a soon-to-be has-been. A friend of Morrison's revealed that he, in spite of his titanic ego, experienced "great periods of insecurity where he'd feel he was a fraud." Lennon holed up in his Dakota cell for five years, suffering the same Nowhere Man impostor syndrome, the scourge of so many great artists. Cobain—though a part of him felt like "a boy wonder" and, as his wife put it, "too good for everybody"—in the end felt drained, obsolete, and just "too fucking sad."

And then there was the leader of the Grateful Dead. Compared to the other six, Jerry Garcia was the poster boy of mental health. Some called him "the closest thing to a perfect human being," others "the Buddha." He wasn't manic or twitchy; he beat and berated no one; he remained relatively unparanoid and unbummed; he shunned the spot-light; and in spite of the deification by Deadheads, he said, "No matter who you are, you know yourself for the asshole you are."

Though Garcia had, early on, vowed never to "grow up," arguably he was the only one of the Seven who did indeed grow up. True, in the end, Morrison, Cobain, and Lennon, in particular, gained some per-spective on their adolescent egocentrism, alienation, and anger, but they were still victims of the resulting compulsions that, ironically, helped make their music so powerful. In "Borrowed Time," Lennon sang "When I was younger, living confusion and deep despair . . . full of ideas and broken dreams," then in the last verses, "Now I am older . . . less complications, everything clear." But in "Scared," he sang, "Hatred and jealousy, gonna be the death of me. I guess I knew it right from the start." As for Garcia, carrying considerably less psycho-logical baggage than the others, he managed to outgrow the damaging madness of youth while retaining in his music its boundless energy, idealism, and freedom.

But after his "long, strange trip" inside the belly of the beast, the Buddha of rock and roll at last paid the price for the insanity that was superstardom.

Of all the stars, the one who was most complex was of course the King himself. He had a God complex, a mother complex, and an obsessive/compulsive disorder. He was a bipolar, a paranoid, a schizoid. He was an insomniac, a hypochondriac, and a fetishist. Throughout his life, he insisted that he had serious medical conditions, but he didn't count these among them. Being a world unto himself, what might have been called crazy by lesser mortals was normal for him. Whatever therapy he felt he needed, he got from his local druggists.

When he ran low on his meds, Elvis tended to get more seismic than usual. "His temper could give Darth Vader a run for his money," remembered his daughter, Lisa Marie. Elvis pulled guns on his retain-ers regularly. When his aunt almost shot one of his favorite Guys, he threatened to "kill that bitch, sew her cunt up and throw her over the damn wall!" And when he had to deal with more serious problems, such as feedback on stage, he once told his soundman, "Shut that damn sound off, Felton, or I'll take your kidney away from you." By this time, he did indeed need a new kidney, as well as several other organs.

On the other hand, Elvis had his angelic side. He was kinder to and more generous with his fans than any other star in history.

But, revealing how crazy it all really was, the King's old and trusted friend, Lamar Fike, betrayed a secret about him which lay beneath the grand facades of most of the others too.

"Elvis was the most insecure human being I've been around in my life. He took the cake. He was destiny's child, but he was never prepared to be what he was."

4

ELVIS PRESLEY

January 8, 1935–August 16, 1977

TCB

The King is cruising at 120 miles per hour up the Santa Monica Freeway in his black Dino Ferrari. His twin .45s are in his show gladiator belt buckled over his black, perspiration-soaked DEA jumpsuit. His derringer is in his boot, his Thompson machine gun under the seat, and cocaine-soaked cotton balls fill his nostrils. His kid stepbrother, David Stanley, is riding shotgun. The young man has never seen him in such a state.

Elvis broke down the door of his room in the middle of the night, "Get your gear, we're goin' head huntin'," he'd ordered him. "We're gonna kill those sonsabitches!" It's November 1976. Elvis has just completed another grueling national tour, but he seems to be ready for some real breakneck action tonight.

Since leaving their beach condo, David, though ordinarily psyched for predawn adventure, has been trying to talk his stepbrother down. It's not the speed that bothers him: not only is Elvis a seasoned DUI driver, he is a Hollywood-trained *Spinout* professional. And it's not the firepower that fazes him either: Elvis has packed heat for years and is a bona fide peace officer. He carries badges from more than fifty police departments coast to coast, not to mention his Federal Bureau of Narcotics shield. No, what bothers David is that this is the first time he's seen real murder in Elvis's eye.

"They call that gratitude?" he shouts above the Spyder's 335 horses. "I gave them shitheels everything. Every motherfuckin' thing!"

They'd gotten Cadillacs, .357s, gold and diamonds, not to mention more women than any mortal man had a right to. And he'd just offered them a hundred grand not to go through with it. Sinatra had even offered his "influence" to kill the deal. But the King, who'd always preferred Nancy to her father, had told Frank that he was perfectly capable of taking care o' business His Way. Wasn't that his favorite motto engraved on "Captain America" lightning bolt gold necklaces he'd given the ingrates: TCB?

"They ain't worth a bullet, Elvis," his kid brother keeps pleading. "Nobody'll believe that crazy shit!"

The King puts the Ferrari to the mat. He's pulled his shields on speeders in the past letting them go with a stern warning and an autograph. But this will be his first collar on felons, not to mention Judases.

The trouble all got started recently in Tahoe when a skunked real estate salesman paid sixty bucks to get into Elvis's Sahara suite for a private party. Shoved from the door by the bodyguards, he started fooling with the suite lights at the fuse box down the hall. Next thing he knew, he was in the dark and the star's posse—the "Guys"—were using his face as a speed bag. After having his jaw set and his lips sewn back on, the crasher sued his assailants for $6 million.

This wasn't the first time the Memphis Mafia had landed Elvis in court, but it was certainly hardest on his dwindling fortune. What was worse, they were starting to meddle in some very personal business of his.

So he had his old man, Vernon, fire them, which he was happy to do since he'd always hated their freeloading asses anyway. All three of them: Red and Sonny West, plus the house karate instructor, Dave Hebler. The bodyguards were given one week's severance pay. It wasn't as generous as the King had been with them in the past, but he didn't expect their names to be on a drugstore tell-all, *Elvis: What Happened?*

Hebler had been an easy fire, but the Wests were another matter. Elvis had gone to high school with Red, and the badass football star had TCB'd some Memphis rednecks who had tried to punch Elvis out and scalp his revolutionary hair. Through thick and thin, the West cousins had had the King's back for the last sixteen years. Not that there hadn't been a rough patch or two.

Though Elvis was best man at Sonny's wedding, he later bedded his bride, which led to divorce. But when the singer lost his own wife, Priscilla, to the Polynesian karate man, Mike Stone, it was Sonny he turned to for help. "The sonuvabitch has to die!" he told him. "Kill the nigger!" Sonny refused the job, throwing away the M-16 automatic Elvis had shoved at him.

Now cousin Red was in the hot seat. Elvis often said, "Red is anger!" and knew he could count on him in a pinch. And indeed he could. Red dropped a dime on Vegas and arranged a hit on Priscilla's lover for ten grand. But by the time Red completed the negotiation and asked his boss to green-light the contract, the King had simmered down. "Aw, hell," he shrugged, "let's just leave it for now."

In spite of Red's devoted service, his employer still found it necessary to remind him of the pecking order now and again. Not long after the aborted Stone hit in '72, Elvis woke his bodyguard up in the middle of the night, insisting that he take him to the dentist. Though Red didn't refuse, he'd just dropped a fistful of sleeping pills. In order to liven him up, the King shoved the business end of a 30-06 into his chest.

"Elvis," said Red with deep regret, "after all these years, I never would have believed you'd point a gun at me." Then, holding his ground, he continued, "Go on, you bastard, pull the trigger. Kill me!" The King, a 7th degree karate black belt, had dropped the gun with a mischievous wink to Red's sometimes better half, Sonny.[1]

This wasn't the first time the star had had to straighten out his employees, even the oldest, James K. Caughley, Jr., aka "Hamburger James." Hamburger was called Hamburger because of all the burgers, popsicles, and other health foods he had served his insatiable boss over the years. He also picked up the King's prescriptions, he kept his wardrobe and jewelry in order, and he changed the sheets in hotel rooms after his boss had another "accident."

Imagine Hamburger's surprise then, when he found himself in a Vegas Hilton suite one evening, with his employer's .45 at his temple.

---

1. In *Elvis: What Happened?* as told to Steve Dunleavy (New York: Vintage, 1991), Sonny wrote that he had taught Elvis always to keep the first chamber of his guns empty, for safety reasons. He related how Elvis once, in a rage, pulled the trigger on a guy who barged in on him in the bathroom. "Jesus, thank God, he didn't have a bullet in that chamber," Sonny wrote, "otherwise he would have blown the man's head clean off his shoulders."

Recently, Elvis had decided that Hamburger was ripping him off—pocketing his jewelry and forging checks. After rounding up the Wests and his other deputies, he intercepted Hamburger in the Vegas airport preparing to take off. Flashing his federal narcotics agent shield to the gate attendant, Elvis and his posse cuffed Hamburger, read him his Miranda's, then rifled his briefcase, coming up with a .357 magnum and a $20,000 ring. They browbeat him back at the hotel, threatening him with a ride out to the desert. When Hamburger blubbered that he'd just taken the ring for safekeeping, Elvis reclaimed his property, fired him, and called it a night.

The King had scored his Bureau of Narcotics and Dangerous Drugs (BNDD) badge from the president himself, Christmas 1971. Nixon had declared drugs "America's Number One Problem." Elvis handwrote him a letter denouncing the Beatles and Jane Fonda, and offering his services as "ambassador" to America's troubled youth. Nixon invited him to the Oval Office. The singer arrived in a black suede jumpsuit and a purple velvet cape festooned with gold chains. The ensemble was accessorized with amber aviator shades that muted his Revlon eye shadow and mascara. According to one source "he looked like Dracula."

"You dress pretty wild, don't you?" observed the Quaker chief executive.

"Mr. President," responded the medicated King, "you got your show to run, I got mine."

After the summit, both shook hands for a photo op before a bank of American flags. Nixon had given Elvis his narcotics badge; the King had given Tricky Dick a commemorative Colt .45 revolver. (He'd offered Spiro Agnew a Colt .357 snub nose, but the vice president—who later resigned due to income tax evasion—turned it down on principle.) Elvis also tried to offer his services to the man whom he considered "the greatest living American"—J. Edgar Hoover. The transvestite FBI head, however, refused the King an audience due his "exotic dress" and the length of his hair.

When Elvis returned to Graceland and proudly flashed his narcotics badge to his stepbrother, David, the teenager smirked, "Did you buy it?"

"That's not funny!" snapped the deputized King. "I am the ears and eyes of President Richard Nixon!"

*   *   *

Like he always does, Elvis carries his narc shield now as he blazes up the Santa Monica freeway to Sonny and Red West's Hollywood hideout. In the unlikely event he is pulled over at this hour by the CHP, the badge will prove that he is working undercover.

A few weeks ago, he'd had a high-ranking law enforcement associate call the Wests and offer them a golden parachute if they would abandon their budding literary careers. They declined. So he'd taken it upon himself to phone Red personally to talk some sense into him. Red was unreceptive. On top of that, he'd gone and *taped* the conversation. So having exhausted every diplomatic avenue, what was the King to do? It wasn't just his own career at stake here—it was his reputation. If they wanted to play hardball, so could he. He'd wanted to lure the Judases back to Graceland for a taste of Tennessee justice, but the chicken livers were now sandbagging it out on the coast. Did they actually think his long arm of justice couldn't reach them there? Well, they didn't know the King so well after all.

"They ain't worth a bullet, E!" his deputy keeps pleading.

David, now twenty-three, has been on his big brother's payroll ever since high school. "My role was that of bodyguard-headhunter badass," he wrote in his book, *Raised on Rock*. Elvis felt the boy was well qualified for this position since his father had been the personal bodyguard to General George C. Patton himself.

A quick study, David has become quite adept at defusing the irascible King. But on this predawn morning he seems to be at his wit's end. Then he gives it one last shot, appealing to the only person his brother still seems to care about now.

"Elvis," he cries, grasping the driver's arm. "What about your little girl? Better she read that you were a druggie than a killer, man!"

The singer clutches the wheel of the Ferrari, jaw flexing, eyes fixed. Suddenly he stands on the brakes, and the car comes to a smoking halt on the freeway shoulder.

Head bowed, Elvis begins to weep. "You're right. You're right! My baby needs me!"

The King takes a moment to collect himself. His dyed black hair is down in his face and his 280-pound bulk is soaked with sweat. He towels himself off, then reaches into his DEA windbreaker and produces his makeup kit. Inside are his credit cards and prescriptions. He pops a handful of his midmorning "protocol" from Needle Nick: Quaalude, Placidyl, Valmid, Demerol, Dilaudid.

"Let's go home," he sighs, exhausted.

He already has another plan. More prudent though less satisfying than TCB with Sonny and Red's asses personally. Besides, his investigators have told him the cousins have sealed documents and photos in a safe deposit box, to be revealed in the event of an "untimely demise" after the release of their book on the 19th anniversary of his mother's burial.

What Elvis doesn't realize is that in only ten months time he will be lying in a 900-pound copper box without his organs or his brain, but at last with his beloved Satnin again.

SATNIN

Elvis Aaron Presley had inherited his bone structure from his beautiful daddy, Vernon, and his disposition from his excitable mama, Gladys, whose parents, Bob and Doll, were first cousins. Gladys's eldest brother, Tracy, born deaf and dumb, had the mind of an eight-year-old. He could walk a mile on his hands, but often complained "I got my nerves in the dirt." His kidneys shut down when he was 49. Gladys's younger brothers, Travis and Johnny, were heavy drinkers, prone to gunplay, and both came to early ends as well. Vernon's father was a loose-cannon alcoholic too, and his daughter, Dixie, Vernon's sister, died of tertiary syphilis in a mental hospital.

Elvis's generation was no more stable. His first cousin, Bobby, punctured his intestines after eating safety pins, while his father, Travis, was in prison with Vernon. After a psychiatric discharge from the Army, he was run over and crippled by a drunk outside Graceland. In the end, Bobby, age 27, swallowed a fatal dose of rat poison. Elvis's other cousin, Junior, regularly threatened to murder people and died in an alcoholic seizure at 29. Junior's brother, Robert, met his maker after falling or jumping into a vat of molten chrome in a Tupelo plating factory.

Bobby's brother, Billy, who went on to become his cousin Elvis's most trusted employee, would later say of his kin, "It felt like somebody threw a hex on us."

But Vernon and Gladys Presley—18 and 22, respectively, when married—believed that their own boy would be different. Very different. Vernon would later tell a story about blacking out at the instant of his son's conception, then, regaining consciousness, seeing the night sky thronged with brilliant blue stars. Though from humble backgrounds—both Vernon and Gladys were from a long line of Mississippi moonshiners and sharecroppers and had depended on the state to pay the $15 delivery fee—they believed that their only child was the One. If not the Second Coming himself, then certainly part of the advance team.

As a boy, the future King lived alone and on welfare with his doting mother, a part-time seamstress, while his daddy and Uncle Travis did time in the Mississippi State Penitentiary at Parchman for forging a check on a $4 hog sale. Even when Vernon returned, he was a withering presence in the household dominated by his formidable wife who called him a "work-shy, steer-coddled jellybean."

Gladys never let Elvis out of her sight; they fawned over each other, they petted each other, and they developed a language all their own. The boy called his mother "Satnin" after her satiny smooth skin. Prone to violent nightmares and somnambulism, Elvis slept with Satnin until his teens. Vernon was often out of town, pounding nails or running shine. The trio was like the Mary, Jesus, and Joseph trinity: Vernon Joseph was around for the nativity, but he was never heavily involved.

A voracious Marvel Comic reader, Elvis dreamed of becoming a Tennessee state trooper and fighting the forces of evil. Meantime, he loved to sing gospel with his mother at the First Assembly of God and at their riverbank revivals. "When I was four or five," he recalled, "all I looked forward to was Sundays." His insular world was broken when his father was caught running hooch again, and the family fled the sleepy Tupelo for the housing projects in the metropolis of Memphis.

Here, Gladys gave Elvis his first guitar. To go with it, he got a pompadour and some flashy getups from Lansky's clothes emporium, which catered to black musicians. "Somebody's gonna beat the hell out of him and peel them nigger outfits right off his hide!" his cousin Billy warned his mother. Though this did almost happen at Hume High School, Elvis could not be discouraged. He was a born stylist like his Grandpa Jessie Presley, the "peacock" womanizer who regularly abandoned Grandma Minnie Mae and squandered their pennies on pearl-button blazers. Keeping her dog on the porch, Gladys didn't put up with the same shenanigans from Vernon.

Though Elvis had never been the student, Gladys, who had only reached third grade, was proud when her son graduated from Hume High in English, History, and Industrial Arts, then became a machinist the very next day. In his sophomore year, the boy had worked at Loews Theatre, but was fired for punching out another usher over the concession girl who had been stealing candy for him. Even in high school, though he'd never been popular with the other boys, the future King had made quite an impression on the fair sex.

A few years later, Elvis, now a delivery driver for Crown Electric, strode into Sam Phillips' Sun Studio and made an impression on the record producer's young secretary, Marion Keisker, formerly Miss Radio Memphis. She had seen many pickers and crooners come and go, but there was something about this one—shy, soft-spoken, sensitive, stunningly handsome.

"And what kind of singer are you, sugar?" asked Marion.

"I sing all kinds," muttered Elvis.

"Who do you sound like?" she went on.

"I don't sound like nobody," he said.

Then she heard his sweet, plaintive voice on "My Happiness." He paid Marion $3.25 for the recording that he told her was a present for his mama. When Sam Phillips returned to the studio later, his secretary made him sit right down and listen to the young truck driver's tape. Phillips, who had once predicted he could make a million dollars if he could find a white man who sounded like a Negro, invited the boy back for an audition. After a listen, he decided that the singer had promise, but his main impression was something else entirely.

"He felt so inferior," recalled Sam years later. "His insecurity was so markedly like that of a black man."

But this insecurity, at least on the face of it, was short-lived. "That's Alright Mama," recorded by Phillips in 1954, enjoyed instant and continuous airplay, earning Elvis a spot on the *Slim Whitman Show*, the *Louisiana Hayride*, and at country music's Vatican, the *Grand Ole Opry*. The next year, Johnny Cash and Buddy Holly were the openers for his Elvis Presley Jamboree. Then came the monster: his first RCA single, "Heartbreak Hotel," sold a million copies and topped the national charts in 1956. That fall, 60 million viewers watched his first appearance on *The Ed Sullivan Show*.

In a single year, Elvis had gone from "The Hillbilly Cat" to "Elvis the Pelvis." Finally—after Ed Sullivan told America he was "a real decent, fine boy"—*Variety* crowned him "The King of Rock and Roll."

Nobody had seen the like of him—black or white—on stage. Not Holly or Haley, nor even Domino, Diddley, or Berry compared. Elvis shook, rattled, and rolled like a man on fire; he wailed and he howled as if overtaken by the rapture. "His energy was incredible," said Roy Orbison, after seeing him perform in Odessa, Texas. "There was just no reference point in the culture to compare it."

It wasn't just the King's volcanic energy, but the raw sexuality of it that drove the crowds to frenzy. Though Elvis insisted, "I don't make no dirty movements," Cardinal Spellman and Frank Sinatra disagreed. But his act was the blossom of the most flamboyant theater of all: Southern evangelism. At Tupelo's Assembly of God, the young Elvis had heard testifying in tongues, and he had seen sinners overtaken by the spirit, swooning to the floor, doing the first break dancing. "Music," he said, "should be something that makes you gotta move, inside or outside." Having always claimed gospel as his favorite, he brought it to nonchurch-going folk, delivering it with the fervor of a natural-born preacher.

The likes of "Heartbreak Hotel" and "Love Me Tender" especially moved one group. Said Elvis's first bodyguard, "It's crazy the way women react." They fainted during performances, they tore at his clothes, and they lipstick graffitied his Caddy with phone numbers. Soon he got his first death threat from a steer-coddled husband. Then an unemployed steelworker, whose smitten wife had just left him, was fined $19.60 for attacking the young King.

"He never thought he was gonna be a monster," said his friend, Lamar Fike. "It was scary to him. Very, very scary."

Only one person was even more scared: his mother, Gladys. In his nightly calls to her from the road, Elvis hadn't told Satnin about the death threats, but she had only to look out the window of the house he'd just bought her to see bobby-soxers scrambling over her fence. Since she kept a wary eye on the newspaper too, he'd had to fess up to nearly crashing in his airplane. While flying to Texas, his prop lost an engine but managed an emergency landing, sparing him the fate that would soon befall his friends Buddy Holly, Richie Valens, the Big Bopper, and Patsy Cline.

Though Gladys was tickled with the new house and the pink Cadillac, nothing was worth the life of her beloved boy. The fact that he was away from home all the time now, fighting mobs and running himself ragged, she blamed on one person: the Colonel.

An illegal Danish immigrant, Tom Parker had started his career as a dogcatcher in Florida, then graduated to show business by founding The Great Parker Pony Circus, featuring "The Honorary Colonel Tom Parker and His Dancing Chickens." The huckster soon abandoned poultry to become a country music promoter in partnership with Hank Snow—then managing Elvis.

What really got Gladys hot was how this rotund, cigar-chewing, circus barker had started right off calling her boy *"my* boy," riding roughshod over her, and acting like she should be grateful for the hired help. Worse, her malingering empty-headed husband, Vernon, *did* kiss the Colonel's ass and spent Elvis's new fortune with delight, seeming not to care one wit for his health and safety.

Gladys was relieved when her only son came home from the road, bought Graceland for her, and reunited the family. She, Vernon, Grandma Minnie Mae, Aunt Delta, Uncle Vester, Cousin Billy, and other kin moved in with Elvis, along with their menagerie of farm animals.

For a short time, the Presley clan enjoyed their Camelot on the estate. The 21-year-old King built a go-cart racetrack, a full-sized roller coaster, and a shooting range. He and the family staged watermelon seed-spitting contests, firecracker fights, and go-cart races. Then, after midnight when Gladys was in bed, the Memphis police department would close off Highway 61 outside Graceland's Music Gates, and Elvis and the boys would race their Harley hogs. But, as always, the fun would come to an abrupt end when the Colonel would call Elvis back to the road.

During one of his absences, a friend of the family, Frank Richards, dropped by Graceland for the first time and said to Elvis's mother, "I guess you must be about the happiest woman in the world!"

"You got it wrong," she spat. "I'm the most miserable woman in the world. . . . I'm guarded. I can't buy my own groceries. I can't see my neighbors."

She was already pining for the days before the mansions, the roller coasters, and the Cadillacs. Her only link to it now was her chickens that she fed every day off the back stoop while downing her vodka and pep pills and waiting for her boy to come home again. Then in the spring of 1957, hardly a year after moving into Graceland, one of her worst fears was realized: the Army called Elvis.

She knew he didn't want to go. And he didn't *need* to go. Sal Mineo and other stars had pulled strings, and he could too. But his manager wouldn't hear of it. It wouldn't be good for his boy's image, said the Colonel. He was an all-American boy, said the Colonel. People would love him even more in uniform, said the Colonel. Besides, if he took the candy away from the fans for a little, they'd want it even more when he gave it back. Meantime, while Elvis was serving his country, he promised to keep his boy's career alive. Now Gladys loathed the Colonel.

The Army agreed to delay Elvis's induction until he finished his fourth movie, *King Creole*. He had just attended the premiere of his second, *Jailhouse Rock*. At twenty-two, he was now the same age his father had been when he'd been sent upriver to Parchman. For Gladys, the movie was a preview of a real prison sentence for her son: the Army.

As soon as *King Creole* wrapped, Elvis left for basic training in Arkansas. When he was about to be shipped overseas for active duty, his mother fell gravely ill. Diagnosed with hepatitis and liver damage, Gladys suffered severe nausea, headaches, weakness, and depression. She deteriorated quickly in the hospital, and Elvis was granted emergency leave to see her. Within days of his arrival, his mother passed away.

"Oh, Satnin, I wanna go with you!" he sobbed at the funeral, seizing her casket and refusing to let go.

He spent the last nine days of his leave crying in his room, clutching and kissing her pink housecoat.

PYGMALION AND THE GUYS

Elvis, who said he wanted to be treated like any other soldier, lived off base in Germany with what was left of his immediate family: Vernon, Grandma Minnie Mae, and his sidekicks, Red West and Lamar Fike. The Army paid him $122 monthly to supplement his monthly $400,000 from the Colonel who, true to his word, was keeping the King solvent stateside. Though the singer felt "shafted and drafted," the Army introduced him to his two favorite future pastimes: sharpshooting and karate. Private Presley was also introduced to a certain special fourteen-year-old girl.

The daughter of an Army colonel, Priscilla Beaulieu, was stunningly beautiful. But to Lamar and others, what was most striking about her was her resemblance to a young Gladys and to Elvis himself. Later, he would call her Satnin. She called herself his "Pygmalion."

She later wrote, "Elvis relished the role of recreating me. Like a sculptor, he could shape my image and design my demeanor in ways that would bring him delight."[2]

While Elvis reincarnated Gladys in Priscilla, Vernon replaced Gladys with Dee Stanley, the wife of General Patton's bodyguard. The vivacious blonde, an avid Elvis fan, came onto Vernon like gangbusters, and the long deprived moonshiner fell head over heels. Dee divorced her husband in short order, and she and Vernon got hitched as soon as Elvis finished his tour and returned to Graceland. Disgusted by his father's infidelity to his dead mother, Elvis refused to attend the wedding. His father had eaten of the forbidden fruit, so he banished him and his temptress from Graceland.

As for Elvis, though he returned to his steady girlfriend, Anita Wood, he regularly wrote to his Pygmalion overseas. He persuaded the Beaulieus to let her celebrate Christmas with him at Graceland. When she arrived jetlagged from the overseas flight, "He gave me prescription pep pills which he had been taking for so long," recalled Priscilla. "He even called them 'helpers.' He swallowed them like candy." Later, when she couldn't sleep, he fed her some Placidyls. "A variety of pills were his constant companions," she went on. "They did much to change the emotional weather. I was still learning who he was."

When Priscilla returned to Germany after the holiday, her stepfather, Colonel Beaulieu, recalled, "Her eyes looked like two pissholes in the snow. I was worried."

Still, he allowed his daughter to return to Graceland to live. Elvis had phoned him personally, begging for his permission, promising to enroll Priscilla in Immaculate Conception High School. Convinced that the star was a complete gentleman and intended to make an honest girl of his daughter when she came of age, Colonel Beaulieu gave his consent.

Elvis was now spending half his time in Hollywood. *Jailhouse Rock* and *King Creole* had been box office hits, so, resuming his career, Elvis decided to concentrate on the acting. His first post-Army movie was *GI Blues*. For the next nine years, he did three pictures annually, working for a few months on each with his beautiful co-stars. Between musicals, he returned to his Pygmalion at Graceland.

---

2. David Ritz, ed., *Elvis, by the Presleys: Intimate Stories from Priscilla Presley, Lisa Marie Presley, and Other Family Members* (Memphis, TN: Elvis Presley Enterprises, 2005).

After Priscilla graduated from Immaculate Conception in 1963, she pleaded to go with Elvis to Hollywood. The town was rotten to the core, a veritable Babylon, he told her—in short, no place for a girl like her. He had taken her to the Memphian Theatre to see some of his hits, such as *Girls! Girls! Girls!* with Stella Stevens, *Fun in Acapulco* with Ursula Andress, and *Viva Las Vegas* with Ann-Margaret. Priscilla asked him what he did off the set, and he told her he just killed time with the Guys, watching TV, practicing a little karate, and shooting a little pool.

Priscilla had never understood the Guys, much less why everybody called them the Memphis Mafia. "I don't like to sit alone too much and think," Elvis once admitted. As his *Jailhouse Rock* co-star, Anne Neyland, had observed, "He's one of those people who cannot be alone. He feels he has to surround himself with close friends as a sort of protection against loneliness." Priscilla understood this, especially since Elvis had been an only child—but the Guys seemed to be more than just the brothers he'd never had.

The original core Guys were Billy Smith, Red and Sonny West, Joe Esposito, Charlie Hodge, and Lamar Fike. Billy was Elvis's favorite cousin, the only normal son of Gladys's crazy brother, Travis. Cousins Red and Sonny, excitable Memphis redneck boys, were Elvis's bouncers, drivers, and all-around Man Fridays. "Diamond" Joe, "the Yankee" hustler from Chicago, was the tour manager and treasurer. Charlie, former Lilliputian lead singer for the Foggy River Boys, was the King's dresser and musical advisor. Lamar—a three hundred pound Presbyterian Jew from Mississippi who wore yellow cowboy boots and whom E called "the great speckled bird" and "Buddha"—was the Falstaff and court jester of the group. "I'm a character," he said, speaking for the others as well. "I've never been a normal person." The five things the King most valued in an employee were: unerring fidelity, an insatiable appetite for taking his shit, the ability to kick ass, a bent sense of humor, and sartorial style—in that order.

Having few of these fine qualities personally, Priscilla soon found herself at loggerheads with all the Guys except Diamond Joe who, in spite of his eccentricities, at least knew how to handle money and hold his drugs. She'd met Joe, Red, and Lamar in Germany, then Billy, Charlie, and a few others at Graceland—and found them weird. What she couldn't understand was why Elvis had to live with them, spend every waking hour with them, and keep them on call even when he slept.

And what exactly, Priscilla wondered, did the boys all do together out in Hollywood? At Graceland she'd watched them race their Vettes and hogs, play football, throw cherry bombs at each other, and shoot their guns. A kid at heart, Elvis loved to play. But as his Pygmalion knew, he didn't play well with others unless his rules were followed. "The unwritten rule in the kingdom of Elvis was simple: let Elvis win," said his cousin, Patsy. Priscilla had seen it firsthand in cards, "If he wasn't winning, he'd cheat and accuse *you* of cheating."

In the spring of '65, the King at last begrudgingly agreed to bring "Cilla," as he called her, out to the coast. Now in his spiritualist phase, he took her to The Self-Realization Fellowship where he'd been studying. His hairdresser, Larry Geller, had gotten him into metaphysics and given him texts ranging from *The Autobiography of a Yogi* to *The Tibetan Book of the Dead.* He had confided to Geller, "I swear to God, no one knows how lonely I get and how empty I really feel." By this time, he was even considering quitting show business and becoming a monk.

"Enough of this spiritual searching!" his manager raved after hearing that the hairdresser was helping Elvis contact his dead twin brother. "Enough with these books on mind control and meditation! Enough with Larry Geller!"

For once, the Guys agreed with their nemesis, Colonel Parker. "Geller turned Elvis upside down," said Lamar. "He's like plastic. You could make toys out of that bastard." The Guys called him Swami, Rasputin, and The Brain Scrambler.

Parker at last exorcised Geller and persuaded Elvis to abandon enlightenment and shoot *Tickle Me.* Before she left Hollywood and was sent back to Graceland, Cilla got a glimpse of Elvis's home away from home, a Frank Lloyd Wright creation formerly owned by Rita Hayworth and the Shah of Iran. Maybe it was just all the Guys lounging zombie-eyed around the pool with their boss's "fans," but Pygmalion got the feeling that the place was some kind of "bachelor pad," as she called it. Her suspicions were confirmed when she intercepted a perfumed note to her husband that was signed *Lizard Tongue.*

What on earth *did* go on there? Was her creator and the love of her life, for all his spirituality, living inside one of his movies?

In fact, truth stranger than fiction, the action inside Elvis's Perugia Way sultanate was better than *Harum Scarum* and *Girls! Girls! Girls!*

He *was* swimming, shooting pool, and watching TV, but not stag.

One night the Guys counted 152 aspiring actresses in line for the casting couch. With only six Guys and one King, this worked out to about twenty-one apiece, eclipsing even Hefner's ratio nearby at Playboy West. The star had pick of the litter and would take two to four to chambers. The leftovers were divided between the castrati.

Not one to check ID, the King favored golden-locked sweet sixteens in snow white panties. But a reckless deflowerer of virgins he was not. "15'll get you 20," was his motto and he didn't intend following his father's footsteps upriver. Besides, according to Cousin Billy, Natalie Wood, Peggy Lipton, Cybill Shepherd, and others sex had never been—"a big thrill" for him. A fondler and cuddler, the Guys called him "The King of Foreplay." Due to his conditions and medications, he could not always rise to the occasion. But when he did, Lamar noted that he would often rupture his uncircumcised foreskin. Also, having a deadly fear of paternity suits, he had become the fastest withdraw in the West.

The King, however, did oblige many of his co-stars as a professional courtesy. He came very close to marrying a few—notably Ann-Margret and Nancy Sinatra—but monogamy had never been his strong suit, and he didn't intend to move to Utah.

Woefully, many men never live to realize even the least of their fantasies, but the King was not one of them. "He had every fetish there was," said Lamar. He had an onanist's fixation about goldilocks hair and a mandarin thing for "sooties"—clean, white, little feet. Through a two-way mirror in his pool house bullpen, he monitored the aerobic workouts of the Guys with his female fans. In his bedroom he enjoyed watching art films of Scandinavian girls getting it on with livestock.

Then there was Scatter. The singer had adopted the forty-pound, three-foot chimpanzee from a Memphis cartoonist who had introduced him to the forbidden fruits of groupies. Though Elvis and the Guys drank only Pepsi at their parties, they served Scatter scotch until the chimp started skirt diving. In the midst of the pandemonium, Elvis's pet mynah bird cursed the lubricated chimp, "Fuck you! Son of a bitch!" The King particularly delighted staging in his game room no-holds-barred WWF smackdowns between strippers and his randy mascot. Otherwise, he chauffeured Scatter, dressed in a bowler and bow tie, around Hollywood in the Rolls. But finally the Guys got tired of the chimp trying to tag team while they were in the saddle. Lamar, especially sensitive to interruptions, tried to electrocute the chimp in the bathtub. So in the end, Elvis sent his pet back to Graceland to join Priscilla in the Tower. Here in an air-conditioned laundry room, Scatter, once the life of the King's parties, died of neglect.

By 1966, Priscilla, now twenty-one, was impatient for a commitment from Elvis. She found an unlikely ally in the Colonel himself, a champion of family values. Parker told his boy that this six-year flirtation was becoming a public embarrassment. He needed to make an honest woman of Priscilla for the sake of his "fine, decent boy" image, if nothing else. So deferring to his manager once again, Elvis proposed to his Pygmalion on Christmas Day.

The battle lines were now drawn for the King's future and his heart. On one side were Priscilla, the Colonel, and Vernon; on the other were the Guys. For the Guys, a married Elvis would mean an end to their bachelor paradise on the coast. But more than this, they didn't cotton to Priscilla. "She didn't want anyone around who didn't kiss her ass," said Marty Lacker. He and the others had little trouble kissing Elvis's ass, but they drew the line when it came to Priscilla's. Marty also called her "cold as ice" and a "penny-pincher." At least she acted that way toward him and the others because she considered them leaches, as did both Vernon and Colonel Parker. Elvis lavished Cadillacs, Harleys, gold chains, and guns on them, and they accepted the gifts in lieu of real salaries since, as Red pointed out, "We were all busier than a one-legged man in an ass-kicking contest." Priscilla had also noticed that her fiancé was most generous with the help when shopping under the influence. So the Guys were happy to fill his prescriptions, she thought.

Elvis assured his worthies that there was no statute of limitations on engagements. He'd get married when and if he was good and ready. When he told this to Cilla, a fight erupted; he stormed up to his room and nearly OD'd. By the spring of '67, the King of Rock and Roll—finally buckling under Vernon's and the Colonel's pressure—was at the altar in Vegas, kissing his bride and kissing his life good-bye. Priscilla had drawn up the guest list and the Memphis Mafia, except for Joe and Marty, was conspicuously absent. Then, after a one-day honeymoon in Palm Springs, the new Queen returned to Graceland and did some much overdue spring-cleaning: she kicked the Guys out.

In short, Mrs. Presley had won; the Guys had lost. For now.

The bride—whom Elvis now called Satnin—got pregnant immediately. Soon after the announcement, he told her he wanted a trial separation. The split ended at Christmastime when Elvis gave her a Cadillac. Then he returned to L.A. to shoot *Clambake*. The Guys had now been reduced to a skeleton crew and Satyricon parties were history. So Elvis played with Nancy Sinatra. Cilla gave birth to Lisa Marie that winter, and Nancy graciously gave the baby shower.

Elvis, burned out on a decade of beating up bad guys, getting the girl, and singing in between, was now itchy to get back to reality: rock and roll. In late 1968, a billion viewers watched his TV comeback special. In preparation, he'd gone on a crash diet said to have involved one of his New Age elixirs: daily injections of protein extracted from the urine of pregnant women. In July of the following year, for his first live performance in Vegas, he was paid $1.5 million for a week's work. Before the curtain went up on premiere night, "Elvis was as nervous as Hitler at a packed Bar Mitzvah," said Lamar. But the performance was a killer and put the King on the cover of *Rolling Stone*.

Elvis toured almost continually for the remaining nine years of his life, logging 1,145 gigs. He enacted a "No Wives on Tour" decree. After everybody boarded the tour plane, Elvis presided over a solemn wedding ring removal ceremony. His father, Vernon, still married to Dee, also participated in the rite.

The only bachelor roadie was Elvis's kid stepbrother, David Stanley. As soon as they arrived at their first stop in New York City, the King buzzed David's room and barked: "Get up to my suite immediately!" When the seventeen-year-old arrived, he found his big brother on the couch with four scantily clad professionals. "Girls, I give you the boy," he told them. "Bring me back the man!"[3]

Meanwhile, déjà vu all over again: The Queen was at Graceland wondering what her liege and his courtiers were up to now. She was also concerned that her husband hadn't made love to her since Lisa Marie's birth. "I remembered him telling me some time in the past," she later wrote, "that he just couldn't have sex with a woman who'd had a child." The full truth was worse. "I'll give you Elvis's relationship with her in a nutshell," Lamar said. "You create a statue. And

---

3. Perhaps Elvis felt this was the least he could do for his young brother since he had been hitting on David's high school girlfriends for some time. He had also seduced the young wife of David's brother Rick, which led to divorce. As for David, he married in 1974, but Angie divorced him a few years later due to tour infidelities. In the same year and for the same reason, his mother, Dee, divorced Elvis's father, Vernon.

then you get tired of looking at it." Only a month after his Pygmalion became a mother, he told Lamar, "You know I really don't like Priscilla anymore."

As for his new daughter, "Lisa was just another trophy for him," said Lamar. "Parenthood didn't change Elvis at all."

When the King returned home and Cilla again complained of being lonely, he proved himself a normal man after all: he told her she needed a hobby. He set her up with a dance teacher and karate teacher, then hit the road again. When her husband came back to Graceland for the Christmas of '71, he knew something was awry in Camelot when Cilla refused a new Fleetwood Cadillac from Santa and asked for $10,000 instead. Then she packed up her cash and her baby and drove out to Hollywood to rendezvous with her karate instructor, Mike Stone.

Elvis filed for divorce, citing "irreconcilable differences." Priscilla wanted a queen-sized alimony. "That no-good, greedy fuckin' bitch!" raged Elvis. "Dammit, I gave her enough!" In the end Mrs. Presley received $2 million outright; $250,000 for her share of their L.A. house; $6,000 per month for ten years; $4,000 per month alimony; $4,000 monthly child support, plus 5 percent of her husband's publishing companies.

Elvis signed the final papers in the fall of 1973. Days later, he suffered his "Divorce OD"—a double dose of "Vitamin E" prescribed by Dr. Nick.

VITAMIN E

I take Vitamin E.
—Elvis, when asked by a reporter how he continued to look
  so youthful

In the early years of his stardom, Elvis did speed to gear up for his performances, and sleeping pills to wind down. In the Army, he'd taken "Prellies" for all-night guard duty. During his Hollywood stint, he packed coke-soaked cotton balls in his nostrils to keep his spark up and to control his consumption of fried bacon and banana sandwiches. Speed in turn created a dependence on liquid Demerol for sleep. In the 70s, to weather the blowback from touring, heartburn romances, and general craziness, his favorite Vitamin E became Dilaudid, a potent synthetic morphine generally reserved for amputees, burn victims, and terminal cancer patients.

Ever the law-abiding citizen, E never acquired his vitamins from street sources. He always went to bona fide, licensed doctors. By the end of his life, the King had countless physicians from Memphis to Vegas to L.A. The most prolific prescriber among them was Dr. George Nichopoulos. Between 1970 and 1977, Elvis paid Dr. Nick—who moonlighted for Jerry Lee Lewis and other stars—more than $200,000 for his services. He also bankrolled the doctor's $750,000 Memphis mansion and financed a racquetball club for him.

The King was equally magnanimous with his other MDs. He gave his favorite Vegas physician, Dr. Elias Ghanem, a Mercedes as well as a $42,000 Stutz Blackhawk. As a token of his gratitude, the Lebanese doctor built a private getaway for his patient on the top floor of his Las Vegas house. Here the King could escape the frenzy of the Strip and enjoy on-call injections.

Though once an inexhaustible rock-and-roll warhorse, Elvis started canceling gigs and was repeatedly hospitalized for "fatigue." When he did perform, he would sometimes forget the words to his songs, digress into incoherent monologs, or break into uncontrollable, hysterical laughter. After a near fatal narcotic OD in St. Louis in '72, his father and manager hired two veteran detectives to find out what kind of vitamins their boy was taking and who was prescribing them. John O'Grady, aka "the Big O," was a retired L.A. narcotics agent with over 2,500 drug busts under his belt. Jack Kelly was a former head of L.A.'s DEA division.

Soon enough, the O'Grady-Kelly team tracked down Nick, Ghanem, and Elvis's other health-care providers. The detectives provided Vernon and Colonel Parker with a full report. After the Divorce OD, O'Grady urged immediate intervention. Vernon and O'Grady checked Elvis into the Memphis Baptist Hospital where he underwent a two-week methadone detox for Dilaudid addiction.

His physicians found that the singer suffered from Cushing's Syndrome. Symptoms of this condition include inflamed or "cushingoid" tissue, weight gain, "moon face," abnormal perspiring, fatigue, decreased libido, anxiety, mood swings, and severe depression. Cushing's is a hormonal disorder sometimes caused by the body's own excessive secretion of cortisol to combat abnormal stress; but more often, it is caused by excessive intake of cortisol drugs (prednisone, cortisone, etc.) for serious systemic diseases such as lupus. In the mid-sixties, Elvis had complained of severe joint pain, especially in the knees—one of the first signs of lupus, an inflammatory, degenerative disease of the autoimmune system triggered and exacerbated by stress. Elvis went on to develop pulmonary problems, high blood pressure, skin rashes, rheumatoid arthritis, glaucoma, and kidney infections—classic symptoms of progressive lupus.[4] But in treating it with huge and continuous doses of cortisone, the cure became worse than the disease. Even lesser doses of cortisone commonly cause an insatiable appetite and rapid weight gain—Elvis's nemeses in his later life. Continuous doses of cortisone also commonly cause mood swings—from elation to suicidal depression. In fact, current medical researchers assert that high cortisol levels are directly related to suicidal tendencies. In the 60s and early 70s, however, these and the other devastating side effects of the "miracle" drug were generally unknown. Cortisone was not administered as conservatively as it is today. Moreover, when Elvis wanted relief, he wanted it now and to the hilt.

After narcotic detox, the King hit the road again, this time with Needle Nick. His doctor's job was to "monitor and control" his medications according to a strict six-stage "drug protocol," which seemed more like a prescription for euthanasia than for recovery.

First, hours before a performance, Dr. Nick would give the King a vitamin B-12 "voice shot," herbs, three appetite suppressants, and testosterone. Next, an hour before the performance, voice shot #2, a decongestant with amphetamines—plus, if needed, a hit of Dilaudid. Then, moments before going on stage, Protocol 3: caffeine, Dexedrine, and, if needed, a second morphine chaser. Next, after the show: blood pressure pill, antihistamine, sedative, and diluted Demerol. Then, Stage 5, before bed: Quaalude-Amytal-Placidyl cocktail, plus a laxative and blood pressure pill. Finally, if the King was still restless, the sixth and last daily protocol: another Quaalude-Amytal cocktail.

Otherwise, for his general health, the singer daily filled a champagne glass with eighteen vitamins and downed the multiple with a single swallow. Still, he kept coming down with the "flu" or "Vegas Throat."

"Sorry, folks," Elvis regularly told his audiences now. "I just got up, and I am not really awake yet." The problem was that Dr. Nick's voice

---

4. The King's future son-in-law, the Prince of Pop, Michael Jackson, was diagnosed with lupus in 1984.

shot upper hadn't evened out the downers yet. But the speed was not just to keep him on his feet and coherent: it was for weight control. By this time, he needed corsets and Saran Wrap to fit into his $10,000 jeweled jumpsuits. And his New Age crash diets were no longer working due to the severely constipating effects of the narcotics. So Dr. Nick added powerful laxatives to the protocols, which had an embarrassing side effect. The King regularly soiled his hotel beds and often wore diapers under his Aztec jumpsuits.

Even so, every morning Elvis still enjoyed his six-egg Spanish omelets, with hash browns and twenty strips of bacon. For dinner, he packed away a pound of King Cotton crispy bacon, a quadruple order of mashed potatoes with thickenin' gravy, all of which he stirred together into a baby food batter and ate with his bare hands. For snacks he consumed countless peanut butter and grape jelly sandwiches, fudgesickles, dreamsickles, and jars of yogurt. Sweets were drugs for him, and drugs sweets, and his appetite for both were as insatiable as they were compulsive. His handlers had to watch him closely at mealtimes because he would often black out on his downers, and half-masticated food would have to be extracted from his throat.

"If Elvis hadn't had the Guys around," said Marty Lacker, who sometimes managed to replace his dope with placebos, "he probably would have died fifteen years before he did."

January 8, 1975 was not a good day for Elvis. A Tabloid newspaper celebrated the star's birthday with a photo of the 270-pound sequined star and the accompanying headline: ELVIS: 40 AND FAT! The star was so distressed he had to be sedated and carried to bed by the Guys.

Weeks later, he was rushed to the hospital with "acute abdominal pains." Though he signed in as "Aaron Sivle," his dyslexic pseudonym, the savvy lab techs supplemented their pay by selling his extra urine and blood. His father, Vernon, had a heart attack and soon joined him in the ICU.

After Elvis's release this time, O'Grady persuaded Priscilla—the only one the star would sometimes heed—to check him into San Diego's Scripps Medical Clinic, the Cadillac of detox facilities for hardcore addicts. Her efforts failed. So O'Grady pressured Dr. Nick to cut down on his prescriptions and fill the rest with Sweet 'N Low. Elvis blew a gasket. He fired Dr. Nick. Now Vernon, his son's honorary treasurer, tried an intervention. Elvis fired him too.

"You can't fire me," protested Vernon. "I'm your *father!*"

"You're fired *anyway!*" raged Elvis. Then he laid into the Guys for messing with his meds too. "You're either for me or against me. And I *will* get what I need, goddamn it!"

The only one who seemed to understand this now was his long-suffering girlfriend, Linda Thompson. The former Miss Liberty Bowl and Miss Tennessee had moved into Graceland with him right after Priscilla left. "I was an incredibly maternal presence in is life," she said. Elvis called Linda "Mommy," and she called him "Little Baby Buntin'." She obediently injected him with his vitamins and had saved his life more than once when he passed out and aspirated on food.

Linda took a brief sabbatical to clear her head. Elvis wasted no time finding her replacement in Sheila Ryan. But the stunning young model had only been with him a few days at Graceland when "all of a sudden you graduated into Mother," she recalled. "You were expected to take care of him." Sheila gave him his pills, hand fed him Jell-o, and read him to sleep. When she left him to marry actor James Caan, Linda came back to find Baby Buntin's situation even more desperate than before.

Finally, Elvis suffered a third near fatal narcotic cocktail overdose. He was aboard his new jet, the *Lisa Marie*, en route home after another grueling Vegas run. He suddenly collapsed, choking, "I can't breathe! I'm not gonna make it. Land!" The Guys strapped an oxygen mask on him as the pilot dove. Upon landing, he was hospitalized again at Memphis Baptist for "extreme fatigue." The date was August 16, 1975. He would die exactly two years later.

This was the last straw for Linda Thompson. Saying she "objected to his entire lifestyle and his entire person," she left Graceland to pursue an acting career, as had Priscilla and Sheila.[5]

Linda's objections were not limited to her lover's substance abuse. He'd almost killed her. Elvis was in the habit of shooting TV sets, chandeliers, and other nuisances in his hotel rooms. He'd recently targeted a porcelain owl in his Vegas penthouse; he'd missed, and the slug went through the wall into the bathroom, inches from Linda who was on the toilet. "What in God's name was that!" she cried, barging out into the living room. He'd shot her yellow Ford Pantera for not starting a while ago, but now this was going too far.

"Hey, now, Hon, just don't get excited," chuckled the King, laid out on a sofa with his shooting iron.

Another girl had once had a close call. At a Palm Springs pajama

---

5. Linda would become a regular on *Hee Haw* and marry Olympic medalist, Bruce Jenner.

party, Elvis and a teenage fan got to doing champagne glass shots of Hycodan, a narcotic cough syrup. The next afternoon, Charlie Hodge succeeded in slapping his boss back to consciousness. But the girl hardly had a pulse, her pupils were fixed, and she had begun to turn blue. At the hospital, her stomach was pumped, and she was injected with stimulants. After a seventeen-hour coma, she came to—luckily without brain damage. Colonel Parker used all his Palm Springs connections to squelch publicity and a police investigation. The girl's mother was offered hush money.

If there was anything—other than the superhuman pressures of being himself—that had driven Elvis to self-medication over the years, it was certainly the loss of the mothers in his life: first Gladys, then Priscilla, then Linda. His drug abuse began after the death of Gladys; his dangerous habit began after his divorce from Priscilla; and his self-destructive addiction began after Linda left.

During the second stage, deejay Wolfman Jack asked the King: "What's it like being Elvis Presley?"

"I'll tell you what, Jack," the star replied. "It's very, very uncomfortable."

ZOMBIE

My life is over. I'm a dead man!
—Elvis, after reading an advance copy of *Elvis: What Happened?*

During the last years of his life, the King of Rock and Roll came to hate touring but continued to do so out of financial necessity. In 1974, he did 152 shows, earning $7 million; but he remained $700,000 in the hole. Nearly broke by the end of '76, he borrowed $350,000 against Graceland. His record sales continued to fall and his tour receipts to dwindle. The more bummed he got about it, the more stoned he got and the more he shopped.

"He was getting rid of money like it was going out of season at sundown," one of his managers said.

He spent tens of thousands on guns: on a single day during Christmastime, he blew $19,792 on thirty-two handguns from Kerr's Gun Shop in L.A. His year-end jewelry tab at Lowell Hayes of Memphis was $880,000. He blew even more on cars for girlfriends, family, and fans. One day he shelled out 140 grand for fourteen gift Cadillacs.

When it came to jets, the King pulled the stops. "He had airplanes out the ass," said Lamar. While waiting for a million-dollar custom renovation of his sky palace, the *Lisa Marie,* he bought four spares in one day, including a Lear, an Aero Jet Commander, and a Lockheed Jet-Star. The fourth, a Grumman Gulfstream G-1, he gave to his manager, the Colonel, though by this time he didn't particularly like him, and feelings were mutual. Elvis needed multiple jets, not just for touring, but for exigencies. He used one to express his "vitamins" to and from Memphis, Vegas, L.A., Palm Springs, and wherever he happened to be performing. He once used another to airlift seventy Fools Gold Loaf peanut butter sandwiches, at $49.95 apiece, from Colorado to himself and his entourage in California.

Then there were his annual seven-figure charitable donations, not to mention his band and staff payroll, plus cash disbursements to family, friends, and hangers-on. On top of this were his pharmacy bills, his detox bills, his Graceland bills, his wardrobe bills.

Near the end, the financial Atlas toyed with the idea of an identity switch. After his facelift and eye job in '75, he told Billy he'd met a guy in the hospital who was having plastic surgery to look like *him.* "I think I'm going to swap places with him," Elvis told his cousin. "He can have all this shit, and I'll just take the everyday, normal life." But, like most of his other schemes, he let this one go after taking more Vitamin E complex.

By this time, the Colonel felt Elvis—with all the detoxes, concert cancellations, lawsuits, and coma girls—was "getting to be more trouble than what he was worth." Rumor had it that the former huckster and carnival psychic was ready to sell out his contract with the singer to cover his multimillion-dollar table tab in Vegas. Parker didn't share any of his boy's vices, but he did have a gambling problem. The casino of life had paid him off well: he'd collected the mother lode on Elvis. But Vegas hadn't been quite so kind to him. "He was good for a million a year," said a casino pit boss. The Guys had seen him drop $250,000 on a single roulette roll.

Coincidentally, just as the Colonel was thinking of dumping Elvis, Elvis was thinking of dumping him. Parker's 50 percent cut stuck in the star's craw. Also, Elvis had badly wanted to do a quality movie, and when one had finally been offered—the lead in Barbra Streisand's *A Star is Born*—the Colonel had turned it down. Worse, Elvis knew he could make a fortune touring Europe, but Parker, an illegal alien, refused to arrange it, fearing the INS would arrest him returning to the States.

Still, in spite of their mutual distaste for each other, the pair stuck together—each fearing bankruptcy without the other. Though a dinosaur and an inflated Liberace in the last year of his life, Elvis kept touring and the Colonel kept booking him. Meanwhile, they both hoped no more shit would hit the fan.

But hit the fan it did with the disastrous trifecta: first the $6 million lawsuit against the Guys, then Vernon firing the Guys, then the Guys exposing Elvis as a junkie in their the tell-all, *Elvis: What Happened?* The situation would have gotten a good deal more complicated had E's stepbrother David not dissuaded him from killing the Judases.

Afterward Elvis flew the *Lisa Marie* back to Graceland for some much needed R & R. Here he hatched a new, less drastic plan to discredit the book. He'd do another tour, and, on the last night, he would bring to the stage Dr. Nick himself who would explain to the fans his patient's very real medical needs without going into unnecessary details about lupus, cortisone poisoning, hormone replacement, and Schedule II protocols. Then Elvis would announce his engagement to his beautiful new fiancée, Ginger Alden. He'd have a Supreme Court justice perform the ceremony and invite leading politicians to the festivities.

This seemed like a workable image rehabilitation in his more sober moments, but later at night, the King couldn't help but fall victim to a mind-numbing pessimism and weariness.

Truth be told, he didn't even really want to marry Ginger Alden now, though he'd been head over heels when first meeting her. "Ginger sugar," he'd said, "you're burning a hole through me!" He told Dr. Nick she reminded him of his mother. Indeed, she was a Priscilla clone. Ginger had visited Graceland at the age of 5 and Elvis had treated her to a ride on his roller coaster. Sixteen years later, the King, on bended knee in his bathroom, slipped a $70,000 engagement ring onto her finger. But his infatuation had quickly faded. He discovered that Ginger, now Memphis's reigning Miss Public Safety, was fickle, temperamental, self-centered, and, he was convinced, having an affair with his stepbrother David.

Ginger was also disillusioned. Her fiancé wasn't the King, but a fading star who was constantly, she complained, "getting zonked out of his mind." And she hated touring with him. No sooner had she gotten back to Graceland than she refused to go with him to a Nashville recording session. The King fired shots over her head as she beat a retreat for the Lincoln Mark V he'd given her. "He was going to go ahead and slowly kill himself no matter what I did," Linda later said. "I couldn't make him happy, and I knew he wasn't going to change. So I left."

The Guys had a different take on the situation. "Ginger probably added to Elvis's downfall," said Marty Lacker. "She was always disappointing him. She didn't love him."

"Ginger didn't give a rat's ass about him," said Lamar with his customary euphemism.

Elvis had always said a man needs three things to be happy: Someone to love; Something to look forward to; and Something to *do*. He didn't love Ginger; he didn't look forward to anything personally or professionally; and he definitely didn't want to tour ever again. In one of his last performances, after his grand *Thus Spake Zarathustra* entrance, he had collapsed on stage, wept, and been carried out.

Just before he was scheduled to leave Graceland for the new tour, he called his stepbrother up to his room.

"David, I want to say good-bye," he told him.

"What do you mean?" asked his kid brother.

"The next time you see me," replied Elvis, "I will be in a different place, a higher plane."

David Stanley left without a word, taking this for just more of his famous brother's "drugged-out rambling."

ATTACK 3

> If I'd gone back up to E's bedroom, I might have found him. But I was abusing drugs too . . . I think it'd be safe to say I had enough Demerol going through me right then to sedate Whitehaven. So, instead, I went back to my own room and shot up.
> —Ricky Stanley, Elvis's stepbrother explaining to *People* magazine why he failed to find the body earlier

It's about 8:30 in the morning when the intercom sounds in Ricky's room. Though he's supposed to be on duty, he's been out cold since he delivered E his second prescription packet at around 4 A.M. Next door, his brother, David, isn't stirring either. It doesn't seem like anybody is up yet at Graceland—not Vernon, Dee, Uncle Vester, or anybody else.

The intercom just keeps buzzing.

Jimi Hendrix at Monterey Pop Festival, June 18, 1967.
(Photo by Jill Gibson/Michael Ochs Archives/Getty Images)

Hendrix in Hawaii, with Noel Redding, Mitch Mitchell, and friends, October 1968. (Photo by Michael Ochs Archives/Getty Images)

Janis Joplin, 1970. (Photo by Michael Ochs Archives/Getty Images)

Janis performing, 1970. (Photo by Tom Copi/Michael Ochs Archives/
Getty Images)

Jim Morrison, collapsed on stage, Frankfurt, Germany,
September 1968. (Photo by Michael Ochs Archives/Getty Images)

Morrison in church, 1970. (Photo by Michael Ochs Archives/Getty)

Morrison in Hollywood hills, with Pamela Courson, 1969.
(Photo by Estate of Edmund Teske/Michael Ochs)

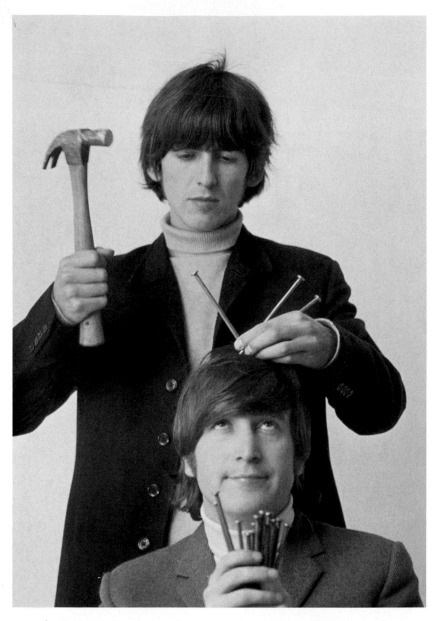

John Lennon, nailed by George Harrison during a studio session in Chelsea, London, March 1966. (Photo by Robert Whitaker/Hulton Archive/Getty Images)

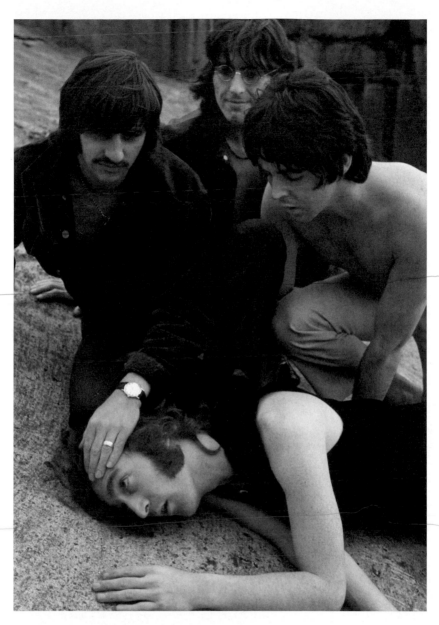

Lennon and the Beatles, London, July 1968.
(Courtesy Tom Murray USA)

Private Elvis Presley, with Vernon and Gladys, spring 1958, shortly before his mother's death. (Photo by Hulton Archive/Getty Images)

Elvis in concert, Asheville, North Carolina, July 1975.
(Photo by Michael Ochs Archives/Getty Images)

Kurt Cobain, live MTV performance, with *In Utero* mannequin angel, December 1993. (Photo by Jeff Kravitz/FilmMagic)

Cobain with Courtney Love and daughter, Frances Bean, at MTV
Music Video Awards, September 1993. (Photo by Paul Harris/Getty
Images)

Cobain (*right*) with (*from left*) Frances Bean, Courtney Love, lawyer Rosemary Carroll, and manager Danny Goldberg, at MTV Music Video Awards, September 1993. (Photo by Jeff Kravitz/FilmMagic)

Jerry Garcia and the Grateful Dead in concert. (Photo by Robi Cohn)

Garcia (*center*), reluctant Grateful Dead leader, with (*from left*)
Bob Weir, Bill Kreutzmann, and Phil Lesh, in San Francisco, 1968.
(Photo by Michael Ochs Archives/Getty Images)

It finally stops when a light-but-urgent knock sounds at the door of the master bedroom. Suddenly, the door cracks open. Then a whisper from outside into the darkness within—"Lord knows what's happened to those boys!" says Aunt Delta Mae, Graceland's housekeeper. She hands over a third packet and it's snatched up. "There you go, hon," she says. "You get yourself some rest now and I'll see to them damn boys."

Elvis's Graceland medication packets differ from his six-stage, on-tour protocol from Dr. Nick. Administered hours apart, they are three nearly identical narcotic cocktails which the Stanley brothers call "Attacks 1, 2, and 3."

The King tears open the new packet, downs its contents, then gropes through the darkness back to bed. Ginger is curled up on a corner of the nine-foot-diameter platform. She hasn't moved since Ricky dropped by a few hours ago and gave her something to take the edge off her menstrual cramps.

Elvis collapses on the bed, leans his head back against the black quilted Naugahyde headboard, and waits for Attack 3 to kick in. It is a bright, already sultry Memphis morning, but huge air conditioners keep the room frigid and the crimson drapes are drawn. The only light is provided by lava lamps, the enormous TV set perched over the bed with the volume off, and the closed-circuit screen tuned in to the Graceland Music Gate where fans are already beginning to congregate, hoping to catch a glimpse of the King today.

He glances down from the screens toward the night table. On it is a photograph of Gladys who was laid to rest this very day, nineteen years ago. The anniversary of his mother's funeral has not become any easier for the singer, and he remembers it as if it were only yesterday. How he had combed her hair in the open casket, how he had caressed her satin hands, her feet, her face.

Still restless, the King struggles to his feet and inches toward the bathroom, gripping the furniture for ballast. He's annoyed that Ricky, David, and the others aren't answering the buzzer this morning. Due to his weight and medications, it's often necessary for them to carry him to the bathroom.

Ginger stirs as he opens the door. "Precious, I'm going to go to the bathroom and read for a while," he says.

"Okay," she murmurs groggily, "but don't go to sleep."

"Don't worry, I won't," he says, closing the door of his inner sanctum behind him.

His bathroom, where he is accustomed to spending hours, has a wide-

screen TV, two phones, an intercom, and shelves with his favorite reading material. He picks up *Sex and Psychic Energy*,[6] and settles down
on his enormous toilet with its padded seat. As he thumbs through
the erotic picture book, he begins to nod off, Attack 3—Quaaludes,
Placidyl, Valmid, and Demerol—beginning to finally kick in. But suddenly he's feeling very hot and itchy. The sensation first came on after
his midnight dental appointment. He'd been administered codeine for
a cavity repair. While lying awake in bed waiting for the delivery of
Attack 3, he'd swallowed the entire codeine prescription the dentist
had given him, plus six extra Dilaudids Ricky had delivered just before
crashing himself.

Soon he's beginning to perspire heavily, he's dizzy, and he can't
catch his breath. Just like it had been exactly two years ago when he
was suffocating on his airplane.

Suddenly, he gasps, flings the book from him violently, collapses, and
smashes his head on the floor. Flailing, he bites his tongue in half, and
his mouth fills with blood, which overflows onto the crimson carpet.

Hours later, just after noon, a timid knock sounds on the closed bathroom door.

When there is no reply, the door opens and Ginger Alden—smartly
dressed, carefully coiffed and madeup—is standing there, statue still,
eyes widening.

A book lies on the red shag carpet, and, scattered around it, are
cologne bottles that have been knocked off the bathroom counter. Just
beyond them lies Elvis Presley. His gold pajama bottoms are around his
ankles, his limbs are rigid, his mouth is agape, his severed tongue is
black, and his skin is livid blue. "He was on his left side with his knees
drawn, and his hands underneath his face," recalled Marty Lacker. "He
was almost in a praying position."

Ginger dashes to the phone. She calls her mother first. Then, according to Billy Smith, she calls Jim Kirk, a reporter for the *National
Enquirer*.[7] At last, she picks up the in-house phone.

---

6. Elvis mythology has it that the last book he picked up was on the Shroud of
Turin.

7. In Alanna Nash's *Elvis and the Memphis Mafia*, with Billy Smith, Marty Lacker,
and Lamar Fike (New York: Harper Collins, 1995), Smith states that he concluded
this as a result of a bugged interview with Kirk after Elvis's death. Moreover, "We
guess she [Ginger] called him [Kirk] twice and struck a deal with him for her story
and a page-one fee, for $105,000."

Momentarily, she is with Al Strada, Elvis's valet, and Joe Esposito, his road manager. They are stooped over Elvis, slapping his face, shouting hysterically. Joe tries mouth-to-mouth resuscitation while Al calls 911.

By the time the paramedics arrive, they have no idea that the body on the floor is that of Elvis Presley. One would later recall that the patient, due to the lividity, appeared to be a huge black man. This was not the first time the paramedics had received an anonymous emergency call from Graceland.

The room is in pandemonium as the EMTs try to revive Elvis. Everyone is there now: David, Ricky, Marty, Aunt Delta Mae, Charlie Hodge, Vernon, and Dr. Nick himself. Little Lisa Marie bursts in, crying, "What's wrong with my daddy?" but is quickly hustled out.

"Do something! Do something!" Aunt Delta Mae is sobbing.

"Breathe, Elvis! Breathe!" begs Charlie Hodge. "Don't die! Please don't die!"

"Oh, no! My son is dead!" wails Vernon. He begins desperately grasping for him. "Son, I'm coming. I'll be there! I'll be meetin' you there!"

Only his stepbrothers, Ricky and David, stand by speechless. As does Al Strada. For months now they'd been making bets as to when Elvis would die. Al takes one of the medics aside and tells him what they all already know. "We think he OD'd."

Later David Stanley would confess: "No one can tell me that he did anything but commit suicide." Then, he added: "Yes, it took him two years to finally do it, and yes, his heart did give out, but it was suicide, plain and simple." Gazing down at the lifeless body now, remembering Elvis's final words to him only days before, David says, "You son of a bitch!"[8]

The body of Elvis Presley is taken to Baptist Memorial Hospital in Memphis and admitted as Mr. John Doe. Though it is clearly lifeless, trauma surgeons make heroic attempts at revival. They try open heart message. They pump the stomach. They perform an emergency thoracotomy, suctioning the vomit from the windpipe and inserting a tube to reinflate the lungs.

All to no avail.

The King of Rock and Roll is declared dead at 3 P.M., August 16,

---

8. David Stanley, *Raised on Rock: Growing Up at Graceland*, with Mark Bego (UK: Trafalgar Square, 1997).

1977. In fact, he had died six hours earlier while everyone at Graceland was asleep.

A complete autopsy was performed.[9] The chest cavity was opened. The heart was found to be enlarged and "like brown flab." The liver was also severely deteriorated, as were the arteries—sure signs of lupus and radical substance abuse. The colon, four times the average size, was impacted with chalklike fecal matter. The top of the head was sawed off and the brain removed. No signs of blunt trauma or foul play were discovered.

The pathologists disposed of the organs and sewed the body back up empty. Then it was sent to the embalmer, cosmetician, and hairdresser—Larry Geller himself—for open casket viewing.

Dr. Nick, who was on hand for the autopsy, insisted that the cause of death was "cardiac arrhythmia, coronary artery disease, hypertension, and diabetes mellitus, plus fatty liver." Chief pathologist, Dr. Jerry Francisco, concurred with the heart attack theory and signed the death certificate.

"Basically, it was a natural death," Francisco announced that evening at a press conference, Dr. Nick sitting beside him. "It may take several weeks to discover the exact cause of death. The precise cause may never be discovered."

A cover-up was already in progress. The contents of the singer's stomach were destroyed without being analyzed. No coroner's inquest was ordered. The medical examiner's notes, toxicology report, and photos disappeared from the official files. And, ever the faithful "lifer" till the end, David Stanley had disposed of all the drugs and syringes in Elvis's room before investigators arrived.[10]

Other cause of death theories abounded, even in the Memphis medical community. Some said Elvis died of lupus, others of bone cancer, others of stroke. Still others believed he had been murdered by Mike Stone, Dave Hebler, or another martial arts expert.

The truth did not surface till nearly two years later, the result of an intensive ABC News investigation and several private investigations. The most notable of these examinations was carried out by retired

---

9. Elvis had refused an autopsy for his mother, insisting he didn't want to know how she died.

10. "There were millions and millions of dollars wrapped up in Elvis's various insurance policies," explained David. "If they even got a whiff of the theory that Elvis died of a self-induced drug overdose then a fortune was at stake."

Memphis detectives Charles C. Thompson II and James P. Cole, who would reveal their findings in *The Death of Elvis: What Really Happened.*

According to Thompson and Cole, ten controlled substances were discovered in Elvis's bloodstream, though not originally reported.[11] In short, the true cause of Elvis's death was "Poly-Pharmacy"—the deadly interaction of these narcotics.

The most virulent ingredient in the mix was codeine, to which Elvis was allergic. Sixteen times the average therapeutic dose was discovered in his liver and twenty-three times the average dose in his kidneys. Elvis knew quite well that he was allergic to all but mild doses of codeine, but he had clearly taken an enormous quantity. And Elvis, a pharmaceutical expert, certainly knew this could be a fatal mix with his three Attack packets of narcotics.

Toxicologist Dr. Randall Baselt stated that the codeine alone could have killed him. He would have gone into anaphylactic shock and been unable to breathe.

"Elvis suffocated," later confirmed his own physician, Dr. Elias Ghanem. "Anytime a person bites through his tongue, he's suffocating."

POSTMORTEM

Twenty thousand mourners passed through the Music Gates to view the King of Rock and Roll lying in state at Graceland, which was thronged with five tons of flowers. Sixty thousand more lined Elvis Presley Boulevard awaiting their turn to bid their idol good-bye. When the Music Gates were closed at dusk, a riot nearly ensued. The funeral procession, led by sixteen white Cadillacs, was miles long.

Shortly after the internment, Elvis's father, Vernon, took his stepson aside. "David," he said. "I've got to ask you a question. Did you kill my son?"

David could hardly believe his ears.

"The last conversation I had with Elvis," continued Vernon, "he said you and Ginger were having an affair."

---

11. Codeine, Morphine, Quaalude, Valium, Valmid, Placidyl, Amytal, Nembutal, Carbrital, Demerol. Dilaudid would also have been detected had his stomach contents not been destroyed.

David begged his stepfather to believe that nothing of the kind had ever happened and that he, like Vernon, had only had one thing in mind, always: Elvis's welfare.

Vernon was satisfied. For years, he too had tried in vain to control his son's self-destructive habits. Nor did he have any doubts about who had fed those habits. Nevertheless, protecting Elvis's image was still the order of the day. So Vernon had allowed Dr. Nichopoulos to be one of his son's pallbearers. But he intended to settle scores.

Not long after Elvis was laid to rest, Dr. Nick was at Memphis's Liberty Bowl football game when his companion, Dr. Charles Langford, suddenly collapsed, stricken by a bullet to the shoulder. The police failed to apprehend the assassin in the crowded stadium.

Hearing about the incident, Elvis's father was disgusted. "They shot the wrong damn doctor!" he told Ginger's mother afterward.

Vernon died of heart failure the summer of the following year. He was laid to rest beside Elvis and Gladys at Graceland.

The graves had been moved from Forest Hill Cemetery to Graceland the previous fall after three men tried to dig up Elvis's coffin to prove that it was empty and that the King had risen.

The King did indeed rise. He sold more records after his passing than the already unrivaled quantity he had during his life. Total sales currently exceed a billion. In the 80s he was inducted into all three halls of fame: Rock, Country, and Gospel—the triple crown bestowed on no other recording artist. Also without precedent, he has had ninety-seven gold albums, fifty-three gold and platinum singles, and 385 hits. As if this were not enough, he starred in thirty-one movies, some among the top-grossing films in their time.

Few disagree that Elvis Presley was among the greatest, if not the greatest, entertainer of all time. "I am not the King, Jesus Christ is the King," he declared. "I'm just an entertainer . . . That's my whole life. To my last breath." He was the only one of the Seven who was a true solo entertainer, in the classic sense. But an entertainer of unrivaled range and power: he could croon like Crosby and Sinatra; he could rock and roll like Little Richard and Jerry Lee; and he might have approached Dean and Brando had he been given the parts. The secret of his legendary success was not only his ambition, which he called "a dream with a V-8 engine," but his inestimable talent that he called "being able to sell what you're feeling." No entertainer before or since has been able to telegraph their feelings the way Elvis did, enthralling audiences young and old throughout the world. Stars unanimously pay tribute to him, not only as an indispensable inspiration, but as the founding father.

"If there hadn't been an Elvis, there wouldn't have been the Beatles," said Lennon.

"Elvis is the best ever, the most original," said Morrison. "He started the ball rolling for us all."

"No one, but no one, is his equal, or ever will be," said Jagger. "He was, and is supreme."

That he himself owed a debt to black musicians, Elvis was the first to acknowledge. "Nobody paid it no mind 'til I goosed it up," he admitted. "I got it from them." But he did far more than "goose it up." Said Al Green, "He broke the ice for all of us." Said Little Richard, "He opened the door for black music."

As Bruce Springsteen observed, where Dylan "freed the mind," Elvis "freed the body." But more than bringing the physical, the primal, the sexual to rock and roll, he electrified it with a soulful passion and love that moved people like no other music had. He loved his audiences more than any other entertainer, and that love came through in songs he and his fans believed came from a power greater than himself.

"My voice is God's will," said Elvis Presley, "not mine."

Interlude: Mr. D

Down in the graveyard where we had our tryst . . .
Lord, I was dancin', dancin', dancin' so free!
Dancin' with Mr. D.
   —Jagger and Richards, "Dancing with Mr. D"

Linda Thompson once asked Elvis what his greatest character flaw was. "I'm self-destructive," he replied. "But there's not a lot I can do about it." She and many other loved ones desperately tried to help. But they found that they couldn't do anything about it, either.

"I think that over his final two years, Elvis consciously killed himself," wrote David Stanley. "He killed himself because it was his last great act of humiliation towards himself . . . to prove to himself that he was just a human being. . . . His death finally humanized the King of Rock and Roll."

The same could be said of the other stars.

When Janis was beginning her singing career, she wrote her parents, "I'm sure you're both convinced my self-destructive streak has won out again . . . but I do plan on coming back to school." A few years later, after her twenty-fifth birthday, Janis wrote another letter home which began, "Twenty-five? I never thought I'd even survive this long."

In spite of achieving the fame she so craved, the Queen of the Blues suffered "the most complete abysmal empty isolation that the heart can know," wrote Myra Friedman. She had told Myra, "I only live to perform. That's the only time I feel. . . . Man, if it hadn't been for the music, I probably would have done myself in."

Though Janis often talked about doing this, she tried to pull herself from the black hole. "You may not end up happy, but I'm fucked if I'm not going to try," she said. "That's like committing suicide the day you're born, if you don't try." But in the end, as with Elvis, there was not a lot she could do to save herself.

The others were suicidal too. "Jimi had talked to me about suicide and death a lot," said Eric Burdon. Cobain, who wanted to entitle Nirvana's fourth album, *I Hate Myself and Want to Die*, was fond of doing photo ops with pistols in his mouth. Robby Krieger, recalling one of Morrison's "depression trips," confessed, "He just didn't think it was worth it anymore and life was horrible . . . so we spent all night talking him out of killing himself." As for the upside of self-euthansia, Morrison's mentor, Nietzsche, said, "It is always consoling to think of suicide: in that way one gets through many a bad night."

Lennon was no stranger to bad nights himself. When he was separated from Yoko in the early 70s, he admitted to trying to "drown himself" with the biggest boozers in the industry. "But, Jesus, I had to get away from that," he told an interviewer, "because somebody was going to die. Keith Moon did. It was like who is going to die first." Though he left his sidekicks in L.A. and returned to New York, there he started chasing his vodka with heroin. "My goal was to obliterate my mind so I wouldn't be conscious. I think I was suicidal on some kind of a subconscious level." He regained some stability after reuniting with Yoko. But toward the end of his life, according to his diaries, he was doing smack again and giving thought to throwing himself out the window of his cell in the Dakota. After one of his beloved Persian cats, Alice, did fall to her death from his window, his young son, Sean, had asked him, "Why don't you go out the window, Daddy?"[1]

Jerry Garcia wasn't as self-destructive as Lennon or the others. But after more than three decades on the road, he got that way. In those years he had watched many bandmates and friends self-destruct, but believing in the sanctity of freewill, Garcia had never intervened. Early in the Grateful Dead's career, their lyricist, Robert Hunter, wrote the Ten Commandments of Rock and Roll. The tenth read, "Destroy yourself physically and morally and insist that all true brothers do likewise as an expression of unity."

The death trip of each star was rooted in many different things, but in the end, there was one commonality: terminal regret. Though idolized by millions, each had fallen short of his greatest ambition.

Head in the lap of his girlfriend Linda Thompson, the King mourned, "How will they remember me? They're not going to remember me. I've

---

1. John Green, *Dakota Days* (New York: St. Martin's, 1983).

never done anything lasting. I've never done a classic film." Though Lennon wanted to "conquer the world again," he told a confidante, "They've got me nailed in a coffin called the past. . . . They've made me into another Elvis and I don't even own the rights to the fucking songs." Morrison, who had always wanted to be a great poet like his heroes Rimbaud or Blake, said, "I'd like to write something of great importance. That's my ambition—to write something worthwhile." Hendrix wanted to abandon performance and compose a completely new kind of music combining symphony, jazz, and improvisational rock. In spite of her brilliant last album, *Pearl*, Janis said, "I'm not a star. I'm just an old chick with a loud voice." As for Cobain, "I can't enjoy it anymore. I'm too crazy, empathetic. I'm sorry beyond words."

The stars' regrets weighed on them heavily and fueled their drug habits. In the last days, they all looked posthumous, even Garcia. Of the Dead's last tour, his bandmate, Phil Lesh, recalled, "Jerry looked, acted, and sounded as if he were already at death's door." Ten years before this, the guitarist hadn't been much healthier. At a gig in '84, he appeared "not just dead but like a creature who'd returned from beyond the grave," said writer Robert Greenfield. "His skin seemed to glow a dull gray green."

As we have seen, none of the Seven had expected to die of old age anyway. As for Elvis, few of his relatives had enjoyed longevity, and he didn't expect to either. In his final years, the King became ghoulishly curious. "His fascination with human corpses is downright terrifying," said Sonny West. The singer often visited graveyards and dropped in on mortuaries to watch embalmings and corpse cosmetic makeovers.

Since the stars anticipated meeting the Reaper sooner rather than later, there was a sense of resignation and even of relief for some. "People fear death even more than pain," said Morrison. "It's strange that they fear death. Life hurts a lot more than death. At the point of death, the pain is over. Yeah, I guess it [the End] is my friend."

Lennon was of the same mind. "Being dead is really not so bad," he told his spiritual advisor, John Green. "Take my advice and get through the dying part as quickly as possible. Then you're dead and everything is alright."

Most hoped for a quick and brilliant transition. Inspired by *The Tibetan Book of the Dead*, Lennon expected—as he sang in "Tomorrow Never Knows"—to "relax, sit back . . . and surrender to the shining void." Morrison wanted to vanish "like a fiery comet—whoosh, and I'm gone!" Cobain imagined he would "go out in a flame of glory." Garcia blew out a candle and said, "That's the way I'm going to go."

As for the actual sensation of dying, Morrison was the most curious of all, wanting to "taste it, hear it, smell it." Lennon, who believed he was destined to be shot, asked his assistant's uncle, a gunshot victim himself, "how it feels to take a slug." He might have asked Mal Evans, but his close friend, gunned down by the LAPD in 1972, hadn't lived to tell about it. Or he might have asked Peter Fonda for the specifics. The actor, who had accidentally shot himself as a boy, dropped acid with John at a party and told him, "I know what it's like to be dead." The Beatle wrote "She Said She Said" and put the line in a lover's mouth: "She said, 'I know what it's like to be dead' . . . and she's makin' me feel like I've never been born."

The only one of the Seven who did clinically die and come back to tell about it was Jerry Garcia. While in a four-day coma, the Dead's guitarist flatlined. He described the state as "a tremendous struggle in a sort of futuristic spaceship vehicle with insectoid presences . . . big beetles rushing into tubes." Years before, when his keyboardist, Pigpen, cashed out, Jerry was envious. "That motherfucker," he told bassist Phil Lesh after Pig's wake, "now he *knows.*"

Elvis, Janis, and Kurt, having suffered numerous near fatal ODs between them, had come almost as close to the Reaper as the comatose Jerry. In this sense, each had experienced pre-deaths and had miraculously survived to live the lives of cats.

None of the Seven believed the end was the end, so their dances with death seemed less dangerous from the resurrection point of view.

"Meet you in the next world, don't be late," sang Hendrix.

Elvis looked forward to being "on a higher plane" and still watching over his loved ones.

"Hang around for THIS?" exclaimed Garcia, grabbing his gut, "You've got to be kidding. When I'm dead, I'm OUTTA here!"

"The dead are newborn awakening, with ravaged limbs and wet souls," Morrison sang in "American Prayer." "Who called these dead to dance?"[2] The lyrics were no doubt inspired by the words of his favor-

---

2. Arguably, Morrison was the forerunner of 80s and 90s Death Metal groups such as Megadeth, Metallica, Morbid Angel, Napalm Death, Anthrax, Suicidal Tendencies, and so on.

ite philosopher, "Let us beware of saying that death is the opposite of life," wrote Nietzsche. "The living being is only a species of the dead, and a very rare species."

Many rock legends have physically burned out or come very close because they had been unable or unwilling to separate their explosive onstage persona from their lives. Hendrix, Morrison, Janis, and the others, would never have become legends had their lives and their performances not been the same. They died by rock because they had *lived* by rock. "For me, it was never really an 'act', those so-called performances," Morrison told an interviewer. "It was a life and death thing."

He and the others were like aerialists working without nets, unlike their more cautious colleagues. "Rock'n'roll is like a drug," Neil Young pointed out. "I don't take very much, but when I do rock'n'roll, I fuckin' do it. But I don't want to do it all the time 'cause it'll kill me." Bruce Springsteen's secret of survival was staying, in his words "very concerned about being in control." Said Jagger, "Anything worth doing is worth overdoing." But like Young, Springsteen, and the other rock survivors, before overdoing it, Jumpin' Jack Flash always made sure his parachute was secure. Not so with most of the Seven. Each was a rock-and-roll Icarus; both for themselves and for their breathless audiences, wearing a parachute would have taken all the exhilaration out of their spectacular death-defying skydives.

Besides, each was a fatalist. When your time is up, it's up, they believed. The Reaper laughs at the cautious. So waiting for their number to come up, each danced with Mr. D in the meantime. It was a dance of material destruction: smashing guitars, trashing hotel rooms, shooting TV's, inciting riots, and, most exhilarating of all—crashing cars.

The history of rockers and their car wrecks, fatal and near fatal, is long and rich. Race car driving and playing rock and roll have much in common, not the least of which is the marriage of danger and excitement. Most stars would agree with Mario Andretti, "Except for death," said the champion racer, "everything else is a minor injury."

Elvis totaled his first Cadillac in 1956 and would have many more close scrapes. But that didn't stop him and the Guys from playing Chicken in their Harleys at 120 miles per hour on Elvis Presley Boulevard.

In addition to all the guitars and hotel suites he smashed up, Hendrix totaled six Corvettes in two years. Once, hurdling down the winding roads of Benedict Canyon, the unlicensed, severely nearsighted Jimi nearly flew off a cliff. He walked away from his Stingray cantilevered on a tree and promptly bought himself another.

Janis's Porsche Cabriolet Super C with its psychedelic paint job "was her pride and joy," remembered her producer, Paul Rothchild. "We both had Porsches. We'd race along Sunset Boulevard and Laurel Canyon. She was a lot crazier than I was—and I was *nuts*. She'd go against traffic on blind curves, with the top down, laughing, "Nothing can knock me down!"

Jerry Garcia who, like Lennon, lost his mother in a car accident, miraculously survived a crash of his own before founding the Grateful Dead. Later on, he was again spared when his BMW slammed through a freeway divider into oncoming traffic. Near the end, Phil Lesh, who had survived three near fatal crashes himself, made the mistake of driving with a pissed-off, DUI Garcia to a detox facility. "To this day, I don't think I've ever been so frightened in a car," wrote Lesh. ". . . I had to wonder if Jerry was feeling suicidal—or murderous. I was shaky, and sweating bullets."[3]

Cobain enjoyed destroying stuff as much as the next guy, especially Strats, amps, stages, tour buses, and whatever five-star hotel was foolish enough to book him. As for driving, the son of the Texaco mechanic told *The Advocate*, "I'm not that bad a driver, and I get in a wreck almost every day."

The most colorful and adventurous Mr. D demo derby partner was the Lizard King. In his Mustang Shelby GT, the ghostly Blue Lady, he parked on the railroad tracks and played Chicken with locomotives. Otherwise, he bailed out of speeding cars and jumped into the middle of freeway traffic, playing matador with semis.

From the ordinary mortal point of view, this might have seemed like the *Titanic* looking for an iceberg. But Morrison and his ilk had a different perspective. Each seemed to believe that, since an early end was their fate, they—like Achilles, Crazy Horse, or Evel Knievel—were immortal before the clock struck twelve.

Lennon thought he was driving with karmic insurance, too, at least in the beginning. During the filming of *Help!* in the Caribbean, he, Paul, George, and Ringo, chased each other around at 100-plus miles per hour in rented Cadillacs. "It was a terrific feeling smashing up all those shiny limos," recalled John. Returning home, George bought a

---

3. Phil Lesh, *Searching for the Sound*.

Ferrari, and John—though almost legally blind—decided he had to have one too. Pitting his Dino against his friend Pete Shotton's Spitfire, he enjoyed what he called "the most fantastic kick I've had in ages!" while Pete described the experience as "the most hair-raising experience of my life." Riding shotgun with the Beatle was even worse. "John was an appalling driver," wrote Cynthia Lennon whom he gave a VW bug. "His passengers suffered a hideous roller coaster ride . . . at breathtaking speed." After shutting down Shotton, John took on Ringo in the drummer's Facel Vega, but retired from NASCAR after nearly crashing into another motorist at 150 miles per hour. Finally, he traded the Ferrari in for a Rolls after his racing rival and fellow kamikaze, Tara Browne, ran a light and drove his Lotus through a lorry in Kensington. "He blew his mind out in a car," sang John in "A Day in the Life" on *Sgt. Pepper's*, "he didn't notice that the lights had changed."

But soon the Beatle nearly suffered the same fate. Driving his Austin Maxi with Yoko and their kids, he was grooving on the Scottish countryside when a ditch suddenly ambushed him. "We're alive!" he cried, scrambling out from under the upside-down coupe with Yoko, her daughter Kyoto, and his son Julian.

He got seventeen stitches and a sculpture out of it. Yoko installed the wreckage on a pedestal outside the living room of their Tittenhurst Park mansion, calling it "A Tribute to Survival."

As if the stars were not preoccupied enough with Mr. D, most received regular notes from him in the form of death threats. Generally, the number was proportionate to the star's fame. Elvis got the most, with Lennon a close second, followed by Garcia, Morrison, and Hendrix. Janis and Kurt were largely ignored maybe because potential assassins felt that they were doing a good enough job killing themselves.

Elvis didn't get too concerned about his early death threats because they were mostly from boyfriends and husbands who couldn't take a little competition. The JFK assassination changed the King's tune. He now started collecting guns and bodyguards. Then, when the Manson murders went down, it was "as serious as a six-car pileup," recalled Fike. Hearing that he was on Manson's hit list,[4] Elvis, playing Vegas at the time, packed everybody up and took cover at Graceland. Now

---

4. Charles Manson, an aspiring rock musician inspired by the Beatles' *Helter Skelter*, had also threatened Hendrix and Lennon.

his gun collection turned into an armory worthy of Fort Dix, and his employees became the Secret Service.

"Goddammit, if anybody ever assassinates me, I want you guys to get to him before the police do," he ordered them. "I want you to pull his eyes out, rip his throat apart, and kill that son of a bitch!"

Since childhood, Elvis had been plagued with nightmares about manglers and murderers. He later became nocturnal due to his paranoia. "I stay up all night, and I have my friends with me, and I feel comfortable," he would later reveal. "In the morning when everybody else is up, I feel safe because it's daytime—and then I can go to sleep." Even then, he would sometimes crawl into bed with one of the Guys.

If the Manson murders woke up the King, a few months later Altamont roused the rest of the rock community. The Grateful Dead, an organizer of the free concert along with the Rolling Stones, refused to play after the Hell's Angels' homicidal mayhem set in. Now the great post-Altamont guns-for-guitars swap began. Jagger and Richards, whom the Angels put a contract out on, started packing heat and security teams.[5] So did Zeppelin, the Who, Dylan, and all the other major acts. The days of "All You Need is Love" had given way to "Let it Bleed" and "Sympathy for the Devil."

Although Jerry Garcia, a longtime friend and champion of the Angels, left the speedway unscathed, plenty of death threats came his way in the next twenty years. By the time he got his last one before an Indiana concert in 1995, he'd become stubborn. Security begged him to cancel the Dead show but he refused, saying, "There's no way I'm going to let that stop me; hell no. I've been getting crackpots all my life."

Like Elvis, John Lennon got his first death threats early on. They came from drunk German sailors whose girlfriends he scored at the clubs or from the ones he rolled for Deutschemarks in the back alleys of Hamburg. But he didn't get his first official notice until '66 after the Jesus-Beatles comparison. He took the threat pretty much in stride until, soon afterward, a psychic told him he would be shot down during his upcoming U.S. trip. "I was totally paranoid the whole time," he said of the Beatles' last visit to the states, which he dubbed "The Jesus

---

5. According to a 2008 BBC documentary, the motorcycle gang hatched a plot to assassinate Jagger in 1969 at his Long Island holiday retreat. Attempting an assault by sea, they might have succeeded had their boat not capsized during a storm.

Christ Tour." "Everywhere we played I was just waiting for something dreadful to happen." Onstage in Memphis, he heard a firecracker go off that he mistook for a gunshot. "My immediate reaction was to check meself to see if I'd been hit," he recalled. "Fucking hell," I thought. "At least they haven't gotten me!"

Hardly had the Fab Four returned to London with relief when their manager, Brian Epstein, suffered a near fatal narcotic overdose. A year later, he committed suicide. John, in his Transcendental Meditation period then, seemed stoical, saying, "The Maharishi told us that death is just an illusion, and we mustn't get depressed about it." Besides, by this time he was funeral numb. "I had the feeling that anybody has when somebody close to them dies," he went on. "There is a sort of little hysterical, sort of hee, hee, 'I'm glad it's not me.' . . . I've had a lot of people die around me and the other feeling is, 'What the fuck? What can I do.' "

It was almost like Elvis when he confessed that his greatest flaw was being self-destructive "but there's not a lot I can do about it."

The Beatles hired a medium to contact Epstein's spirit, but "it was all bullshit," said John. In Brian's effects he stumbled on a final tape recording by his manager that terrified him. "It was barely recognizable as a human voice," wrote Pete Shotton, "alternately groaning, grunting, and shrieking." After Brian's death, John began to have nightmares. According to his diary, he dreamed of being "trapped in a maze full of giant spiders." In another dream, he "stashed decapitated heads in a garden." In a third, he saw "shrieking lobsters on dinner plates."

By the end of his life, according to his assistant, Fred Seaman, John was suffering recurring nightmares about a violent death. In one of the last, according to his diary, he dreamt of "reading in his own obituary . . . that he had been charged with his own homicide at the Dakota."[6]

---

6. Geoffrey Giuliano, *Lennon in America: 1971–1980, Based in Part on the Lost Diaries* (New York: Cooper Square Press, 2000).

5

JOHN LENNON

October 9, 1940–December 8, 1980

DOUBLE FANTASY

> People say I'm crazy doing what I'm doing.
> Well, they give me all kinds of warnings to save me from ruin.
> When I say that I'm o.k., well, they look at me kind of strange;
> Surely you're not happy now you no longer play the game.
> —John Lennon, "Watching the Wheels"

In 1980 John Lennon and Yoko Ono hired ex-FBI agent Douglas Mac-Dougall to handle their security. Aside from the death threats John had received over the years, kidnappers had recently threatened his young son, Sean. At the time the couple contacted MacDougall, they were launching "a media blitz like you've never seen," as John called it, for their long-awaited collaborative album, *Double Fantasy*. So, understandably, they were concerned about their safety.

MacDougall told Yoko that their current security measures in New York were dangerously inadequate. He recommended the Lennons hire two armed bodyguards to ride in their limousine between the Dakota and the Record Plant, their recording studio across town. Failing this, he suggested they station one bodyguard at the studio and another at the apartment. Yoko promised to get back to the retired FBI man after conferring with her husband.

In an interview with the *Daily News*, Yoko revealed John's and her daily recording schedule as well as their route to and from the studio. MacDougall was furious. He told Yoko that publicizing details like this was "an open invitation to every wacko in the country to come after you!" Yoko pointed out that her first concern was "selling records." She also informed MacDougall that she and John had decided against his suggestion for bodyguards.

When the *Double Fantasy* producer, Jack Douglas, asked John why he and Yoko had rejected MacDougall's plan, he replied, "It's my rationale that if they're gonna get ya, they're gonna get you anyway. First they kill the bodyguard."

John had just emerged from a five-year "househusband" hibernation at the Dakota, he had just turned forty, and was experiencing a new lease on life as a non-Beatle. "I'm happy to be forty years old," he told Douglas. "I'm in the best shape I've ever been in my life, and I feel the best I ever felt."

True, he had a hole in his septum from snorting too much cocaine and heroin during his sabbatical. But now he was clean at least of smack, and he was scheduled for a surgical repair after *Double Fantasy* was launched. Then he planned a Broadway show about Yoko and him, as well as other albums, the first to be with Ringo.

But John Lennon had always been prone to oscillations in mood and outlook. In spite of his apparent optimism, he'd recently confided to Douglas that his days "were numbered" and that he was living "on borrowed time." In a burst of creativity while vacationing in Bermuda that spring, he composed "Living on Borrowed Time," after the Bob Marley song of the same name. "That's it!" he told his assistant, Fred Seaman, when first hearing the tune. "That's the phrase I've been looking for. That's going to be my first new song!"

John had been preoccupied with the idea of an early demise even as a Beatle. Philip Norman[1] recounts an incident in 1964 when a friend, the beautiful socialite Sonny Freeman, told John about how her father was shot dead by a Nazi soldier; John replied that he'd always had a premonition that he, too, would be shot at a young age. Several years later, the Beatle played Musketeer Gripweed in the comic film noire, *How I Won the War*, and when he was shot and bloodied under enemy fire, said, "I knew this would happen."

---

1. Philip Norman, *John Lennon: The Life*. (New York: Ecco, 2008).

Death had already claimed many of his closest friends and relatives: his mother, Julia; his Uncle George; his best friend, Stu Sutcliff. Then, in 1968, the Beatles' manager Brian Epstein fatally overdosed. After Epstein's death, John held séances. He had always been fascinated by the otherworld and the metaphysical.

Yoko had inspired this fascination. In the seventies, she consulted many occultists—from exorcists, to astrologers, to tarot readers. While in a trance, her first New York psychic, Frank Andrews, told her: "Your husband sleeps in blood. . . . I don't feel he has a happy ending. I see him covered in blood." Though Yoko didn't relay the information to John, she encouraged him to consult Andrews personally. Finally agreeing to a private meeting at the Dakota, his first and most urgent question to Andrews was, Will I make it to forty?

"Till at least forty-four," replied the clairvoyant.

But shortly after her husband's 40th birthday, Yoko consulted several other psychics. One told her she saw a "long-haired woman . . . crying like crazy."

At 5 P.M. on December 8, 1980, John, having just finished a phone interview with a San Francisco radio station, emerged from the Dakota with Yoko. On the way to the limo at the curb, he was accosted by a pudgy, bespectacled young man holding out his new album. Where fans were concerned, the Beatle had always wavered between impatience and indulgence. In an obliging mood that day, he signed the album "John Lennon, 1980."

"Thanks, John!" the exhilarated fan finally stammered. Then he watched his idol disappear in the limousine.

In one hand, Mark David Chapman held his signed *Double Fantasy*. In the other, inside his jacket pocket, he clutched a five-shot .38 snub nose revolver.

WATCHING THE WHEELS

People say I'm lazy dreaming my life away.
Well, they give me all kinds of advice designed to enlighten me.
When I tell them that I'm doing fine watching shadows on the wall,
Don't you miss the big time boy you're no longer on the ball. . . .

No longer riding on the merry-go-round.
I just had to let it go.
—John Lennon, "Watching the Wheels"

John Lennon and "Mother," as he had called Yoko since the birth of Sean five years before, were on their way again to the Record Plant where they were mixing her new single "Walking on Thin Ice." *Double Fantasy* had just been released three weeks before to mixed reviews. Yoko was already concentrating her efforts on the launch of her solo career.

That morning, the Lennons had posed for the famed Annie Leibovitz *Rolling Stone* cover photo: a naked, skeletal John lying curled in a fetal position around an impassive, fully clothed Yoko. Weeks before, Mother had arranged another photo-op, this time a video for *Double Fantasy*. John straddled Yoko, "dry humping her for thirty minutes with grim determination," according to Fred Seaman.[2]

The couple hadn't had sex in some time. And though John wasn't keen on the exhibitionism, he left all career promotional details up to Mother. Not only did he hate business, but he had always feared making decisions of any sort.

He confided to Fred that his indecisiveness dated back to a boyhood trauma. His father, Freddie, in the merchant marine, returned to Liverpool after an extended voyage and insisted on moving the family to New Zealand. His wife, Julia, then pregnant with another man's child, refused. So the couple told their five-year-old to decide whom he would stay with. At first the boy chose his father, but when his mother started for the door, he ran after her, crying desperately. He had always resented his parents for forcing him to choose between them and attributed not only his indecisiveness but his divided nature to this. One half of him became a withdrawn monk, he said, the other half an attention-starved "performing flea." As for being a performing flea, part of him came to revel in it, the other part to hate it.

"I resented performing for fucking idiots," he told *Rolling Stone* in 1970. "One has to completely humiliate oneself to be what the Beatles were, and that's what I resent. . . . It happened bit by bit, gradually, until this complete craziness is surrounding you. . . . I remember what it's all about now, you fuckers—fuck you!" The fans' craving for a Bea-

---

2. Fred Seaman, *The Last Days of John Lennon* (New York: Birch Lane, 1991).

tles' reunion upset him even more. "Do we have to divide the fishes and the loaves for the multitudes again? Do we have to get crucified *again*? Do we have to do the walking on water *again*?"

It was with apparent relief that after ten years with the Fab Four, then another five solo, Lennon abandoned his performing career and became a monk. He felt everything he'd done since *Imagine* in 1971 was "dog shit." And he told his tarot reader, John Green, "My muse is gone. Poof! Up the chimney. Up your ass. Gone." But the final decision for his withdrawal had been Yoko's.

"The big plan is that I do nothing for the next four years," he told another confidante, Sam Green, in 1978. "Mother says that everything I do is doomed to failure until the year 1982. That year, according to the numbers, I'll conquer the world again. Before that, if I try anything, I'll fall on me face."

Yoko's numerologists must have changed their numbers since her husband came out of his retirement in 1980. By then, he was itchy to return to the studio. "Mother warned me that this is a high-risk period," he had explained to Green. "I have to cool it until she lets me come out of hiding—hopefully in the fall."

And let him come out of retirement in the fall she did.

But after finally winning his U.S. citizenship in '76, exactly how *did* John Lennon spend the last four years of his life besides, as he told *Playboy* magazine, "baking bread and raising my son"?

John spent his days and nights in his private bedroom, smoking Thai stick, chewing mushrooms, and snorting coke or China White heroin. "I kept to my rooms and delved into my favorite subject: me." Aside from meditating, he watched TV, read, listened to Muzak (often Beatles covers), and slept with his three black Persian "aristocats": Sasha, Misha, and Charo.

The "intellectual Beatle" had always been keen on the telly. His favorite shows were *Dallas*, *Three's Company*, and *The Tonight Show*. His reading habits were also eclectic. He was drawn to books about saints, martyrs, mystics, and ancient civilizations—Egyptian, Celtic, and Viking, especially. Due to his seafaring heritage, marine adventure such as Thor Heyerdahl's *Kon Tiki* fascinated him. To keep his edge, each day he tried to digest several pages of "difficult" books, such as Joyce's *Ulysses*. Otherwise, he consumed pop magazines and newspapers. His favorite news section was the obituaries.

John only emerged from his room, often naked, for meals. He lived on a 750-macrobiotic-calorie diet, supplemented with an occasional breakfast goodie. Ever since he'd once been called the "fat Beatle," he'd become obsessed with his weight. The coke took care of his appetite, but when he overindulged, he stuck a finger down his throat, as did his anorexic wife.

While he sipped tea and sneaked a toast with marmalade, the 130-pound John often delivered stoned rants. His favorite diatribe was on assassination conspiracies. Knowing that he had been under FBI and INS surveillance due to his radical activism,[3] he feared the same fate as RFK and Martin Luther King. "Who the hell cares who killed that nigger," he raved to his Dakota housekeeper, Marnie. "What matters is the SYSTEM!" He insisted that Sirhan Sirhan and James Earl Ray had been brainwashed and were the pawns, not the real perpetrators.

Yoko was seldom present for his polemics, preoccupied as she was with business. John complained that his wife made little time for him or Sean. "The queen is in the counting house counting all the money," he sang in "Cleanup Time." "The king is in the kitchen baking bread and honey. No friends and yet no enemies."

Yoko worked in her own private rooms and seemed to be on the phone 24/7. Managing John's and her career as well as running their Joko Productions, specializing in avant-garde films, was only part of her business life. Playing "the money game," as she called it, she had become an avid investor in real estate, dairy cows, antiquities, and art. To ensure that the acquisitions of her company, Pentacles, were auspicious, each required phone conferencing with her astrologers, tarot readers, and numerologists. Before she bid on a house, Marlene Wiener, her New York real estate psychic, had to okay its vibes by laying hands on Polaroids of the property. The same clearances were required for her other acquisitions, from Matisse canvasses to Egyptian artifacts, including *The Golden Lady*, a three-thousand-year-old mummy for which she paid $300,000, convinced that it was her former incarnation.

---

3. This began in 1969 with Yoko's and his Amsterdam bed-in for peace. Months later, his song "Give Peace a Chance" was sung by a half-million antiwar demonstrators in Washington, DC. Lennon went on to befriend Yippie founders, Abbie Hoffman and Jerry Rubin, and to headline benefit concerts for White panther, John Sinclair, as well as Black Panther, Bobby Seal. The FBI amassed a 281-page Lennon dossier, which was not fully released until 2006.

Yoko was an insatiable shopper as was her "Imagine no possessions" husband. They spent afternoons emptying Manhattan shops until their limo was at capacity with clothes, antiques, electronic equipment, and the like. On one particular afternoon, unforgettable to animal activists, the couple dropped $300,000 at Bergdorf Goodman for twenty fur coats. The bulk of their purchases were relegated to their storage rooms, which their staff regularly sacked.

Their shopping Sherpa, Fred Seaman, described the couple as "kleptomaniacs who paid." His friend, Robert Rosen, characterized Yoko as "a New Age Capitalist monster."[4] In 1968 when the Apple boutique closed, she had filled John's Rolls with free clothes before any of the Beatles themselves had made their own selections. Lennon had recently written "I Am the Walrus," and would later reveal to *Rolling Stone*—

"I was the Walrus, whatever that means. We saw the movie *Alice in Wonderland* in L.A., and the Walrus is a big capitalist that ate all the fuckin' oysters."

The Lennons took two trips to Japan. Returning there as the prodigal daughter with her legendary husband, Yoko arranged introduction parties with her well-to-do family and friends. John was often a no-show, holing up in their hotel suite watching Japanese TV. When Yoko succeeded in outing him, he made drunken pronouncements at posh restaurants such as, "Ya know, what they say about the Japanese is right! They all *do* look alike." Yoko was mortified. "Which is the preferred term for these people," her husband continued boisterously, casting his eye about him at the stunned restaurant patrons, " 'nip' or 'gook'?"

Yoko called the trip short and returned to New York where she vowed to her housekeeper, "I'll get him for this! I'll get him!"

As for John, he was relieved to be back in his room with his Thai stick, his American telly, and his three cats. "If he doesn't come out of that room," Marnie warned Yoko, "he's going to turn to mold!"

"We're going to treat him like the fungus he is," declared Yoko. "Keep him in the dark and feed him horseshit!"

Lennon now had only one real confidante: Fred. His man Friday supplied him with his modest worldly needs: books, magazines, marmalade, cat litter, pharmaceuticals, and more tea. He also protected him from run-ins with fans, which John called "close encounters of the fourth kind." After being in his service for some time, Fred felt he

---

4. Robert Rosen, *Nowhere Man*.

had become more than an employee, a friend. John was quick to disillusion him.

"I don't have any friends," he said. "Friendship is a romantic illusion."

"When John needed company, he bought it," wrote Rosen. "Having no friends was freedom. . . . One good day per week was the most he dared to hope for."

But in this last chapter of his life, was it possible that John Lennon was truly alone?

A LITTLE HELP FROM MY FRIENDS

What do I do when my love is away
(Does it worry you to be alone?)
How do I feel by the end of the day
(Are you sad because you're on your own?)
No, I get by with a little help from my friends.
—Lennon and McCartney, "A Little Help from My Friends"

When John Lennon met Paul McCartney at a country fair gig in 1957, he was annoyed to find that the fifteen-year-old knew more chords and did a better Little Richard "Be-Bop-a-Lula" too. Though John's band, the Quarrymen, needed a bass player, he later recalled, "It went through my head that I'd have to keep him in line if I let him join." A few years later, after Paul, George, and Ringo had become the Beatles, John already had his hands full maintaining his leadership and keeping the ambitious and prolific Paul in line.

Together, the two whited the black American blues and became the Shakespeares of rock and roll's Elizabethan period. But what was to become the century's greatest songwriting team was never so much a collaboration as a "sibling rivalry," as John later put it. Even in the early days, Lennon and McCartney didn't really write together: one would compose a tune; the other might make small changes. The duo was a synergy of opposites: if McCartney provided the sugar, Lennon added the salt; if McCartney created silly love songs, Billy Shears and "Rocky Raccoon," Lennon created the "Revolution," "Walrus," and "Helter Skelter."

In short, if Paul made the Beatles popular, John made them profound.

The Lennon/McCartney rivalry intensified after the death of their manager, Brian Epstein. Epstein had been their ballast and their buffer. In the early days, he and John had vacationed together in Spain while Cynthia was delivering Julian. "It was almost a love affair," recalled Lennon. "It was not consummated. But it was a pretty intense relationship." Later, after *Sgt. Pepper's*, Brian—drug addled, depressed, and feeling irrelevant—feared the Beatles would sack him. "My life became a succession of mental illnesses and sordid unhappy events," he confessed. Then his father died, and he wrote, but didn't send, a suicide letter to his mother. A month later he was found at his country estate, suffocated, and overdosed.

"After Brian died, we collapsed. Paul took over," said John.

"They could never agree on anything," remembered Apple executive, Tony Bramwell. Ego started becoming more important than success. John automatically blackballed any of Paul's suggestions, Paul killed George's, George rejected John's."

But, finally, Paul did indeed win out. The concepts behind *Sgt. Pepper's*, *Magical Mystery Tour* and *The White Album* were almost entirely his. During the *Let It Be* sessions, John was playing second fiddle and bitterly resented it. "When Paul was feeling kindly, he'd give me a solo," he recalled. "I pretty damn well know we got fed up being sidemen for Paul." The only nice thing he could say about his former collaborator was, "He's a good PR man, that's all. He's about the best in the world."

The other Beatles had a different view of the rift. For them, it had less to do with the loss of Brian than the ascendancy of Yoko. "Yoko was pushing him [John] out of the band," said George. John didn't disagree: "The old gang of mine was over the moment I met her," he told *Playboy* in 1980. The Beatles had always had an unwritten rule about keeping wives and girlfriends out of the studio. The intrusion of Yoko—who fancied herself a superior artist to all—went beyond the pale: she became a shadow, an advisor, and a creative dominatrix.

In the day, the Beatles had been more than brothers—they were a quadraphrenic hit machine. "Paul was the face, I was the smart one, George was the spirit, and Ringo was the heart," he said. They balanced each other well: John and George were the introverts; Paul and Ringo the extroverts. As the "smart one," John was the unstable element. Yoko succeeded in breaking the atom by convincing him of what he'd always felt deep down: that he was the only real artist in the group and that the others, especially the popster Paul, were suffocating him creatively.

John told *Rolling Stone*, "I could no longer artistically get anything out of the Beatles, and here was someone [Yoko] who could turn me on to a million things."

Having no illusions about Yoko's subterfuge, Paul and the others hated her for it. And John hated them for hating her. To cope, he and Yoko started doing heroin. "We sniffed a little when we were in real pain," he admitted. "We took H because of what the Beatles and others were doing to us."

The Fab Four saw little of each other in the final days, especially Paul and John. They circulated in the exclusive social circles of their new highborn wives: Paul in Linda Eastman's coterie of town and country bohemians; John in Yoko Ono's cabal of revolutionaries and junkie artistes. And their wives, both Sarah Lawrence alumnae, loathed each other.

Before the official Beatle breakup, even the peacemakers had tantrums and stormed out. Ringo left during the *White Album* sessions but returned two weeks later. George split during the *Get Back* period and was back in a few days. John's turn came nine months later, in 1969. "I'm breaking the group up," he told the other three. "It feels good. It feels like a divorce!" His recent divorce from Cynthia had been a great load off, but this was even better. Paul begged him to delay a public announcement so as not to hobble the sales of *Abbey Road* that was about to be released.

But no sooner had McCartney debuted his self-titled solo album the following spring than *he* made the breakup announcement. Feeling outmaneuvered and betrayed again, Lennon seethed. He was in a London hospital at the time, recovering from a nervous breakdown and heroin addiction. His memory of recently hurling bricks through the windows of Sir Paul's St. Johns Wood mansion after a taxing day with the barristers was small consolation. Said Paul, "I was never out to screw him, never. He could be a maneuvering swine, which no one ever realized." John soon vented his spleen in "How Do You Sleep." "Those freaks was right when they said you was dead, . . ." he sang. "You live with straights who tell you, you was king. . . . The only thing you done was Yesterday. . . . The sound you make is Muzak to my ears."

The Plastic Ono Band Album, a primal assault on McCartney

Muzak, was unadulterated, in-your-face Lennon. "I wrote all about me, and that's why I like it," he told *Rolling Stone*. "It's me! And nobody else." He called it *Sgt. Lennon*. The censored album cover of his first recording with Yoko, *Two Virgins* (1968), illustrated this "me-ness" in full blossom: it was a naked photo of the couple, John partially erect. With this he was merely proving what he had sung as a Beatle: "Everybody has something to hide except for me and my monkey."

He tracked Paul's and George's more modest efforts with a nervous and malevolent curiosity: as *McCartney* and *All Things Must Pass* climbed the charts, *Plastic Ono* fell. John and Yoko's conviction was confirmed: their art was pearls before swine, and the fans *were* "fucking idiots." Still, a fame junkie from ten years of adulation, the solo Clever One expected to have his cake and to eat it too: he wanted to be an true artist *and* popular. He softened the edges on his next album, *Imagine*, and came as close to this as he ever would.

He called *McCartney* "rubbish" but allowed that some day his ex-collaborator might produce a great work on his own. As for creating masterpieces, "In me heart of hearts," Lennon told *Rolling Stone*'s Jann Wenner, "I wish I was the only one in the world." Though his ego was big enough for its own zip code, it still felt claustrophobic. He readily admitted that he was a "fuckin' egomaniac" and vowed never again to work with another egomaniac: Paul.

Meanwhile, Beatle "reunion" hopefuls were teased. George, still on speaking terms with John after the split, asked him to join his Bangladesh concert. Though John initially agreed, he backed out at the last minute when finding out McAsshole might show up for the benefit along with Ringo. George, who had done many things for John since the split, never forgave him. The hostility became mutual when George released his 1980 autobiography, *I Me Mine*, scarcely mentioning his bandmate: "I did everything for that fucker!" railed John.

The guitarists, however, agreed on one thing in retrospect: "Being a Beatle was a nightmare," declared George.

"The Beatles were the biggest bastards on earth!" pronounced John.

Even before the group's first success, their fifth member, Stu Sutcliff, warned his sister, "Keep away from the Beatles because they're a bad lot, completely lacking in moral fiber." Sutcliff, who fancied himself "the James Dean" of the group and even cuter than the Cute One, had regular brawls with McCartney on stage in Germany.

Paul shed few tears when Stu left the group to pursue his painting career.

"The Beatles were the most ruthless of all," said a fellow musician at the time. "No one was going to stand in the way of their success." After the breakup, Lennon and McCartney turned that ruthlessness against each other. But Paul never bore quite the same animosity toward Lennon, as Lennon toward him. After all, Paul, the interloper, had stolen the Beatles from John, the founder, not the other way around.

Late in the seventies, just before going on tour to Japan with Wings, Paul tried to extend the olive branch to his old mate. When he phoned the Lennons from his New York hotel, Yoko as ever took the call. Paul told her he had just scored some "dynamite grass" and suggested he and Linda drop by the Dakota and share the peace pipe. Yoko declined. In closing, Paul mentioned that, while in Tokyo, he and Linda would be staying in the Hotel Okura Presidential Suite. Yoko was beside herself. So, too, was John on hearing the alarming news. The McCartneys were trying to poison their "hotel karma," John explained to Fred Seaman. This was *their* suite. "If Paul and Linda sleep there, we'll never have peace when we return to that room!" But he hadn't given up hope, "I've talked to Mother and she's working it out."

Days later, Paul was busted for pot at the Tokyo airport. Yoko had contacts with the customs officials in her homeland.[5] When Lennon got word that McCartney's jail keepers were ordering him to sing "Yesterday" over and over in his cell, he was hysterical. "We could get him off like that," he told Fred with a snap of the fingers. "Mother's got all these connections. But, of course, he would never ask for help. It would be beneath him."

So now that the days of a little help from friends were gone, did John have anyone to stand by him? Or, in the end, had he become what he had always feared:

A Nowhere Man?

---

5. Yoko, however, refused to take responsibility. "It's a pity, really," she told John Green. "I like Paul! I think of him as a friend."

PORNOGRAPHIC PRIESTESS

> She's the teacher and I'm the pupil. She's taught me everything
> I fucking know . . . she was *there* . . . when I was the nowhere
> man.
> —John Lennon, 1980 *Playboy* interview

> After Yoko had a measure of control over John . . . she was to
> undergo a startling metamorphosis from a timid, fumbling
> mouse to a strong-willed, domineering tigress.
> —Lennon's friend, Pete Shotton

Her father was a cousin of the Emperor of Japan, her mother an heiress
to the banking fortune of the esteemed Yasuda family. She attended
the royal Gakushuin school with the crown princes, one of whom had
a crush on her. "She never felt happy unless she was treated like a
queen," recalled her classmate in the drama club.

As a girl, Yoko Ono declared that she was the reincarnation of the
legendary 16th century Samurai general, Hideoshi Toyotami. "He was
very clever, very strong and always victorious," she said. Known for his
ruthlessness, the general had decapitated and piked his nephew, and
had crucified Franciscan missionaries. Believing that her "rounded"
fingertips were identical to Hideoshi's, she predicted she would "take
over the world one day."[6]

During World War II, Yoko's father, Isoko, was imprisoned in a POW
camp in Saigon. After the war, their fortune restored, the Ono family moved to New York where Yoko enrolled in the prestigious Sarah
Lawrence College. Soon estranged from her parents who disapproved
of the lowborn bohemians she befriended here, she immersed herself in
avant-garde art. "I was doing all that [art] just to prevent myself from
going mad," she said. The last straw for her family came when she
dropped out of college in 1956 and married a penniless pianist, Toshi
Ishiyanagi.

The girl who had been raised by twenty servants, now became a
waitress and part-time calligraphy instructor while trying to establish herself in the performance art world. Failing to gain recognition,
she tried several times to jump out her apartment window. Finally,

---

6. *Yoko Ono*, Jerry Hopkins.

she confessed, "I took an overdose of pills. I was feeling that I always wanted to die."[7] Her parents committed her to a mental institution in Tokyo.

She was rescued from the hospital by Tony Cox, a New York artist, sax player, and beguiling Svengali. Together, the couple returned to New York and lived ménage a troix with the compliant Toshi. In 1963, Yoko divorced the pianist, married Tony, and bore him a daughter, Kyoto. While Tony cared for the baby and became "like Yoko's servant," as one acquaintance observed, Yoko resumed her art career with renewed determination. The banker's daughter devised unique ways to marry her art with commerce: she offered two-hundred shares of herself for $200 apiece; she built a coin-op mechanical dog which barked and wagged its tail; she charged £200 for an apple pasted on a black canvas.

Fights began to break out between the frustrated artist and her emasculated househusband. "They were always trying to kill each other," recalled Tony's friend, Alfred Wunderlick. In their 1971 custody battle for Kyoto, Tony testified that Yoko had once stabbed him with scissors, and another time held a broken bottle to his neck. But in their more harmonious moments, they continued to brainstorm on creative marketing schemes.

Finally in 1966, Yoko accepted an invitation to participate in a "Destruction in Art" symposium being held in London. Before leaving New York, she told her fellow Happening artist, Allan Kaprow, that she had "a close interest in the Beatles." Then she added "half-laughingly, 'I'd like to marry John Lennon.' "

By that fall, Yoko Ono was staging an art happening at London's Indica Gallery. The Beatles were about to start recording *Sgt. Pepper's Lonely Hearts Club Band*, and John, a former art student, would occasionally drop in on such avant-garde openings. "I got word that this amazing woman was putting on a show, and there was going to be something about people in black bags," he later recalled.

Even by this time, Yoko Ono, though obscure, considered herself one of the greatest artists of the century or, as John liked to put it, "the most famous unknown artist." Later, she was to claim she had invented Conceptual Art, Minimalist film, the Happening, and Flower Power. Though hungry for recognition, she considered society "a bunch of assholes."

Yoko's Indica show featured a Box of Smiles, a Sky-TV, a Crying Machine, and other curiosities. The artist introduced herself to her future husband by handing him a white card that read, BREATHE. John paid an imaginary five shillings (he didn't carry cash) to pound the first real nail into her virgin *Hammer and Nail* painting. In the following days, the Beatle received a blizzard of notes, begging for patronage. "If you don't support me, that's it!" the artist wrote. "I'll kill myself!"

Though aloof at the outset, John soon warmed to the artist, realizing that she was "as barmy as me." After entertaining Yoko, six years his senior, in the back of his Rolls, he became personally besotted, calling her "me in drag." Their relationship climaxed after they recorded their first duet—later called *Two Virgins*— at his manor while his wife vacationed in Greece.

John unburdened himself of Cynthia for £100,000, his monthly income at that time. Yoko's husband was almost as costly. Though, according to biographer, Jerry Hopkins, Tony would give Yoko a divorce only "if she signed an agreement giving him fifty-percent of everything she got from John," the grifter settled for £40,000 to cover his debts, plus a stipend to move to the Virgin Islands.

Before eloping to Gibraltar with his new bride, John dropped in on his Aunt Mimi. After one look at Yoko, Mimi asked her nephew, "Who's the poison dwarf?"[8]

By the next week, Mimi, with millions of others, saw front-page snapshots of her nephew's Amsterdam honeymoon "bed-in" for love and world peace. To some, their activism seemed selfless and well-intentioned. To others it seemed the opposite. "No opportunity to grab headlines, no matter how inane or scandalous, went unexplored," wrote the Beatles' biographer Robert Spitz.

The Lennons released three albums, as well as many equally forgettable art films, in the next three years. Meanwhile, Yoko suffered annual miscarriages. The first occurred weeks after John's London drug bust in 1968. Although Yoko told her assistant, Arlene Reckson, that a severe beating from the singer triggered it, her doctors considered her many past abortions the major cause. Also, she and her husband

---

8. "I am a small woman because people repressed me when I was young," Yoko once declared. "My bones stopped growing. Did you ever realize that the great aggressors in the world, Napoleon, Hitler, are all physically small people who have been repressed?" She went on to explain, "I grew up in a family where my father wasn't there, and my mother was a monster. My country was destroyed by war. My feelings and my work have never been respected, and people think that all I've ever done is marry John Lennon and spend his money."

had become heavy heroin users. The second miscarriage occurred in the fall of '69 after her methadone detox. The third came a year later while she and John were undergoing Primal Scream therapy in L.A. Dr. Arthur Janov, the founder, treated the couple personally and recommended that John, for his mental health, leave Yoko.

Though John wouldn't hear of it, the blush was off the rose. "I don't want to fuck her anymore," he complained to his manager, Alan Klein, who had championed him during the Beatle legal battles. "When I married her I thought she was a real wild broad. Yoko is a *prude!*" During their courtship she had been the beguiling free spirit like his mother, Julia; now she had turned into a cold, implacable matriarch like his Aunt Mimi.

The star became withdrawn, started doing more smack, and seduced Yippie Jerry Rubin's girlfriend one night. "John was complaining he wasn't getting laid enough," said his producer and confidante, Jack Douglas.

So Yoko was galvanized to action. She called in her dedicated young assistant, May Pang. "John and I are not getting along," she confessed to May. "We've been arguing. We're growing apart." She predicted that he would start going out with other people, adding, "If he should ask you to go out with him, you should go." The chaste May was speechless. "You should have a boyfriend," continued Yoko in a motherly tone. "Wouldn't you rather see him with someone like you than someone who would treat him rotten?"

In mandarin fashion, Yoko handpicked her husband's concubine. No sooner had he left for L.A. with May than his wife took up with her studio guitarist, David Spinozza. Now, without John to mother, she could at last spend full-time launching her solo music and art career in New York.

John's "Lost Weekend" in L.A. was fourteen months of carousing, snorting, and brawling with brief intermissions for several projects including a fifties rock 'n' roll record with Phil Spector. One night he got so violently drunk that the gun-toting, Wall-of-Sound producer and his bodyguards were forced to lash him to a bed with neckties. When he finally managed to tear himself free, he was wailing: "Yoko, you slant-eyed bitch! You wanted to get rid of me! All this happened because you wanted to get rid of me! Yoko, I'm gonna get you!" Then he broke into tears and cried, "Nobody loves me. Nobody loves me!"

In a rare sober moment at the end, John finally declared, "I don't want to be fucked up again. It scares the hell out of me!"

He needed stability. He needed home. He needed Mother again. He had repented his old ways and wanted to turn over a new leaf. "I was a real pig," he confessed. "The pressures of being a pig were enormous. They were killing me."

But would Mother take her penitent husband back? After all, she considered herself the wounded party, not John. She "kicked him out," she later told an interviewer, because "I felt castrated . . . emasculated." He did his best to counter his wife's insecurity on this account by telling her, "Do you know why I like you? You're like a bloke in drag. You're a mate."

Proving her goodwill at last, Yoko allowed John an audience at the Dakota to plead his case. When all of his entreaties were greeted by her stony silence, he asked, "Whaddaya want me to do, Yoko? Suck your cock?" She betrayed a Mona Lisa smile but held fast. She still had hopes that her career would survive without him. So she left on tour to Japan. The concerts in her homeland were not well attended. She later declared that the many empty seats were in fact occupied by the ghosts of children killed in the World War, cheering her commitment to peace. Even so, her feelings of "being a fish on a cutting board" were confirmed.

Yoko retreated to New York and barraged John with calls as she had during their courtship. But John, comfortably ensconced with May Pang on Sutton Place, was the one playing hard to get now.

Yoko finally persuaded the prodigal husband to return to the Dakota for a miraculous smoking cure (he had a tubercular hack from a two-pack-a-day habit) that involved magic herbs and hypnosis. A zombie-like Lennon returned to May Pang to declare, "Yoko has allowed me to come home." Then he rubbed an herbal potion on himself and May, saying it was a "present" from Yoko. Sickened by the oil, May took it to a Santeria shop specializing in black magic herbs. Identifying it as a sulfur, arrowroot, and chili powder concoction, the proprietor told her "whoever gave this to you must really hate you."

The Lennons were remarried in a Druid ceremony on their anniversary. Soon afterward, Yoko gave John miraculous news: she was pregnant. They had had intercourse only a few times since their reunion. Doctors had given him little hope of insemination due to his low sperm count. And Yoko, now forty-two, had had serial miscarriages. In fact, she told him she wanted an abortion, but he wouldn't hear of it.

"Okay," she agreed, "I'll carry it but, after that, the baby is your responsibility." Yoko delivered Sean Ono Taro Lennon two months

prematurely by Cesarean on October 9 (1975), John's birthday. She sub-
scribed to the Asian superstition that a child born on a father's birthday would inherit his soul.[9]

After the birth of Sean, John got off the merry-go-round and abandoned his career to become a full-time father. His retirement was disturbed by three untimely deaths. First, his favorite aunt, Mater, had
passed away. Then Mal Evans, John's ex-roadie, went berserk and was
killed in a suicide-by-cop shootout with the LAPD. Finally, his father,
Freddie Lennon, died of stomach cancer in a London charity ward for
the indigent.

Speaking of his abandonment by Freddie as a young boy, John said,
"I soon forgot my father. It was like he was dead." Having read about his
famous son in the newspaper, Freddie reappeared twenty years later on
the set of *Help!* With mixed feelings John welcomed him back because
"he's a bit wacky, like me." Trading on his son's fame, the retired seaman recorded an abysmal album, then eloped with his nineteen-year-
old girlfriend, Pauline, whom John had given a room in his attic as well
as a job. Later, Freddie attended *The Magical Mystery Tour* party where
he and his son "danced drunkenly together, while I was thoroughly
miserable," wrote Cynthia in her memoir.

Six years later, John, a new Primal Scream graduate, invited Freddie
to his thirtieth birthday party at Tittenhurst Park. No sooner did the
retired sailor arrive with Pauline and their infant child than John went
berserk, threatening to have him buried at sea for betraying him as a
boy. "Keep to your fuckin' self and get out of my life!" he screamed.
When his little half-brother began to cry in terror, his fury peeked,
"See what will happen to him if you lock him away from his parents
and shut him up with a fuckin' madwoman [Aunt Mimi]! He'll end up
a raving lunatic, like me!" He raved that he was destined for an early
end just like Jimi Hendrix, Jim Morrison, and Janis Joplin because "I'm
bloody mad! Insane!"

Freddie beat a quick retreat, never to see his famous son again.
Fearing for his life, he wrote an account of the horrific encounter and
handed it to his lawyer in a sealed envelope which read, "To be opened
only in the event I disappear or die an unnatural death."

Since divorcing Cynthia, John had rarely visited his own first son,

---

9. She also froze Sean's placenta, intending to consume it later (obsessed with aging
she took many youth elixirs), but the maid accidentally defrosted it.

Julian. Whenever a meeting was arranged, Yoko usually managed to sabotage the plans. Finally, when John was in L.A. with May, Cynthia, taking advantage of Yoko's absence, called and asked, "Do you know you have a son?"

John flew the boy to California and took him to Disneyland for a day.

As for his own father, John had six years to chill since the Tittenhurst blowout. So when, in 1976, he got word that Freddie had terminal stomach cancer, he gave him a brief farewell telephone call. Then, at Mother's suggestion, he went on a forty-day postmortem cleansing fast. At the same time, completing his monastic vows, he became celibate.

"Now, John," instructed Yoko, who was still carrying on with Spinozza, "if we don't fuck, you'll become psychic. We should try."

Lennon had become comfortable with his teacher-pupil marriage and raged at those who found it unnatural. "You think I'm being controlled like a dog on a leash because I do things with her, then . . . fuck you, brother and sister!" he told *Playboy* magazine. Not only did he believe "Mother is usually right about things," but he felt she had great psychic powers. In 1977, Yoko had traveled to Cartagena, Colombia, to meet a legendary seven-foot-tall witch by the name of Lena. According to her consort and liaison, John Green, the banker's daughter paid Lena $60,000 and made a pact with the devil—to do "everything" for her, including cursing all her enemies and giving her a "money bush."

Detracting from Yoko's psychic power not to mention her business acumen, though, was her heroin addiction. She knew she had to detox again but how could she keep it from John? She dispatched him to their Long Island estate and, for his further spiritual development, assigned him a ten-day vow of silence. He resisted his urge to phone Mother by rereading Gordon Liddy's inspirational book, *Will,* wherein the Watergate burglar boasts of unflinchingly cooking his palm over lit matches. Meantime, back at the Dakota, Yoko was detoxing and sleeping with her handsome bisexual antique dealer, Sam Green.

While exiled in Cold Harbor, John was overtaken by his old romantic seafaring dreams. He suddenly decided that, after spending years in his room watching TV, he'd like to sail across the ocean as his father and grandfather had done. But he feared that Mother, ever safety-minded, would forbid it. After all, he had no nautical experience.

But not only did Yoko enthusiastically support the idea, she also let him rent the sailboat and hire the crew himself. She insisted on only one thing: that he follow the course dictated by her numerologist-directionalist, Takashi Yoshikawa. Takashi, who ran the Taste of Tokyo restaurant downtown, was the leading American practitioner of *katu-tugai*, or directional taboos. Yoko had been consulting him for years and credited him with masterminding her reconciliation with John. Having recently detected an "evil cloud" in John's aura, Takashi told Yoko that to dispel the specter it was imperative John sail in southeasterly direction to Bermuda—directly through the Devil's Triangle.[10]

The occultist Yoko was surely aware of the nautical misadventures here. Since 1945, more than a hundred ships and a thousand people had disappeared in these waters. John's mystical number, Nine, figured (alone or by addition) uncannily in many episodes. Among them: in 1945, the Navy bomber squadron, Flight 19, disappeared at 29°N 79°W on a course of 270°; in 1963, the Marine tanker *Sulphur Queen* vanished with 39 sailors aboard; in 1968, the nuclear submarine, *Scorpion*, with a crew of 99 went missing. To the scientific-minded, these may seem nothing more than random coincidence, but surely not to Yoko and her numerologist, Yoshikawa.[11]

Just before the voyage, John told Yoko's card reader, John Green, "According to the numbers, the thing for me to do is take a little cruise down to Bermuda. So spake the oracle of the East." But, he added: " . . . a little ship and a little crew strikes me as a little dangerous . . . like tempting fate." He called the plan "thoroughly reckless" and "totally off the wall," and concluded, "The part that bothers me the most is that Yoko is so insistent that it's the thing to do."[12]

Could it have been that his wife, The High Priestess of the Happening, was arranging the pieces for the ultimate Happening—the magical disappearance of a magical husband in a storybook place? "All of my

---

10. *John Lennon: The Life*. Philip Norman.

11. Some investigators believe that the unpredictably volatile waters are the result of powerful seismic activity. Famous psychic Edgar Cayce, whom Yoko admired, asserted that the mythical lost continent Atlantis, said to be destroyed in an earthquake, was located here. Other investigators attribute Triangle incidents to the disturbance of electro-magnetic fields found in only one other place: the Dragon's Triangle or "Devil's Sea" off the coast of Japan. So many sailors were lost here that, in 1952, Japan designated it as a danger zone and sent out a ship to investigate which itself vanished with its nine scientists.

12. *Dakota Days*. John Green.

work in fields other than music have an Event bent," she had once said. " . . . My events are mostly spent in wonderment." It wouldn't be the first time her art was born of a fateful event— they had almost died in a car accident years before and, to John's delight, his wife had turned the smashed car into a sculpture. Later, his bloody spectacles would grace the cover of Yoko's first album as a widow.

In early June—the beginning of hurricane season—John Lennon bid his wife and young son goodbye and set sail for Bermuda, through the Triangle. The craft was the *Megan Jaye,* a 43-foot sloop, skippered by Cap'n Hank, an ex-rock promoter who had worked with Big Brother. Aboard was a crew of four, including John.

His fear that this was a "dangerous," "thoroughly reckless," undertaking hadn't abated. But he was exhilarated and hopeful, too. For five years, guided by his wife, he had lived as a virtual monk in the Tower, hoping for psychic and even supernatural powers; but, as he told John Green, his muse had abandoned him and he hadn't been able to write a song. Creatively dead in the water, he desperately needed a jolt of fateful adventure which would either be the end of him or a true rebirth. As he waved goodbye to his family and friends before flying to the docks, he cried, "See you in paradise!"

The *Megan Jaye* was only out a few days before she hit heavy weather off Cape Hatteras, known as "the Graveyard of the Atlantic." Clinging to the masts, riding the twenty-foot swells, John was scared shitless at first. But soon the sea blood of his forefathers welled up and he threw his arms to the thundering sky, "Take me away, God! I don't give a shit!"

The voyage from Rhode Island to Bermuda was to take five days. Back at the Dakota, Fred Seaman counted each one. Meanwhile, Yoko had Green do many tarot readings. By the eighth day, still without any report from the *Megan Jaye,* Seaman desperately wondered, "What if John's boat had disappeared in the Bermuda Triangle?" That same day, Japanese Prime Minister Masayoshi Ohira died of a heart attack. The next day was not only Friday the 13th but a Mercury retrograde in John's sign. Seaman had also noticed an odd new ornament on Yoko's desktop: a skull in a glass case.

Late that Thursday, Green was conferring again with Yoko when the phone rang. Answering, Yoko turned away from her psychic, listened, replied in monosyllables then hung up. Then, according to

Green, "with a face full of pain" and after "collecting" herself, Yoko told him: "Well, I guess you will be pleased to hear that all your little fears about the safety of the family were ill founded."

Now anchored in Bermuda after the tumultuous eight-day voyage, John told Mother over the phone that he'd had the bloody best time of his life. The seas had almost taken him down in the yellow submarine to join the Atlantians and lost sailors. But now he was on terra firma, reborn. His creative juices were flowing again, he was composing songs and was anxious to get back to the studio. "I was tuned into the cosmos, and all these songs came!" he told her. He begged Mother to fly down with Sean and Fred for a joyous reunion in paradise. She told him she was too busy just now, but would send his boys ahead.

While John had been at sea, Yoko had been on Fire Island with Sam Green. She and Green—whom John had dismissed as a "fag" and a "useless sycophant"—were making marriage plans. "I'm bored with John," she had told her other gay confidante, Luciano. "I'm tired of the Lennon name, and tired of living in his shadow. As soon as the album is off the ground, the marriage is over. I'm planning to leave him." She and Sam had been reviewing the Lennon assets in order to ensure the maximum divorce settlement. To minimize complications, they were also preparing to move John's belongings from the Dakota before he returned. Meanwhile, the singer didn't understand why his wife kept promising to join him in the Caribbean, but always canceled trips due to last-minute business developments.

"Communication's lost. Can't even get you on the telephone. I feel you slipping away," he wrote in "Losing You," a new tune for *Double Fantasy*. "You didn't have to tell a white lie. You knew you scored me for life. . . . Ain't no doubt about it. I'm losing you."

But in "Starting Over," a pathetically hopeful husband sang, "Our love is still special. Let's take a chance and fly away somewhere alone. . . . When I see you, darling, it's like we both are falling in love again. It'll be just like starting over."

When Yoko at last visited John and Sean in Bermuda later that summer, "she treated them both with an icy reserve bordering on contempt," wrote Fred. And she returned to her affairs in New York within days. "No wonder that she bitterly resented John," concluded Seaman. "Without him, Yoko was just an eccentric lady with no money and no power—and for this she would never forgive him." In fact, according to author Geoffrey Giuliano, she had told her associates, "How can that oaf be so successful when I am so much more talented and educated?"

Ever the pragmatist, she decided to delay the divorce until the completion of *Double Fantasy* (named after a spectacular two-headed iris Lennon saw in a Bermuda flower show). "John's stuff isn't all that good," she told John Green. "I want this record to make people think of Yoko and John, not John and Yoko. Then it will be easier to make them think of Yoko only. That's my real goal, an independent career. . . . Think of John as an old star who is fading and me as the new star on the horizon."

CAPTAIN NEMO

May hatred be appeased in that savage heart! . . .
If his destiny be strange, it is also sublime.
—Jules Verne, *Twenty Thousand Leagues Under the Sea*
(last lines)

Mark David Chapman's father, formerly an Air Force staff sergeant, worked for an oil company, led a Boy Scout troop, and taught guitar at the YMCA. Mark's mother was a nurse. His father beat his mother. Inside the wall between their bedrooms, he began hearing the voices of "the Little People," urging him to protect his mother. The withdrawn, unathletic boy was bullied at school too. In his junior year, he ran away from his home in Decatur, Georgia, and became a carnival security guard in Miami for two weeks.

Returning home, he got heavily into drugs and the Beatles, especially John Lennon. Then in 1971, Chapman, now sixteen, found the Lord and began working as a door-to-door evangelist. On Sundays he played guitar and spoke in tongues at his local Pentecostal church. That summer he became a counselor at the YMCA camp. All the children loved him and called him "Captain Nemo."

A fierce champion of the oppressed, Nemo was the creator of his fantastical submarine, the *Nautilus*, in *Twenty Thousand Leagues Under the Sea*, Mark's favorite book besides the Bible. Jules Verne named his hero after the Scottish motto *Nemo me impune lacessit*, meaning "No one provokes me unpunished." *Nemo* is Latin for "no one" and Greek for "I give what is due."[13] Chapman would later tell court-appointed

---

13. It is also the name the Greek adventurer and avenger Odysseus used.

psychiatrists that his summer as counselor Captain Nemo with the YMCA kids was the happiest time of his life.

After graduating from high school, Chapman—continuing the Lord's work through the YMCA—traveled to Chicago, briefly to Lebanon, then to a Vietnam refugee camp in Fort Chaffee, Arkansas. But suddenly his fortunes reversed. He enrolled in Georgia's Covenant College, failed out, and his fiancée there left him. Beginning to hear the voices of his Little People again, he resolved to move to Hawaii and kill himself after "a last fling in paradise," as he would later tell his psychiatrists.

Arriving in Honolulu, Chapman attempted to asphyxiate himself in a rental car. But the makeshift vacuum cleaner hose from the exhaust pipe melted. He was treated for severe depression at Castle Memorial Hospital. Afterward, he took a part-time security job there and, in his spare time, played guitar for patients. His faith weakened, his new Bible was now *The Catcher in the Rye*, which a YMCA friend had lent him.

The famous J. D. Salinger novel was narrated by a young man, Holden Caulfield, dedicated to saving children from the "phonies" of the adult world, catching them in the rye before they jumped over "the edge of some crazy cliff." Holden kept himself from going crazy by talking to his dead brother, Allie, and by fantasizing about jumping on a nuclear bomb or killing the subverters of youth. His teacher had warned him about taking a fall into a bottomless pit, saying, "You're not the first person who was ever confused and frightened and even sickened by human behavior." Even so, Holden went off the cliff he was trying to save everybody else from. He told his story from a psychiatric hospital, after suffering a nervous breakdown.

The story was a cloud parting for Mark David Chapman in the Hawaii sanitorium. Holden Caulfield's story was his story. He *was* Holden Caulfield. Just as he had been Captain Nemo, defender of the innocents, he was now the catcher in the rye. Having protected only a handful at the Y camp, he now felt that a whole generation of young needed a savior. After all, as he would later tell his wife, he was "meant for greatness, to be someone big." Of all the phonies and false prophets deceiving and exploiting the young now, who was the biggest? Who was the Goliath?

Chapman had always idolized John Lennon. He played *Imagine* on his guitar for children, for the homeless, and for the sick. But he couldn't forgive or forget what Lennon had said about the Beatles being bigger than Jesus. Then, while in Hawaii, he'd read a library book[14] about his former hero, which revealed the patrician lifestyle of the workingman's hero. "He told us to imagine no possessions," Chapman later told biographer Jack Jones, "and there he was, with millions of dollars and yachts and farms and country estates, laughing at people like me who had believed the lies and bought the records and built a big part of their lives around his music."[15]

When, in their last major interview, the Lennons were asked by *Playboy*'s David Scheff about their politics and wealth, John confessed his "guilt for being rich, and guilt thinking that perhaps love and peace isn't enough and you have to go and get shot or something." Yoko conceded, "Yes, you have to play the money game." Lennon often called life "a game." "Play the game of existence to the end," he sang in "Tomorrow Never Knows." "Keep on playing those mind games forever, raising the spirits of peace and love," he sang in "Mind Games." He likened his celebrity life to a chess game, telling Fred Seaman that he was the king "and every encounter with pawns weakens me."

"Game, my ass," said Holden Caulfield, the catcher in the rye. "Some game. If you get on the side where all the hotshots are, then it's a game, all right—I'll admit that. But if you get on the other side, where there aren't any hotshots, then what's a game about it? Nothing. No game."

It was no game for Mark Chapman, either. He was no hotshot. He knew all about being a nobody. But like his alter ego Holden, "I'm sick of not having the courage to be an absolute nobody." Sure, Lennon had sung about being a Nowhere Man himself, but he'd turned himself into a hot shot in his *game* of existence. Then he talked about being bigger than Jesus. Jesus who was *The* hotshot. But Jesus didn't act like a hot shot or talk about nobodies and pawns "weakening" him. Christ, the real savior, the original catcher in the rye, had no problem hanging out with nobodies. In fact, he preferred their company; he couldn't stand hotshots and phonies. And if there was one thing Chapman knew, had Jesus ever been tempted to call life a *game*, he certainly changed his mind on his last Friday.

---

14. Anthony Fawcett, *John Lennon: One Day at a Time: A Personal Biography of the Seventies* (New York: Stein & Day, 1983).

15. Jack Jones, *Let Me Take You Down: Inside the Mind of Mark David Chapman, the Man Who Killed John Lennon* (New York: Villard Books, 1992).

Mark Chapman came to hate John Lennon. True hate is born of true love betrayed. John Lennon was a phony masquerading as a catcher in the rye, and for that sacrilege, he had to die.

Before meeting his appointment with destiny, Captain Nemo decided to retrace the itinerary of Jules Verne's other adventure, *Around the World in Eighty Days.* As fate would have it, he fell in love with his travel agent, Gloria Abe. Like Yoko Ono, Gloria was the daughter of a wealthy Japanese banker. Returning from his whirlwind trip, Mark married Gloria, and she converted from Buddhism to Christianity for him.

But soon his fortunes were again reversed. He was fired from his job at Castle Memorial Hospital, rehired, and then fired again. He now became a condominium night watchman, but, due to his volatile and erratic behavior, was dismissed from this position as well. He went on to do security work elsewhere, but only sporadically and part-time. Gloria became the main wage earner, and Mark a humiliated house-husband, who was now drinking heavily and falling into fits of rage. "The only place you could go for privacy was the bathroom," Gloria later told *People* magazine, "and so often at night I'd go in there and lock the door and just cry."

Broke, Chapman borrowed thousands from his father-in-law and from his mother who had joined him in Hawaii after divorcing her abusive husband. Just as the Lennons invested in art, so now did Chapman with his borrowed funds. His favorite acquisition was a sentimental family scene by Norman Rockwell, former chief illustrator for the Boy Scouts. Aside from collecting art, he busied himself harassing Hare Krishnas in downtown Honolulu and robocalling the local Church of Scientology whispering, "Bang Bang! You're dead!" Meanwhile, he had contacted the Hawaii attorney general's office to inquire about legally changing his name to Holden Caulfield.

Signing out for his last security job, Chapman scrawled the name "John Lennon" instead, then scratched it out. He now bought a .38 revolver from a Honolulu gun salesman by the name of Ono.

Then he flew to Holden's hometown, telling Gloria, "I'm going to New York to make it all different."

He walked the city streets for several days, thinking about jumping off the Statue of Liberty. At last he saw a matinee of *Ordinary People,* a movie about the struggle and deliverance of a suicidal boy who blames himself for the drowning of his brother. Emerging from the theater, Mark called Gloria from a phone booth, telling her, "I'm coming home, I won a great victory. Your love has saved me!" He assured her that he had "capped the volcano."

He flew back to Hawaii. But he hadn't been home long before Gloria was awakened in the middle of the night. She heard her husband screaming above Beatles' music:

> *The phony must die, says the Catcher in the Rye.*
> *The Catcher in the Rye is coming for you.*
> *Don't believe in John Lennon.*
> *Imagine John Lennon is dead, oh yeah, yeah, yeah.*
> *Imagine that it's over.*[16]

INSTANT KARMA

Instant Karma's gonna get you
Gonna knock you right on the head
You better get yourself together
Pretty soon you're gonna be dead.
—John Lennon, "Instant Karma"

John it seemed *had* become psychic on his own, or with Yoko's help. He had recently confided to his fellow musician, Jesse Ed Davis, that a violent death was his "karmic destiny" because he had lived a violent life. The composer of "Give Peace a Chance" had beaten people in his younger years. When club emcee, Bob Wooler, had teased him about his "honeymoon" with Brian Epstein in Spain, Lennon had broken his nose, ribs, and collarbone with a shovel. "I could have really killed him," he told a BBC journalist, "and that scared me." Earlier, he had kicked his best friend, "the Fifth Beatle" Stu Sutcliff, in the head, which later he feared resulted in a fatal brain tumor. And the composer of "Woman Is the Nigger of the World" had battered Cynthia, Yoko, May Pang, among others.

In "Getting Better," he confessed "Me used to be angry young man. . . . Man I was mean but I'm changing my scene. . . . It's getting

---

16. Jack Jones, *Let Me Take You Down.*

better all the time (can't get no worse)." In one of his last interviews, the former Beatle explained, "It is the most violent people who go in for love and peace. . . . I am a violent man who has learned not to be violent and regrets his violence."

But he didn't believe his repentance would save him from the immutable laws of karma. He obsessed about being shot, considering it, according to Fred Seaman, "a modern form of crucifixion."

After every verse of his song, "Come Together," the Beatle had screamed, "Shoot me!"

But for the ever-mercurial John, all that seemed behind him now. After five long years in purgatory, his muse had finally returned to him, giving him a new lease on life—not only his own life, but his life with Yoko in double fantasy.

Not so long ago, he had been haunted by repeated death threats, the last coming in a posted note. "The police can only protect you briefly," it read. "We can wait for a year or two years. Then we will be back. We will kill you. Maybe we could kidnap your son."

More than two years had passed now, and he had shaken his paranoia. "I should thank this terrorist really," he told John Green. "He's given me an excellent lesson in why I really ought to live my life one day at a time and each day as the last."

Now he felt truly liberated. In his December 6 BBC radio interview, when Andy Pebbles asked about his "security," he confessed, "It took me two years to unwind. I can go right out this door now and go into a restaurant. You want to know how great that is?"

And in his other major interview shortly before, the star stressed that he had no interest in collecting the "prize" just yet. "The biggest prize is when you die—a really big one for dying in public," he told *Playboy*'s David Scheff. "Okay: those are the things we are *not* interested in doing."

The morning has come at last. It is December 8, an unusually warm, springlike day in New York. The early sun pours through the drapes in his Sheraton Hotel suite. Freshly showered and already in his overcoat, Mark David Chapman is standing at the bureau, carefully arranging his altar in front of the mirror. To the left he places a snapshot of himself, smiling broadly, arms around Vietnamese refugee children at Fort Chaffee. Next to it he lays down his Y supervisor's hand-printed letter of praise for exemplary service. Behind these, he scotch tapes to the mirror the *Wizard of Oz* poster he picked up downtown yesterday, the one of Dorothy wiping away the Cowardly Lions tears before she taps her emerald slippers and flies back to Kansas from Emerald City. Then he picks up the Sheraton Gideon Bible, opens it to the Gospel of John title page, and prints in bold letters LENNON after it. He steps back and beholds his display proudly, imagining all the reporters crowding the room, snapping pictures. Finally he puts on his cap, reaches into his suitcase, withdraws the .38 Charter Arms revolver, and slips it into the inside pocket of his overcoat.

As Chapman sets out from the Sheraton on foot, across town John Lennon is enjoying his after-breakfast Gitane and cappuccino at La Fortuna, his favorite neighborhood café. Yoko is reviewing with him her arrangements for yet another busy day of interviews and photo sessions for *Double Fantasy*. What he's really wondering about are the reviews, but he makes a habit not to read them unless she insists he do so. The reviews for the album are mixed at best. Yoko has no intention of showing him the one from *Melody Maker*, in particular, calling the album "a godawful yawn . . . reeking with self-indulgent sterility." She's not mentioning the numbers either: it reached #8 on the charts in the first week; now it's fallen to #21. She just tells him they need to step up the publicity blitz and give *Rolling Stone* a good cover later this morning. John groans. This is not his favorite part of the business. With his reemergence, the fans in front of the Dakota are growing. Only yesterday, Sunday, he'd had to chase after some pudgy nerd with glasses who wouldn't stop shooting pictures of him. Yoko managed to call him off. "If anyone gets me, it's going to be a fan!" he told her, letting the kid go.

As Mark Chapman makes his way past delis and roasted chestnut carts, beneath the canopy of the sunlit skyscrapers, he hears the weeping of his own dear wife, Gloria. He'd left her in tears at the Honolulu airport gate. He'd had an appointment with a psychiatrist only days before, but he failed to show up. He assured Gloria that he was returning to New York to find a job and make a new life for them both. But he keeps hearing her crying, which again gives way to the voices of his Little People. "Please, think of your wife," they plead. "Please, Mr. President. Think of your mother. Think of yourself."

Pressing on across town, he suddenly spots a bookstore and hurries in. Momentarily, he emerges with a fresh copy of *The Catcher in the Rye*. Sitting down at a streetside café table, he opens the clean red cover, takes out his ballpoint pen, and writes on the inside cover: "This is my statement." And he signs it Holden Caulfield.

It's 11:30 A.M. now and John Lennon is lying naked on the floor of the White Room, curled in a fetal position around a fully clothed Yoko Ono, staring blankly at the Dakota ceiling. At the periphery of the umbrellaed spots, *Rolling Stone*'s Annie Leibowitz circles the couple with her camera exclaiming "Yes! . . . Hold that. . . . Great!"

Six stories below, Mark Chapman, standing at the front of a small crowd of fans now, is peering up at the gothic, high-gabled edifice of the Dakota. Under his arm he holds *The Catcher in the Rye* and a new copy of *Double Fantasy*. Though it promises to be an unseasonably warm December afternoon, his long green overcoat is still buttoned, his green scarf wrapped round his neck, and his gloves on. Holden himself had been dressed just this way on his arrival in the city. Except he had worn a red deer hunter's cap. His alter ego could only find a fake fur model to complete his costume.

After Liebowitz takes her leave with historic celluloid, her subjects have a quick bite to eat in the kitchen, then retire to Yoko's office for a phone interview with Dave Sholin, a San Francisco radio personality. "We're either going to live or we're going to die," John tells him. "I consider that my work won't be finished until I'm dead and buried—and I hope that's a long time." Only a few weeks before, during his marathon talk with *Playboy*, he had been interrupted by a scream outside the Dakota. "Another murder at Rue Dakota!" he had cracked.

Outside, Mark Chapman keeps waiting. He has seen Lauren Bacall, Mia Farrow, and Paul Simon himself duck out from the building, but still not the prize. He bides his time chatting with a regular visitor, Jude Stein, as well as to a young local photographer, Paul Goresh, who has succeeded in snapping the Lennons here several times. Suddenly Jude alerts him to an elderly woman emerging from the lobby, hand in hand with a young boy. Jude presses forward introducing her new friend to 5-year-old Sean Lennon. Captain Nemo bows down and tenderly shakes his tiny hand.

"He was the cutest little boy I ever saw," the former YMCA counselor would recall. "It didn't enter my mind that I was going to kill this poor young boy's father, and he wouldn't have a father for the rest of his life. I mean, I love children. I'm the catcher in the rye."

Soon after the boy is gone, a limo pulls up. Momentarily, the black iron gates are thrown open and John and Yoko Lennon materialize surrounded by their staff. Chapman is immobilized. Goresh shoves him forward. Suddenly, he finds himself standing in front of John Lennon himself, holding out his album and a pen. The star hastily autographs the album.[17]

"Is that all you want?" he asks the fan. Yoko is already in the idling limousine, the passenger door still open. "Is that all you want?" he asks a second time.

"Yeah . . . thanks, John!" Chapman stammers at last.

"I was just overwhelmed by his sincerity," he later recalled. "I had expected a brush-off, but it was just the opposite. I was on cloud nine. And there was a little bit of me going, 'Why didn't you shoot him?' And I said, 'I can't shoot him like this.' I wanted to get the autograph."

Their limo drops the Lennons off across town at the Record Plant. They spend the next six hours mixing Yoko's first solo single, "Walking on Thin Ice." "I may cry someday, but the tears will dry whichever way," sings Mrs. Lennon, "and when our hearts return to ashes, I'll be just a story."

They work till 10:30 that evening, John insisting on getting the recording just right. Yoko suggests they go out for a late dinner at the nearby Stage Deli, but John wants to return home to tuck Sean in. "See you tomorrow morning, bright and early!" he calls to his producer, Jack Douglas, as he leaves. But Douglas is disturbed. He later reveals to biographer, Sandra Shevey, that John had been talking strangely in private that afternoon. "I think John knew his life was over," he told Shevey. "He knew something was definitely wrong that afternoon. . . . He said he'd be more famous than Elvis when he died. He was talking about death all that day. He said, 'Don't tell Yoko.' He was explicit."

Mark Chapman is alone now at the Dakota, a solitary sentry. He'd pleaded with his new friends, Jude and Paul, to stay on but they have gone home to bed, wishing him luck with John again. As the cars and cabs speed past on 71st Street, he chats with the Cuban doorman, José Perdomo, about his world travels, his work with refugees, his career in security, the Bay of Pigs, and the JFK assassination. He still holds his autographed *Double Fantasy* and his novel.

In his overcoat pocket, the revolver weighs heavily. He's never fired the weapon. Will it work? And what about his aim? He'd taken a marks-

---

17. In 2003, it was purchased for $525,000, making it the most valuable LP ever sold.

manship course for his security work and had scored well above average, but that was years ago. He relies on the bullets: his .38 is loaded with hollow-point slugs, the kind that explode inside the body.

Suddenly, he turns toward the curb, eyes widening. The long black car with the opaque windows glides to a stop only feet away. Yoko exits, followed by her husband, carrying a tape recorder. As Lennon brushes past Chapman, he gives him a sudden hard glance.

"He printed me," the gunman would later confess. At that instant, "I was praying to God to keep me from killing Lennon," he went on, "and I was also praying to the devil to give me the opportunity, because I knew I would not have the strength on my own."

Gloria cries louder. "Please, Mr. President, please," plead the Little People, "think of your wife." Do it, do it, DO IT! screams another voice.

He rips the revolver from his coat and drops down in a combat squat, "Mr. Lennon!" he shouts.

John doesn't have time to turn to the voice before four slugs tear through his back. "I'm shot!" he chokes, staggering six steps and collapsing inside the concierge's booth, blood spraying from his lips.

Chapman drops the gun to the pavement. "Do you know what you've done!" cries José, rushing for him, kicking the weapon across the pavement. Heart racing, hearing a woman's sobs inside the hotel foyer, Chapman begins pacing, flipping through the pages of his gospel, trying to focus on the words.

He is still trying to read when two squad cars scream up. As the first team of policemen rushes him, he drops *The Catcher in the Rye* and *Double Fantasy* and throws his arms up crying, "Don't hurt me. I'm unarmed. I acted alone!"

The second team of officers, Bill Gamble and James Moran, dash into the concierge's booth where Yoko is huddled over her husband, sobbing.

John's eyes are glazed and blood gushes from his mouth and chest as Gamble and Moran carry him to their squad car and lay him out on the backseat, knowing they can't wait for an ambulance.

"I'm not afraid of dying," John had once said. "It's just like getting out of one car and into another." He'd also told Fred Seaman that, when dying, one's life replays itself in one's mind in backward, chronological order.

John Lennon spends his last moments on the backseat of a speeding NYPD squad car. The phantasmagoria of the city lights flashes through the windows on his fixed pupils as the blood pours from his chest and the officers call to him as if from a dream, "Are you John Lennon? Do you know who you are? Are you John Lennon?"

But their voices are drowned in the wail of the sirens. Then he hears another voice, his own, echoing within him and without him, louder and louder:

> Turn off your mind, relax and float downstream
> It is not dying, it is not dying
> Lay down all thoughts, surrender to the void
> It is shining, it is shining.

POSTMORTEM

Newspaper taxis appear on the shore,
Waiting to take you away.
Climb in the back with your head in the clouds,
And you're gone.
—Lennon and McCartney, "Lucy in the Sky with Diamonds"

Attempts to revive John Winston Ono Lennon were futile. He was pronounced dead shortly after arrival at Roosevelt Hospital by chief medical examiner Dr. Elliott M. Gross. He had lost nearly all his blood.

Yoko had her husband cremated. Her security man Douglas Mac-Dougall delivered the body from the funeral home to the Ferncliff Mortuary Crematorium. Julian had wanted to view the body, but it was reduced to ashes before he arrived from London.

The woman who only fourteen years before had begged for his patronage lest she kill herself, inherited half of Lennon's $30 million estate outright and was named executor of the balance that was placed in trust. Though she had refused MacDougall's security measures before the assassination, she paid $1 million for her own protection in the following year.

On the very next day after the assassination, the widow ordered Jack Douglas back to the studio to dub her husband's lyrics over prerecorded David Spinozza guitar parts. "She rattled on like a drill sergeant," said the producer, so grief stricken he was nearly incapable of working.

On Sunday, December 14, 100,000 fans congregated in Central Park, and Mayor Koch ordered flags throughout the city to be flown at half-mast. Yoko Ono asked the crowd to "pray for John's soul" during a ten-minute memorial silence.

Double Fantasy quickly rose to Number 1 on the charts and won a Grammy for Best Album of the year.[18] On the cover of her next solo album, *Season of Glass,* appeared a photo of Lennon's blood-stained spectacles beside half a glass of water. The cover of her 1982 follow-up album, *It's Alright (I See Rainbows),* featured a shot of Ono in wrap-around sunglasses, looking toward the sun and, on the back, an image of Lennon's ghost looking over her and their son.

In the years to come, the widow would release two books, three albums, three hundred hours of lost Lennon tapes, mugs, T-shirts, sweatshirts, kites, rugs, and Lennon drawing posters. Her latest album, *Yes, I'm a Witch,* is a collection of remixes and covers of previous work.

"Whatever her wishes," wrote *Rolling Stone* in 1984, "her identity has switched irrevocably from Yoko Ono, Avant-Garde Artist, to Mrs. Lennon, Keeper of the Flame."

Said the widow: "For ten years I was the devil. Now I'm an angel. Did the world have to lose him to change their opinion of me?"

Six months after the murder, Yoko married her assistant, Sam Havadtoy, in a secret ceremony in his native Hungary. The couple separated in 2001.

At the command of God, Mark David Chapman rejected an insanity defense and pleaded guilty to the murder of John Lennon. "I deserve to die," he said. But he was sentenced to twenty years to life in Attica State Prison. Here he re-embraced Christianity and was exorcised of six demons. "They were the most fierce and incredible things you ever saw or heard in your life," he said, "hissing, gurgling noises and different voices right out of my mouth."

He didn't, however, blame his crime on the demons. Nor was there a simple reason for the murder. As his biographer, Jack Jones, pointed out after more than two hundred hours of interviews with him in Attica, Chapman as Holden Caulfield considered Lennon the "ultimate 'phony.' " By "killing him he could stop the rock star from leading astray another generation of innocent youth," wrote Jones.

On another level, his real target had been his violent father. "I

---

18. In 1982, Jack Douglas sued Yoko for $750,000 in unpaid royalties. The court awarded the album's producer $2.5 million.

wanted to go hold a gun to his head, make him beg, blow him away," Chapman told prison psychiatrists. "Perhaps I was getting him back by killing John Lennon."

Though Jones conceded that this might have been a partial underlying motive, Chapman had also confessed that he had fantasized about not only killing just a father figure but wiping out multitudes with a nuclear device. Instead, wrote Jones, he murdered "someone that most of the people in the world identified with . . . thus hurting us all."

On yet another level, prison psychologist, Dr. Daniel Schwartz, diagnosed Chapman as a schizophrenic with a narcissistic personality disorder. Indeed, the prisoner went on to explain to Jones, "I was an acute nobody. I had to usurp someone else's importance, someone else's success."

Referring to himself in the third person, he told Larry King during his 1992 telephone interview: "Mark David Chapman was a walking shell who didn't ever learn how to let out his feelings of anger, of rage, of disappointment. Mark David Chapman was a failure in his own mind. He wanted to become somebody important, Larry. He didn't know how to handle being a nobody."

Surely such Lennon songs as "Nowhere Man" and "I'm a Loser" had resonance for the former youth counselor and security guard, especially since, from an early age, he had felt destined to great things. "He's as blind as he can be, just sees what he wants to see," sang the Beatle, "Nowhere Man can you see me at all?"

He didn't and couldn't. "I saw him as a cardboard cutout on an album," Chapman confessed to the police. "And now I've come to grips with the fact that John Lennon was a person."

The irony is of course that John Lennon had thought of himself as a Nowhere Man during low points in his life. "Doesn't have a point of view, knows not where he's going to. Isn't he a bit like you and me?" In this sense Lennon was murdered by his own brother who had never escaped his own nihilism—who had never been redeemed by success as he, Lennon, had. "It's getting hard to be someone, but it all works out," he sang in "Strawberry Fields Forever." But it hadn't all worked out for Chapman. As he told Jones, "I was 'Mr. Nobody' until I killed the biggest Somebody on earth."

Some, however, dismiss such psychologizing, convinced that the CIA or FBI was behind the assassination of John Lennon and that his murderer was a Manchurian Candidate. Lennon's son, Sean, is among these believers. "Anybody who thinks that Mark Chapman was just some crazy guy who killed my dad for his personal interests is insane, I think, or very naive," he insists.

When Larry King asked Chapman about such theories, he bluntly replied, "Hogwash."

The conspiracy theories are based on Chapman's involvement with the YMCA and a supposed connection between the organization and the CIA. As a Y counselor, Chapman had briefly visited Lebanon where the CIA allegedly ran "assassin camps." Conspiracy theorists believe that Chapman (like Oswald and Sirhan Sirhan before him) was "programmed" to assassinate political subversives such as Lennon. This programming was reactivated several years later, they believe, by a catalyst word or phrase that came from *The Catcher in the Rye.*

Even if the far-fetched mechanics of the theory are accepted, its foundation is flawed. The New York FBI had closed their file on Lennon in 1972, saying that he had renounced his former radicalism.[19] Indeed, he had said he was "sick of being in the crusades." "But when you talk about destruction," he sang in "Revolution," "don't you know you can count me out." Moreover, in 1975, before his retirement, he told *Rolling Stone* magazine he was "jumpy and nervous even commenting on politics." When he resurfaced in 1980, he was effectively apolitical. If there had been a conspiracy to assassinate him, it surely would have been set in motion during his activism throughout the Nixon administration, not at the end of the benign and far less paranoid term of President Carter (whose inaugural ball Lennon attended).

After conducting an extensive investigation, the NYPD concluded that murder conspiracy theories had no merit.

Whatever the truth is, John Lennon's dying wish was at least realized.

"I just have one hope," he confessed near the end, "that I die before Yoko does because we have become so much of an equation together that I don't think I would have the strength to go on without her. Oh, I don't mean I would commit suicide; I just mean life would be so empty. I hope I die before Yoko, because if Yoko died I wouldn't know how to survive. I couldn't carry on."

What would have become of the star had he not been murdered has

---

19. Even before this time, it was noted in his FBI file: "Lennon appears to be radically oriented, however, he does not give the impression he is a true revolutionist since he is constantly under the influence of narcotics."

been the subject of much speculation. Most insiders agree that Yoko intended to divorce him. A divorce would have been more devastating to him than their eighteen-month separation five years before, which sent him into a self-destructive meltdown.

After hearing of Yoko's intention to divorce John, Fred Seaman worried that "the shock might send him reeling back into seclusion and terminal depression." While composing "Losing You" and the other songs for *Double Fantasy* in Bermuda, John felt "that she was slipping away. It drove me crackers." He had never been without close female companionship in his life and simply couldn't handle being alone. Throughout his separation from Yoko, in spite of May Pang's devoted companionship, he had drugged himself to oblivion.

But even if he did survive the loss of Mother, on whom he had become utterly dependent, would he have gone on to "conquer the world again" alone, his one great ambition? Not even McCartney has come close, though, of all the Beatles, he was and is the greatest populist. Lennon might have created another *Imagine*—his greatest album in his own estimation and that of most critics—but it would never have remade him a "king" much less the messiah that he once thought he was.

Would John Lennon have survived on the memories of once having been a king? Not even his idol, the King himself, whose throne the Beatles had stolen, had survived that.

Yet his body of work as it stands, with no addition, is incomparable in its breadth, depth, and humanity. He brought an unequaled wit, incisiveness, and imagination to music. Above all, at the core of his work was a moral dimension that went well beyond the social and political protests of such luminaries as Guthrie, Baez, or even Dylan. In this, he became the conscience of a generation striving for justice and freedom.

More than any other artist, John Lennon, in spite of passing self-deceptions, was unflinchingly honest with himself in the end. "Just give me a little truth," he sang. He revealed truths that others couldn't see or hadn't the courage to tell. Not just truths about the world as he saw it, but about himself. Like all men, he had feet of clay, but he was the first to admit his imperfections, his confusions, and his fears. He confessed that he'd been a violent man and had hurt others, but he'd repented and strived for redemption in love. "No one you can save that can't be saved," he sang. "Nothing you can do, but you can learn how to be you in time."

When he came to his end at the hands of a lost soul, it had been more than ten years since he had written the beautifully innocent "All You Need Is Love." And in this time, through all his struggles, he had learned that true love wasn't so "easy" after all, but a divine life force hard won in the face of mortality.

"I tried so hard to stay alive," he sang on *Double Fantasy*. "But the angel of destruction keeps on houndin' me all around. . . . They say the Lord helps those who help themselves. . . . Lord, help me, lord. . . . Help me to help myself."

Interlude: Soul

Fame is the soul eater.
—Jerry Garcia

According to his song, "God," John Lennon stopped believing in everything after the Fab Four breakup—the Beatles, the Bible, Buddha, Jesus. Everything. Except "Yoko and me—and that's reality . . . now I'm reborn. I was the Walrus but now I'm John."

He'd arrived at a definition of God as *a concept by which we measure our pain.* And God knew, Lennon had always had plenty of that before, during, and after Beatlemania. "The bigger the pain, the more God you look for," he said.

So God grew bigger and bigger for him until, near the end, he declared, "Well, if there is a God, we're all It." But in a kind of nuclear metaphysics, the big became little and universal personal. "You've got to get down to your own God in your own temple," he'd come to believe. He'd started doing this with the Maharishi. But after a month, he and the other Beatles abandoned the guru. When the holy one asked why, John replied, "If you're so cosmically conscious, as you claim, then you should know why."

Lennon suffered no frauds or fools. So he became an atheist about everything except "Yoko and me." But his wiser half wasn't even sure about his wife. "You're getting phony," he sang in "Losing You," echoing Holden Caulfield, his assassin's hero. That left just his maker and him, and he was ready for the reunion, crying to the sea storm, "Take me away, God!" Years before, he had seen a UFO hovering over the Manhattan horizon. "I kept shouting, 'Over here!'" he recalled. "Take me with you! I'm ready!"

Elvis had been ready too. "It was as if he wanted to die . . . just to see the other side," wrote his stepbrother David Stanley. "And it all goes back to a spiritual thing. I think E's death was so spiritual because he wanted to know." In fact, Elvis, a firm believer, *did* know. He just wasn't sure about the details. He wore both a crucifix and the Star of David because, "I wouldn't want to be kept out of heaven on a technicality."

"I believe in the Bible," he went on to explain. "I believe that all good things come from God. I don't believe I'd sing the way I do if God hadn't wanted me to." One of his favorite Bible verses, as well as Lennon's, was "What profiteth a man if he gains the world, but loses his soul?" And he had an answer of sorts: "Adversity is sometimes hard upon a man," he said. "But for one man who can stand prosperity, there are a hundred that will stand adversity." In short, prosperity was the King's cross.

His mother had told Elvis he was the One and he knew he had a mission. "He'd get up on the table and preach; he'd gather us all around," Priscilla remembered. "He was Moses with a cane coming down the mountain or John the Baptist greeting the Savior." Red and Sonny West, whom he called his "disciples," recalled how their boss updated scripture during these impromptu Graceland sermons. "Moses came on down from the mountain, and how he got down was the burning bushes directed his ass on down!" Another time, he proclaimed, "A rich man's chance of getting into heaven is like a camel's ass trying to get through the eye of a needle." Often he would begin his sermons on an ominous note, "Whoa, all ye motherfuckers, of kind thoughts and good deeds."[1]

Then there were the celestial signs. Thirteen years before his death, Elvis was driving to the City of Angels through the Palestinian landscape of Arizona. Beside him sat Larry Geller, his hairdresser guru. Elvis slammed on the brakes, jumped out of his tour van, and dashed into the desert, arms thrown heavenward. "I see Stalin's face up there!" he cried to Geller. "My prayers have been answered! I have seen Christ and Antichrist, and I know what I have to do!"

The King began studying with Daya Mata[2] at the Self-Realization

---

1. Red West, Sonny West, and Dave Hebler, *Elvis: What Happened?*

2. Sri Daya Mata, now ninety-four, still heads the fellowship, based on the teachings of Yogi Paramahansa Yogananda. Born Faye Wright in Salt Lake City, in 1914, Daya Mata is descended from a prominent Morman family, among the founders of The Church of Jesus Christ of Latter-Day Saints.

Fellowship in Malibu. "It's what we all need, a break from the craziness," he told Priscilla. One day he and his disciples, the Memphis Mafia, sped up the Pacific Coast Highway at a 100-plus, E in the lead on his
Harley Electra Glide, the guys drafting on their Triumph Bonnevilles,
roaring into the Hindu sanctuary. The King was taking a much-needed
break from the shooting of *Harum Scarum* down in Hollywood. Greeting her holiness, Daya—whom Sonny said "reminded Elvis a lot of his
mother"—he came right to the point: he had been seeking "a higher
level of spirituality" all his life. She advised him to go slow on Jacob's
ladder. But the ever-impatient King told her, "I want to get there now. I
want a crash course. There have to be shortcuts."

Though Daya insisted there were no shortcuts, he soon began hearing the voice of Jesus in the song of birds at Graceland. He came to
believe that he could hypnotize people with a glance and to heal children with a touch. He bought FDR's yacht, *Potomac,* and donated it
to St. Jude's Children's Hospital in Memphis. He gave away much of
his fortune to complete strangers. In the spring of 1967, he released
How Great Thou Art. The gospel album included hymns he had sung
as a boy at the Assembly of God church in Tupelo: "There is no God
but God," "Reach out to Jesus," "He is my everything." The following
year, on the night his daughter Lisa Marie was born, he called Nancy
Sinatra and, overwhelmed with gratitude for his many blessings in a
world where so many others knew only hardship, he told her, "I should
have been a preacher. I should have stayed with the church."

Later, having suffered several near fatal overdoses and sensing that
he was living on borrowed time, the afterlife was never far from Elvis's
mind. He assured family and friends that he would find a way to communicate with them from beyond the grave. Taking solace in this, his
fans founded The Church of Elvis the Divine. Hours before his death,
he urged his stepbrother Ricky who had just delivered him his midnight narcotics, to kneel down and pray with him.

"Dear Lord, please show me the way," Elvis prayed. "I'm tired and
confused, and I need your help." Then, turning to his stepbrother, he
said, "Rick, we should all begin to live for Christ."

Jimi Hendrix had a Christian burial, like Elvis. But both were part
Cherokee, a tribe rich in searchers and visionaries. Like the King, the
Voodoo Child claimed to be a messenger too. "I've wanted to go into
the hills sometimes, but I stayed," he told an interviewer. "Some people
are meant to stay and carry messages." In this, he wasn't submitting to

the sixties guru epidemic, but earnestly believed in the transformative spiritual power of his "sky" music.

Just as Lennon had called the disciples "thick and ordinary," Hendrix called the Ten Commandments "a drag," and believed that the Catholic Church was "vomiting over the earth." His message was not dogmatic or denominational. "My music is electric church music," he said. "I am electric religion." The Dead's Phil Lesh echoed this, writing, "Every place we play is church. When we play, we're prayin'." The spiritual advisor for both Hendrix and the Dead was Rolling Thunder.[3]

Jimi's second album, *Axis: Bold As Love* came from *The Book of the Hopi.* In it, the Creator Spider Woman orders her disciples "to go about all the world and send out sound." The sound of true soul music. Two months before his death, Hendrix traveled to Hawaii to conduct the Rainbow Bridge Vibratory Color-Sound Experiment on Maui's Olowalu Volcano, the Polynesian holy site of the Crater of the Sun. Dressed in shaman's garb, he retired to a medicine tent and, there, with the other participants, consumed LSD. Just before the experiment, an aged German fortune-teller, Clara Schuff, told the star he was descended from Tibetan royalty and that in his next incarnation he would teach the magical astrology of Tibet.

Most of the other stars, as well as their wives or significant others, dabbled in the occult. Lennon and Morrison were married in Celtic ceremonies. Yoko considered herself a witch, as did the second Mrs. Morrison, Patricia. Monika Dannemann was an obsessive student of clairvoyant metaphysics. Like Yoko Ono, Courtney Love "surrounded herself with a coterie of soothsayers," wrote her biographer, Melissa Rossi. In the end, she "called psychics across the country, searching for astral information" about her missing husband. The stars and their mates did daily tarot, astrological, or numerological readings.

Hendrix was a great student of numerology himself. He spoke at length about mystical number systems with Dannemann who recounted these discussions in *The Inner World of Jimi Hendrix.*

St. Augustine had called numbers "the Universal language offered by the deity to humans as confirmation of the truth." Lennon, Presley, and Hendrix planned their schedules and their travels by the numbers,

---

3. The Shoshone medicine man, born John Pope, once cured Jerry Garcia of pneumonia, several times spiritually "cleansed" the Fillmore and other concert venues, and later became the inspiration of Dylan's 1975 Rolling Thunder Review tour.

and screened their friends and assistants according to them too. Each was a devotee of Cheiro, the father of modern numerology.[4]

Each attached enormous significance to his personal number, the sum of their month-day-year birthday numbers. Both Elvis and Jimi were powerful 8s—the number, according to Cheiro, of both "domination, control, and achievement," as well as of "fatalism" and "loneliness." Lennon called himself a 9—the number of creative, universal consciousness.[5]

The Doors were into numbers too. Jim was a 1; co-founder Ray, a 9. Ray called this "the Dionysian and Apollonian balancing act. . . . The snake biting its own tail. The Ouroboros. The wholeness." Dionysius was the body, the impulse, the id; Apollo was the intellect, the order, the superego. Morrison found more significance in these pagan symbols than in Christian ones. Detecting no moral authority in the universe, much less in human affairs, for him the Judeo/Christian God of the commandments was dead. Only Nietzsche's Superman survived.

A musical shaman like Hendrix and Garcia, Morrison called himself "an oracle, a priest . . . a ventriloquist of God." For him, "God" was not a beneficent or wrathful Who or He, in Whose image man was created. Rather God was an omnipotent, cosmic What—an infinite, eternal impersonal force at the heart of all things—from the amoeba to the galaxies. In this sense, Morrison dismissed Christianity as a myopic moral religion born of the idea that death is a punishment for sin, and eternal life only achievable through contrition and worship of a martyred divine intermediary. Instead, the spiritual orientation of Morrison—as well as that of Hendrix, Garcia, and Lennon too—was closer to a nondogmatic Buddhist or existential point of view in which death was not an end of life but merely a change or dissolution of form. So Morrison was spiritual, but not religious. As his precursor, Nietzsche, said, "After coming

---

4. After an apprenticeship in India, Cheiro, aka William John Warner, an Irishman, read the palms and the numbers of early-twentieth-century notables from Oscar Wilde to Thomas Edison, to King Edward. After his own reading, skeptic Mark Twain, confessed, "Cheiro has exposed my character to me with humiliating accuracy."

5. Numerological coincidences abound in the world of rock death. Jimi Hendrix, Janis Joplin, Jim Morrison, Kurt Cobain, and Brian Jones all died at age 27, equaling the cosmic 9. Elvis and blues pioneer, Robert Johnson, died on the same day, as had soul brothers, Jim Morrison and Brian Jones. Lennon was shot on Morrison's birthday.

into contact with a religious man I always feel I must wash my hands."
Then he added, "In heaven, all the interesting people are missing."
Though the philosopher and the singer may never have rendezvoused in
heaven, they surely met in some other less exclusive dimension.

And the head of the Grateful Dead is surely with them. Though
Jerry Garcia was as much a spiritual rebel and loner as Morrison or the
others, he was the unofficial Buddhist of the group. If God is a bank in
which Jesus saves, Moses invests, and Buddha plays the market—Jerry
was a player too and took his inspiration from every corner of the cosmos. Some Deadheads even called him the Buddha. Which he hated.
If some of his colleagues got into self-deification, the guitarist wanted
none of it. After he was resurrected in 1986 and Deadheads started
calling him a saint, he said, "I'll put up with it until they come to me
with the cross and nails." But the more the star insisted he was "just
a guy who plays guitar," the more everybody genuflected. Eventually,
he got down to the "temple" inside, like Lennon. "There is a road, no
simple highway, between the dawn and the dark of night," he declared,
"and if you go, no one may follow, that path is for your steps alone."

That road was longer for Garcia than for any of the others. In the
climax of the Grateful Dead's last performance, he brought tears to the
eyes of everyone at Chicago's Soldier's Field when he wailed the chorus
of "So Many Roads" over and over:

> So many roads to ease my soul . . .
> All I want is one to take me home.

Born not only of the blues but of gospel and soul too, rock music has
provided plenty of the sacred and the profane over the years. Stars have
been torn between both.

"It's hard work saving rock and roll," said U2's Bono.

"You got to serve somebody!" sang Dylan.

"Work me, Lord. Work me, Lord. Please don't You leave me," sang
Janis, her father an atheist, her mother a Sunday school teacher. "I
don't think I'm very special. . . . But I don't think you're gonna find
anybody . . . who could say that they tried like I tried. The worst you
can say about me is that I'm never satisfied.

Her friend Pat Nichols said Janis was "a very spiritual person" but
was "afraid to let others see that."

Other stars were afraid to show it too. Some are even believed to have sold their souls. The original legend has it that rock's Abraham, Robert Johnson, did so at the crossroads, only to be fatally poisoned at age 27. Fearing damnation for playing "the devil's boogie-woogie music," the Reverend Little Richard abandoned rock and roll twice. Jerry Lee Lewis, believing his Job-like misfortunes—the deaths of his wives, his sons, his mother, as well as his own close scrapes with the reaper—were payback for his Great Balls of Fire rock, also briefly abandoned the stage with the help of his fallen cousin, Jimmy Swaggart. A disciple of Satanist Aleister Crowley, Jimmy Page allegedly made a pact with Lucifer for the success of "Stairway to Heaven." "Walking side by side with death, the devil mocks your every step," sang Robert Plant. After the song topped the charts, the "Zeppelin Curse" descended: Page and Plant were nearly killed in a car accident; Plant's five-year-old son died mysteriously; and, finally, Zeppelin's drummer, John Bonham, fatally OD'd. Though the Stones' "Satanic Majesties Request" was a commercial failure, Brian Jones was murdered in his swimming pool a year later, then came "Sympathy for the Devil" at Altamont, then Jagger and Bianca wed in a Balinese voodoo ceremony, sacrificing multi-colored chickens "for luck."

Though Hendrix dabbled in the dark side, too, by all accounts he never sold his soul. But, his first girlfriend, Faye Pridgeon, said he worried about "some devil" in him. "He was so tormented . . . with something really evil," she recalled. ". . . He used to talk about having some root lady or somebody see if she could drive this demon out of him."

Lennon, horrified by his own past violence and misdeeds, briefly became a Jesus Freak and even contacted the Bakkers' 700 Club several times. Protesting his earlier "antireligion" reputation, he declared, "I'm a most religious fellow. I was brought up a Christian and I only now understand some of the things that Christ was saying in those parables." He fantasized about searching for "The Spear of Destiny" that had pierced Christ's side; he pledged all future musical proceeds to world peace; and he even tried the vows of St. Francis. When deliverance still eluded him, John—a spiritual omnivore like Elvis—even fasted in the name of Allah for a few days. In the end, his prayers unanswered by any god, he feared that he had sold his soul.

"There was a time in my life when I would have given anything to be on top, anything. Nothing stopped me," he confided to his spiritual advisor John Green. "And who's the devil that I sold out to?" he went on. "The God Almighty public! That's the god I pray to." He explained that as a Beatle he had "channeled the public's love into music." But after the group disintegrated "now that I'm truly and totally hooked, they won't deal! They've got my soul, what else is there?"

Cobain, who hero worshipped Lennon, felt much the same toward the end of his life. He'd gone through a very brief Christian period in his teens, soon converting to his ABORT CHRIST—GOD IS GAY Protestantism. With his friend Dylan Carlson, a student of Eastern religions, he began studying Shiva, the Hindu God of Destruction; and with his wife, Courtney, who kept a personal Buddhist shrine in the house, he delved into the dharma and karmic realms too. His friend with whom he'd wanted to collaborate, Michael Stipe of REM, sang, "up in the spotlight, losing my religion," expressing Cobain's own feeling well. In the end, the young star's belief was disbelief. He felt that he had lost not only his religion but his soul. He longed only for an end to the pain, as did Lennon. "Nirvana means freedom from pain, suffering and the external world," he'd explained after founding the group, "and that's pretty close to my definition of Punk Rock."

But when punk stopped freeing Cobain of the pain, it nailed him to its crossbeam. "Rinkydink God. For putting me on this earth," he sang in "Downer." "Death in mind. Nurse!"

Death, life's eternal mystery, is the mother of religion. In the end, Kurt Cobain was taken by her in the form of the only person whom he had always loved, trusted, and believed in: his soul mate.

The Book of Genesis tells the story of the birth of death. When Adam and Eve ate the forbidden fruit of knowledge, they saw good and evil, and God condemned them to "return to the dust from which they came." Banished from Eden, they had only each other for comfort now. Husband and wife till death did they part. Soul mates.

The first to meet his Maker was their favorite son, Abel, killed by his jealous brother, Cain. So man's first death was a murder. God made Cain "a wanderer" of the world but gave him a mark so no one would kill him in retribution: he was cursed to live to the end with his unforgiving conscience, his parents' legacy. And with that punishment, the first son must have cried, as one of his marked daughters later would after murdering her own soul mate and the voice of his generation:

I'm Miss World,
Somebody kill me
Now I've made my bed I'll lie in it
I've made my bed I'll die in it
I made my bed I'll cry in it.

6

KURT COBAIN

February 20, 1967–April 5, 1994

WHY?

His wife lay in the dried blood where the body had lain. Beside her was a pile of potting soil, with a handwritten note on top. It ends:

"KEEP GOING, COURTNEY. I LOVE YOU, I LOVE YOU."

Draped in her husband's blood-splattered corduroy jacket, she crawls across the floor. She seizes a fragment of the matted scalp and clutches it to her breast. "Are you there, are you there, are you fucking anywhere?" she cries again. "Are you an angel now? Fuck you!"

The body of Kurt Donald Cobain has been moved from the greenhouse of his Lake Washington estate to the funeral parlor. Here the widow visits him for the last time. She gently strokes his waxen face and snips off a lock of his cherubic blond hair. She unzips his pants and clips a strand of his pubic hair.

"WHY?" she keeps wailing.

She seemed to have answered this herself in her MTV interview an hour ago. She said her husband's final note read, "It's not fun for me anymore, I can't live this life." In another interview that Saturday morning of April 9, 1994, Courtney Love urged the MTV viewers to share her emotion: "Everyone who feels guilty, raise your hand!"

At the Sunday candlelight vigil for her husband, her grief turned to anger. "He's such an asshole. I want you to say 'asshole' really loud!" she urged the 7,000 mourners. After she read the part of the suicide note about his not wanting to be a rock star anymore, she cried, "Shut up! Bastard. Why didn't you just enjoy it?"

Finishing her videotaped message to his fans, Ms. Love had one last request, "Just tell him he's a fucker, okay? Just say, 'Fucker, you're a *fucker*. And that you love him.' "

She had told reporters that she had done everything to prevent a suicide. A week before, her husband had escaped from a detox retreat in L.A.; she filed a Missing Person report with the police, telling them that he had a gun. Then she hired a private detective to find him before he turned it on himself.

Tom Grant, a retired LAPD officer and now a prominent detective with many high-profile celebrity cases to his credit,[1] worked tirelessly to find the missing star. But even before the body was discovered, many days in decomposition, Grant had concluded that there was more to the case than met the eye.

After the hasty cremation of the singer, the detective urged the Seattle Police Department to reopen the case as a possible homicide. He had many concerns—among them that Cobain had more than three times the lethal dose of heroin in his system, that the shotgun at his side had no identifiable fingerprints, and that the "suicide" letter was not entirely in his handwriting.

He was also puzzled that the letter was addressed to BODDAH.

AH, PUNK!

This is what I was looking for. Ah, punk rock!
—Kurt Cobain, fifteen, after seeing the Melvins perform

Kurt Cobain called himself "an extremely happy child" until the age of nine.

"Things just lay down before me," he later recalled. "I didn't have any problems. There were no obstacles." During this period, the boy believed he was an alien sent from another planet to study earthlings.

---

1. In addition, he would later work on the Paula Jones and Monika Lewinsky cases.

His best friend was a fellow extraterrestrial by the name of "Boddah." Amused by the fantasy at first, his parents set a place at the dinner table for Boddah. Finally, becoming concerned that their son wasn't spending time with real children, they told him Boddah had been drafted and had vanished in Vietnam.

Then, in 1976, Don Cobain, an auto mechanic, and Wendy, a homemaker, were divorced.

I HATE MOM. I HATE DAD, Kurt graffitied his bedroom wall.

Wendy won legal custody of her son and tried her best as a single parent. "I was totaled out on him," she told Michael Azerrad.[2] "My every waking hour was for him." Though a small, meek boy who hated sports, he became prone to violence and backtalk. Without friends, he adopted stray and wounded animals. Wendy took him to a psychologist who prescribed Ritalin for his hyperactivity and tantrums. Finally, at her wits end with the unmanageable boy, she sent him off to live in the trailer park with his father and grandparents. "As my bones grew they did hurt. They hurt really bad," Kurt sang in "Serve the Servants." "I tried hard to have a father. But instead I had a dad."

Don Cobain could be an impatient disciplinarian. He had once thrown his misbehaved son, age 6, across the room. He was especially severe with the boy in public. Once when Kurt spilled his water glass in a restaurant, Don seized him by the head, rapping him with his knuckles. "Fuck him for that!" Kurt told Azerrad. "Accidents weren't allowed. . . . We had to be perfect all the time."

Still deeply attached to his father, he begged him after the divorce not to get remarried. To pacify the sensitive boy, Don promised, but broke his word. "After that," recalled Kurt, "I was one of the last things of importance." He had little further contact with his father for the rest of his brief life. Like Lennon, Morrison, and Garcia, he felt fatherless.

Early on, the future icon of the Gen X decided he was fated to be either a great artist or a rock musician. In kindergarten, he drew perfect Donald Ducks, Plutos, and other Disney characters. By early teens, he was producing lifelike vaginas, fetuses, and devils. Later, after an arrest for public drunkenness and graffiti, he spent his jail time drawing nudes that he sold to fellow prisoners for masturbation.

In high school, Cobain's precocious art abilities led him to film-

---

2. Michael Azerrad, *Come as You Are: The Story of Nirvana* (New York: Main Street Books, 1993).

making. One of his Super 8 shorts was called *Kurt Commits Bloody Suicide*. In it he pretended to cut his wrists with a crushed soda can.

"I have suicide genes," he told schoolmates.

Kurt's genetic instability rivaled that of Elvis. Two of his fraternal great-uncles had fatally shot themselves. A third great-uncle died of a cerebral hemorrhage after toppling drunk down a staircase. His maternal great grandfather stabbed himself in the stomach in front of his family and later perished in a mental hospital.

"I'm going to be a superstar musician, kill myself, and go out in a flame of glory," Kurt told a friend after deciding that his future was not in art after all, but rock and roll. Not classic rock, not metal rock, but the kind of rock that expressed his entire childhood—the manic energy, the isolation, the rejection, the hurt. The *rage*.

Kurt got his first guitar from his Uncle Chuck, a drummer for the Beachcombers, a local Top 40 cover band. Though it was a secondhand Japanese acoustic, it became the fourteen-year-old's prize possession. He began taking lessons from the Beachcombers' guitarist who soon gave him an Ibanez electric and taught him how to play his favorite song, "Stairway to Heaven."

In 1985, two weeks shy of graduation, Cobain, like Hendrix, dropped out of high school. His mother, with whom he was living again by then, told him to get a job or get out. His father agreed to take him back if he agreed to give up his music and go into the military. Kurt took the Navy entrance exam, scored well, but refused to enlist. Evicted by both his father and mother now, he became homeless. "I played the 'tough love' thing on him," Wendy later confessed. In the next years, he slept under bridges and in cars, jails, and the spare rooms of ten different families.

The only thing that sustained Cobain now was his dream. "All my life, my dream has been to be a big rock star," he said. But he wasn't sure what kind of rock star. He had grown up with the Beatles, Abba, ELO, Queen, and Zeppelin. Though they were his favorites, their music lacked something. The missing link was finally revealed to him when he heard the Ramones, the Sex Pistols, and Aberdeen's underground heroes—the Melvins. After quitting high school and his parents, Kurt became a Melvins' roadie. The group's leader, Buzz Osborne, introduced him to other punk artists including Flipper, MDC, and the Butthole Surfers.

Controlled substances were sacrament for the punks. As a teen,

Kurt consumed great quantities of booze, pot, and acid. When nothing else was available, he did glue, cough syrup, or aerosol cans. "I saw him spray antiperspirant down his throat," said a friend. "He had a positive genius for misusing toiletries."

In 1987, he formed his first band, Fecal Matter, which, after a personnel change, became the future Skid Row. The trio included Kurt on guitar, Krist Novoselic on bass, and Aaron Burkhardt on drums.[3] They were all the children of divorce. Burkhardt lived on welfare with his mother. He was "a magnet for trouble," as Kurt approvingly noted, having once driven through the display window of the local ShopRite. "Novie," a 6-foot-7-inch gawky giant, had an equal appetite for destruction especially when on one of his "cartoon land" jug wine drunks. He described himself as "weird and maladjusted . . . and really depressed" in those days. The son of a Croatian truck driver, he lived with his mother, Maria, above her beauty parlor and made ends meet painting houses and working at Taco Bell.

The punk trio made its debut at a farmhouse in Raymond, Washington, a redneck logger town much like Aberdeen, which Kurt described as "Twin Peaks without the excitement." It turned out to be a Michelob blowout for yuppies, as Burkhardt recalled. A wasted Novoselic, covered in vampire blood, enlivened the evening by jumping in and out of the windows and chasing the guests. Afterward, Cobain kicked off the set with "Downer," his own composition about the B-side of homelife and growing up.

"Hand out lobotomies," went the chorus, "To save little families."

When the audience screamed for Zeppelin, Black Sabbath, and Beastie Boys' covers, the front man dove into "Spank Thru"—an autobiographical tune about jerking off.

The gig was cut short when irate boyfriends rushed the bandstand under a rain of Michelobs. Cobain beat a retreat outside to find his bassist already in the parking giving golden showers to the fans' cherried-out pickups. The future Nirvana managed a narrow escape in Novie's thrashed VW.

Kurt was now hooked on show business.

---

3. Burkhardt, who would become known as Nirvana's Pete Best (the Beatles first drummer) was soon fired. The band exhausted four more drummers until finally settling on Dave Grohl (now the Foo Fighters' front man) in 1991.

* * *

To Cobain's regret, his first trio netted no groupies. He had always been shy around girls. By age 20, he had suffered a few aborted liaisons. According to his journal, his first was with "a half-retarded girl" in her father's house. "I tried to fuck her but I didn't know how," the sixteen-year-old confessed.

He was giving suicide more serious thought by now but was determined "not to go out of this world without actually knowing what it's like to get laid."

At seventeen, he had chaperoned two goth girls back to his mother's double-wide for a Romilar cough syrup nightcap. While one puked and passed out in the front room, he managed to bed the other—but no sooner than his mother burst in and went ballistic. "Get that slut out of here!"

Kurt and Wendy hadn't exactly seen eye to eye since the divorce. She'd started partying with guys half her age, and all his friends had the hots for her. "He hated his mom," said his best friend, Dylan Carlson, "he thought *she* was a slut."

Wendy finally settled down and married an alcoholic longshoreman, Frank, who beat the shit out of her and terrorized Kurt. One night after Frank blacked out, Kurt stole his guns and threw them in the Wishkah River where he often camped out. He rescued them the next morning and pawned them for his first guitar amp.[4]

Frank had called Kurt a faggot ever since he'd seen him lose his first wrestling tournament in the 102-pound division. After becoming a star, Cobain would confess to *The Advocate*,[5] a gay weekly, that he considered himself a homosexual in high school—at least "in spirit." "I started being proud of the fact I was gay, even though I wasn't," he clarified. ". . . I used to pretend I was gay just to fuck with people. Once I got the gay tag, it gave me the freedom to be able to be a freak and let people know that they should just stay away from me." His first close friend in high school, Myer Loftin, a gay artist, "basically saved me from wanting to kill myself half the time," he went on, concluding, "If I wouldn't have found Courtney, I probably would have carried on with a bisexual lifestyle."

Several years later, however, Ms. Love would tell *Out* magazine that her husband had "made out with half the men in Seattle," and went on

---

4. A handful of his crematory ashes were later scattered in the Wishkah.

5. Kevin Allman, "The Dark Side of Kurt Cobain," *The Advocate*, February, 1992.

to insinuate that he had been intimate with Michael Stipe of R.E.M.[6] In his biography, *Kurt Cobain*, Christopher Sandford relates that the star himself confessed to a friend in L.A. that "he'd had sex with three or four men." *Penthouse* magazine reported accounts of an affair with "a well-known male artist" in L.A. Otherwise, the star was known to frequent gay bars on both coasts and while touring in Europe. Finally, a Seattle acquaintance, speaking anonymously, declared that in his last years "Kurt was frustrated trying to go straight. He wanted out of that marriage [to Courtney] so bad . . . it killed him." In 1992, performing in Reading, England, he dedicated a new song to Love that had only three words, "I'm married. Buried."

Earlier in his career, Cobain had been mischievous about his sexual orientation. A pioneer of in-your-face punk theater, he began cross-dressing on stage. He did his 1991 MTV performance in a yellow silk ball gown. At a Nirvana photo shoot, he appeared as Scarlet O'Hara. He took meetings with his producer David Geffen in a pink bathrobe and his wife's panties. At Nirvana's first gig on *Saturday Night Live*, he Frenched his bass player, Krist Novoselic. In Newcastle, he told the crowd, "I am a homosexual, I am a drug user, and I fuck potbellied pigs." In his journal he wrote, "I'm lactating. . . . My breasts have never been so sore." Moreover, the King of Grunge summed up his general orientation with his first Nirvana T-shirt logo: FUDGE PACKIN', CRACK SMOKIN', SATAN WORSHIPPIN' MOTHERFUCKERS.

Though Cobain delighted in baiting homophobes and in doing many pro-gay benefits besides, he was, according to another acquaintance Frank Hulme, "deeply embarrassed by the rumor he was gay." Said another L.A. friend, he "never got over the shame, beat into him in Aberdeen, of being queer." When Eddie Veder's chick told him at a gig, "Kurt, Eddie says you suck dick," he threatened to "beat him to shit" with his Mustang guitar. Instead, he kicked Veder in the groin, then collapsed in a bowl of dip on the backstage buffet.

Unlike Pearl Jam's Veder, Guns N' Roses Axl Rose, and Kiss's Gene Simmons, the King of Grunge slept with only a handful of female

---

6. In 2001 the singer, who had formerly called himself "an equal opportunity lech," revealed to *Time* magazine that he was "a queer artist." Explaining the delayed admission, he said, "I was being made to be a coward about it, rather than someone who felt like it really was a very private thing." Stipe is the godfather of Cobain's daughter, Frances Bean. As for Ms. Love, she came out as a lesbian at Elton John's AIDS benefit in 1996.

groupies. "Kurt was passive, and enjoyed playing the traditional girl's roll in bed," confessed one of them, ". . . the chick did the work." In the interview that he later regretted, Cobain told *The Advocate:* "I've always been a really sickly, feminine person anyhow, so I thought I was gay for a while because I didn't find any of the girls in my high school attractive at all. But I'm really glad that I found a few gay friends, because it totally saved me from becoming a monk or something."

Cobain's first real girlfriend was Tracy Marander, a coquettish trailer beauty much like his mother. He moved into Tracy's apartment in Olympia, the scenic capital of Washington, which he called a "Peyton Place Utopia where everybody fucked one another." A graveyard shift waitress at Boeing, Tracy supported him while impatiently waiting for a break in his career. She often took him out to dinner and bought him presents, which made him feel guilty. They shopped together "like a married couple," he would later recall, and he became increasingly frustrated that they couldn't do more "artistic things" together. For her part, Tracy became frustrated at his antisocial attitude, not to mention his resistance to employment. "I was a monk," he admitted, echoing John Lennon. "I've always been that way." The future star's monastic activities in Tracy's apartment included playing guitar, scrambling his DNA, spacing on afternoon soaps, caring for his menagerie (five cats, four rats, two rabbits, many turtles, and a cockatiel), and creating porno punk art.

His high school friend, Myer Loftin, dropped by his crib and described it as "a found-art museum, with dolls and figurines smeared with shit, weird pop culture artifacts, and a statue of the Virgin Mary with its head cut off."[7] Kurt's surrealist montages were populated by aliens with shrunken penises, fetuses in gutters, and horned women whelping and defecating. All his canvasses were varnished with what he called his "secret ingredient": his cum.

"Look, you can see how it glistens!" he enthused to Tracy when she returned from Boeing to view the latest masterpiece. Another time, she found the refrigerator pasted with a photo collage of grocery store deli specials and gynecology text close-ups of malignant vaginas.

---

7. Later, he would transplant to the cover of *Incesticide* his winged female mannequin with exposed organs. Her life-sized sculptural reproduction became a Nirvana stage prop.

"Kurt was fascinated by things that were gross," the waitress pointed out.

When Cobain still wasn't making rent with the fledgling Nirvana, much less his Art Brut, Tracy pressured him into a nine-to-five. He began cleaning medical offices for $4.75 an hour plus perks—whatever drugs he could liberate.

The only work experience of the future King of Grunge was janitorial: after dropping out of Weatherwax High, he'd become a floor sweeper there (later the inspiration for the old man sweeping in Nirvana's *Teen Spirit* video). But Kurt had never been the type to bring his job home with him.

Just as his mother had always fruitlessly pestered him to clean up after himself, Tracy was constantly leaving him smiley to-do Post-its on the cold cut and cunt-laden frig. But Kurt had always taken an artist's pride in squalor. "It was a very smelly, very odorous place," he had boasted of the little bungalow he had rented before moving in with Tracy. A delivery boy for the *Daily World* experienced this firsthand, "The stink almost knocked me out," he reported. "There were turtles crawling on the floor, and dolls hanging up by their necks from the ceiling."[8]

The squalor of Cobain's surroundings, of course, had nothing to do with his modest means. The soon-to-be millionaire would routinely ghettoize his five-star suites; his tour bus, said one roadie, "stank of something worse than shit"; his mansion was said to have reeked of rotten food, feces, and vomit. When the Seattle police responded to a 911 call at his home, they were overwhelmed by "the sheer filth and air of decay." Courtney's biographer Melissa Rossi wrote, "The squalor was so extreme that one newly hired maid walked in and promptly ran back out, screaming 'Satan lives here!' "[9]

---

8. Cobain's obsession with the olfactory later paid off with Nirvana's first hit, "Smells Like Teen Spirit." Teen Spirit was a female hygiene deodorant. Cobain's favorite novel was Patrick Suskind's *Perfume* about a sociopathic perfumer who disembowels a French virgin and tries to extract the scent of primordial life from her remains.

9. Years later, turning over a new leaf, Ms. Love decorated Hole stages with a glittering banner that read: "Cleanliness is next to Godliness." In 2008, she advertised on MySpace for an "insanely clean" housekeeper. "Agencies suck and I'm sick of pigs who steal," she explained, apparently forgetting her own history of kleptomania. "So, fuck it—why not try MySpace? . . . I'm insane."

Kurt was equally casual about his personal hygiene. He rarely bathed or brushed his teeth and avoided eating apples because they made his gums bleed so badly. He was a true romantic of the repulsive. To the psychologist his scatophilia may have indicated a less than trouble-free toilet training, if not self-loathing. But it was ironic that the future Father of Grunge chose to be a janitor, though not a particularly energetic one.

In the fall of 1989, Kurt retired from janitorial work and recorded Nirvana's debut album, *Bleach*, for Sub Pop Records, a small Seattle punk label. He had sent a demo tape to countless labels, including in the packages his art miniatures, as well as used condoms filled with the dead flies he would scrape from the many fly strips that hung from his bedroom ceiling. In spite of his unique packaging, he had no takers. Then Sub Pop's Jonathan Poneman, the northwest punk aficionado, heard "Love Buzz," signed Nirvana, and sent the group overseas on a shoestring tour in a dilapidated bus.

Returning home, a penniless Cobain was turned down for a dog kennel shit-scooper gig. Then, with his bass player, Krist, he tried to launch his own cleaning business, Pine Tree Janitorial. He was saved from the enterprise when Sub Pop sent Nirvana on a U.S. *Bleach* tour in the summer of 1990.

This tour was such a success that by the end of it Poneman predicted that Nirvana might become "bigger than the Beatles."

Cobain returned to Olympia and dumped his patroness, Tracy Marander. Though hurt, she felt relieved too. She'd recently discovered that Kurt had started shooting heroin while recording *Bleach*. As a janitor, he'd bleached hospital floors. Now, a junkie star, he bleached his dirty needles.

HIS HEROINE

I've met the coolest girl in the whole world.
—Kurt Cobain

"Heroine," as he called it, became Kurt Cobain's steady woman after Nirvana's second European tour. "I decided to use heroin on a daily basis," he wrote in his journal, "because of an ongoing stomach ailment . . . that had literally taken me to the point of wanting to kill myself. For five years I would experience an excruciating burning, nauseous pain in the upper part of my stomach. . . . I consulted fifteen different doctors, and tried about fifty different types of ulcer medication. The only thing I found that worked were heavy opiates."

Cobain tasted the first fruits of stardom when he signed with Geffen's Virgin Records. He spent half his $3,000 advance during a Toys"R"Us shopping spree. Afterward, he shot smack, then shot out the windows of the Washington State Lottery Building with his new BB gun.

This was surely one of the happiest days in the young man's life. At last, he had nearly everything he'd always dreamed of—a major publishing deal, cash, toys, and every opiate under the rainbow.

He only lacked one thing. But not for long.

When they first met at the Satyricon club, in Portland, Oregon, 1990, she slugged him in his burning stomach and—having three inches and thirty pounds on him—wrestled him to the floor. "I thought she looked like Nancy Spungen,"[10] he later recalled. "I probably wanted to fuck her that night, but she left."

A year later, their paths crossed again at a Butthole Surfer/L7 concert in L.A. Courtney Love had just suffered an ugly breakup with Billy Corgan, founder of Smashing Pumpkins. She had been watching Nirvana's chart numbers since '88 and had recently sent Kurt a heart-shaped box (later to become the title of his popular song) containing a porcelain doll—one of his "corpse baby" art fetishes. Of their reunion backstage at the Palladium, she recalled, "We bonded over pharmaceuticals." They both shared each other's Hycomine cough syrup. Then they had another wrestle—"Just a mating ritual for dysfunctional people," Courtney called it. The couple rendezvoused five months later at a backstage *Nevermind* release party in Chicago, then finally dispensed with foreplay in Kurt's room back at the Days Inn.

Before a live performance of "Teen Spirit" on the British TV show *The Word*, Cobain announced: "I just want everyone in this room to know that Courtney Love, of the pop group Hole, is the best fuck in the world."

Courtney called Kurt "Pixie Meat," after his elfin body and his thing for the Pixies. She later said she had a "girl boner" for Pixie Meat, especially after *Nevermind* knocked Michael Jackson's *Dangerous* off the top of the charts in January 1992. But their relationship was more than commercial or physical. Courtney was the first chick Kurt could re-

10. The platinum blonde ex-stripper and groupie of the Sex Pistols.

ally talk to. "Bi-polar opposites attract," he wrote in his journal. Aside from punk and drug shoptalk, they discussed their parallel childhoods and argued about who had had the shittiest.

Courtney Love Michelle Harrison was born in San Francisco on July 9, 1965. Her father, Hank Harrison, was an early manager of the Grateful Dead (bassist, Phil Lesh, was Courtney's godfather). Her mother, Linda Carroll, was a psychologist and an heiress to the Bausch & Lomb eye care fortune.

The Harrisons divorced several years later. Linda won custody, alleging, among other things, that Hank had dosed their three-year-old daughter with acid (a charge he vehemently denies). Courtney, however, soon proved to be more than a handful even straight. "She was her mother's worse nightmare," wrote her biographer and friend, Melissa Rossi.[11] The moody, volatile Courtney was placed in analysis and diagnosed with hyperactivity, ADD, and mild autism. She would later assert that she had been molested not only by her father, Hank—aka BioDad—but by her mother's third husband, Frank Rodriguez, as well as her therapist Dr. Pharr, who tried to "re-parent" her through Gestalt rebirthing techniques. Later, the girl was shuffled between boarding academies, foster homes, and reform schools, which took her from Oregon, to New Zealand, to Australia, then back. Like Kurt, Courtney had from an early age been plagued by deathly nightmares and became suicidal. She hated her younger sisters and was forbidden to play with them. Biographer Poppy Brite,[12] recounts an episode in New Zealand when Courtney, then about ten, cut herself with blades of grass and thought of jumping off a cliff.

At twelve, she was arrested for shoplifting a KISS T-shirt at Woolworths and sent to Hillcrest Reformatory in Portland, Oregon. Her caseworker called her "the most shrewd, cunning, devious person" she had ever treated. Her mother said she "hated school" and "hated everything." Courtney called herself "a demon child." One day at Hillcrest she would later remember, "I knifed a girl because I didn't like her looks." Her favorite book was *Lord of the Flies*, about marooned En-

---

11. Melissa Rossi, *Courtney Love: Queen of Noise* (New York: Pocket Books, 1996). Though Love originally asked her Portland friend Rossi to write the biography, she later threatened her with a lawsuit unless she made more than a hundred corrections in the manuscript, which her lawyers enumerated in a twenty-eight-page document.

12. Poppy Z. Brite, *Courtney Love: The Real Story.* (New York: Touchstone, 1997).

glish schoolboys who turn cannibal. Her literary interests extended to poetry as well. Went a typical teenage Love sonnet:

> *I'll destroy anyone in my way.*
> *I'll kill every lousy lay—*
> *Coz I got my eye on a Future Date.*

At sixteen, Ms. Love traveled to Japan and worked as a stripper in "the white slave trade," as she called it. Soon deported, the teenager took her thong and pasties to Alaska. Her role model now was Nancy Spungen. Like Courtney, Nauseating Nancy, as the press called her, had a rich psychiatric history, was suicidal, and prone to homicidal violence. Fittingly, she hated everything except punk music and smack. Courtney would later audition to play her heroine in *Sid and Nancy*, but to her disappointment, she won only a supporting role in the 1986 movie.

On turning legal age, Ms. Love moved to Liverpool on the $800 per month stipend from her Bausch & Lomb trust. Immersing herself in the avant-garde music scene, she got into acid, smack, and balling the movers and shakers. In spite of her stint in the sex slave trade and her assertions of molestation by multiple fathers, she said she lost her virginity to Michael Mooney of Echo and the Bunnymen. Mooney later claimed to have no such memory. Moreover, Hank Harrison, in Ireland at the time, recalled that his daughter was hooking on the streets.

At thirteen, Courtney had come back into BioDad's life, having not seen him since the divorce ten years before. Her mother had told her Hank was dead. The reunion was not a happy one. Of their time together in Ireland, Harrison, in his 2002 title, *Kurt Cobain: Beyond Nirvana* wrote, "I had to accept her heroin, her opportunistic lesbianism . . . and her foul mouth—without qualification. . . . I had to be her whipping boy, a role that Kurt eventually filled." He declared that she had "a demented hatred of men," which he felt originated from her belief that he had abandoned her.

Shuttling back to England, Courtney soon bedded Julian Cope, founder of the psychedelic, post-punk The Teardrop Explodes. Years later, in 1991, Cope would run this ad in the trades:

FREE US FROM NANCY SPUNGEN–FIXATED
HEROIN A-HOLES WHO CLING TO OUR GREATEST
ROCK GROUPS AND SUCK OUT THEIR BRAINS.

Asked by an interviewer to translate, Cope said, "She [Courtney] needs shooting, and I'll shoot her."

Abruptly leaving Liverpool, Courtney, now nineteen, returned to the states. When between situations, she boarded at her father's California house in the early eighties. Harrison recalled that she threatened to kill him several times, and said she had given his toothbrush to an HIV-infected friend. She also nearly burned his house down. "Pyromania was her name and fire was her game," he wrote. Explaining his tolerance, he went on, "She mistook my love and guilt feelings for weaknesses. . . . In her jungle, dickheads like me get eaten for snack food."

Leaving her father and California, she took up with twenty-seven-year-old glamrocker Rozz Rezabek-Wright, flamboyant front man for Portland, Oregon's Theatre of Sheep. Calling her "The Black Tornado" and "my cure for happiness," Rozz soon decided that the cure was worse than the disease. Courtney—though she would have much experience with it—never reacted well to being dumped. "I stole for you, I lied for you, I prostituted myself for you," she told the ingrate before destroying his apartment. Then, dressed in a Theatre of Sheep T and black lingerie, she slashed her wrists with a razor blade. It was Valentine's Day, 1983.

On the rebound, she married punk rocker "Falling James Moreland," the self-described "Eddie Fisher of punk rock." Known for salty lyrics and his onstage gymnastics in a cocktail dress and fishnet stockings, Falling James soon became disillusioned with his bride. "I thought I was marrying the female Johnny Rotten. Instead I got this right-wing Phyllis Diller."

Moreland knew the honeymoon was over when his wife set his bed on fire while he was sleeping, and then promised to have "the living shit" beat out of him for $200. "She was fucked up on drugs most of the time," he confessed. "She could get uncontrollably violent. . . . And she seemed to know a lot about hit men." The final straw for James came when Courtney got knocked up, kept shooting smack, and got an abortion. Then she annulled their Vegas marriage. By this time, more than a few people were encouraging her to leave Portland. According to Melissa Rossi, a group of neo-Nazi skinhead girls kidnapped her, drove her near the Canadian border in Bellingham, and threw her out on the highway, naked.

Returning to L.A. she began her singing career with Faith No More.

The hardcore death rock band dumped her after only four shows, during one of which—as a tribute to Iggy Pop—she rolled in broken bottle glass and set her hair on fire.

In the next five years, Courtney went through a succession of chick groups, notably Sugar Baby Doll, the Pagan Babies, and Babes in Toyland. At last in 1989, she succeeded in forming her own group, Hole, with guitarist Eric Erlandson.

The following year Ms. Love met Pixie Meat for the first time.

After their dysfunctional mating rituals climaxed at the Days Inn in the fall of 1991, Kurt and Courtney became the unofficial First Couple of Punk. Both were heroin addicts. Friends disputed who made whose habit worse. But all agreed that—as similar as both their backgrounds were—neither was a healthy influence on the other.

"You guys are like a natural disaster," a friend told Kurt.

Asked another, "Are you guys Sid and Nancy?"

Kurt and Courtney took this as a compliment. Their predecessors had proved themselves to be the prototypical punk Romeo and Juliet, when the smacked-out Sid stabbed Nancy to death with a hunting knife before she had an opportunity to do the same to him.

The new first couple was a volatile pair too. When *Rolling Stone* later asked Kurt the secret of their relationship, he replied: "It's like Evian water and battery acid. Mix them and you get love."

The truth was, due to their childhoods in hell, they shared a single powerful emotion: hate. I hate mom, I hate dad, wrote the nine-year-old Kurt on his wall. "She hates school, she hates everything," Courtney's mother later said. Courtney noted how Kurt had "a nearly bottomless disdain for his own audience." Kurt didn't disagree. He talked to Michael Azerrad about "hating people so much" and having "a personal vendetta against them . . . because they didn't live up to my expectations." Sympathizing, his future wife collected a list throughout her life of the people she hated and wanted to kill. In short, the couple found a measure of love in hating people together. And it was the basis of a working relationship until the levy broke and they started hating each other.

Loathing, if not fear, was central to the nihilistic punk ethic. Punks were Gen X Holden Caulfields who took his anger and alienation to the max. The more pissed, fed up, and fucked up you were—the cooler you were. The more repulsive you looked and behaved, the more attractive you were. Most importantly, you couldn't give a shit about anything, except fucking people up before they fucked you up. This pragmatic attitude was doubly powerful in the synergism of a punk couple.

But Kurt and Courtney's love wasn't all loathing. Though Kurt was a force to be reckoned with on stage, offstage he tended to angst out in a corner, even at his own parties. He loved how his heroine sucked the oxygen from a room and messed with everybody's heads. The MO didn't matter: a bottle over the head, a gob in the face, a Sylvia Plath quote, a militant feminist Susan Faludi rant—different strokes for different folks. His future wife had a low tolerance for being ignored. Her "mouth . . . was like a chainsaw, it ripped through anything in its way," wrote Rossi. Courtney agreed: "I'm not a woman, I'm a fucking force of nature." As she also pointed out: "I like there to be some testosterone in rock, and it's like I'm the one in the dress who has to provide it." By contrast, in his "suicide" letter, Cobain called himself "an emasculated, infantile complain-ee," and on *Nevermind* sang about being "neutered and spayed."

In short, Ms. Love had what Cobain did not: balls. Which helped resolve his sexual identity problems, at least for the moment.

From her side of it, Courtney admired Kurt too. He had a hit record, which is more than his predecessors—Cope, Rezabek, Falling James—could say.

Further proving that their relationship wasn't all negative, the couple made one positive, if surprisingly conventional, decision early on. One day after shooting up together after a pro-choice benefit in L.A., the couple stumbled on a dead bird while out on a nature walk. Plucking three feathers, Kurt gave one to Courtney, keeping the second for himself. "And this one," he said of the third, "is for our baby we're gonna have." Courtney gave him a peck on the cheek. "We should breed," she agreed. "It's better than having a monkey."

By the time *Nevermind* topped the charts, Courtney told Kurt she was pregnant. In February 1992, on a cliff overlooking Waikiki Beach, he gave Courtney Michelle Harrison Rodriguez Menely Moreland Love yet another name. The bride wore an antique lace dress of Frances Farmer's.[13] The groom wore green flannel pajamas. He later

---

13. The alcoholic, schizophrenic actress from Seattle—later institutionalized and administered electroshock treatments—was the couple's heroine. Cobain paid tribute to her with his *In Utero* song, "Frances Farmer Will Have Her Revenge on Seattle."

explained that he commonly wore pj's "in case Mr. Sandman should come knocking." Rather than put up with "inane" and "boring" things, as he called them, "I'd rather just be asleep . . . or in a coma." He'd always had narcoleptic tendencies. But in spite of doing smack before exchanging vows with his bride in the Hawaiian sunset, he managed to stay awake. The nuptials didn't bore him, nor did the idea of becoming "a punk rock daddy."

In fact, Kurt delighted in the idea of fatherhood. But he feared that he and his bride would have a "flipper baby" like the amphibious infants he had drawn as a boy. Each had a $300-a-day junk habit. So in Courtney's second trimester, they underwent a prenatal "hotel detox" at the Holiday Inn. This was to be the first of many dry outs for Cobain and the second of many for Ms. Love. The regimen involved methadone, sleeping pills, diarrhea, and telegraphic puking.

Afterward, Kurt was relieved to see sonograms of a seemingly normal fetus, which reminded him of a "little bean."[14]

Frances Bean Cobain was born in August 1992. Deeming Kurt, then twenty-five, and Courtney, twenty-seven, "unfit parents," Child Services took custody of the infant. The move was the result of a *Vanity Fair* expose, "Strange Love," labeling Courtney as an addict, an unfit parent, and a "train-wreck personality." Meanwhile, the *Globe*'s front-page headline read: "ROCK STAR'S BABY BORN A JUNKIE!" Courtney seemed to have feared worse, wailing during the delivery, "You will only have *one* head!"

Devastated by the press coverage, Kurt broke into the maternity ward with a gun. He threatened to take his and his wife's life according to a rumored suicide pact. In the end, the Cobains decided on a more prudent course. Courtney barraged "Strange Love" author, Lynn Hirschberg, with death threats. Meanwhile, Kurt told the only writer he could still trust, Michael Azerrad, "First I'm going to take her dog and slit its guts out in front of her and then shit all over her and stab her to death." Saying she was "terrified for her life," Hirschberg refused to speak further about the Cobains.

But the journalist had already collaborated with British writers, Victoria Clarke and Britt Collins, who were writing a book about Nirvana. Though Kurt had okayed the project, when he found out Clark had talked to Hirschberg, he left this message on her phone: "If anything

---

14. His other favorite video at the time was a black market clip of Pennsylvania state official, R. Budd Dwyer, blowing his brains out.

comes out in this book that hurts my wife, I'll fucking hurt you. . . . I'll cut out your fucking eyes, you sluts . . . parasitic little cunts! . . . I could throw out a few hundred thousand dollars to have you snuffed out, but maybe I'll try it the legal way first!"

And Ms. Love had her man's back now that he was at last showing some balls in defense of her honor: "I will never fucking forgive you," she wrote the authors. ". . . I will haunt you two fucking cunts for the rest of your life. . . . You're going to wish you've never been born." The punk diva would later pummel Hirschberg at the 1995 Oscars ceremony, as well as smash Collins with a glass and hair-drag her from an L.A. bar.[15]

As for Kurt, he had usually avoided physical confrontations. But now, with his wife's encouragement, he seemed to be turning over a new leaf. "I'm not as much of a hippie as some people would want me to be," he declared after the Hirschberg episode, "I could blow somebody away easily. No problem." He concluded: "When people unnecessarily fuck with me, I just can't help but want to beat them to death."

Till now people hadn't really fucked with Kurt. True, his parents had screwed him, he'd been beaten up at school, and rednecks had called him a faggot and dissed his music; but the Hirschberg attack and the big brother theft of his own child was a fuckover of an entirely different order. Yet it was an inevitable reality of fame: living in a carnivorous fish bowl, sacrificing your private life, becoming a public commodity. Kurt Cobain, little known a year before, was now, like it or not, a millionaire megastar voice of a generation. His dream was already becoming a nightmare.

Three weeks after his daughter was taken from him, Kurt begrudgingly agreed to headline the MTV Video Music Awards, insisting on playing his new song, "Rape Me." "Rape me, Hate me," it went. "Do it and do it again. Waste me. Rape me." MTV freaked, fearing it might bum the Teen Spirit fans. Kurt opened with the first chords of "Rape

---

15. In his 2008 book, *Bumping into Genuises: My Life Inside the Rock and Roll Business* (New York: Gotham, 2008), Danny Goldberg, the Cobains' manager and friend, expanded on Hirschberg's allegation of prenatal drug abuse, saying that an abortion had been recommended. "The doctor tried to give clinical advice," he wrote, "suggesting to Courtney that it was not a great idea to have a baby while dealing with addiction."

Me" anyway, then segued into "Lithium," singing, "I kill you. I'm not
gonna crack."

The Cobains spent the next six months, plus $240,000 in legal fees,
struggling to get Frances Bean back. To avoid cracking or killing anybody in the process, Kurt composed songs for Nirvana's fourth album,
In Utero, which he had wanted to call *I Hate Myself and Want to Die*.
As a precondition for regaining custody of their daughter, Child Protective Services ordered the Cobains to enter a thirty-day drug rehab
and to submit to random urine tests. After completing the program in
March 1993, the couple at last took their baby home.[16]

"I can't tell you how much my attitude has changed since we've got
Frances," an ecstatic Kurt told the *Los Angeles Times*. "Holding my
baby is the best drug in the world."

In fact, since the birth of his child, no sooner did Cobain graduate
a detox program than he fell off the wagon again. Just two months
after regaining custody of Frances, Kurt OD'd in his Seattle house and
might have died had Courtney not called the police.

The star was to overdose twelve more times in the remaining ten
months before a shotgun was put into his mouth.

MISS WORLD

> Can't look you in the eye
> I am the girl you know
> I lie and lie and lie
> I'm Miss World
> —Courtney Love, "Miss World"

Nirvana finished recording *In Utero* at the same time they won their
baby back. According to its producer, Steve Albini, Courtney had been
a "Yoko Ono fixture" at the recording sessions. "I don't feel like embarrassing Kurt by talking about what a psycho hosebeast his wife is,"
he went on, "especially because he knows it already." Courtney knew

---

16. In 2003, Ms. Love experienced déjà vu: her daughter was again taken from her
until she completed another rehab. When she regained custody nearly two years
later, she thanked the court for "helping me deal with a very gnarly drug problem,
which is behind me."

it, too. "Just call me Yoko Love," she said. ". . . They all hate me. Everyone just fucking hates my guts."

Due to the huge success of *Nevermind*, she persuaded Kurt to renegotiate his contracts. Under the original agreement, proceeds were divided equally among Nirvana's three members. After the renegotiation, Kurt received 75 percent of the music revenues and 100 percent of lyrics—effective retroactively. A half-million-dollar royalty refund was also demanded of each. The deal did little to strengthen Courtney's already brittle relationship with bassist Krist Novoselic and drummer Dave Grohl. Nirvana almost broke up.

Months before, Kurt had told an interviewer that Courtney was "really good friends" with both Krist and Dave, except for "the bad blood" after the *Vanity Fair* expose. This was the post-*Vanity* spin control Kurt speaking. Good friends was a stretch; bad blood was a euphemism. In fact, Krist and Dave had become increasingly disgusted and frustrated with Kurt's debilitating addiction, reinforced by Courtney's own. After the Hirschberg article, Krist's wife, Shelli, with his tacit approval, ignited the tinderbox by denouncing Courtney as an irresponsible junkie mother. When Courtney forced the contract rewrite, financially gelding Novoselic and Grohl, they had little doubt that this was one of her paybacks. Nor did the bad blood subside, as Kurt had suggested. On their last tour, Krist and Dave traveled in their own tour bus. In the end, they spurned Courtney's memorial service for Kurt, holding one of their own.

"Since Courtney had entered Kurt's life," wrote Rossi, "few of his friends knew who he was anymore." Musician Tad Doyle, who had toured with Nirvana numerous times, told *Melody Maker*, "She's out of control. Wherever trouble is, she'll find it or make it. . . . She's disgusting." Her employees didn't seem to like her either, and feelings were mutual. In less than two years, she hired and fired fifty nannies for her daughter. After she had finally made peace with *Vanity Fair* and allowed them to eulogize her in their 1995 cover feature, with her customary candor she told them, "Everybody wants to see me dead. But I'm not going to die. I'm a cockroach."

But if Courtney was alienating others, by the time *In Utero* came out, she was beginning to alienate her husband as well. Though the issues between them were many and complex, they reduced to a simple one: fame. Kurt hated it; Courtney loved it.

"If I could have predicted what was going to happen to me a few years ago," said Kurt, "I definitely wouldn't have opted for this kind of a lifestyle."

"I love attention, I love the trappings of it all," declared Courtney. "To say you hate the trappings, you're an asshole and a liar."[17]

The bachelor who had contentedly lived in his battered blue Dodge when *Nevermind* was rocketing to the top of the charts, only months later was a married man driving in limousines and sleeping in presidential suites with his wife. After they were evicted from the Four Seasons and every major hotel in Seattle for vandalism, they purchased a million-dollar estate on Lake Washington next to Starbucks' chairman Howard Schultz. Later, the Cobains were seen "snarling at each other like wild dogs" at the American Dream Car dealership. At Courtney's insistence, they drove off the lot in a new black Lexus, which an embarrassed and disgusted Kurt returned days later.

From Kurt's point of view, he may have owned a Lexus and a mansion—but the price of this was the public owning *him*. His soul was too high a price for what he hated and his wife loved. Moreover, he felt creatively straitjacketed by his fans' demands for more angst-ridden *Nevermind* punk anthems. He was exhausted by his touring schedule. And though a part of him felt like "an untouchable boy genius," another felt unworthy of the international attention lavished on him. "People are treating him like God," explained his publicist Nils Bernstein, "and that pisses him off." Which is why he had started trashing his five-star hotels with such zeal. "We were feeling weird because we were being treated like kings," he told Azerrad, "so we had to destroy everything."

But his frustrated rage fed on a deeper well. Being rich and famous violated the most fundamental punk law. The Seattle punks had already branded him with the scarlet letter: "Sellout scum." But they still bought his music and flocked to his shows as if to watch him hang himself on his corporate puppet strings. He'd done his best to shake free. In April 1991, for his first *Rolling Stone* cover shot, he'd worn a special tee: CORPORATE MAGAZINES STILL SUCK. Then he cursed his competitors—Guns N' Roses and Pearl Jam—as sellouts themselves. Meantime, he pressed his case in every interview, complaining about

17. Later, after becoming a Golden Globe–nominated actress, she expanded on the point: "You can't go on being a punk when you've had loads of plastic surgery and waltzed up the red carpet."

how "the innocence of underground music has been lumped in with the corporate idea of what underground is."

He might have more easily shed his cross of celebrity had his wife not been so intent on keeping him nailed to it. He could have blamed his "trappings of fame" on her, and it may have flown. But this would have put him in the even more untenable position of confirming that he was her wind-up husband—another slander that was eating him alive. "There's definitely not manipulation going on in this relationship at all," he told *The Advocate.* "It really sickens me to think that everyone assumes this." Years before, Lennon had been even less diplomatic about Yoko's influence over him, telling *Playboy,* "You think I'm being controlled like a dog on a leash. Fuck you, brother and sister!"

This is exactly the attitude Courtney told Kurt to adopt: Fuck 'em all! She hadn't worked ten years in strip bars and punk dives to get weak-kneed when it was all starting to pay off. And what about Kurt's dues for the punk blues? From her point of view, he'd swept a few floors, played with his turtles, jerked off on a few canvasses—then suddenly the mother lode dropped into his lap and he started whining.

The girl with the most cake had no patience for this. It almost made her want to do him a favor and put him out of his misery. It wouldn't be murder. It would be euthanasia.

Though they now had their baby back and Nirvana sales were exploding, the First Couple of Punk had now begun to fight as often and violently as their predecessors, Sid and Nancy.

Courtney filed her first assault charge against Kurt in June 1993. According to her, she and Kurt had had words about his house guns, she then threw a glass of juice in his face, and he tried to strangle her. But she took responsibility and insisted on being arrested herself. Another dispute now broke out over who would be cuffed and booked. Kurt chivalrously prevailed, spent hours in the King County jail, then was released when his wife declined to press charges. The police, however, confiscated his WMDs: two .38 pistols and a semiautomatic assault rifle.

Though Courtney was experiencing no difficulty spending Kurt's millions, she'd lately gotten into the habit of throwing kitchenware at him while calling him "useless" and a "loser"—much as his mother had years before. So now he did what he'd done back then: he hit the road. He went on a European tour for *In Utero.* He hated the idea of going to an uncivilized land where he had no dope connections and nobody "could fry a decent burger"—but he needed the money no less than the marital sabbatical.

Kurt called Courtney from Munich and their conversation turned into a shouting match. Courtney, traveling with Frances, was in London doing pre-publicity for her new Hole album, *Live Through This*, to be released in a month. Kurt had heard rumors that she was sharing her suite with her former lover, Billy Corgan. Cobain had always loathed "Billy the Pumpkin," as he called him.[18] After slamming down the phone on his wife, he called his lawyer, informing her he wanted a divorce. He told the same thing to his old friend, Buzz Osborne, front man for the Melvins who opened the Munich show for Nirvana that night. The next day, on doctor's orders, Kurt canceled the Nirvana tour due to bronchitis, laryngitis, and exhaustion. No wonder his voice and stamina were strained when singing, "My girl, my girl, don't lie to me. Tell me, where did you sleep last night? . . . I'm going where the sun don't ever shine—I would shiver the whole night through."

Canceling the Learjet she'd chartered to take Billy and her down to Majorca, Kurt's dutiful wife flew instead to Rome and rendezvoused with him at the Excelsior Hotel. On arrival, a conflicted Kurt gave her red roses and a chunk of the Roman coliseum, almost the way Lennon had sung both "Losing You" and "Starting Over" to Yoko on *Double Fantasy*. Courtney's reception was chilly. She preferred Billy Pumpkin. With this last rejection, Kurt handed her a three-page letter. She later told her private detective, Tom Grant: "It was mean to me . . . not really nice. It talked about getting a divorce." But committed to the long term, she later told a reporter, she fellated her husband that night and spit his semen into a cup. She later froze it but, as it turned out, not at a cold enough temperature for posterity.

Early the next morning, an ambulance sped from the Excelsior to Umberto Polyclinic hospital, bearing a fully madeup Courtney and a comatose Kurt. The star's stomach was pumped and he awakened twenty hours later. His first two words to his wife at his bedside, scrawled on a notepad due to the tubes down his throat, were: "FUCK YOU." Then he asked the nurse for a strawberry shake.

---

18. Weeks after Cobain's death, Courtney reunited with Corgan, cohabiting with him at Canyon Ranch detox resort in Arizona. In 2005, Corgan collaborated on her *Nobody's Daughter*. In 2006 she built a wing off her West Hollywood house for him.

Dom Perignon and sixty hits of Rohypnol—the date rape drug—were found in Cobain's system, usually a fatal dose. Just before leaving for Rome, Ms. Love was interviewed by *Select* magazine in her London hotel room and had there "a box of Rohypnol on her big mahogany table." At that time, the sleep aid was available over-the-counter in England. Charles Cross, whom the widow later authorized to write her husband's biography, wrote that Kurt had his own U.S. prescription for the medication and filled it before his Rome overdose.[19]

If true, whose Rohypnol prescription, then, did Cobain consume? Did he swallow the sixty pills knowingly; or was the tasteless, fast-dissolving drug slipped into his champagne glass?[20]

Courtney insisted on the former, later (after Kurt's death) calling his three-page divorce letter a "suicide note." Paraphrasing it, she said Kurt wrote: "You don't love me anymore. I'd rather die than go through with a divorce." The letter was never presented to Rome authorities. The only people to see it were Seattle Police Department detectives. "She said it was a suicide note, but it wasn't," stated an SPD source. "It was a rambling letter, which was very unflattering to her." She confessed to burning the letter shortly after her husband's death.

Cobain's treating physician, Dr. Osvaldo Galletta, told Max Wallace and Ian Halperin, authors of *Love and Death* and investigative reporters: "We can usually tell a suicide attempt. This didn't look like one to me." Janet Billig, a Nirvana manager, confirmed Galletta's position: "Kurt insisted it was not a suicide note. He just took all of his and Courtney's money and was going to run away and disappear." Geffen Records, too, issued a statement that the incident was "accidental." Cobain confirmed this, but refused to discuss the incident further. In fact, his memory of the incident was probably impaired, since Rohypnol overdoses commonly cause prolonged confusion and amnesia. "Cobain doesn't know what happened to him," Dr. Galetta confirmed at the time. "He hasn't gained complete control of his memory."

But if Courtney had slipped Kurt the drug, why then had she called the ambulance? By her own admission to *Rolling Stone* magazine, she found her husband comatose on the hotel room floor at 3 or 4 A.M. She

19. Susan Wilson's biography *Hole: Look Through This* (London, UK: Music Sales Corp., 1996), however, states that the prescription filled was Love's. The couple also commonly took other prescription antianxiety medications including Klonopin, Xanax, and Valium.

20. Due to the criminal abuse of Rohypnol as an incapacitating substance, its manufacturer added a bright blue dye to the chemical in 1998.

did not call the ambulance until 6:30 and never provided an explanation for the delay. Earlier that morning Geffen Records had received a phone message from "a female identifying herself as Courtney saying Kurt was dead."

"If he thinks he can get away from me that easily, he can forget it," Mrs. Cobain told *Spin* magazine after her husband regained consciousness at Umberto hospital. "I'll follow him through hell."

LIVE THROUGH THIS

I'm all I wanna be
A walking study in demonology.
—Courtney Love, "Celebrity Skin"

I might lie a lot, but never in my lyrics.
—Courtney Love

Eldon Hoke, aka El Duce, is three sheets to the wind, propped against the door of the Rock Shop, a punk vinyl dive in West Hollywood. It's a balmy evening, December 28, 1993. A white limo pulls up, the chauffeur opens the door, and a gloriously disheveled platinum blonde emerges. She meanders over to the shop window, blowing smoke to the sky. She knows Duce through Hole's drummer, Carolyn Rue, who had a thing with his guitarist, Sickie Wifebeater, back in 1989.

"El, my old man's been a real asshole lately," she tells him. "I need you to blow his fucking head off."

The front man for the Mentors, who has more experience singing about this kind of gig than doing it, asks if she's serious.

"As a fuckin' heart attack," she replies. She offers him fifty grand and a plane ticket to Seattle.

Second Lady, Tipper Gore, gave El Duce and his bandmates—Sickie and Dr. Heathen Scum—their fifteen minutes in 1985 when she read their "Golden Shower" lyrics on the Senate floor.

"Bend up and smell my anal vapors. Your face will be my toilet paper."

Since then the Mentors' popularity had tapered off, and the porn metal rocker found himself moonlighting at the Rock Shop and taking whatever other paying gig came his way to support his alcohol and pharmaceutical needs.

"Fifty grand?" he says. "Up front?"

She smiles then offers him a bonus.

But El is a man of principle: "Forget the bj, just gimme the fuckin' bread."

He hands the blonde a business card. She says she'll be in touch.[21]

Three months later, after Courtney returns to the states from Rome, she phones the Rock Shop asking for El Duce. According to Wallace and Halperin, the store manager, Karush Sepedjian, tells her El is on tour with the Mentors and can't be reached. "She was all frantic," recalled Sepedjian. "She says, 'I need to talk to him. He's got a job to do!' "

Joe Mama, a friend of hers, says the same thing at around this time, calling her "freaked out" and "scared." Is this because, as Detective Grant believes, that the Rome overdose was not an accident after all, but a failed murder attempt? Is it because Kurt—in spite of his overdose impairment—is determined to divorce her and cut her out of his will as he's threatened?

When filmmaker, Nick Broomfield, later asks the Cobains' nanny, "What was so strange in those last weeks?" she replied, "There was way too much will talk. Major will talk. She [Courtney] just totally controlled him . . . every second that she could.[22] Added Peter Cleary, one of Kurt's Seattle friends, "She was always hurling abuse at him, even in public. . . . She would call him a dumb fuck all the time. He would just stand there and take her abuse. . . . He was like a baby."

But Kurt struggles mightily to break free in this last month of his life. After returning to Seattle from Rome, he tells Courtney he's killing the golden goose, Nirvana. He's also turning down $9.5 million to open the Lollapalooza festival. And he refuses to let Hole fill in for Nirvana. In short, he's done with her. He's done with everything. He wants his soul back.

Courtney is so pissed she can't see straight. But the best defense is

---

21. Three years later, Dr. Edward Gelb, the FBI's top polygraph expert, wired Eldon Hoke up for *Hard Copy*, to determine the veracity of this story. Gelb twice asked Hoke: "Did Courtney Love ask you to murder Kurt Cobain?" Both times the polygraph recorded his "Yes" 99.91 percent reliable. Gelb, who tested O. J. Simpson (who failed badly), concluded that Hoke's response was "completely truthful" and "beyond possibility of deception."

22. Outraged by Broomfield's investigation into murder theories in his documentary expose, *Kurt & Courtney*, Courtney succeeded in preventing its showing at the Sundance Film Festival in 1998.

an offense, as she always believed. So she orders her attorney, Rosemary Carroll, to find "the meanest, most vicious divorce lawyer." She also wants to know if the prenup agreement she signed can be voided. Yes, but only in the event of infidelity, counsel replies. Ms. Carroll's head is now spinning with conflict of interest. She's just gotten off the phone with Kurt who has ordered her to find *him* a divorce lawyer, to write Courtney out of his will, and to dissolve Nirvana. In short, her star client is not only committing professional suicide but railroading his wife's career in the process.

Rosemary gives diplomacy a shot. She suggests marriage and drug counseling to both her clients. She knows too well that, in spite of all the detoxes, each again has a killer junk habit. She stalls on the divorce and the will, hoping they get help before things get ugly.

But ugly comes only ten days after the Cobains return from Rome. Responding to a 911 call on March 18, 1994, the police race out to the Lake Washington mansion to find Cobain locked in the bathroom and Ms. Love in an agitated condition outside. She tells them that her husband is threatening to shoot himself. But when he opens the door, he has no gun and says she threatened to kill *him*. The cops, weary of responding to 911s from the Cobain residence, warn Courtney about making false statements. But they confiscate Kurt's guns anyway.

A week later, his wife springs another surprise on her beleaguered husband still in a roofie haze. He returns home to find a crowd inside: his managers; record label executives; a drug counselor; his daughter's nanny; his best friend and dealer, Dylan Carlson; plus Courtney. An intervention. Almost everyone present has his or her own substance abuse problem. Three are bona fide junkies. He sees that this isn't a smack junkie intervention, but a money junkie convention. Due to his drug habit, they're worried that Kurt is trying to detox from their own favorite fix: money.

His managers take turns counseling and cajoling Kurt. The strung out mother of his child has the last word of solicitous concern: "This has got to end . . . You have to be a good daddy."

"Who the fuck are all of you to tell me this?" Kurt snarls, then storms upstairs to refresh his own high and play his favorite video game, *Mortal Kombat*.

But before he leaves, Courtney tells him if he doesn't clean up, she'll have no choice but to take their eighteen-month-old daughter.

Frances is the only living thing Kurt cares for anymore. Through her he can almost revisit the innocence and happiness he had known so many years ago as a young boy. His baby is his last surviving hope and lifeline. Without her, he knows he is lost.

Realizing he'll never get custody of Frances in his condition, Kurt checks in to the Exodus Recovery Center in Marina del Rey. Exodus is the alma mater of David Crosby, Steven Tyler, Joe Walsh, and many others.

Cobain finds the experience of being evangelized by hippie burnouts "disgusting." He spends forty-eight hours in his 6- by 9-foot cubicle enduring counselors and smoking in the rec room with Butthole Surfer, Gibby Haynes. Finally, he goes AWOL. The date is April 1, 1994—April Fools' day.

Meanwhile, across town, his wife is in dueling detox at the Beverly Hills Peninsula. She has her trump card with her: Frances.

After escaping Exodus, Kurt leaves a phone message for Courtney at the Peninsula. He takes the last Delta flight to Seattle and taxis to his Lake Washington house. Here he runs into his daughter's live-in nanny, Michael "Cali" DeWitt. Cali is a junkie. He is a former lover of Courtney's. A castrati, he follows orders. Cali accompanied Courtney to Rome. Some believe he was the one who called in her Rohypnol prescription. Some say Kurt hated him; some say Kurt liked him. Some believe he fired Cali and kicked him out of the house that night in Seattle. Others believe they shot up together and talked.

Anyway, the next morning, Saturday, Courtney is still multitasking from her Peninsula suite. She cancels Kurt's credit cards. She calls the Rock Shop again. Then she thumbs through the Yellow Pages for private detectives.

Back in Seattle, several witnesses see Kurt driving with a blonde in his old blue Dodge. The blonde is likely one of two people: Kaitlin Moore, his heroin dealer and possible lover, or Kat Bjelland, the Babes in Toyland guitarist, who is now staying out at the Cobains' country cabin in Carnation.

Tom Grant is one of the few private detectives in L.A. answering his phone on Easter Sunday, 1994. Courtney summons him to her hotel. After telling the PI she'll "sue the fuck" out of him for any breach of confidence, she hires him to find Kurt. Grant urges her to reveal any leads she might have about her husband's whereabouts. She's clueless, she insists. Kurt's earlier phone message slips her mind, as well as a call from Cali, telling her Kurt had dropped by the Lake Washington house Saturday around midnight. So an unsuspecting Grant proceeds with the search from scratch.

On Monday morning, Courtney calls the SPD. Identifying herself as Wendy Cobain, she files a Missing Person report, insisting her "son" is "armed with a shotgun" and "suicidal."

Just before entering rehab, Kurt had purchased a Remington .20 gauge with his friend Dylan Carlson. Due to the recent SPD gun confiscation, the weapon was registered in Dylan's name. And, due to a recent burglary at Lake Washington, Kurt said he wanted the gun for protection. According to Wallace and Halperin, he'd also told Dylan his life was in danger. When Dylan was later asked by Grant if Kurt was suicidal, he had replied, "No, not at all. He's under a lot of pressure, but he's handling things pretty good." Cobain had "all sorts of plans" after rehab, Dylan added. He was composing new songs and planning a collaborative album with R.E.M.'s Michael Stipe.

The Exodus staff psychologists treating Kurt hadn't considered him suicidal either. Before he left the facility, his friend Joe Mama visited him and said, "I was ready to see him look like shit and depressed. He looked fucking great!" Kurt had recently told *Rolling Stone*'s David Fricke that the chronic stomach problems which had tormented him for years and made him suicidal had finally been correctly diagnosed as scoliosis and cured by a prescription.

"I'm eating!" he told Fricke. "I've never been happier in my life."

On Tuesday, April 5, Hole's album, *Live Through This,* is released. Courtney, insisting she is too busy in L.A. to join the search personally, sends her guitar player, Eric Erlandson, to Seattle to look for Kurt. Eric checks the Lake Washington house, then their Carnation property twenty miles away. But he comes up dry.

Meanwhile, neither Tom Grant in L.A. nor his partner in Seattle has found any trace of Kurt either. So on Wednesday, Courtney orders him to fly to Seattle to conduct yet another search, this time with Dylan. The two visit the Lake Washington mansion late that afternoon. Like Eric the day before, they find no one. Cali is gone, but the TV is still on in his room as if he has left abruptly, avoiding them. Tom and Dylan return a second time after midnight. It is raining heavily and they don't check the greenhouse, thinking it an unused storage area.

On Thursday morning, the pair drives out to the Carnation cabins for a look around. Meanwhile, Courtney, furious to hear Cali has left his post at Lake Washington, phones the strung out junkie at his girlfriend's Seattle apartment and orders him to return immediately. Cali obeys. Shortly after arriving, he leaves a note on the staircase banister that reads, "Kurt—I can't believe you managed to be in this house without me noticing. You're a fuckin' asshole for not calling Courtney. . . . Get it together to at least tell her you're o.k., or she is going to *DIE*."

After Courtney speaks with Cali from Rosemary Carroll's office, she returns to hotel detox at the Peninsula. But she accidentally leaves her backpack behind. Looking inside, Carroll finds one of her client's to-do notes to herself. It reads, "GET ARRESTED."

Soon, an anonymous 911 call is made about a possible drug overdose in Ms. Love's Peninsula suite. Rushing in, paramedics find the walls splattered with blood and vomit, and the diva herself splayed on the floor in a "distressed state."[23] Though she quickly recovers at the Century City Hospital, she is arrested for drug possession. She insists that she has just suffered an allergic reaction to her Xanax prescription. As for the white powder the police found in her suite, it's not heroin after all but Hindu good luck ashes.

Released on a $10,000 bail, she phones Dylan Carlson in Seattle. It's now nine o'clock Thursday evening. She tells him she's just had an OD and an arrest, but it's all a misunderstanding. Now, back on the case, she orders him to return immediately to Lake Washington with Grant to search a secret closet for Kurt's new shotgun.

Why hadn't she revealed this closet before their first search? wonders Grant.

He and Dylan return to the Lake Washington house yet again. They uncover no gun in the secret closet. And Cali is again AWOL. But they do find his note to Kurt on the staircase banister.

Did Courtney send him to the house for the express purpose of find-

---

23. According to Wallace and Halperin on the day of Cobain's disappearance, Courtney paid an inside AP source to plant a phony overdose story in order to force Kurt to contact her. She revealed to Grant the follow-up story she had planned for AP: "What I can say is that [Kurt] left rehab. . . . I got very depressed and had to be hospitalized for some sort of nervous breakdown. . . . I mean, how's that for spin? It's gonna appear that I attempted suicide. Even if it says I OD'd on Xanax and booze, that would be fine, but if it says heroin, I'm in deep shit." Then "the chameleon press whore," as she described herself, told Grant, "You know, I've been dealing with the media a long time."

ing this note? wonders Grant. Could it be used as some kind of alibi later? The detective is beginning to feel now, more than ever, that "this whole thing smelled really rotten."

Earlier that Thursday, before her "overdose," Courtney had taken care of one other important bit of business: she called Veca Security Systems, currently installing alarms at the Lake Washington house, to put in a motion detector on the greenhouse the next day.

When her day's work is at last done, Ms. Love checks out of the Peninsula and—lest anyone think she's not committed to getting clean—moves into the Exodus Recovery Center that her husband left five days before.

The next morning, Friday, she awakens in her cubicle to find Rosemary standing in the doorway, trembling, speechless.

Courtney clutches her hands to her face. "HOW?" she sobs.

By that evening, the widow Cobain is crawling across the bloody floor of the Lake Washington greenhouse, wailing "WHY?"

The alarm electricians she had ordered to the greenhouse had discovered her husband's body early that morning. It is in full rigor mortis.

The coroner estimates that the star has been dead since Tuesday.

Grant, however, later estimates that Cobain has been dead since Easter Sunday.

CAMERON AND HARTSHORNE

Both SPD chief homicide detective, Sgt. Donald Cameron, and his colleague Dr. Nikolas Hartshorne, chief medical examiner, immediately concurred that this was an "open-and-shut case of suicide."

The widow's detective was doubtful. To him, the evidence did not appear to support the official conclusion. Grant thought he was the only skeptic until Wallace and Halperin arrived on the scene.

First, there was the matter of the overdose. The medical examiner's office found 1.52 milligrams per liter of heroin in Cobain's system—three times the maximum lethal overdose for a hardcore addict of normal weight. Cobain weighed 115 pounds.

"I've never seen anybody with his levels," Denise Marshall, deputy coroner in Colorado, told Wallace and Halperin. "It's just staggering."

A heroin overdose of this magnitude, she and other forensic experts asserted, would have immediately incapacitated Cobain. He would have been incapable of putting away the syringe and other paraphernalia in the cigar box found at his side, much less placing the shotgun in his mouth and pulling the trigger. He would have instantly lost consciousness, probably even before injecting the full shot. In past ODs, needles had to be extracted from the arm of an unconscious Cobain. This dose was substantially stronger than its predecessors.

"With gun suicides, you always see the victim still gripping the barrel of the gun," Hartshorne told the journalists. He had to pry the shotgun from Cobain's hands. "That's a sure sign the wound was self-inflicted. That kind of evidence doesn't lie."

However, not all forensic experts agree on this phenomenon called Cadaveric Spasm.

"From my experience," Marshall told Wallace and Halperin, "everything about this case points to a staged scene, somebody trying to make a murder look like a suicide. . . . Cadaveric Spasm can still occur in a homicide."

Marshall envisioned a scenario like this: Valium or Rohypnol was slipped into Cobain's root beer can. (A three quarter full can of Barq's root beer was found next to his body, but disposed of by the SPD without testing it for drugs or prints.) As he lost consciousness, he was injected with a "hot shot"—the immense heroin overdose. The syringe and paraphernalia were returned to the cigar box at his side. The perpetrator then placed the shotgun in the unconscious Cobain's limp hands. Placing his own hands over them, he pulled the trigger. Cobain's fingers, nerves still firing, instantly contracted around the trigger in Cadaveric Spasm.

Was there any way to confirm or rule out such an MO?

"The photos should tell the story," asserted Marshall. "You see, if somebody actually held Kurt's hand around the gun and pulled the trigger, some of the blood would probably have splattered on their hand, leaving a void on Kurt's. You can analyze that void in the photos and determine whether or not it was a staged suicide."

"I'd have to see the photos," agreed Vernon Geberth, former Bronx Homicide Task Force commander. "The photos tell you everything."

Both 35mm and Polaroids were taken by the SPD. Even if they hadn't shown a telltale blood splatter "void" on Cobain's hand, they would certainly have shown what detectives had already admitted:

that a pool of blood was found at his feet, not his head. The body had to have been moved after the shot.

Grant, as well as Wallace and Halperin, filed a Freedom of Information request to view the photos. The request was denied. Shortly after Grant made the request, Don Cameron sent his commanding officer an internal memo. It read in part, "Courtney Love has gone to her attorney with concerns over the release of any crime scene photos. Courtney's attorney, Seth Lichtenstein, called and asked if the photos could be destroyed to prevent any mistaken release."

Aside from the photos, what about fingerprints? Other than Cobain, at least two other people handled the Remington .20 gauge: the gun dealer and Dylan Carlson. But the police found only four "latent"—unidentifiable—prints. Likely, therefore, the gun was wiped down. The house, usually dirty and in disarray, was also scrubbed. When Dylan arrived there, searching for Kurt, he told Grant, "I've never seen the house this clean before." Cobain was never one for neatness and grooming himself, but according to the electrician who found his body, "Kurt's hair looked like it had been combed by a hairdresser. It was all spread out nice and even."

As for the pen stabbed through the "suicide" note, the police found no prints of any kind, latent or otherwise. Therefore, the pen, like the gun, was wiped down, or gloves were used. NBC's *Unsolved Mysteries* hired top international handwriting experts, Marcel Matley and Reginald Alton, to examine the note. Both concluded that Cobain wrote the bulk of the 500-word document, but not the first and the last four lines.

The first line read, "To BoddAH"—his imaginary childhood companion. The last four lines read:

Please keep going Courtney
For Frances
For her life, which will be so much happier
Without me, I LOVE YOU! I LOVE YOU!

The note itself, however, had nothing, explicitly or implicitly, to do with the addressee, nor with his wife or child. The letter was an apology to Nirvana fans: "I haven't felt the excitement of listening to as well as creating music . . . for too many years now. . . . I feel guilty beyond words about these things. . . . I can't fool you. Any one of you." It is signed "Kurt Cobain." It seems, therefore, to be a letter of retirement from Nirvana and perhaps the music business altogether.[24] The idea of suicide was absent except for the last four lines in forged handwriting.

Whose forgery?

Besides the "Get Arrested" reminder, Carroll discovered one other item in Courtney's backpack: a sheet of paper on which she had been practicing different styles of handwriting for each letter of the alphabet.

In spite of all this, Sgt. Cameron insisted that Cobain could not have been murdered because the greenhouse French doors were locked from the inside and a stool wedged behind. But as Grant pointed out, the lock was a simple twist type that could have been pulled shut from the outside. As for the stool, police later admitted that it was, in fact, across the room and not wedged against the doors.

Then there was the matter of the credit card. Examining Cobain's wallet, SPD detectives found his Seafirst MasterCard missing. In the days after Cobain's death, numerous charges—for goods and cash advances up to $5,000—were made and rejected. Because the card was canceled, Seafirst could only track the times of the rejected charges, not the places. The SPD never looked into who had stolen the card, nor did they ever find it. Nor did they investigate Cobain's police report, just before his death, that the tires of his Volvo, parked below the greenhouse, had been slashed. Had someone intended to restrict his mobility?

A week after Cobain's death, Grant presented some of this evidence to Cameron. But the SPD chief homicide detective remained adamant: "Nothing you've said convinces me this is anything but a suicide." When Grant asked if he might see the crime scene shots, Cameron replied, "We don't develop photographs of suicides." Then why take them?

In 1995, the *Orange County Register* called Cameron, asking if he had investigated the missing credit card and who might have used it. "We're not going to comment until we figure out what Grant's after," replied the detective.

---

24. Nivana bass player, Krist Novoselic, confirmed this to Cobain biographer, Charles Cross: "The band was broken up." Drummer, Dave Grohl, made the same admission on the *Howard Stern Show* in 1998. "Teenage angst paid off well, now I'm bored and old," wrote Cobain in "Serve the Servants." And in the October 1993 *Rolling Stone* interview, Cobain declared, "We've got to the point where things are repetitious. I'll be totally forgotten in five years."

Cameron stated publicly that he was prepared to reopen the case should credible evidence be shown indicating murder. Three years later, Wallace and Halperin traveled from Montreal to Seattle with a BBC camera crew with just such evidence. It included the 99.8 percent certain polygraph of Elton Hoke stating that Courtney Love attempted to contract him to kill her husband. Though Cameron was at his desk and apparently unoccupied, he sent another detective out to tell the journalists, "That case is closed. Now leave." When the two offered to hand over their evidence file for Cameron to review at his leisure, the detective ordered them to leave immediately or be arrested.

Was Cameron protecting someone?

The homicide detective and Courtney had known each other for several years. They had a working relationship. She said she got "brownie points" for tipping off his colleague, narcotics detective Antonio Terry about Seattle dealers, some of them her own.[25] In exchange, Narcotics gave Courtney immunity, and Cameron provided her helpful professional advice. When she showed him Kurt's Rome "divorce" letter, calling it suicidal, the detective returned it, advising her, "This will never do you any good. I'd get rid of this if I were you."

In 1999, after thirty-eight years with the force, Sgt. Cameron was charged with conspiracy to steal $10,000 from the department. There were two hung juries. The second voted eleven to one to convict. The prosecutor did not retry because the two-year statute of limitations had run, preempting criminal charges. Cameron retired from the SPD.[26]

But what about the medical examiner, Dr. Nikolas Hartshorne? Why had he so quickly concluded with Cameron that this was an "open-and-shut case of suicide"? He and Courtney had history too. He first got to know her during medical school in 1988 when, moonlighting as a rock promoter, he put together a punk bill at Seattle's Central Tavern. Nirvana was the opener for Leaving Trains, the band of James Moreland, Courtney's first husband. She later described Hartshorne to Grant as "my rock-and-roll medical examiner." He, in turn, described Courtney to Wallace and Halperin as a "great girl."

When the journalists asked Hartshorne if being the chief medical

---

25. Two months after Cobain's death, Detective Terry was ambushed and fatally shot by two dealers.

26. Cameron died in 2007. His obituary in the SPD's *Guardian* newspaper described him as "the finest death investigator ever of the Seattle Police Department and maybe the nation and/or the world. That's no exaggeration. He was a true genius and renaissance man . . . [and] truly a legend in his own time."

examiner in the Cobain case might represent a conflict of interest, he responded: "Absolutely not." But when Grant asked Courtney about Hartshorne, she declared, "As long as Nikolas is the coroner, I'm not afraid."

She added that Hartshorne refused to give him, Grant, the autopsy records because "he's angry at you." He considered the detective's homicide theory "ludicrous." Even so, Grant asked Courtney if she might get the records from her friend. She agreed to do so when having dinner at the doctor's house in 1995. However, she failed to obtain the records.

Hartshorne, known as "Dr. Death," was killed seven years later in a BASE (or building, antenna, scan, earth) jumping accident off a Swiss cliff known as "The Nose."

Finally, there is little evidence that Cameron or Hartshorne had considered one last detail of the case: motive. Again, Kurt had been in the process of filing for divorce and removing her from his will. Courtney had told Grant she would consent to a divorce only if she could prove spousal infidelity, voiding the prenuptial agreement. She herself was having an affair with Smashing Pumpkins' Billy Corgan, part of the reason Cobain was seeking a divorce in the first place.[27]

"Kurt was worth more to Courtney dead than alive," Grant concluded. Where Courtney the Divorcee would have been a professional disaster, Courtney the Widow was a gold mine. Others came to the same conclusion.

"I'd bet a year's salary that he was murdered," declared Denise Marshall, coroner.

"I don't think she did it, but I think she *had* it done," said Kurt's grandfather Leland.

"She didn't want the divorce, so she had him killed," agreed Courtney's father, Hank Harrison. "Face it, she's a psychopath." He also showed Grant a letter his daughter sent him years before, stating, "I'm going to marry myself a rock star, and kill him."

Grant urged Kurt's widow to take the test. "I'll do a bloody polygraph for you, if you keep it a secret," she told him. She never did so. Instead, she asked Grant to commit to a Confidentiality Agreement,

---

27. Weeks after Cobain's death, Love moved into the Canyon Ranch detox resort in Arizona with Corgan. Soon she took up with Trent Reznor. After the Nine Inch Nail star left her, she threatened him and splattered his hotel room with bloody tampons.

insisting, "Everyone who works for me has to sign it." The detective, however, declined. "I'm not going to sign anything that could interfere with my investigation," he told her.

But most other insiders consented to her gag order. Krist Novoselic and Dave Grohl did so in order to collect the royalties owed them by the Cobain estate. Kurt's mother, Wendy, may have done so after her daughter-in-law bought her a $400,000 house. Kurt's best friend, Dylan Carlson, may have done so as well. Although he consented to a brief interview for Broomfield's documentary, the filmmaker found him "to be evasive and in a very defensive position." Moreover, as a heroin dealer, Carlson was surely careful not to displease Courtney lest she turn him over to her friends in narcotics at the SPD. As for Cali DeWitt, she told Grant that her former lover signed her agreement, adding that she had given him $30,000 for drug detox. But she wasn't sure where. "Cali went to rehab in El Paso, or Georgia . . . no, he's in L.A. with friends," she told her detective. Later that year, she secured DeWitt a talent scout job with her record label, which soon ended when he assaulted a programmer. Ms. Love's former nanny—whom Grant believed was a co-conspirator in Cobain's murder—is now the president and sole employee of his own punk label, True Love records.

Two months after the death of Kurt Cobain, the body of Kristen Marie Pfaff was found in the bathtub of her Seattle apartment. Pfaff had been the bass player for Hole. The coroner of the case was again Courtney's "rock-and-roll medical examiner," Dr. Nikolas Hartshorne. He recorded the cause of death as "Acute Opiate Intoxication."

Pfaff had just undergone a successful detox program in her hometown of Minneapolis. "Kristen stopped doing drugs the day Kurt had died," her mother, Janet, stated. "She was devastated. . . . It was a big wake-up call for her."

After Kurt's death, Pfaff had quit Hole, left Seattle, and returned to Minneapolis. "These people are all crazy," she told a former band member. "Let them find another idiot to play the bass. I'm history."

"She wasn't really quitting Hole," said her mother, "she was quitting Courtney."

Courtney had harassed Kristen during the *Live Through This* sessions. Kristen was "beautiful and smart," everyone agreed. A classically trained musician, she proved a superior composer and player to Courtney. Courtney complained that she and Kurt were "connecting too much." Though not romantically involved—Pfaff had a long-term affair with Hole guitarist Eric Erlandson—the two were close friends and enjoyed discussing art and music.[28]

When Kristen returned to Seattle in a U-Haul to collect her belongings from her Capitol Hill apartment, "She sounded as chipper and happy as she'd ever been," recalled a friend whom she phoned that night. "She couldn't wait to get back to Minneapolis."

Eric Erlandson briefly visited her that night. Kristen's brother, Jason, believes that her ex-lover may have delivered a "going-away gift from Courtney . . . of dirty (uncut) heroin."

Soon after her body was discovered in the bathtub the next morning, Eric returned with Courtney. After they left, Kristen's journal was found—with pages ripped out.

Janet Pfaff called the SPD urging them to look into the death of her daughter. But "they told me they couldn't investigate every heroin death in Seattle because in those days people were OD'ing every day," she said, "and they just didn't have the manpower."

"It concerns me and my family greatly that Dr. Hartshorne did the autopsy," Janet Pfaff went on. "I've heard all about his close friendship with Courtney. It's a conflict of interest. It scares me."

HOKE AND WRENCH

Elton Hoke, aka El Duce, was about to go onstage at Al's Bar in downtown L.A. with his new band Courtney Killed Kurt, formerly the Mentors. It was April 1997, more than three years since Courtney allegedly offered him $50,000 to kill her husband. He shared a corner table with Brent Alden who was writing about the L.A. punk scene. "Duce was acting very freaked out," Alden recalled. "He had heard that he might be in danger. He said, 'People get buried in cornfields. People get lost in swamps.'"

---

28. Courtney had never dealt well with romantic competitors. Of Kurt's ex-girlfriend, punk rocker, Mary Lou Lord, she said: "There are five people in the world that, if I ever run into, I will fucking kill and she is definitely one of them." Just after her marriage to Kurt, she phoned Mary Lou to inform her: "I'm gonna cut your head off and shove it up your ass—and Kurt's gonna throw you in the oven." Two years later, she actually did run into Mary Lou on Sunset Boulevard and gave chase, screaming: "I'm gonna kill you!"

Thirty-six hours later and a mile away, El Duce's body parts were found on the Metroliner train tracks and on the grill of the Sacramento Flyer.

The last person to see Duce was one Allen Wrench, front man of the eponymous Allen Wrench. According to his website, "Punk Rock's Most Important Band" was dedicated to "all four rock essentials: Satanic Worship, Alcoholism, Spousal Abuse, and Self-Destructive Drug Use!" Wrench's own record label was Devil Vision Records. His debut CD was *My Bitch Is a Junky*.

By his own admission, Wrench made no money from his music. But he had recently built a $100,000 recording studio in his house. A national jujitsu and judo champion, Wrench apparently moonlighted to keep the wolf from the door.

The night after Duce spoke with Alden about "people getting buried in cornfields," he found himself in Wrench's Corvette driving to the neighborhood liquor store near the train tracks. Duce and Wrench were punk partners from the early days. But Wrench was not feeling particularly friendly toward Duce on this particular evening. The drunken Duce had recently identified to British filmmaker, Nick Broomfield, the real murderer of Kurt Cobain.

Allen Wrench.

"It was naming me in the *Kurt and Courtney* movie," Wrench later told Wallace and Halperin. "I was fairly pissed off."

The journalists asked Wrench if, by the time he dropped Duce off at the liquor store, he'd "forgiven" Duce for fingering him. "After I read the newspapers the next day, it was okay," laughed Wrench. "Problem solved."

Seeming to enjoy playing cat and mouse, Wrench denied any involvement in Cobain's and Duce's deaths one moment; then, the next, he dropped a lead with a wink and nod.

"Nice little spot," he told Wallace and Halperin, showing them the secluded bend of train tracks where Duce met his maker. It was out of eyeshot, he explained, and no one could hear a struggle due to nearby traffic noise. "The thing about train wrecks is that they kind of make it difficult for a forensic investigation," Wrench continued. "It's not like you have a body to examine. . . . There's nothing left but fucking juice."

As for the death of Kurt Cobain, Wrench was equally cryptic. "Perfect assassinations always look like suicides," he pointed out.

When the journalists pressed him for an off-the-record statement,

Wrench at last conceded, "Okay, off the record, I whacked him." Then he smiled: "Nobody will ever know how he died. That's the fun of it."

POSTMORTEM

The widow Cobain washed the clothes her husband died in and wore them for days. She made plaster casts of his delicate hands. She had the monks of the Namgyal Buddhist Monastery in Ithaca, New York, make sculptures with his crematory ashes. She gave his shotgun to Mothers Against Violence who melted it down.

Tom Grant pressed on with his investigation. The widow tried, without success, to get the detective's license revoked. She took out a *Publisher's Weekly* ad threatening "to sue the skin off" any publication that repeated Grant's allegations. Her record company, Gold Mountain, announced in industry magazines their intent to sue anyone who supported the detective. Later, during her 1995 trial for the battery of two fans, the defendant whispered to the prosecutor, "Can I be O. J. and you can play Christopher Darden?"

The singer/actress went on to be a Golden Globe nominee for playing Larry Flynt's wife in the 1996 Milos Foreman biopic. She also won critical praise as Andy Kaufman's wife in *Man on the Moon*. But in recent years, Hollywood studios have reportedly avoided casting her due to her drug problems and volatile behavior, making it nearly impossible to insure her for a production. Magazines other than *Vanity Fair* have also become skittish about the controversial star. After she set fire to £8,000 worth of custom designer outfits, then rolled naked for photos, *Q Magazine*'s editor Paul Rees, observed: "Courtney Love is a genuinely pathetic, tragic story. She's obviously someone who is deeply troubled and deeply out of control. She's certainly the most genuinely unhinged person I've ever dealt with."

For offstage productions, Ms. Love has checked into hotels under the name of "Mary Magdalene" or "Blanch DuBois." In spite of the charade, while staying at New York's Royalton Hotel, she received a note from a fellow guest that read: "You killed Kurt Cobain." Melissa Rossi wrote of another time when Hole was playing Portland and a Nirvana fan shouted: "You killed Kurt!" His widow stormed offstage, spitting, "I'm not playing anymore. You can blame [that] little fucker!" When another fan begged her to return, she punched her in the mouth. But return she did, tongue-lashing Portlanders while pelting them with cold cuts from her dressing room. The fan filed assault charges. The concert promoters wrote her a check for the misunderstanding.

Kurt Cobain died before his divorce petition and new will—removing Courtney—were filed. She inherited the entirety of his multimillion-dollar estate. She called this her "blood money." Her future earnings have dwarfed the original payout. In 2006, the annual income of the Cobain estate was $26 million, placing it atop of the Forbes list, above Elvis Presley.

Shortly before her husband's death, Ms. Love told Tom Grant that she aspired to be the first female recording artist to earn a million-dollar contract. The ambition was realized with Hole's *Live Through This* that went platinum and was voted "Album of the Year" by *Rolling Stone*, *Spin*, and the *Village Voice*. Friends of Kurt have stated that he composed much of the material for the album, though his widow denies this. She went on to release numerous projects, the most successful of which were *Celebrity Skin* (1998) and *American Sweetheart* (2004) on which Billy Corgan collaborated.

During the course of her career, Ms. Love has been interviewed many times, but refuses to discuss her husband's death. She has also generally declined to comment on her serial arrests for drug abuse and assault in the last fifteen years. Her stormy romantic life has been well publicized: she has vandalized the apartments of former lovers—notably her former manager Jim Barber and Trent Reznor of Nine Inch Nails. "If she died tomorrow I wouldn't shed a tear," said Reznor. "She's a very evil person." She herself has said little about these incidents except to note, "I'm pathologically competitive with men."

In spite of her wealth, the widow claimed to be "on the verge of applying for food stamps" in 2004: she alleged that members of her entourage had embezzled $20 million from her. Several years later she regained solvency after selling 25 percent of Nirvana's song catalog for $50 million. She had also collected seven-figure payments for her husband's *Journals* (2002) and her own memoir, *Dirty Blonde* (2006). In 2007 she held a Christie's auction for Kurt's belongings. That year she made fifty-three New Year's Resolutions, three of which were:

Do not be a doormat in a relationship again.
Know that Kurt's spirit is tended to and tend to it daily.
Understand who my enemies are.

Regarding the last resolution, she had threatened to sue Wallace and Halperin; her father, Hank Harrison; her biographer Melissa Rossi; filmmaker Nick Broomfield; Tina Brown and *Vanity Fair*; as well as others, who she believed had portrayed her unflatteringly. "I am God and my lawyers are my twelve disciples, do not fuck with me," she warned her detractors. With her "blood money," she has employed more lawyers than the apostles since the group must not only protect her reputation but defend her against her many arrests for assault, vandalism, and drug abuse.

The Los Angeles Department of Children and Family again took Frances Bean from Ms. Love in 2003, due to drug charges. She regained custody of her daughter two years later. In 2006, during an *i-D* magazine interview, Frances denounced the "lies" about her mother in the press. Later that year the teenager posed for *Elle* magazine wearing her father's cardigan sweater and the pajama pants he was married in. For her sixteenth birthday in 2008, her mother reportedly spent $323,000 for a "suicide theme" party at the House of Blues on Sunset Strip in Hollywood. Prizes were given out for those who looked "the most dead." Revealing her special bond with her daughter, Courtney declared, "She's a gay man trapped in a woman's body, like me."

Cobain's widow recently announced that she herself was suicidal because someone had stolen his leftover ashes. Originally, she had spread a handful in the Wishkah River and had given two handfuls to the Namgyal Buddhists. She had kept the rest in a bear-shaped handbag, saying, "I used to take them everywhere with me just so I could feel Kurt was still with me." But, hardly had she announced their loss, than her publicist revealed that they had not been taken after all. Supplementing her efforts to feel that Kurt was still with her, Ms. Love had a *K* tattooed on her stomach. She also said that she continues to write letters to him.

Krist Novoselic and Dave Grohl, after years of silence, asserted that Courtney "appropriated" Kurt's work to further her own career. The ex-Nirvana members, who went on to form successful groups of their own, described her as "irrational . . . self-centered, unmanageable, inconsistent, and unpredictable."

Even so, the memory of Kurt Cobain and his revolutionary music is cherished by his fans independently of his widow's apparent exploitation of it. Just as his legendary predecessors became touchstones of the 60s generation, so Cobain became the voice of its children. It was a voice of raw intensity rivaling that of Janis Joplin, but the inner demons that fueled it were of a very different sort. If Janis sang from a broken heart, Kurt sang from a broken soul struggling to make itself whole in the purge of his music. There was no sound and fury like his. "The worst crime is faking it," he'd always said. In the end, when he thought he was faking it, just going through the motions, he quit. But by now he was a star, something he viewed as the ultimate fakery, the ultimate emptiness. He tried to become the anti-star. While some denounced him as a sellout and a hypocrite, for most his anti-stardom made him even more of a star. Until, in the end, he said:

"If you die you're completely happy and your soul somewhere lives on. I'm not afraid of dying. Total peace after death, becoming someone else is the best hope I've got."

Interlude: Love

You really like rock 'n' roll
All of the fame and the masquerade . . .
And all the money honey that I make, but
Do you love me?
   —Sung by Kurt Cobain, composed by Kiss

I'd rather be hated for who I am,
than loved for who I am not.
   —Kurt Cobain

"All you need is love!" sang Lennon.

But this was the one thing neither he, Cobain, nor any of the others had in their last days. The Seven were easy to worship. But too often faithless, temperamental, childish, selfish, they were not easy to love. Even so, each had been fortunate enough to find a person who did indeed love *them*, not their legend. Yet, tragically, they abandoned these souls, gravitating to those who used them and helped bring them down.

Tracy Marander, a cafeteria waitress, loved and supported Kurt while he was a struggling musician. Singers Mary Lou Lord and Tobi Vail did too. He abandoned them after his overnight success, marrying his "heroine," Courtney Love. Few understood why. "God is love. Love is blind. And so am I," Kurt explained in his journal. In the end "Love Gun" was the star's epitaph. "No place for hidin', baby. No place to run," he sang. "You pull the trigger of my Love gun."

How was it that the star had surrendered himself to this woman with such abandon? As we have seen, they both found fertile common ground in their loveless childhoods. They mirrored each other, at first enamored with the reflection, but in the end repelled. Even so, Cobain couldn't break free. "Broken hymen of your highness I'm left black," he sang in "Heart-Shaped Box." "Throw down your umbilical noose so I can climb right back." Observed Melissa Rossi, "Kurt found in Courtney the mother he'd never really had." But soon "Courtney seemed to have tired of being his mother and his human shield. . . . [She] was ready to have a career of her own."

Ms. Love felt she was his artistic equal, if not his superior, and deeply resented his success and her comparative obscurity. That he fled success was even more galling to her. So, she returned to her former lover, Billy Corgan, who loved success as much as she did. But, for Kurt, this was a betrayal as devastating as when his parents had divorced and abandoned him.

Without Courtney he was utterly alone, except for his three-year-old daughter, Frances. But his wife was taking her away from him too. He had no one left, no one to fall back on. In the end, he was estranged from Krist and Dave, and most of his other former friends. "Friends," he said, "are just a known enemy." His last friend was Carlson, his heroin dealer. He had many homosexual encounters, but no relationships that were lasting or that provided him with the kind of love, fidelity, and security he so needed in his tormented life.

His hero, John Lennon, suffered a similar predicament. Few understood why the former Beatle became so utterly dependent on Mother. But he had explained it well in the many songs he wrote to Yoko Ono. In *Double Fantasy's* "Woman," he thanked her for understanding "the little child inside the man" and for showing him "the meaning of success. My life is in your hands," he sang. Like Courtney Love, Yoko may have begrudgingly fulfilled this nurturing role early on to gain an emotional foothold, but in the end, she was desperate to throw off the maternal yoke, declare independence, and pursue her own career. Like Courtney, too, the competitive Yoko resented John. He was just a pop star; she was an artist in the tradition of the historic greats, she believed. He was just a poor Liverpool boy who had dropped out of a little art academy; she was a Japanese aristocrat who had graduated from the finest institutions.

But underneath his devotion, John had his own reasons for resenting Yoko. "She accelerates my failure and I hate her for that," John told John Green during his fallow period in the Dakota. ". . . . She's supposed to be strong when I can't be. Instead she hides." Green countered, "She's hiding from you because you've made it expressly clear

you don't want her around." Yoko insisted that John, fearing his career might be eclipsed by hers, humiliated and undermined her. On
the other hand, John feared that he might become like Yoko's first
husband, Japanese composer Toshi Ichiyanagi. "I divorced him," said
Yoko, "because there was nothing more in him for me to take." She
may have felt the same way with her third in 1973.

"Yoko kicked me out!" said John. She had just released her first solo
album, *Feeling the Space,* including such songs as "Woman Power,"
"Angry Young Woman," and "She Hits Back." Her husband, composer
of "Woman is Nigger of the World," understood. Having never been
without a woman himself, John fled to L.A. with Yoko's surrogate,
May Pang. To further buffer himself from the solitude he knew could
kill him, he joined the oblivion express fraternity of Moon, Starr, and
Neilson. But to Lennon, like Cobain, friendship was "a romantic illusion." For him it was a temporary alliance, not a bond of love. "Please
help me, I'm drowning in a sea of hatred," he sang in "Dream #9,"
in *Mind Games,* recorded just after the separation from Yoko. These
could have been Cobain lyrics. As for his purgatory in L.A., John told
an interviewer, "The reaction to the breakup was all that madness. I
was like a chicken without a head." So he abandoned the devoted May
Pang and returned to Mother.

Seven years before, he'd abandoned Cynthia with the same stoic
abruptness. Cynthia had loved him unconditionally from beginning
to end in spite of his abuses. He sued for divorce on the grounds of
infidelity, though he had betrayed her countless times and she him
not once. Most of the Beatle's liaisons had been one-night stands, but
his Yoko sentence lasted fourteen long years. When Cynthia had asked
him who was stalking him in London, then barraging him with letters
during their Maharishi trip, he told her she was just another "weirdo
artist . . . wanting money for all that avant-garde bullshit."

After they returned from India, the singer evicted Cynthia from the
house and gave his assistant Magic Alex[1] a white Mercedes to hand
deliver his Dear John letter. Cynthia pleaded for civility and a private
divorce settlement, but John now communicated only through his lawyers who offered her £75,000. When she finally succeeded in contact-
ing him personally, he snapped, "That's like winning the pools [Lotto],
so what are you moaning about? You're not worth any more!"

---

1. When he wasn't running personal errands for John, Magic Alex tinkered with his
inventions such as his antigravity machine and Ferrari-powered flying saucer.

Then—as Cobain had done with Nirvana—Lennon divorced his brothers: the Beatles. "John's in love with Yoko, and he's no longer in love with the other three of us," Paul said. But this wasn't entirely true. John told *Rolling Stone* that though he couldn't "forgive" Paul and George for their animosity toward Yoko, "I can't help still loving them either."Nor is it true that Yoko broke up the Beatles: in the end, they simply no longer shared a unified creative vision. But she did, intentionally or not, accelerate the splintering of that vision.

"Until Yoko Ono arrived," wrote Pete Shotton, "John never lost his almost desperate need to surround himself with close male friends: to remain, as always, the leader of the gang."[2] Similarly, Elvis was "the Boss" of his own boyhood gang, the Memphis Mafia. Besides Pete, John's two closest friends were Brian Epstein, the Beatles' manager, and Stu Sutcliff, the fifth Beatle. Brian died soon after Yoko arrived on the scene, Stu well before. Some insiders claim John had sexual relations with both. "Contrary to the opinion that Brian was on the make for John," wrote biographer Sandra Shevey, "it was John who attempted to involve himself with Brian." After the "Spanish honeymoon" in '63, John told Shotton, "I let him toss me off. . . . What's a fucking wank between friends?" But many believed there had been more to the liaison than a wank, especially when John later confessed that he "had loved Brian more than any woman." Unable to be more forthcoming about the relationship, after their vacation John wrote, "You've Got to Hide Your Love Away." As for Stu, John told another confidante, Beatles' PR man Derek Taylor that the two had been intimate in Hamburg.[3]

The only real male friend Lennon kept after Yoko's arrival was Pete. His old school chum took charge of the Apple boutique. But soon Pete, like the others, found it impossible to coexist with the possessive and volatile Yoko. After several blowups with her, Pete threatened to quit, but "John would panic and beg me to stay on," he wrote. "Without me, he would insist, he had nobody." Finally, finding the situation intolerable, Pete did indeed leave John and the two would never reunite.

Toward the end, self-exiled in the Dakota, John told his tarot reader,

2. Pete Shotton and Nicholas Schaffner, *John Lennon: In My Life*.

3. Geoffrey Giuliano, *Lennon in America*. This biography as well as Albert Goldman's *The Lives of John Lennon* (Chicago, IL: A Capplla Books, 2001) and Sandra Shevey's *The Other Side of John Lennon* (London, UK: Pan MacMillan 1990) include numerous other documented examples of Lennon's bisexuality. The only title that categorically dismisses such stories is the Yoko-approved book by Ray Coleman, *Lennon: The Definitive Biography* (New York: McGraw Hill, 1985).

"I don't have friends, . . . *We* [Yoko and me] have friends. So I go out and rent a friend." His favorite rental friend by this time was a comely Asian masseuse, Kimi, with whom he enjoyed regular rubdowns at his Cold Harbor residence.[4] As for Platonic friends, John told John Green about a certain "drinking buddy" whom he declined to name. "I had an opportunity to be a real friend," he confessed. But when his buddy had surgery for cancer, John failed to visit him. "I don't even know if he died or not," he said. "That's how I am."

During his eighteen months with May Pang, "May and John seemed genuinely in love," said an acquaintance. But the "jealous guy" went into a rage one night when he thought May was flirting with teen heart-throb, David Cassidy. "I always knew you'd cheat on me!" he cried. "I don't want to be in love. It hurts too much!" But the devoted May hadn't hurt him, Yoko had. She had arranged the separation, and he felt abandoned in the way he had by his mother years before. "Nobody loves me!" he wept.

His first son, Julian, knew the feeling. The boy had hardly seen or heard from his father since the divorce, except for unsigned Christmas and birthday cards. "Dad's always telling people to love each other, but how come he doesn't love me?" he asked his mother, Cynthia.

John's relationship with his second son seemed much closer, at least in the beginning. Just as Cobain had called his daughter "the best drug in the world," after the birth of Sean, John was "high as the Empire State Building." Celebrities can be abnormally attached to their children since intimacy with outsiders—fans, flatterers, hangers-on—can be nearly impossible. Their child, being a mirror, can also appeal to their narcissism. Moreover, a child can afford a parent a vicarious second childhood, which can be particularly fulfilling if the parent never had one of their own or had an unpleasant one. So, that Cobain and Lennon were in love with fatherhood, is not surprising. But for the househusband, John, the delight was soon eclipsed by the burdensome responsibility. "I tried the father bit and blew it," he later confessed. "I hated the role, and then I started hating the kid."

From Sean's side of it, feelings became mutual. "I think of my dad as a huge asshole," his beautiful boy said. "He was a macho pig in a lot of ways and he knew it. . . . That was his only saving grace. He tried to

---

4. Yoko claimed that John had never employed prostitutes and that he didn't even know what a brothel was. There is ample evidence to the contrary, dating back to the Beatles' wild nights in Hamburg's Herbertstrasse red-light district.

overcome it." The boy explained that Yoko's song, "Death of Saman-tha," on her *Approximate Infinite Universe* album, was ". . . all about dad having sex with some girl at a party where my mom was." "Their relationship really ended there," recalled Rubin, the party host. A little later, John reportedly had a quickie with Linda McCartney. Yoko en-joyed her own flings, too, and contented herself with the idea that "a lot of men around John have been attracted to me." These included not only Paul McCartney but Mick Jagger who she said had tried to move into the Dakota to be near her.

John and Yoko remarried in 1975. But unlike their blissful bed-ins seven years before, their second honeymoon was short-lived. "They plagued each other with petty assaults and fabricated disasters," wrote John Green. They were depicted in the London's *Sunday Mirror* as "one of the saddest, loneliest couples in the world . . . who have everything that adds up to nothing."

Jimi Hendrix called Kathy Etchingham, "My girlfriend, my past girlfriend, and probably my next girlfriend. My mother and my sister and all that bit. My Yoko Ono from Chester." Even so, according to Kathy,[5] he had "thousands" of casual relationships and had beaten her. After his death, Kathy helped settle his affairs and devoted her life to finding out who was responsible.

During his starving period in Harlem, the woman who loved and supported him was Sam Cooke's ex, Faye Pridgeon. Next came Linda Keith, Keith Richard's ex, who helped launch his career. "His elaborate double life backfired on him," she said, "because there was no depth to any of his relationships." One of the few women the guitarist failed to bed was Marianne Faithfull whom Mick Jagger dumped after her sui-cide attempt and six-day coma. "Once you start to care about anything or anybody, it always fucks up ambition," wrote the "As Tears Go By" chanteuse in her memoir.

Hendrix, too, avoided fucking up ambition with emotional attach-ments. Like Lennon, he felt that love "hurt too much." In the end, the composer of "Cry of Love" said he'd like to get married but "I'd really hate to get hurt. That would completely blow my mind." He proposed to many women—Kathy Etchingham and Kirsten Nefer among them—who would never have hurt him, but he soon abandoned them all. He stuck with only two: Devon Wilson, "the Cleopatra of Groupies" who inflamed his jealousy and fed his drug habit, and Monika Dannemann,

5. Kathy Etchingham, *Through Gypsy Eyes* (London, UK: Orion, 1998).

who helped kill him and tried to use his legacy as a stepping-stone for her career. It was a familiar theme: Yoko Ono had done the same with Lennon, Courtney Love with Cobain, Ginger Alden with Elvis, Seth Morgan with Janis, Deborah Koons with Garcia.

Like Lennon and Cobain, Hendrix abandoned his male friends. He had no greater friend than Chas Chandler, the manager who sacrificed everything to make him a star. Jimi left Chas for Mike Jeffery who ripped him off, got him busted, poisoned his later bands, and helped kill him. Hendrix said he only had two friends besides a few roadies: Noel Redding and Mitch Mitchell. Yet his bandmates were paid a pittance, abused, and run ragged. "I love you deeper than you could ever imagine," he wrote them in a letter of apology. "Please help me as I would love to help you." But by then, the guitarist was too preoccupied with his own survival to help even those whom he professed to love.

By this time, he had two illegitimate children by two women whom he had long ago left behind. Unlike John and Kurt, his fatherhood was not a source of delight or of renewal, but of guilt. Though he expressed a desire to have a family, he never took the time to meet his children.

Who, then, did the composer of "Love or Confusion" have in the end?

Said Jerry Garcia, "I never saw him without half-a-dozen weird people hanging around him—vampires and shit."

Said Jethro Tull's Ian Anderson "I couldn't get anywhere near him because he was surrounded by a phalanx of very sinister people."

In his last days, Jimi poured his heart out to his Auntie May who, through her Baptist church group, had taken him in as a child. "True friends do not allow you to destroy yourself," she told him.

Tears came to his eyes, and he said, "Auntie, I really want you to do some serious prayin'."

Later on, the King did some serious praying too. Throughout his career, he sang about love more than anybody—"Can't Help Falling in Love," "Burning Love," "Love Me Tender," "I Love You Because." But what did Elvis Presley really know about love?

Like both Jimi and John, Elvis's only true love had been his mother. His twin brother had died in the womb. "I grew up alone," he said. "I guess my mother—and my father, too, of course—were trying to make up for that by giving me enough love for both."

Elvis spent the rest of his life trying to replace his mother. As we have seen, both his wife, Priscilla, and his fiancée, Ginger Alden, bore a striking resemblance to Gladys as a young woman. Elvis had tried to mold them both into what his mother had been. Priscilla had wor-shipped him and catered to his every whim. But to him, she was never so much a lover and wife as a trophy. He cheated on her regularly. When she left, she took their three-year-old, Lisa Marie, with her. Elvis said many times how much he adored his daughter, but according to the Guys, she had become little more than a plaything.

Of the King's countless women, surely the most devoted and long-suffering had been Linda Thompson. She'd seen him at his worst but still stayed. He called her Mommy. At last, she had to flee for the sake of her sanity.

Elvis immediately replaced her with another caregiver. For his en-tire life, he—like Jimi, Jim, John, Kurt, and Jerry—had never been with-out a woman. Briefly infatuated with some, he gave cars but never real love. In fact, his women were like his cars—beautiful, luxurious, but quickly exhausted and traded in. He'd had plenty of one-night stands, but old-fashioned at heart, the King was the record holder for beauty queen live-ins. After Linda left Graceland, model Sheila Ryan was next in the queue. Then Diana Goodman, Miss Georgia; then Melissa Black-wood, Queen of the Memphis Southmen; then Jo Cathy Brownlee, the Memphis Grizzlies hostess; then Ginger Alden, Miss Mid-South and Miss Traffic Safety. All his domestics agreed that the star was into be-ing mothered, not sex. The Queen of the Southmen spoke for all when, as she escaped Graceland in her courtesy car, she cried, "This is all just too much for me!"

Elvis seemed to have greater love for the Guys. Though the originals—his cousin Billy, and his schoolmate, Red West—were at his beck and call 24/7 for many years, he paid them little. Explained Red, "It was almost as if it was a requirement to work for him that you had to be broke. He thinks if you get enough money together, you can pull up stacks and leave him because you don't need him anymore and, above all, he needs to be needed." Still, as compensation for "putting them through hell," as Elvis put it, he gave the Guys guns, cars, and houses. But ever suspicious of their motives for sticking with him, Elvis regu-larly tested their loyalty. On one occasion, he spread thousand-dollar bills over his bed, left the room, then watched to see who might try to pocket one. On another, he pressured them into arranging the murder of the man who cuckolded him.

Like Yoko and Courtney, Priscilla thinned the ranks of her hus-band's stand-in brothers early on. Though they regained the King's fa-vor after the divorce, the West cousins got fired and wrote a tell-all about their boss, which they insisted they'd done for love and concern, not payback.

Red and Sonny wrote of their boss, "We were like brothers. But, in the end, it just worked out that we meant nothing to him." This shouldn't have been a surprise since he had forewarned them years before, "I'm in charge here and if anyone wants to say different, then I may get hurt but somebody is going to die." The singer replaced the Judases with his stepbrothers, the Stanleys, but Ricky Stanley, too, came to the same bitter conclusion as the Wests. "Elvis really didn't have any true friends," he wrote.[6]

So in the end, the King, like most of the other stars, was both friendless and loveless. Gone were the days when he could feel love just by looking in the mirror. He no longer saw the beautiful Narcissus, but the vacant-eyed behemoth that he had become. The only one who remained at his side was his twenty-year-old fiancée, Miss Public Safety, who as Lamar put it, "didn't give a rat's ass about him." Ginger's first phone call, on finding his corpse on the bathroom floor, was to the *National Enquirer*. "If Linda Thompson had been with him, he wouldn't have died that night," wrote Sonny.

Elvis's rival, Jerry Lee Lewis, who shared an equally ill-starred love life, provided the epitaph: "He killed himself over a broad." The Killer never mentioned which one. Ginger? Priscilla? His mother? Or all three?

Jim Morrison's love life, or lack of it, reflected that of Elvis, Lennon, and Cobain. He had a thing about his mother, too, but not a thing called love. In his prime, he, like Elvis, could look in the mirror and see the man of his dreams. Otherwise, true to the pattern, the composer of "Love Me Two Times," "Love Her Madly," and "Hello, I Love You," abandoned those who cared for him and gravitated to those who brought him down. He dumped Ronnie Haran, Gloria Stavers, and Patricia Kennealy. Finally, he escaped to Paris with his common-law wife, Pamela Morrison, whom Mrs. Morrison II (Patricia) called "a slut, a junkie, a whore, and . . . a murderess."

Said Jim, "Real love amounts to letting a person be what he really is. . . . A true friend is someone who lets you have total freedom to be yourself." He called the Doors his friends and brothers until

---

6. Rick Stanley, *Caught in a Trap*, with Paul Harold.

they sold "Light My Fire" to Buick. Then he called them "associates." But his drinking buddy, Tom Baker, the burned-out ex-porn star, condemned *him* for being the sellout. "You're no good, Morrison, no good at all," he regularly told him from above or below a table. "Everybody hates you!"

Later on, Morrison wasn't even feeling the love from his gay partners on and off the Strip. One of them, Freddie, was blackmailing him for palimony. Perhaps his only true friend now was Max Fink, the lawyer who saved him from Freddie and at least twenty paternity suits. Though the Erotic Politician was a pusher of the romantic envelope and a no-holes-barred adventurer, he assured his lawyer that "I'm not a queer" and that "I did it [Freddie, and others] for my career." The bisexual Lennon, Cobain, or Joplin may have said the same of their own extracurricular activities.[7] Even so, the common root was a craving for real intimacy and trust that eluded them all, regardless of their partners' personalities or genders.

"Hatred," declared Jim, "is a very underestimated emotion." Many of his acquaintances agreed. They either loved to hate him or hated to love him. Pamela Morrison was in the second group. After another vicious fight, the mischievous Jim asked Pam if she still loved him "at least a little." She finally admitted "maybe" then screamed, "But I hate myself for it!" Jim always kept her in limbo: one day he would give her a Jaguar or a boutique; another day he would give her the clap, lock her in a burning closet, or kick her out of bed because "she looked so much like my mother." But the thing he'd always loved about Pam was that she could be even crazier than he was, at least when playing Russian roulette with their guns or cars.

The Morrisons boasted an "open relationship," just as most of the other stars did. With the advent of "free love," possessiveness and jealousy were considered old-fashioned, uncool. Most believed in playing the field, but not on an equal-opportunity basis. As we have seen, though a prolific cheater himself, Lennon beat up Cynthia and May when suspecting them of infidelity, just as Jimi had Kathy Etchingham. Elvis put a contract out on the man who cuckolded him. Courtney's

---

7. Noel Redding wrote that Hendrix also had bisexual tendencies. In their *Playboy* feature (November, 2005), Alana Nash and former Colonel Parker assistant, Byron Raphael reported a rumor that Elvis had been intimate with his friend actor Nick Adams (who fatally overdosed in 1968). Other authors have suggested that Adams was bisexual and had had a relationship with James Dean, among others.

flagrant affairs crushed Kurt, and Courtney, though she considered herself the paradigm of a liberated woman, threatened to kill several of Kurt's girlfriends.

When Mrs. M I (Pam) first met Mrs. M II (Patricia), she assured her successor she and Morrison hadn't "balled for over a year" and that she was totaly "cool" with her. Patricia didn't buy it. "Basically, she [Pam] was a totally dependent junkie who had nothing in her life but Jim," she wrote, "and she was . . . maniacally jealous and paranoically terrified of losing him."[8]

After the wives' tête-à-tête, their husband arrived. Proving that everything was indeed "cool," the bigamist star engaged them in a ménage a troix game of War in which he quickly devastated their collective forces. Then Pam excused herself to do some junk and amyls, and Jim consummated for the last time with Patricia. Afterward, he told her that he would be leaving for Paris with Pam because "I kind of feel responsible for her. . . . I owe her." But he promised Patricia he would come back to her soon. Then he asked if she'd kill herself if he died in Paris. Because, by this time, he felt that he had only one "beautiful friend" left: The End.

Before leaving to meet his fate overseas, he had that farewell drink with his old nemesis and lover Janis, and the two stars actually hugged.

By this time the Queen of the Blues had had her fill of the Saturday Night Swindle. But of the four serious marriage proposals she'd had, two seemed like true love: Travis Rivers and David Niehaus. She turned down Rivers because she didn't want to miss having fourteen-year-olds. She turned down Niehaus—who didn't even know who she was when first meeting her—because "he's determined to turn me into a school teacher's wife."

While Janis was waiting for the perfect man to show up, she admitted to getting it on "with a couple thousand cats and a few hundred chicks." Her nymphomania—which eclipsed even the satyriasis of Lennon, Hendrix and Morrison—came to full flower in her last five-day tour during which she estimated having sex sixty-five times.

By now having realized, like Hendrix, that caring fucks up ambition, she had abandoned her Big Brother family and their manager, Chet Helms, who had given her her start. She said she'd kill anyone

---

8. Patricia Kennealy-Morrison, *Strange Days*.

who stood in the way of her career. Joni Mitchell wasn't surprised. "She was the queen of rock and roll," the singer told *Mojo* magazine, "then *Rolling Stone* made me the queen of rock and roll and she hated me after that." "Women, to be in the music business, give up more than you'd ever know," the Queen of the Blues told an interviewer. ". . . You give up an old man and friends, you give up every constant in the world except music."

In the end, like Morrison and Lennon, she grieved that no one loved her. Then she ran into the "silver-tongued devil," Seth Morgan, and accepted his proposal of marriage. In the flush of the romance, it didn't occur to her that he meant to use her.

After Janis's death, Morgan went on to marry other girlfriends: the first whose face he paralyzed in a motorcycle crash, the second whom he addicted and pimped out. Before his violent death, he confessed to being "an addictive personality growing up in an alcoholic household," and that throughout his life he had engaged in "the strategic degradation of women" who reminded him of his mother who had drunk herself to death in his youth.

Janis spent her last night at Barney's Beanery trying to drink Seth off her mind. On returning to the Land Mine alone, maybe she'd been thinking about her only true love, David, when she'd recorded "Bobby McGee" days before: "But I'd trade all of my tomorrows for one single yesterday / To be holdin' Bobby's body next to mine."

As the saying goes, a beautiful song comes from a broken heart. Love can break a heart, but so can its masqueraders—infatuation and need. The hearts of these great musicians were broken, but by which? They had been loved, but had they really loved?

A person must love himself before he can love someone else, as another saying goes. Narcissism aside, did any of the stars love themselves—not their dazzling images but themselves alone, as human beings? It can take a lifetime to get to this point because first a person must find out, more or less, who he or she is.

To varying degrees all Seven were dedicated to this search. The deeper the soul, the deeper and longer the search. Unquestionably, these were people of great depth and complexity. So the searches were long, especially for the introspective Lennon, Morrison, and Garcia. But even the less reflective Elvis never stopped asking himself who he was and asking God why He had made him Elvis Presley, adored by millions and yet so lonely. It was a predicament shared by all Seven. Their struggles to find true love gave their music a tormented power, but their isolations grew with their celebrity.

During his separation from Yoko, John had cried, "I'm finally being myself for a change, and nobody wants me!"

"Love cannot save you from your own fate," said Morrison, expressing the fatalism many felt in the end.

Jerry Garcia might have agreed. The love life of this original San Francisco love child had not been any less troubled or confused than that of the others.

Garcia was the marrier of the Seven, but had followed the pattern. He'd had four wives. Number 1 supported him: he left her. Numbers 2 and 3 rescued him from ODs and diabetic comas: he left them. In her eulogy, Number 4 called herself "the love of Jerry's" life: she had taken his money but complained that it wasn't enough, "bringing Jerry to tears," as a friend said.

"A box of rain will ease the pain, and love will see you through," he sang. Although Garcia may have been the oldest and wisest of all, what brought him to the same lonely end?

7

JERRY GARCIA

August 1, 1942–August 9, 1995

LAZARUS

The head of California's thirty-ninth largest corporation is in full diabetic shock. His blood sugar is the second highest the doctors at Marin General have ever seen. His kidneys have been shut down for ten days. He's running a 105-degree fever from a systemic infection. He's in a coma.

But running on reflex, his legendary hands, as if with a life of their own, try to tear out his breathing and IV tubes.

Outside the ICU, the corridor is packed with family, friends, managers, reporters—and the Hell's Angels. The motorcycle gang, providing security, have taken over the entire floor of the hospital.

Only the patient's wife is permitted inside. She's hysterical. He can hardly breathe, the doctors have ordered an emergency tracheotomy, but she won't allow it. She insists that they have already killed him once with a shot of Valium to which he's allergic. "His heart stopped," she would later say. "He died. The hospital didn't want anyone to know this but he died. They had to resuscitate him."

Even if her husband survives, she's been told that he might be brain damaged and unable to walk again. It's not like she or any of the others haven't seen this coming.

Her husband, the leader of the Grateful Dead, has been courting his dark muse for almost two decades now.

Carolyn "Mountain Girl" Garcia had married Jerry in 1981, five years before this hospitalization. They had become lovers in the sixties and had an on-again, off-again relationship since. A former Stanford student, Mountain Girl—or MG, as she was called—had been the girlfriend of Ken Kesey, founder of the Merry "electric acid test" Pranksters.

By the early eighties, two members of the Grateful Dead had already died—one from substance abuse. And for some time, Jerry had been doing smack, coke, and speedballs himself. "I knew that he [Jerry] was playing with dangerous stuff," MG said. "I realized that he could die at any moment." So she told him, "Look, you know you're going to probably croak here or something bad might happen. I'd feel better if we were married."

A Tibetan Buddhist monk performed the ceremony in an Oakland Auditorium dressing room on New Year's Eve. "But it didn't change a goddamn thing," the bride later confessed.

MG returned to her farm in Oregon. Jerry returned to the road with the Grateful Dead and to his longtime tour mistress: heroin.

His habit continued to escalate and his health to deteriorate. By 1984 he was morbidly obese, his cholesterol was over 900, and his feet had swelled two sizes with edema. He looked "not just dead but like a creature who'd returned from beyond the grave," wrote Robert Greenfield[1] who attended his performances at the time. His wife, friends, and bandmates pleaded with Jerry to seek treatment, but he was obstinate.

He called heroin his "medicine." Explaining its therapeutic value, he told an interviewer, "It's the thing of being removed from desire. Every time you do it, you get off. Except for things like forgetting to eat and all the other little things in life. All that shit slips right past you. That's why people die."

Mountain Girl at last resolved to try an intervention. "Get the fuck out of here!" he roared when MG and his bandmates descended on him.

Personal choice had always been inviolable for Garcia: he never messed with anybody else's trip; he refused to tolerate anybody mess-

---

1. Robert Greenfield, *Dark Star. An Oral Biography of Jerry Garcia* (New York: Broadway Books, 1997).

ing with his—even if he had become the heart of a multi-million-dollar corporation on which many had come to depend. A fact he had come to bitterly regret.

But soon he checked into Narcotics Anonymous. On his way there, he pulled his BMW into a no-parking zone in Golden Gate Park and did a speedball. He was arrested for possession of twenty-three packets of heroin and cocaine. This was his third bust.

He spent his detox days painting, running his remote-control cars, building model Uzis and other guns, and watching TV. Emerging clean and revived, he returned to the road. But he soon fell off the wagon again.

At the end of a mini-tour with Dylan and Tom Petty in the stifling summer of '86, he found himself slipping into a peculiar state of mind. "I felt like the vegetable kingdom was speaking to me in Italian and German accents. Potatoes and radishes and trees were all speaking to me," he recalled. "It gave me a greater admiration for the incredible, baroque possibilities of mentation."

No sooner had he returned home when his housekeeper, Nora Sage, found him comatose on the bathroom floor.

The doctors administer more Demerol to the unconscious Garcia while nurses strap his hands so they can't pull the tubes. MG watches in horror as his leviathan, three-hundred-pound frame twitches and kicks on the gurney. He seems to be having a nightmare.

At last he becomes still and his eyes open. He sees his wife and the doctors huddled around him, not saying a thing as if he were deaf. "Why are you looking at me?" he whispers to his speechless wife. "I'm not Beethoven. I'm not deaf."

The hospital is soon in pandemonium—family, friends, bandmates, and Hell's Angels celebrating the incredible news. "The doctors said they'd never seen anybody as sick who wasn't dead," Jerry would later recall. Then he added, "I really felt that the fans put life into me."

But his recovery is slow and laborious. "After I came out of my coma, I had this image of myself as these little hunks of protoplasm." Experiencing what he called "Joycean inversions of language," he has difficulty talking. He must learn to walk again. And he must learn to play guitar again.

His friend and collaborator, Merl Saunders, teaches him. "We started off very slowly," said Merl. "It was just like teaching a baby. . . . It would take maybe two hours for him to do two or three chords."

"He was grateful to be alive," said David Nelson, his bandmate in the New Riders of the Purple Sage. "For him, it was the second time. The first was the car accident in Palo Alto."

The accident had occurred twenty-five years before.

"It was where my life began," said Jerry of the crash that claimed a close friend, yet spared him. "That was the slingshot for the rest of my life."

THE SLINGSHOT

Named after American composer Jerome Kern, Jerome John Garcia was born on August 1, 1942. His father, Joe, a clarinetist bandleader, had played on Mary Pickford movie scores. After being fined by the musician's union for doing a free performance, Joe became a bar owner in San Francisco. Jerry would later call himself "the black sheep of a black sheep."

Jerry's mother, Ruth "Bobbie" Clifford, worked as a nurse at San Francisco General Hospital. She painted, loved opera, and was into astrology, palmistry, and the cosmic historian Immanuel Velikovsky.

Jerry and his older brother, Tiff, enjoyed a carefree early childhood. Then one day Tiff accidentally chopped off four-year-old Jerry's finger when they were splitting kindling.[2]

Just after his fifth birthday, Jerry went on a camping trip to the northern California coast with his parents. He and his mother were sitting on the bank of the Trinity River watching his father fish for steelhead, when suddenly Joe lost his footing and the current overtook him. "I actually saw him go under; it was horrible," Jerry recalled. His father's death, he said, "emotionally crippled me for a long time."[3]

Jerry and Tiff moved in with their maternal grandparents, the Cliffords, while Ruth took over Joe's sailor bar, The 400 Club. Their grandpa Bill was a retired laundry truck driver; their free-spirited grandma Tilly let the boys do as they pleased. A delinquent like Lennon, Hendrix, and Cobain, Jerry would later confess to setting fire to

---

2. The Dead guitarist would later offer to auction off the missing digit for Jerry's Kids [The Jerry Lewis MDA Telethon].

3. Other family members maintain that there were no witnesses to the accident.

the hills and, another time, breaking seventy windows in the back of a police station. "I was pathologically antiauthoritarian," he said.

He credited his seventh-grade teacher, a sci-fi scholar and Vincent Black Shadow motorcyclist, as "the one who turned me into a freak." Jerry had to repeat eighth grade because "I was too smart for school." After being placed in an accelerated program, he became a voracious reader. His favorite books were Orwell's *1984* and Joyce's *Finnegan's Wake.*

Taking after his father, Jerry's great love had always been music. His first instruments were his grandma Tilly's banjo and ukulele. Then, for his fifteenth birthday, his mother surprised him with an accordion that he pawned for an electric guitar and amp. "I was beside myself with joy," he recalled. After seeing *Rock Around the Clock* in 1956, he started practicing incessantly—not only guitar, but saxophone and piano too. "You're going to be a rich and famous rock 'n' roll star someday," his best friend and future roadie, Laird Grant, told him.

Then Garcia made an important discovery that he later revealed to *Rolling Stone.* "I was fifteen when I got turned on to marijuana. Wow! Marijuana. It was great, it was just what I wanted . . . that wine thing was so awful, and this marijuana was so perfect!" To supplement, he scored "candy," as he called it, from street gangs. "He'd have about fifteen different kinds of colored pills," remembered Laird. ". . . These were unknown substances—Ups and Downs and Sideways and Tranks. We'd drop all of that and then go tripping in San Francisco."

At seventeen, Jerry dropped out of high school and joined the Army. "I wanted so badly to see the world . . . Germany, Korea, Japan, *anywhere,*" the antiauthoritarian later explained.

Private Garcia earned decorations for carbine and surface-to-air missile marksmanship. Then he drove missile trucks at the Presidio. He soon tired of "the incompetent leading the unwilling to do the unnecessary in an unbelievable amount of time." So one morning he found himself in a motel room off base trying to convince a GI buddy not to shoot himself. Though his friend was "a total fuckup" and "trouble incarnate," he was also a hot guitarist and had taught Jerry how to fingerpick. When Private Garcia returned to base, he was slapped with an AWOL and court-martialed. Concluding that the young man was "not suited to the military lifestyle," the court granted him a "hardship discharge," just as they had Hendrix at the same time back in Kentucky.

Jerry blew his severance on a thrashed 1950 Cadillac and smoked his way to the hip university town of Palo Alto. There he hung out with artists, folkies, and beat poets. One was a teenage Englishman, Alan Trist, who would later head the Grateful Dead's publishing company; another was a precocious painter and actor, Paul Speegle.

One night, after a party where they'd been playing what they called "death charades," Jerry and Alan piled into Paul's Golden Hawk Studebaker. The coupe was topping a hundred near the VA Hospital when it lost a curve, careened through a fence, somersaulted, and slammed on top of the driver. Jerry, at shotgun, flew through the windshield, breaking his collarbone. Paul Speegle was declared dead at the scene.

"I was a changed person," said Jerry. "It [the crash] was cosmic. . . . It was where my life began. Before then I was always living at less than capacity. I was idling. That was the slingshot for the rest of my life."

Fellow survivor, Alan Trist, agreed. "This was when we were all coming into adult life. It had a profound effect on Jerry. It made him aware of life's fragility. Of how things could be taken away."

Music now became Jerry Garcia's all-consuming passion. Like Hendrix at the same time, he practiced constantly. The two were musicians' musicians. Whereas for others music was a vehicle, for them music in and of itself was the be-all and end-all. The essence.

"That's *all* he did," declared his girlfriend, Barbara Meier. "That's it. He played music. He was totally dedicated."

Jerry met Barbara soon after the accident. The bright, bohemian fifteen-year-old student modeled part-time for Pepsodent. Though Jerry teased her about it, she bought him two guitars with her toothpaste money. They broke up after a few years, but reunited again after Jerry became head of the Dead empire.

The guitarist now took up with Sara Ruppenthal, a Stanford co-ed, peace activist and friend of Joan Baez. Sara soon got pregnant. She and Jerry threw a shotgun wedding in the spring of 1963.

"We stopped being friends basically after we were married," Sara recalled. "Parenthood wasn't something he could participate in." Jerry spent little time with her during her pregnancy. "He lived for music," she continued. "He'd be in a bad mood if he couldn't practice for several hours a day. He was very ambitious. He wanted to do something big. . . . I thought if he had a good woman behind him he could go far."

Sara worked part-time for her father at the Stanford Business School. Jerry brought in a few dollars as a guitar teacher, but spent most of his time gigging with his new bluegrass band, the Wildwood Boys, in South Bay bars, in bookstores, and at hootenannies. "I don't have to grow up and I'm not going to," he told Sara after their divorce based on this irreconcilable difference and his monogamous affair with music.

Robert Hunter co-founded the Wildwood Boys and would become the Dead's lyricist. A University of Connecticut dropout, Hunter was into Tibetan mysticism, Beat poetry, and old-timey bluegrass. The Boys' career high point came at the Newport Folk Festival featuring Dylan;[4] Doc Watson; Peter, Paul, and Mary; and other luminaries. The Wildwood Boys won the amateur bluegrass competition.

Though by this time Garcia was a banjo and bluegrass virtuoso, a musical Renaissance man, he wanted to branch out. Encouraging him in new directions were some new Bay Area bohemians: Phil Lesh, Bob Weir, and Ron McKernan.

A classically trained musician and jazz aficionado, Lesh had studied under John Cage at Julliard; he worked as a mailman and underground deejay, and wanted to be a composer. Weir, a guitar student of Jerry's who had been kicked out of seven private schools, aspired to outdo his idols, the Beatles. The third, Ron McKernan—aka "Pigpen" (after the *Peanuts* cartoon character)—blew killer harp; played Hammond B-3, Dobro, and slide; and, to boot, sang the blues like a Mississippi Delta black man.

Jerry, Bob, and Pig started out as Mother McCree's Uptown Jug Champions. They morphed into the Warlocks when Lesh came aboard in '65. "The Beatles were why we turned from a jug band into a rock 'n' roll band," said Weir after they all watched *A Hard Day's Night*. "What we saw them doing was impossibly attractive."

Pigpen became the lead vocalist of the group, Garcia the de facto leader. "Jerry could be very direct and actually quite cruel to band members if they met with his displeasure," remembered Sara. "People were scared of him. He was a hard taskmaster." Lesh agreed. When first joining the Warlocks, he objected to Garcia because, "This guy has too much power."

But Jerry hated power trips: he just knew not only that the group needed work to become a cohesive unit, but, more importantly, to find out who they really were musically.

---

4. Dylan first played electric here, horrifying folk purists.

BIRTH OF THE DEAD

> The Grateful Dead looked like they were almost dead.
> They were just twenty-year-olds. But a bizarre-looking group of people.
> —Grace Slick, the Jefferson Airplane

Soon after the Warlocks formed, Jerry dropped acid for the first time.

His Wildwood Boy partner, Hunter, had guinea-pigged psychotomimetic (madness-mimicking) drugs at the CIA's Chemical and Bacteriological Lab at the VA Hospital.

This interested Jerry. So as soon as a bluegrass friend laid some Sandoz on him, he and Sara jumped down the rabbit hole. "We freaked out badly," recalled Sara. They managed to drive to Hunter's house. "We beat down the door," she continued, "and woke up Hunter . . . because he had *The Tibetan Book of the Dead,* so clearly he could help us."

After consulting the book identifying the "bardo" states in the itinerary of the soul, he told Jerry and Sara, "It's okay!"

"He just cut through the freak-out and we were so relieved," said Sara. "Of course it's okay! Thanks, man. Sorry we woke you up!"

After that, Jerry started dropping acid religiously. He would tell an interviewer that under the influence of LSD he, like his lyricist, had "ridden up to the heavens and had been shown the face of God."

Not long after that debut trip, Garcia was at Lesh's house with the other Warlocks, smoking DMT. Still dissatisfied with their band name, they were discussing options. Jerry opened Weir's Funk & Wagnall's dictionary at random and found himself staring at *Grateful Dead.* The term came from an old English folktale: a good Samaritan pays for the burial of a beggar who later returns from the dead to save the Samaritan's own life and win him a fortune.

The Warlocks hated the name at first, and they weren't alone. When meeting the Maharishi for the first time, the guru told them: "I must tell you something, children. You must not be calling yourselves 'Grateful Dead.' You must call yourselves 'Eternal Living!' And you must wear silken pajamas."

Rebels to a man, the band rejected the silk pj's and became the Grateful Dead.

"We always thought of it [the name] more as the death of the ego than any specific legend," Jerry would explain. Since ego loss and selflessness are central to tripping, LSD naturally became the sacrament

of the Grateful Dead. And the name solidified their identity: the Dead
became the world's first alchemical, cosmic band.

"Magic is what we do," pronounced Jerry. "Music is how we do it."

As in the folktale, the Dead were penniless until a Samaritan arrived:
Owsley Stanley, "the Johnny Appleseed of LSD." The grandson of Kentucky senator Augustus Stanley, Owsley had been expelled from military school, became an Air Force rocket scientist, then retired to study
Russian, ballet, and to brew his magical compounds. Soon becoming
the largest private producer of LSD, he developed many colorful brands:
White Lightning, Purple Haze, Blue Cheer, and Orange Sunshine.

The chemist first crossed paths with the penurious Dead at a Merry
Prankster Acid Test. A motley assortment of space cadets, the Pranksters were led by the alpha crazy, Ken Kesey. Owsley, aka Bear, provided his head meds for the party; the Dead provided the tunes. "Acid
Tests planted the seeds from which the Grateful Dead grew like Jack's
beanstalk," wrote Carol Brightman.[5] Garcia called the tests, "ordered
chaos."

Bear had an even more dramatic take on the test when it was put to
music that afternoon with the Pranksters. "Garcia's guitar seemed to
come out of the universe and try to eat me alive," he said. "This band is
going to be bigger than the Beatles! That was my thought as I listened
to this incredible cosmic shit they were playing."

The mad scientist trucked the band down to Watts and rented them
Big Pink,[6] a three-story stucco tenement next door to a whorehouse.
Recalled a Dead family member, "Owsley was in charge of paying for
it and, the massive control freak that he was, he controlled every single
thing, down to what we ate." Bear told his band, "We're going to eat
nothing but red meat. And eggs. And we're going to drink only milk.
No vegetables. No fruit."

The only "nonbleeding food group" he allowed was his own produce: purple electric Kool Aid fermented in thirty-gallon garbage pails.
In a two-year period, Owsley cooked 1,250,000 hits of LSD. "We had
enough acid to blow the world apart," Jerry remembered. "Tripping

---

5. Carol Brightman, *Sweet Chaos: The Grateful Dead's American Adventure* (New
York: Clarkson Potter, 1998).

6. Several years later, in Woodstock, New York, Robbie Robertson's group, The
Band, rehearsed in their own funky abode, Big Pink, which resulted in their debut
album, *Music from Big Pink*.

frequently if not constantly. That got good and weird." The Dead's new manager, Rock Scully, once found Garcia under the dining room table hiding from a Tamal Indian shaman ghost who "accused him of ancient outrages perpetrated by the Spaniards against his tribe."

Within months the Dead returned north and moved into a funky Victorian in the Haight. Here, Bob Weir swore off drugs entirely and went on a strict seaweed and rice diet. "My system is now so clean I don't need to use toilet paper!" he boasted to the band.

The only other just-say-no guy was Pigpen, a Ripplehead since the age of twelve. Acid scared the shit out of him. He'd gotten dosed once at the Fillmore East, lost all sensation of his legs and location, and stammered, "I'm transparent. I see it all now. And I don't like what I see." He was rescued from the vision by Dead wet nurses and Wilson Picket records.

The band gigged around town with the Airplane, Quicksilver, Janis's Big Brother, and other friends before scoring a recording contract with Warners whose stable included Frank Sinatra, Dean Martin, Petula Clark, and other less than revolutionary artists. When meeting with executive Joe Smith, the band made no bones about their ethic. "I don't need anything," Garcia told him. "I don't really want anything. I've got instruments; I know I can eat. We're not sacrificing any of ourselves to do business."

"They hated everybody [in business]," said Smith. "They just hated me a little less." Still, the deal almost didn't fly. "They told me I couldn't really understand their music until I dropped some acid," Smith went on.

He told the Dead that understanding a product wasn't indispensable to marketing it. In a word, no. He said being strapped to a gurney on Thorazine wasn't part of his job description. As for the Dead, except for the acidophobic Pig, they shared the Merry Prankster H-bomb ethic about dosing innocents: "Where they go up and where they go down, it's not my department,' says Werner von Braun." The band signed the contract anyway. And in the future, Smith managed to stay straight by seeing as little of the band as possible.[7]

---

7. Years later, when Hugh Hefner had Garcia on his *Playboy After Hours* show, the publisher drank only canned soda, guarded by a personal assistant. Geraldo Rivera was not so paranoid when he had the Dead, Mick Jagger, Grace Slick, and a Beach Boy on his 20/20 *Not Too Old to Rock 'n' Roll* special in 1981. Phil Lesh, who carried acid in a Visine bottle, managed to dose the reporter's champagne.

"The record company was scared of us," said drummer Mickey Hart. ". . . They couldn't eat anything or drink anything around us because they were afraid everything had LSD in it, so they never really showed up."

The band's debut album, *The Grateful Dead*, was recorded in less than a week, with the help of speed, pot, and acid.

By this time, the Dead had an underground following that reached unexpected quarters. While playing New York, they received an invitation.

Salvador Dalí requests your presence at his Exquisite Corpse Brunch in Suite 210 at the Pierre Hotel.

On arrival, the band was introduced to the Spanish painter by Tom Wolfe, author of *The Electric Kool-Aid Acid Test*, who said he'd first met them at an Acid Test. Dali demanded an explanation. "It's where young people take LSD and dance to rock music," explained Wolfe. Whereupon the surrealist shuddered, crossed himself, and exclaimed, "I do not take drugs. I *am* drugs!" The former art student, Jerry, now ventured to ask the master how he achieved such exquisite detail on his *Crucifixion* and *Dripping Clocks*.

"Tiny brushes," replied Dali. "Tiny baby hair, soft as Gala's [his wife's] bottom, made from the pubic hair of capuchin monkeys!" It was then the Dead realized that they wouldn't have to dose the surrealist after all.

Another trippy encounter the group had in its infancy was with the Cherokee shaman, Rolling Thunder. The medicine man had once "smoked" the Fillmore for the Dead, ridding the auditorium of evil spirits. Satisfied with his services, the Dead asked Rolling Thunder if he could heal Jerry of double pneumonia. The guitarist had contracted the disease from sleeping in an old school bus next to his house. The Dead were about to tour.

"Cancel the fuckin' dates," moaned Jerry. "I'm dying here!"

Rather than doing this and hospitalizing him, the Dead summoned the shaman on a house call. Rolling Thunder, who moonlighted for the Union Pacific Railroad as a brakeman, arrived at Garcia's hideaway in the redwoods with his instruments: eagle wing, claw, abalone shells. While the band built a fire, laid out a stone circle, and gutted a chicken, the Cherokee chanted over the ailing star.

Suddenly, according to Rock Scully,[8] "The claw grabs on to Rolling Thunder's arm and the wing stands up by itself!" Just then, unaware of the goings-on, a roadie barges in, crosses the "path of sickness, spins around, and blacks out." Then Rolling Thunder—"taking all of Garcia's poison on himself"—turns green, stumbles outside, and "vomits his guts out."

As for Jerry, his own color quickly returned, and he felt like a million bucks.

Incredulous but grateful, manager Scully told the retching shaman, "Name anything you want, there's nothing I wouldn't do for you!"

"I want your woman," declared Rolling Thunder, without skipping a beat.

Rock's chick, Nicki, had suggested calling in the first place. But Rock asked if he wouldn't prefer instead Jerry's chick, Mountain Girl—since, after all, it was Jerry he cured.

"Hey, Rock, thanks a lot!" cried MG.

"Mountain Girl is too scary," replied the shaman, still eyeing Nicki.

Russian Jewish from New York, Nicki looked rather like a Cherokee. "Listen, guys, it's okay," she announced to the relief of Jerry and everybody except Rock, "I'll handle it."

And so it was that Garcia received yet another new lease on life.

SKULL FUCK

Take a snip of this then play a little riff, don't be afraid to try.
Don't need no airplane to get off the ground, there's more than
one way to fly.
—Garcia and Hunter, "Cocaine"

Before they recorded their second tripping album, *Anthem of the Sun*, the Dead got busted for pot. Everybody was arrested except Jerry who was running errands when the narcs arrived.

"We're a nation of outlaws!" he declared afterward. The incident precipitated the band's exodus from Haight-Ashbury in the summer of 1968. Rock felt they had been "cast out of Eden." But, by now, the

---

8. Rock Scully, *Living with the Dead: Twenty Years on the Bus with Garcia and the Grateful Dead*, with David Dalton (New York: Broadway Books, 2002).

Haight was no longer acid, love, and flowers—but smack, crank, and crime.

The next year the Dead *were busted down on Bourbon Street, set up like a bowlin' pin.* This time it was for acid uppers and downers. Jerry was collared, along with Bear Owsley and seventeen others. Out on suspended sentences, the Dead now released a live album they wanted to call *Skull Fuck.*

"You can't do this to me!" cried Warner's Joe Smith. In deference to the long-suffering executive, Jerry and the band settled for the tepid *Skull & Roses.*

The Dead had begun touring relentlessly. In '69, they did 143 dates. In '70, 145. With the addition of a second percussionist, Mickey Hart, and a second keyboardist, TC Constanten, they had become a Wagnerian jamming band, which blasted a "wall of sound" far beyond anything its original inventor, Phil Spector, had dreamed for "Good Vibrations." Hart, a precocious student of African drumming, added a hypnotic but driving, tribal dimension to the Dead's rhythm. The band was among the first to use two drummers. Improvising brilliantly off each other, Hart and Kreutzmann became known to Deadheads as "The Rhythm Devils." Together with bassist Lesh and "Hammondman" Pig, the four provided the rolling thunder, above which the Garcia-Weir-TC-Godchaux melody and harmony lightning flashed. Every performance of the eight Dead became an unpredictable, soaring collective vision engulfing the audience.

"When the Dead are playing their best," said Hunter, "blood drips from the ceiling in great, rich drops. Together we do a kind of suicide in music."

There was only one problem in their cosmos, or two: Weir and Pigpen. "I don't think that Pig, without being high on LSD, could quite understand the direction the music was going," explained space cowboy, Scully. Still, he thought he was tripping when Jerry—never one to play the heavy himself—ordered him to fire both Pig and Weir too.

Why? Rock demanded.

"Weir for never coming down from Planet Zippy," explained Jerry. "And Pig for never getting off this one."

Weir, who had long since abandoned his seaweed diet, was kiting autistic ragas; and Pig, still nursing Ripple, was stuck down in the twelve-bar blues. So Rock dutifully fired them. But "they just kept coming back," reported Jerry ruefully.

The problem resolved itself when, in early 1973, Pig—age 27, like

Jones, Joplin, Hendrix, Morrison, and Cobain—died of a perforated ulcer and sclerosis of the liver. Jerry was devastated. The tragedy had a cumulative impact since there had been many other fatalities in the extended Dead family recently.

Pig's father had passed away, as had Lesh's. Both Weir's parents came next. Then, in the fall of 1970, Jerry's mother had suffered a fatal car accident. When her German shepherd puppy jumped between her gas and brake pedal, she careened off a coastal cliff, landing in a cypress tree, and died in the hospital soon afterward.

Hardly a week later, Jerry's close friend, Janis Joplin, OD'd. "The payoff for life is death," said Jerry, "Janis was on a real hard path. She picked it, she chose it, it's okay. She did what she had to do and closed her books."

As if these casualties were not enough, the Dead had suffered a huge financial setback and, in 1971, temporarily lost their drummer Mickey Hart. Mickey's father, Lenny, a born-again preacher, had taken over the band's haphazard bookkeeping and straightened things by disappearing with the cash. After gambling $150,000 away in Lake Tahoe, he was arrested in San Diego where he was doing ocean baptisms. He died in prison two years later. His distraught son, Mickey, dropped out of the group for three years.

Garcia weathered these misfortunes by immersing himself in non-Dead music: collaborations with Howard Wales, Merl Saunders, David Grisman, New Riders of the Purple Sage,[9] and, later on, with his own group, the Jerry Garcia Band. The other members of the Dead didn't appreciate their leader's extracurriculars, but for him they were a lifeline. In spite of the debilitating stage fright that plagued him till the end, Jerry had an insatiable appetite for performance and for musical variety.

If Dead concerts were religious experiences for its expanding army of fans, "the Deadheads," they were not always so for Jerry. "We were plumb atrocious," he said of their 1969 Woodstock performance. "It was raining to boot and I was high [on Czech acid] and I saw blue balls of electricity bouncing across the stage and leaping onto my guitar."

Three months later, at the Stones' Altamont concert, Jerry and the band refused to take the stage after the drunk and cranked Hell's Angels' "security men" knocked the Jefferson Airplane's Marty Balin

---

9. In its first incarnation, the country rock group had also included Phil Lesh and Mickey Hart.

unconscious and flogged fans with pool cues, killing one. "It was like hell," Garcia said later, ". . . a nice afternoon in hell." A far cry from the "Gathering of Tribes Human Be-In" the Dead had done two years before in Golden Gate Park where the Angels cared for lost children and everybody was on Owsley Purple.

The times they were a changin' and the Dead's and everyone else's choice of dope was too: if the sixties were pot and acid, the seventies became downers and speed—expanders and elevators versus accelerators and depressives. Jerry had done meth and black beauties recreationally, but coke demanded commitment.

"If anything ruined our lives it was cocaine," said MG. "Jerry and I had fights about it. . . . Coke turned me into a horrible whining Nazi bitch, and I decided it was not my drug *immediately.*"

In the spring of 1973, Jerry was busted again, this time with Bob Hunter. A cop pulled the songwriting team over on the Jersey turnpike for speeding and found a briefcase full of coke.[10]

Years later, on a hot summer day in '80, he nearly got busted again while driving a VW bug on the Oregon interstate. He and Rock were nursing a tank of nitrous oxide when the top blew off. They veered to the side of the road and bailed out, Jerry screaming, "Close the fuckin' door. Save the gas!" The inside of the bug froze up with nitrous. Just as the resourceful Rock was pissing on the door lock to thaw it, Highway Patrol arrived. The cop asked the two nitroused freaks about their NASCAR move to the shoulder. "We hit an icy spot, officer." declared a tweety-voiced Jerry, in the hundred-degree heat. "It's a goddamn mystery!"

By now, Garcia regarded getting busted as an "occupational hazard." "It's like if you're working on a skyscraper," he observed. "If you're paranoid about falling, you shouldn't be working." Given his frenetic touring and recording schedule, natural energy just wasn't enough to keep Casey Jones on track. But doing coke cuts brake lines and pretty soon you're playing Chicken with a wall. So Jerry installed the finest brakes money could buy:

Persian heroin.

According to the New Riders' leader, Marmaduke Dawson, Jerry was first introduced to "Persian" in 1975[11] by a swami friend who ran

---

10. Garcia and his lyricist received one-year suspended sentences.

11. Blair Jackson, *Garcia: An American Life* (New York: Penguin, 2000) puts the date of the Persian introduction later, at 1977.

an ashram. His steady suppliers became two Iranian car-dealer brothers whose father had been the Shah of Iran's police chief. Jerry was not a virgin user. "Heroin had been on the fringes of the Dead's world since the sixties," wrote Blair Jackson. ". . . And the drug even gained a foothold at Mickey Hart's ranch [in the early seventies]." But in those earlier days, he had only "chipped" smack. It wasn't until he was introduced to Persian a decade later that he became seriously addicted.

About 95 percent pure heroin, Persian is smoked—a process called "chasing the dragon." Ancient Persian warriors were said to have heated the gum on their swords and slashed themselves before battle, rendering them less squeamish about being cudgeled or impaled. For the rock warrior Jerry, it took the edge off the coke and helped with his stage fright too.

There was only one problem with Persian, at least for others: "You're really an unpleasant person to be around," his former patron Bear Owsley told Jerry after getting out of jail for the '69 bust.

"I like what it does," Jerry shrugged. In short, it's none of your business—fuck off.

Garcia's dragon partner and procurer was his Sancho Panza, Rock Scully. Rock shipped bindles (small paper packets) of Persian ahead to where the Dead would perform. Jerry refused to play cities where a stash wasn't in place. His bindles became almost more important than his life.

Before a '79 gig at Madison Square Garden, the Dead's management received a note: "Jerry GARCIA dies 2NITE!!"

When Jerry refused to cancel the concert, FBI agents in wigs and yellow tie-dyed tees took position in the first rows. Jerry remained calm during the performance, and it went off without incident. But no sooner did he hurry offstage than he dashed back wild-eyed and shouted over the PA to the departing Deadheads and wigged-out feds:

"WHO THE FUCK STOLE MY STASH? Where's my BINDLE?"

The Dead seldom toured abroad due largely to the difficulty of transporting their leader's medications. But there were notable exceptions.

Jerry had always dreamed of playing the Great Pyramids in Cairo. Fearing a *Midnight Express* gig with Egyptian customs, it remained a dream until a connection of Weir's liberated a Percodan-Demerol-Dilaudid delivery from a pharmaceutical outfit. So in late 1978, Jerry and the Dead family of two hundred—including Owsley, Kesey, basketball great Bill Walton, and others—chartered a jet loaded with meds rivaling Elvis's.

But Garcia's distaste for over-the-border gigs was soon renewed in Toronto. Recalled Rock: "Jerry had to submit to the indignity of being finger searched up his asshole with a rubber glove, which naturally soured him on playing Canada for many years to come."

In '81, Jerry got an SOS from Pete Townshend. The Who had just imploded and canceled their European tour. Pete begged the Dead to replace them. Knowing Garcia refused to perform without his monkey, Townshend assured him that he had already made arrangements for him to be met at the Edinburgh airport by a Persian wholesaler.

When Jerry reached Britain, he found Pete in a bad way. The Who was breaking up, his wife was divorcing him, and he was a million pounds in the hole. Suffering "black fits of depression and suicidal thoughts," according to Rock, Townshend was downing four pints of brandy a day, plus smack. Jerry suggested they drop some Owsley together for a change of perspective. The composer of "My Generation" finally perked up at dawn.

"Fuck me," he stammered, gazing at the fiery horizon and flocking birds. "It's still out there, innit? Bloody Mother Nature, man!"

If the Reverend Lenny (Hart) had put a dent in the Dead's treasury, Jerry's smack habit drove a truck through it. By the eighties, he and Rock were on a $700-a-day Persian diet, each. As for the coke—"God's way of telling you you're making too much money"—they didn't bother with the arithmetic.

Jerry soon developed severe bronchitis and other pulmonary problems from freebasing, chasing the dragon, and chain-smoking Camels. Rock called him "Chief Smoking Moccasin" because Garcia would often nearly set himself and his rooms on fire. And, like most junkies, he was into junk food—downing hot dogs, M&M'S, and great quantities of Häagen-Dazs ice cream, which led to diabetes. Also, like Elvis, Cobain, and other hardcore users, he stopped washing.[12]

"It got to the point where he'd call me up in Oregon," said his daughter, Annabelle, a young teenager at the time, "and nod off while he was on the phone. . . . It was really super awful."

The other members of the Dead, though far from clean themselves, had grown alarmed too. In '85, they fired the pair who they thought

---

12. "You don't like the way I smell?" he asked his friends. "Spray *yourself* with cologne." He couldn't keep girlfriends because they couldn't "handle the stench," according to Rock.

were the worst influences on Jerry: mega-dopers Scully and Trist. But it turned out that Jerry's misery didn't need company. He was more than happy to fix solo. The only one who had the balls to confront him personally was his wife, Mountain Girl, exiled in Oregon with Annabelle. She recalled: "The band members would call me and say, 'God, MG, you've gotta do something.' So I'd drive down there and try . . . but he didn't want to do anything about it. He was really strung out."

"I was pretty out there," Jerry would later admit, "but I was still mainly a maintenance junkie. . . . I was never an overdose kind of junkie. I've never enjoyed the extremes of getting high."

Though he conceded that his habit was "like a black hole," he kept his sense of humor. Running into an old manager, Jon McIntire, his first words to him were: "I've been a stone fuckin' junkie for the last two years. What you been doin?"

Not all of his friends could take this lightly. "He was in terrible shape," said his other lyricist, John Perry Barlow. "Finally I said, 'Sometimes I wish you'd flat die so we can all mourn you and get it out of our system.' "

Garcia walked away without a word and closed himself in his room with a "DO NOT DISTURB" sign on the door.

Then, just after completing the Dead's mini-tour with Dylan in the summer of 1986, he fell into his coma and was rushed to the Marin General.

SECOND COMING

> The flame from your stage has now spread to the floor.
> You gave all you had. Why you wanna give more?
> The more that you give, the more it will take
> To the thin line beyond which you really can't fake . . .
> Fire! Fire on the mountain!
> —Garcia and Hunter "Fire on the Mountain"

Jerry left the hospital after a month. He was now able to walk, though falteringly; he was able to talk without "Joycean inversions"; and he was still re-learning the guitar.

He, Mountain Girl, and their two teenage daughters, Annabelle and Trixie, rented a houseboat upstate on Lake Shasta and enjoyed a family vacation together. Said MG: "He was clean for the first time in how many years? . . . I remember that as being one of the very happiest periods that we ever had."

The family flew to Hawaii. Here Jerry discovered an unexpected natural high: scuba diving. "It takes up some of the space that drugs left, insofar as it's like going to a different world," he said. "It's better than taking drugs. . . . It's a living theater of psychedelia, just incredibly beautiful."

But by the end of that year, Garcia's sabbatical ended. It was the longest rest he would ever have: five months. "We tried being a family again and it worked out for quite some time," said MG. "But nothing lasts and the Grateful Dead had to go back on the road. . . . It was much too soon but Jerry's ego was not going to let him sit in that chair any longer."

The bigger reason was that "the monster" as he called it now— the Grateful Dead machine—needed to be fed. All its employees and hangers-on desperately needed a financial transfusion after five fallow months.

"Garcia's return was greeted as a veritable Second Coming by his fans," wrote Blair Jackson.

Gone were the robotic Dead of the early eighties. At their debut comeback performance at the Oakland Coliseum, the second song Jerry sang was new to the Dead repertoire—a gospel rendition of Dylan's "Forever Young," which was greeted by deafening cheers.

Weeks before, warming up with the Jerry Garcia Band, he had shouted "I WILL SURVIVE!" during "Touch of Grey" that brought tears to fans' eyes. Adding levity to the resurrection, the Dead did a live video featuring life-sized skeleton puppets of each band member, which dissolved into their real selves for the climax.

The Deadheads had returned with a vengeance. A surrealistic parking lot scene blossomed outside the stadiums and coliseums. There were palmists and tarot readers; elixir, amulet, and bong vendors; macrobiotic burrito and electric brownie cooks; tie-dye T-shirt, Jerry doll, and hemp hat hawkers. All that was missing was carob-coated Thorazine. The vendors used their proceeds to bankroll traveling with the band. By the late 80s, or "Mega-Dead" period, Deadheads—hundreds of thousands strong—became their own demographic. They had developed their own dress, slang, and dervish "Spin" dancing. They divided into groups: the Spinners, the Rainbow Tribe, the Gay Deadheads, and "Jews for Jerry." The "Church of Unlimited Devotion" was born.

"The unique organicity of our music," wrote Phil Lesh, ". . . allowed us to meld our consciousnesses together in the unity of a group mind."[13] In other words—spurning the star-driven and egocentric theater of other famous bands—the uniqueness of the Dead's music was in its ego-freeing, spontaneous, and all-embracing nature. The Dead were not performers so much as channelers and lightning rods. They would improvise all night long; other bands played their hits in short sets, often cut shorter when the star was sick, moody, or just pissed off.

In short, the Dead were an "un-star" band. Ironically, though, the personality at the creative and spiritual core of their sound—Jerry Garcia—became a star for being an un-star. At first he regarded this with an amused detachment but, as the years passed, his un-star celebrity came to weigh heavily on him. "Jerry never wanted to be the leader of anything," his manager pointed out. "That was why he never spoke on stage." Said Jerry, "It's always been a matter of personal honor not to manipulate the crowd." He called it a power trip and "a Hitler thing."

In honor of his miraculous recovery from his coma, the band management asked Deadheads not to bring dope to concerts anymore. But Garcia, ever the antiauthoritarian and evangelist of personal choice, protested: "I'm not a cop. I'm not into telling people what to do, *ever*, man!"

Jerry's resurrection from near death catalyzed a marketing bonanza almost unprecedented in pop music. "It's an interesting problem to have, the problem of being too successful," mused the former homeless guitar teacher, now the de facto CEO of California's thirty-ninth largest corporation. "It's one of those things that completely blows my mind." He insisted that the Dead needed to be "de-promoted."

"Oh no. Not more money!" he would groan on seeing another contract or royalty.

His once penniless hippie band was now fabulously wealthy. It was like the Grateful Dead fairytale had come true: the poor beggar returns from the dead to give a fortune to the good Samaritan for burying him. The Dead had buried plenty of the poor since 1970: Pig, Keith, Jerry's mother, Mickey's father, Bob and Phil's folks.

Now in violation of everything he'd believed, Jerry was becoming a Midas, a tycoon, and a brand name. He was not just a stellar musician now—he was an ice cream flavor, a necktie designer, a hotel suite designer, a social icon. In late 1986, hippie ice cream entrepreneurs, Ben

---

13. Phil Lesh, *Searching for the Sound.*

& Jerry, came out with the hi-octane "Cherry Garcia" in honor of the sugarholic who had narrowly escaped a diabetic coma.

More ironic still, Jerry's neckties, emblazoned with psychedelic designs from his DMT trips, became America's number one accessory; by the early nineties, they were being worn by the president, vice president, and many congressional noninhalers. So hot were the ties that J. Garcia Inc. was offered a $5 million boxer shorts deal. But his manager shot it down saying "I don't want people sitting on Jerry's art."

As for Garcia, he was getting seriously bummed by it all. "I liked it when you could just be a musician," he told *Good Times* magazine. ". . . I like to avoid adding to that celebrity bullshit." Confirmed Scully, "He hated the fame that made him into a sacred monster."

When the Dead were inducted into the Rock and Roll Hall of Fame in 1994, Jerry refused to attend the ceremonies. "He didn't think he was worthy," explained his new manager, Sat Khalsa. "All the fame and adulation embarrassed him."

"I'm just a guy who plays guitar," he kept insisting.

But what bothered Garcia more than anything else—far more than having been turned into a commodity, a celebrity, and a CEO—was being considered some sort of a guru. "This scares the shit out of me," he told his boyhood pal, Laird Grant. "Some people at the shows think I'm some kind of a fucking prophet or something. . . . It's like that Manson thing. You get caught up in that kind of power. I don't want it. . . . God, if I could play my music and not have to deal with any of this, it would be the happiest day of my life."

But he couldn't seem to avoid beatification even from his own people. "I loved him more than I loved anything," said Rich Loren, another manager. "I loved him because he was such an almost perfect person. He was unpretentious. He was compassionate. He was humble. In a way, he was a Buddha."

So Garcia kept returning to the dragon because it was the only thing that delivered him from his suffocating fame, his sacred image, and all the people who depended on him. More than that, dope pulled him off the pedestal and deafened him to the clamor around him.

The Second Coming ended when Brent Mydland fatally overdosed on a speedball. There seemed to be a hex on Dead keyboardists. First it was Pigpen in '73. Then his replacement, Godchaux, had a fatal car crash in '80. Now, Mydland in '90. Hart should have been dead too. The drummer had recently driven his Porsche off a cliff and was caught by a single tree, saving him from a three-hundred-foot plunge.

The rest of the Dead, funeral fatigued by now, were philosophical. "Hey, shit happens," they said. "You can't make an omelet without breaking a few eggs." At the burial, one of the pallbearers, wiseacre Weir, pretended to drop Mydland's coffin.

After their '91 tour, the Dead pulled another intervention on Jerry. They knew that he'd stayed clean for almost a year after his coma, but then had begun chipping the Persian until he'd become a full-blown junkie again. It was the Dead's drummer, Bill Kreutzmann, who delivered the ultimatum to the star. "Either you gotta quit this Persian shit or you're fired!"

"Promises, Promises!" sighed Jerry. "Okay, after careful consideration, I'm afraid I have to go with the Persian. Anyway," he continued, "who you gonna hire? It's a lot easier to find a drummer than it is a lead guitar player."

His bandmates didn't need to be reminded that Garcia *was* the Dead. But even if they tried to make a go of it without him, it was all the same to him. After Mydland's death, he'd told them the band wasn't "fun" for him anymore. "We've been running on inertia for quite a long time. . . . In order for it to be fun, it has to keep changing."

But finally bowing to peer pressure, he checked into a methadone program in San Francisco. When he was clean again, he and the Dead went back out on the road with new material, and their fourth keyboardist, Bruce Hornsby.

Hornsby, the perfectionist leader of his own popular band, the Range, soon grew upset with Garcia. "He wasn't listening and starting to run roughshod over people's solos," complained Hornsby, ". . . and the music just seemed strangely lifeless." So after a particularly embarrassing performance in Boston, the keyboardist told him, "I really resent your coming to this gig and not putting anything into it."

"Well, man, you don't understand twenty-five years of *burnout!*" Garcia shot back.

But he got the message. "And from then on, man," recalled Hornsby, "the shit was happening!"

At least until Jerry collapsed again just as he had six years earlier.

THE EMPEROR AND HIS NURSES

In ancient China, you know which kind of patient
is the most difficult to treat? The emperor.
—Yen-wei Choong, Garcia's acupuncturist

Jerry had always joked that if he hadn't gotten into trouble with drugs, he probably would have gotten into trouble with women—which was worse. Opiates stifle libido. Persian had been his old lady for ten years. Divorced or at least separated from it now, he longed for real companionship again.

In 1987, he had taken up with a twenty-seven-year-old Deadhead art student, Manasha Matheson. He'd met her a few years before when she came backstage and gave him a pumpkin she'd carved. "When Jerry had his near death experience," recalled Manasha, "he told me that he promised himself that if he made it, he was going to see me." Rendezvousing with her after a Dylan/Dead gig, he assured her his relationship with Mountain Girl had for some time been platonic.

Manasha soon delivered Jerry's fourth daughter, Keelin. A New Age father, the guitarist suggested that she and the baby move in with him, MG, Annabelle, and Trixie. Manasha declined. But she remained his constant tour companion for several years. At last, his wife had had enough. "In 1990, I gave up," MG said. "I just let go. I realized that it wasn't going to work out."

After she left, Jerry proposed to Manasha. They decided on an Easter wedding. But when Easter arrived, he still hadn't divorced MG and the Dead were scheduled to tour. His fiancée was furious. Her predecessor might have forewarned her. "Having a family is probably going to ruin my artistic career," Jerry told MG years before.

In 1992, Jerry, suffering from congestive heart failure and emphysema, fell into another coma. He had turned fifty only days before. When he came to, he begged Manasha not to call an ambulance. He dreaded a return to the hospital, not to mention the publicity.

His fiancée called his acupuncturist. Yen-wei diagnosed the patient's disease as heart chi exhaustion and toxin (drug) poisoning. Jerry had somehow managed to conceal from Manasha his renewed addiction. Nor had he told her that his other doctors had informed him two years before that he only had two years to live if he continued fixing.

The Dead's autumn tour was canceled. Meanwhile, Yen-wei worked on the emperor three times a week. And Manasha put him on a strict low-fat vegan diet and exercise regimen. Afterward, he was sixty pounds lighter and clean. Hardly had he resumed touring again when he fell off the wagon once more.

Manasha delivered him Sophie's Choice: either the drugs or her. She might have known this was a no-brainer for Jerry. Besides, by this time, he had already rekindled with his old flame Barbara Meier, the Pepsodent model, now a poet. She'd met Jerry again in 1991 on a book tour for her new collection of verse, *The Life You Ordered Has Arrived*. When she saw him for the first time in twenty-eight years, "My heart chakra exploded," she said. Feelings were mutual. "I've never forgotten you," Jerry told Meier. "I've never let go of you. I've always loved you."

Of course, in addition to all his other nondisclosures, Jerry had neglected to tell Manasha about Barbara too. His friends had tiptoed around Manasha, considering her a "control freak," a "space case," and "an intense chick." Jerry hadn't minded in the beginning because, as he'd always said of his women, "I like 'em weird. The weirder the better." Except now, the prospect of dumping Manasha freaked him a little. He confided to Barbara that she might "kill me."

Breakup psychodramas had never been Garcia's trip, anyway, so he resorted to his old MO. He didn't break up with Manasha—he just split. He took Barbara on a Hawaiian scuba vacation, leaving a manager to deliver his ex a "Dear John." When he returned from the islands, Manasha tried to phone several times. Finally, Barbara picked up the phone and snapped, "Don't call here ever again!" and hung up. Then Manasha received notice from Garcia's attorney to vacate his house in thirty days. Jerry would never again see Manasha or their daughter, Keelin.

The romantic aftermath of his second health crisis was a carbon of the first. After his first recovery, he left Mountain Girl, the wife who had nursed him back to health, for Manasha; after his second recovery, he left Manasha, who had nursed him back to health, for Barbara.

Jerry's curtain call with Barbara followed his old romantic pattern. He was happy for a while, but soon became morose and uncommunicative. "Oh, he was vile," she recalled. "He was cold and he was withholding." At first she just thought it was irritability—he was doing hypnotherapy to quit smoking cigarettes. But then he turned into "a real bastard" when she accompanied him on the '93 Dead tour. At last she discovered the reason: he was back with his dragon lady. When she confronted him, he exploded, telling her they were finished.

"I thought we were getting married!" she cried.

"Yeah, well. I meant it at the time," muttered Jerry.

Then he told her the whole truth. "I'm in love with another woman. . . . I can't shake her."

The other woman, Jerry's last, was Deborah Koons. Like Manasha, Deborah had the reputation of being a high-strung control freak. And, like Barbara, she was a retread. He'd had a two-year affair with her in the mid-seventies, which had ended bitterly. "I felt that I'd lost my identity in Jerry's life," she said afterward.

Now Ms. Koons was an independent filmmaker and an astute businesswoman. Many in the Dead family, holding her responsible for the breakup with Mountain Girl years before and with the well-liked Barbara, now, called her "Black Deborah." "With her black hair, black clothing, and black sunglasses, she seemed to be the exact antithesis of MG's hearty, outgoing manner," observed Phil Lesh. Some years before, Mountain Girl had, according to the bassist, wiped "a possessive little smile" off Deborah's face by throwing her against a door and ripping the hinges off.[14]

Jerry and Deborah were married on Valentine's Day, 1994. After the wedding, they continued to live in separate houses. Not long before, Jerry's daughter, Annabelle, asked him for advice on how to make her own upcoming marriage work. "Don't live together, don't see each other," her dad told her. "Have separate houses and have somebody to take care of all your stuff!"

As for the institution of matrimony generally, the star remained old-fashioned. When his drummer's daughter told him she was about to wed, he exclaimed: "That's totally cool! Everyone should try marriage once or twice in his life!"

Now Jerry, breaking his own rule, was on #3. But he had little more than a year left to live and, due to his health and his habits, he must have known it.

Said the Dead's manager, Vince Welnick, "We were all aware he was pretty sick. . . . I think he knew he was dying."

---

14. In the end, the filmmaker would exact her revenge by forbidding MG to attend Garcia's funeral, and by suspending her alimony payments from his estate.

BOX OF RAIN

Walk into splintered sunlight,
Inch your way through dead dreams to another land.
Maybe you're tired and broken,
Your tongue is twisted with words half spoken and thoughts
unclear . . .
A box of rain will ease the pain, and love will see you through.
—Garcia and Hunter, "Box of Rain"

After his marriage to Black Deborah, Jerry collapsed backstage in the middle of a Garcia Band performance in Phoenix. He had suffered another diabetic attack. His doctor advised a renewed health regimen. Jerry ignored the advice. Not that he wasn't alarmed, at least professionally. His diabetic condition, aggravated by carpal tunnel syndrome, was now causing him to lose sensation in his hands.

In early 95, Jerry had a near fatal car accident. He was speeding north on the 101 through Mill Valley, when he lost control of his BMW loaner, ricocheted off the retaining wall, spun, and came to a stop facing oncoming traffic. Miraculously, he was uninjured.

He now took a last and much-needed vacation. He and Deborah enjoyed a belated honeymoon on the island of Bonaire, off Venezuela, a haven for scuba enthusiasts.

That spring, he returned to the road with the Dead and the Jerry Garcia Band. Forgetting the words to his songs, he was now using lyric monitors. Suffering from major hearing loss, too, he needed ear monitors. His legendary guitar solos had become anemic and faltering. For the first time in the history of the Dead, there were harsh critical reviews and thousands of empty stadium seats.

At the Garcia Band's last performance in April, manager John Kahn knew there was nothing left. "It was like he lost interest. . . . He wanted out. He wanted to change his life around."

That summer he embarked on what was to be the last Grateful Dead tour. He did so out of financial necessity. His overhead was enormous now. He paid Mountain Girl a monthly alimony of $20,800. He was putting Barbara through art school. He was covering Manasha's mortgage for her San Rafael mansion, as well as child support for Keelin. And his new high-maintenance wife, Deborah, was going through over twenty grand a month. All this on top of his exorbitant and relentless drug habit.

The Dead of course knew that their leader was off the wagon yet again. But after the unsuccessful interventions of the past, they had now surrendered to what they called, "a resignation born of futility."

On Jerry's last tour, which he dubbed "The Tour from Hell," he received another death threat. Other Dead members wanted to cancel the engagement at Indiana's Deer Creek Amphitheatre. But Jerry would have none of it. Like the Madison Square Garden gig seventeen years before, the gates were filled with metal detectors and undercover cops manned the first rows. Jerry added "Dire Wolf" to the playbill that night, with its refrain of "Don't murder me, I beg of you. Please, don't murder me."

The show went off without incident except when ticketless fans crashed the gates and the cops broke out the tear gas and German shepherds.

The Grateful Dead played their swan song at Chicago's Soldier's Field a week later. The high point of the evening came with Jerry's "So Many Roads" vocal on which he repeatedly wailed the chorus, "So many roads to ease my soul!" bringing tears to the eyes of many.

After the performance, the Dead's manager, Vince Welnick, speaking for the entire band, said: "Thank God it's over."

On return to the West Coast, Jerry checked into the Betty Ford Clinic. He had confessed his addiction to his wife, Deborah, and told her, "My body's shot." She urged him to enroll in the stringent four-week program, and so he did. He withdrew from the clinic after only two weeks and called his friend and collaborator, Robert Hunter.

"Hey, Hunter, it's Garcia. I just got out of the Betty Ford Center!"

"How was Betty?" asked his old acid buddy.

"She was a great fuck, man!" replied Jerry.

But he'd hated her program. They made him go "cold turkey," he told Hunter, they only gave him pills to control convulsions, "and the food—aargh—it makes airplane food seem like gourmet dining. . . . I think the plan is to make you so miserable you don't ever want to go back."

After this last conversation with Hunter, Jerry phoned many other old friends. "He may have been calling people to say good-bye, more or less in a parallel reality way," observed his personal assistant, Sue Stephens.

Said his pal, Alan Trist, after speaking with Jerry for the last time, "He was trying to get out something before he died. . . . He knew he didn't have long and he *had* to do this. There was no sense of regret that he was about to die or of guilt for having created the conditions for his own death."

Jerry now entered Serenity Knolls, a Bay Area holistic health retreat. He had not told Deborah of his plan. On finding out, she was furious. According to his manager, John Kahn, the couple had a "big fallout" the night before he left for Serenity. "She really hurt him in a lot of ways—things about money," Kahn recalled.

"He came over to our house a lot of times almost in tears," explained Kahn's wife, Linda. "He said she [Deborah] didn't have any faith in him. She wanted money in the bank because she didn't think he could go out and make it. . . . That really hurt him."

"The Grateful Dead, the Jerry Garcia Band, his wife, drugs. He really wanted to get away from everybody," concluded John Kahn.

On the evening of August 8, a week after Jerry's fifty-third birthday, Deborah took him to dinner at an Italian restaurant then drove him back to Serenity Knolls.

Just before dawn, a counselor looked into his room and found the star lying on top of his bed in sweatpants and T-shirt "cuddling an apple like it was a baby, with a smile on his face."

The county coroner was called, and Jerry Garcia was pronounced dead of a massive heart attack.

Twenty-three years before, after viewing the remains of his bandmate, Ron McKernan, Jerry had taken Rock Scully aside and told him, "There are just two things I want you to promise me: Don't ever find me in the back of a record store signing records and don't bury me in an open casket."

His wife, Deborah, arranged an open casket funeral for him at St. Stephens Episcopal in Tiburon. The church overflowed with grieving family, friends, and musicians.

"He had a nice little smile on his face," observed one.

"He looked pretty happy," said another.

"He just looked peaceful," thought a third.

Another just said he'd seen him "look worse."

A fifth noted "this look on his face of perplexity."

Carlos Santana eulogized him as "a profound talent who cannot be replaced."

"One of the brightest, most articulate minds of his generation," agreed David Crosby.

Concluded Dylan: "There's no way to measure his greatness . . . or to convey the loss. . . . He really had no equal."

POSTMORTEM

Jerry Garcia left a third of his estate to his widow, Deborah Koons, and divided the remainder among his four daughters; his stepdaughter, Sunshine Kesey; and his brother, Tiff. Claims totaling $38 million were filed against the estate by MG, Barbara, Manasha, and others. In 1996, Court TV televised what *People* magazine called "The War of the Wives." MG sued Deborah for discontinuing her alimony payments. Deborah lost and appealed. In 1998, MG settled for $1.25 million.

The Grateful Dead disbanded. Deadheads mourned and dispersed, but kept the memories alive with thousands of newsletters. Many began following the Dead-inspired jamming band, Phish.

In 1998, Weir, Lesh, and Hart reunited as the Other Ones, which later included Kreutzmann and Hornsby. In 2003, they renamed themselves the Dead. In 2001, Bob Weir founded his own band, Ratdog.

Jerry Garcia continues to cast a long, but benign shadow over his bandmates, his family, friends, and countless fans. Among the stars of rock and roll, he distinguished himself as the only un-star and a musician's musician. Both onstage and off, he shunned theatrics, posing, publicity, and image making. For this reason, he didn't implode in his own myth, and he outlived his colleagues.

A true countercultural rebel artist, Jerry Garcia shunned money and commercialism too, but they ultimately overtook him. Some have called him a sellout. But he had resisted wealth and fame all along and finally threw up his arms in resignation. Above all, to the end, Jerry Garcia remained faithful to the only thing that had ever mattered to him: his magical music.

Epilogue: Life

Eventually you fall through the lowest circle and then you fall into the light.
—Marianne Faithfull

The biggest gift your fans can give you is just treatin' you like a human being, because anything else dehumanizes you.
And that's one of the things that has shortened the life spans, both physically and creatively, of some of the greatest rock and roll musicians.
—Bruce Springsteen

"The more you live, the less you die," was Janis's motto. "You can destroy your now by worrying about tomorrow."

The Seven were of a single mind on this: better one day as a lion, than a hundred years as a lamb, as the saying went. In their one day, each experienced timeless, ecstatic moments the likes of which few ordinary mortals will ever know. But the highs came with crushing lows. If each had known heaven on earth, they had been through hell too. In the dark hours, all had longed for a normal life.

Janis would have chucked it all, she said, for a "white picket fence and an old man who comes home at six." If Morrison had had it all to do over again, he preferred the "undemonstrative little artist plodding away in his own garden trip." Hendrix believed "people who dig ditches don't know how good they've got it." Garcia would have given anything to become "just an ordinary guitar player" again. After the Beatles, John was ready to become "a fuckin' fisherman." The King himself said he was "tired of being Elvis Presley," and regretted that he hadn't become a preacher. In his farewell letter, Cobain wrote: "I haven't felt the excitement of . . . creating music . . . for too many years now."

But, at the outset, all had been possessed by a singular overwhelming ambition: to "make it." Fame comes to some by chance. Not so with the Seven. They all knew what they wanted and each went after it single-mindedly. They had purpose. Some never find a purpose, never fully living but only existing, subsisting, till the end. Not so with the Seven.

But once they made it, they struggled with the fundamental human question. Elvis often asked himself, as did the others: Why am I here? To become rich and famous? To please others? To help others? To fight bad and promote good, love, and peace? To understand? To become enlightened? During the course of their careers, the stars would have replied yes to most of these questions. But in the end, each found the rich, famous, and pleasing others part of it empty.

Arguably, all but Garcia died unfulfilled. The others still wanted something. How is this possible, we ask? Each had the world at their feet. Or did they?

"Fame puts you where things are hollow . . . what you get is no to-morrow," Lennon sang. But what he wanted in the end was "to conquer the world again," this time solo, without the Beatles. "Fame and fortune, how empty they can be," sang Elvis. But, in his last days, he mourned, "How will they remember me? I haven't done a classic film." Janis sang that she didn't think she was "very special," but in "Work Me Lord," sang "The worst you can say all about me is that I'm never satisfied." She hoped that her last album, *Pearl,* would change that. "There's a fire inside everyone of us," she had sung in "Kozmic Blues," "I better use it till the day I die."

The other three died dissatisfied, not because they wanted more of the same, but because they wanted an elusive something else. Morrison dreamed of becoming a legendary poet like Rimbaud and Baudelaire. Hendrix hoped to escape his legal entanglements, leave the stage, and create "sky" music. Cobain wanted to abandon the spotlight, chart a new musical direction, and live with his beloved daughter, Frances.

Only the longest lived of the Seven, Jerry Garcia, died with a measure of tranquility. He had hit speed bumps along the way, very nearly dying twice. But he was the only one except Lennon who evolved, who molted, and who climbed to the next stage until he had given his music everything he had, and it came to full fruition.

Each star had strived for a different thing: Elvis wanted to entertain and enrapture; Hendrix to electrify; Lennon to teach and challenge;

Garcia to enlighten and transport; Morrison to awaken and provoke; Cobain to purge his rage; and Janis to soothe her aching heart. But they all sought to realize themselves in the same thing: rock and roll. Not the tame kind. But the wild kind. The kind that bursts the limits of emotion. The dangerous kind. The kind that captures lightning in a bottle.

"Life'll kill ya," sang Warren Zevon. Especially those who live it and play it to the hilt as a spectator sport. The Seven had such an insatiable lust for life, they amped themselves and turned the dials to the max. Pure life is electricity. To watch any of them perform at their peak was to watch pure, uniquely filtered, electricity. Soon their performances became their lives and their lives their performances. One never knew if it would all end for them in one final explosive spectacle or just a slow burnout. Few in their audiences would have traded the security of their own cautious lives for the dangerous excesses of the stars. But to watch them on the high wire was a vicarious thrill.

The stars agreed that performing could be the ultimate high. Yet, at the same time, it was utterly exhausting. Especially night after night, year after year. Burned out in the end, most longed for the rush of the old days. If it could only again be like when he'd done his live TV satellite *Aloha!* show for over a billion fans worldwide, thought Elvis. Or the Beatles' first appearance on *Ed Sullivan*, thought Lennon. Or "Teen Spirit" on MTV again, for Kurt. Or Monterey, for Jimi and Janis. The Whisky for Jim. The Gathering of Tribes in Golden Gate for Jerry. But the bell only rings once, and these would remain memories for all.

Many felt creatively spent in their last days and longed for the spark they'd once had. The recording of the revolutionary debut albums of Hendrix's Experience, Morrison's Doors, Garcia's Dead, and Cobain's Nirvana had only taken a week each. Creative and destructive energy come from the same source. Once the first wanes, the second begins to take over.

Finally, none could forget the great loves that they had lost: Elvis with Priscilla, Jimi with Kathy, Jim with Pam, Janis with David, John with Yoko, Jerry with MG.

So in spite of their incalculable accomplishments, they all had much to regret. The drugs helped them forget but took away most of what they had left, accelerating their self-destructiveness. Had Hendrix, Lennon, and Cobain not been killed, had Janis and Morrison not OD'd—might they have revived and gone on to create even greater work? Possible, but unlikely.

Each had a sense their time on earth wouldn't be long. This lent their music a desperate power and urgency. Even though their times had been short, each left us with an unforgettable and brilliant body of work. Their early deaths were indisputably tragic. But in the end, most had given all they possibly could, not only inspiring us with their incomparable art, but teaching us through the example of their own lives what it is to reach for the sky and immortality.

As Morrison's mentor, Nietzsche, said, "One has to pay dearly for immortality; one has to die several times while one is still alive."

Other stars have been in the crucible too. Like the God-fearing Shadrack, Meshack, and Abednego of Babylon, they have walked out of the furnace alive. Was it faith alone that saved them, or something even more elusive?

When hearing of the death of Jimi Hendrix his close friend, Eric Clapton, wept, "No! Not him! I wish it could have been me. Not him." He cried all day in his garden. "Not because he'd gone," he later explained, "but because he hadn't taken me with him. It made me angry, I wasn't sad, I was just pissed off."

Like Hendrix, the guitarist known as "God" had a monster habit. "It was like a snort of coke in one nostril, a snort of smack in the other, a pint of cheap wine in one ear, a bottle of Scotch in the other—it was full out," he recalled. ". . . I don't know how we got through it with the amount we were taking. I couldn't do it; I would die now." After Jimi's death, Clapton became a heroin addict. "I want to make a journey through the dark . . . to find out what it's like in there. And then come out the other end," he told his best friend, George Harrison. He spent the next eighteen months in a drugged oblivion at Hurtmore, his Sussex estate, assembling model cars and watching TV, much as Garcia would do.

"I'm a very extreme person and I live in a very extreme way," the guitarist confessed. "I've got this death wish; I don't like life." His friend, Pete Townshend, agreed. "I don't think it's rock unless it is in some way extreme," the Who star said. "Unless you come off totally fucked up and go home completely destroyed, you don't feel like you've achieved anything."

By 1973, Clapton had a £1,000-a-week junk habit. After finally kicking, he became a suicidal alcoholic. Some nights "I sat with a bottle of vodka, a gram of coke, and a shotgun," he wrote in his autobiography. He dried out again, but was soon back to the bottle. In the late eighties, he tried to kill himself, swallowing an entire bottle of Valium. Finally, he successfully detoxed at Hazelton Recovery Center. He said that he had done it for his five-year-old son, Connor, who had tragically died and for whom he had written "Tears in Heaven."

In 1998, Eric opened the Crossroads Center in Antigua, investing millions of his own money for the substance abuse retreat. "I'll be an addict till they put me in the ground. . . . I'm pretty much a monk these days," he says of his new life.

After his treatment, he helped save his friend and fellow guitar legend, Stevie Ray Vaughn. The Double Trouble star had a monster bourbon and cocaine habit that brought him to a German hospital throwing up blood. The doctors gave him a month to live. After detox, he told *Guitar Player* what he had learned. "See this?" he said, pointing to the Jimi Hendrix pin on his lapel: "You know there's a big lie in this business. The lie is that it's okay to go down in flames. Some of us can be examples of going ahead and growing. . . . I hit rock bottom, but thank God my bottom wasn't my death."

The star who wrote the book on rock bottom and lived to tell about it was, of course, Keith Richards. "I was the odds-on favorite as rock's next celebrity death," admitted the Rolling Stone. "It didn't happen, despite everything. I'm a survivor. . . . I come from very tough stock and things that would kill other people don't kill me."

Hadn't Janis and Morrison said the same thing?

"You think you're Superman, don't you?" Keith's lover and shooting partner, Anita Pallenberg, challenged. "Well, you're only Superman when you play the guitar! . . . You're no different than anybody else—you can't handle drugs either!"

After many ODs, Richards realized this and admitted he'd had one thing many others hadn't: Luck. "I've been closer to death a few times more than a lot of people," he allowed. And it showed. "Keith looked like Lazarus before Jesus sorted him out," wrote Stones biographer, Stephen Davis, of his appearance at the height of his addiction in the mid 70s. "It's interesting to be standing there working with someone who's dead," observed Laraine Newman when he appeared on *Saturday Night Live*.

But after years in the belly of the rock-and-roll beast, the "Can't Get No Satisfaction" composer resurfaced like a latter-day Jonah, with a message: "I've lived my life my own way, and I'm here today because I've taken the trouble to find out who I am."

This reveals the greatest secret of star survivors besides luck and a new liver: never losing the *will* to live. Though seemingly as self-destructive as the others, Richards never became so trapped in a suffocating legend that he had a death wish. The Lazarus of rock also admits to having one other thing to thank for his life: Family. "I'm a family man. I'm a grandfather now," the guitarist proudly declares these days. "I'm really a benign sort of old chap." The closest he came to hard drugs since his turnaround was when he snorted his father's crematory ashes. Whether he thought of this as a joke or an inoculation for longevity, he didn't say. But he's ready to go the distance. "The idea of retiring is like killing yourself," he now says. "It's almost like Hari-Kiri. I intend to live to 100 and go down in history."

After ending his consumptive relationship with Anita Pallenberg, he married American model, Patti Hansen, on his fortieth birthday. "I know I couldn't have beaten heroin without Patti," he declared. "I ain't letting that bitch go!" The couple have two daughters. "I'm a cynical, hard-bitten motherfucker—I *have* to be," admitted Richards, "but I got these two little chicks at home who can beat me up every time." Then he added, "What children do to you is grow *you* up."

The other legendary rock diehard is his glimmer twin, Mick Jagger, father of seven. "It's all right letting yourself go as long as you can get yourself back," was Jumpin' Jack Flash's motto. Observed his lover Marianne Faithfull, "Mick is so grounded as a person he never loses his footing. He can be right there next to the person falling off the edge but not slip himself." In fact, he had watched her go down to join Brian Jones. When she awoke from a six-day coma, Jagger sat at her bedside wondering why she had tried to commit suicide.

"If I could stick a knife in my heart, suicide right on stage," he sang in "It's Only Rock 'n' Roll (But I Like It)." "Would it be enough for your teenage lust? Would it help to ease the pain? . . . Would you think the boy is strange?" No. For Jagger, sticking a knife in his heart on stage was an act, a pose, a conceit. For stars like Janis and Cobain, it was real. "We've always done it for the money," said Mick. "Man, if it hadn't been for the music, I probably would have done myself in," said Janis.

Jagger decided survival was a question of disposition: some artists are hardwired for consuming unhappiness, others aren't. He once contrasted himself to the suicidal poet, Antonin Artaud, an inspiration to Faithfull, Jones, Morrison, and others. "As Artaud said, he only had three happy days in his life," declared Mick. "He was an unhappy person, and I'm not. I was just born happy and he wasn't."

Keith begged to disagree on the last point. "Ninety-nine percent of the male population in the Western world would give a *limb* to live the life of Jagger," he pointed out. "To be *Mick Jagger*. He's not living a happy life. To me that's unacceptable." The absurdity of it all boggled his mind. "What's so hard about being Mick Jagger?" he went on. "It's like Bob Dylan's phrase once: 'What's so hard about being one of the Beatles?' . . . I mean, this exaggerated sense of who you are and what you should do and worrying about it so much."

It took Dylan many years to shake counterfeit divinity and declare, "God, I'm glad I'm not me!" The spotlight had been more focused and inescapable for Dylan, a solo icon like Elvis. "The pressures were unbelievable," he said. "They were just something you can't imagine unless you go through them yourself." But he managed to persevere because, "It was important for me to come to the bottom of this legend thing, which has no reality at all. What's important isn't the legend, but the art, the work."

It was even harder for Dylan to stay afloat because, "Happiness is not on my list of priorities. For some reason, I am attracted to self-destruction." But, ultimately, what has kept him going is hope, a last key to longevity.

"What do you have to look forward to?" *Playboy*'s Nat Hentoff asked him in 1996.

"Salvation," said Dylan. "Just plain salvation."

Paul McCartney, another legendary survivor, never forgot John's challenge to him. "He would often say, 'If you find yourself at the edge of a cliff and wonder whether you should jump or not—try jumping.' And I'm afraid I would always say, 'No, man, I'm not gonna jump off that cliff; I don't care how good it is."

While Lennon was exiled in the Dakota, doing smack and falling deeper into the pit of his bitter solipsism, McCartney, on his Scottish farm with Linda and the kids, fed the sheep and chickens, bird watched, and composed his silly love songs.

For the sake of their lives, no less than their sanity, many stars got off "the merry-go-round" for a while like Lennon. Hendrix "hibernated like Yogi Bear," as he said, at his Woodstock estate. Elvis holed up in his room at Graceland. Morrison disappeared regularly. Dylan dropped out for two years after a motorcycle accident that was far less serious than he'd let on. "Being noticed can be a burden," said the songwriter. "Jesus got himself crucified because he got himself noticed. So I disappear a lot."

After Lennon was murdered, George Harrison went into seclusion at his Friar Park estate in Oxfordshire. Later with Dylan, he founded the Traveling Wilburys. The stars of the supergroup changed their names and enjoyed themselves for the first time in years. Dylan became Boo Wilbury; Harrison became Spike Wilbury.

Retiring again to Friar Park, George narrowly escaped John's fate. A junkie mental patient, calling the Beatles "aliens from hell," broke into his house and stabbed him ten times, puncturing his lung.

Harrison had suffered severe drug and personal problems, particularly during the Beatle and immediate post-Beatle periods. His marriage to his second wife, Olivia, was a blessing to him. When she gave birth to their only boy, Dhani, George—having always been insecure about being the only childless Beatle—was giddy with excitement. In celebration, he bought a baby blue Rolls Royce. So protective of his new son was he, that he forbade anyone to touch the infant for months.

Though the "My Sweet Lord" composer never went off the cliff, he'd stood at the edge and taken a long look at what lay below. At one time, he and the others had indeed been almost more popular than Jesus Christ. But he rejected this, knowing that becoming a god in the minds of others or in one's own is a fatal condition. That our life is in being men, and an early death is in losing that humanity. That a man's character is revealed not in what he has achieved with public applause, but in what he has achieved without it. And finally, that a man's life should not be judged by what he has been given—talent or luck but by the hard-won virtues he has gained and grown—courage, kindness, and honor.

When George Harrison was diagnosed with cancer, he fought heroically. But in his last days, he greeted death not as an exterminator but as a teacher from whom he learned the greatest lesson of all: to live contentedly but passionately every day, every moment, as if it were his last.

In the end he said, "I'm not really a musician. I'm a gardener."

The quiet, solitary pleasure of tending his garden was greater than any he had known in stadiums filled with adoring fans.

The questions he asked himself in the final days were not those of a superstar, but those of a man like the rest of us.

"For every human," he said, "is a quest to find the answer to 'Why are we here? Who am I? Where did I come from? Where am I going?' That to me became the only important thing in my life. Everything else is secondary."

Selected Bibliography

1. JIMI HENDRIX

Black, Johnny. *Jimi Hendrix: The Ultimate Experience*. New York: De Capo, 1999.

Brown, Tony. *Hendrix: The Final Days*. New York: Rogan House. 1997.

———. *Jimi Hendrix: A Visual Documentary—His Life, Loves and Music*. New York: Omnibus, 1992.

Burdon, Eric. *I Used to Be an Animal (But I'm Alright Now)*. London: Faber & Faber, 1986.

Burdon, Eric, and J. Marshall Craig. *Don't Let Me Be Misunderstood*. New York: Thunder's Mouth, 2001.

Cross, Charles R. *Room Full of Mirrors: A Biography of Jimi Hendrix*. New York: Hyperion, 2005.

Dannemann, Monika. *The Inner World of Jimi Hendrix*. New York: St. Martin's, 1995.

Etchingham, Kathy. *Through Gypsy Eyes*. London, UK: Orion, 1998.

Henderson, David. *'Scuse Me While I Kiss the Sky: The Life of Jimi Hendrix*. New York: Atria, 1978.

Lawrence, Sharon. *Jimi Hendrix: The Man, the Magic, the Truth*. New York: Harper Entertainment, 2005.

McDermott, John. *Hendrix: Setting the Record Straight*. With Eddie Kramer. New York: Grand Central Publishing, 1992.

Mitchell, Mitch. *Jimi Hendrix: Inside the Experience.* With John Platt. New York: St. Martin's, 1990.

Murray, Charles Shaar. *Crosstown Traffic.* New York: St. Martin's Griffin, 1991.

Redding, Noel, and Carol Appleby. *Are You Experienced?: The Inside Story of the Jimi Hendrix Experience.* New York: De Capo, 1990.

Shadwick, Keith. *Jimi Hendrix: Musician.* San Francisco: Backbeat Books, 2003.

Shapiro, Harry, and Caesar Glebbeek. *Jimi Hendrix: Electric Gypsy.* New York: St. Martin's Griffin, 1991.

Willix, Mary. *Voices from Home.* Seattle, WA: Creative Forces Publishing, 1995.

2. JANIS JOPLIN

Amburn, Ellis. *Pearl: The Obsessions & Passions of Janis Joplin.* New York: Warner Books, 1992.

Caserta, Peggy. *Going Down with Janis: Janis Joplin's Intimate Story.* Secaucus, NJ: Lyle Stewart, 1973.

Cooke, John Byrne. *Janis Joplin: A Performance Diary 1966–1970.* Cobb, CA: First Glance Books, 1997.

Dalton, David. *Piece of My Heart: The Life, Times and Legend of Janis Joplin.* New York: St. Martin's, 1986.

Echols, Alice. *Scars of Sweet Paradise: The Life and Times of Janis Joplin.* New York: Henry Holt, 1999.

Faris, Gerald A., and Ralph M. Faris. *Living in the Dead Zone: Janis Joplin and Jim Morrison: Understanding Borderline Personality Disorders.* Faris Ph.D., privately printed, 2001.

Friedman, Myra. *Buried Alive: The Biography of Janis Joplin.* New York: William Morrow, 1973.

Joplin, Laura. *Love, Janis.* New York: Harper Collins, 2005.

Landau, Deborah. *Janis Joplin: Her Life and Times.* New York: Paperback Library, 1971.

Stieven-Taylor, Alison. *Rock Chicks.* Sydney, Australia: Rockpool, 2007.

3. JIM MORRISON

Ashcroft, Linda. *Wild Child: Life with Jim Morrison.* New York: Thunder's Mouth, 1997.

Bernett, Sam. *The End: Les Derniers Jours de Jim Morrison.* Chez les Editions Privé. 2007.

Butler, Patricia. *Angels Dance and Angels Die: The Tragic Romance of Pamela and Jim Morrison.* New York: Schirmer, 1998.

Crisafulli, Chuck. *Moonlight Drive: The Stories Behind Every Doors Song.* Edited by Dave Dimartino. Music Book Services, 1995.

Dalton, David. *Mr. Mojo Risin', Jim Morrison: The Last Holy Fool.* New York: St. Martin's, 1991.

Davis, Stephen. *Jim Morrison: Life, Death, Legend.* New York: Gotham, 2005.

Densmore, John. *Riders on the Storm: My Life with Jim Morrison and the Doors.* New York: Delacorte, 1990.

Fowlie, Wallace. *Rimbaud and Jim Morrison: The Rebel as Poet.* Durham, NC: Duke University Press, 1994.

Hopkins, Jerry. *The Lizard King: The Essential Jim Morrison.* Medford, NJ: Plexus, 2005.

Hopkins, Jerry, and Danny Sugerman. *No One Here Gets Out Alive.* New York: Grand Central, 2006.

Jones, Dylan. *Jim Morrison: Dark Star.* New York: Viking, 1990.

Kennealy-Morrison, Patricia. *Strange Days: My Life with and Without Jim Morrison.* New York: Plume, 1992.

Lisciandro, Frank. *Jim Morrison: An Hour for Magic.* London, UK: Plexus, 1996.

Manzarek, Ray. *Light My Fire: My Life with the Doors.* New York: Putnam, 1998.

Morrison, Jim. *The American Night: The Writings of Jim Morrison.* New York: Vintage, 1991.

———. *The Lords and the New Creatures.* New York: Fireside, 1971.

Riordan, James, and Jerry Prochnicky. *Break on Through: The Life and Death of Jim Morrison.* New York: William Morrow, 1991.

Ronay, Alain. "Jim And I: Friends Until Death." *Paris Match,* 2002.

4. ELVIS PRESLEY

Brown, Peter H., and Pat H. Broesky. *Down at the End of Lonely Street: The Life and Death of Elvis Presley.* New York: Dutton, 1997.

Curtin, Jim. *Elvis: Unknown Stories Behind the Legend.* Nashville, TN, Celebrity Books, 1998.

Dundy, Elaine. *Elvis and Gladys.* New York: Macmillan, 1984.

Esposito, Joe, Lauren McMullen, and Daniel Lombardy. *Remember Elvis.* TCB JOE Enterprises, 2006.

Esposito, Joe, Joe Russo, and Lauren McMullen. *Elvis, Straight Up.* Vol. 1. Las Vegas, NV: Steamroller, 2007.

Goldman, Albert. *Elvis.* New York: Avon, 1981.

Guralnick, Peter. *Careless Love: The Unmaking of Elvis Presley.* New York: Little Brown, 1999.

———. *Last Train to Memphis: The Rise of Elvis Presley.* New York: Little Brown, 1994.

Henderson, William. *I, Elvis.* New York: Berkeley, 1997.

Hodge, Charlie. *Me 'n Elvis.* With Charles Goodman. Castle Books, 1988.

Keogh, Pamela Clarke. *Elvis Presley: The Man. The Life. The Legend.* New York: Atria, 2004.

Nash, Alanna. *Elvis and the Memphis Mafia.* With Billy Smith, Marty Lacker, and Lamar Fike. New York: Harper Collins, 1995.

Ponce de Leon, Charles L. *Fortunate Son: The Life of Elvis Presley.* New York: Hill and Wang, 2007.

Ritz, David, ed. *Elvis, by the Presleys. Intimate Stories from Priscilla Presley, Lisa Marie Presley, and Other Family Members.* Memphis TN: Elvis Presley Enterprises, 2005.

Schilling, Jerry. *Me and a Guy Named Elvis: My Lifelong Friendship with Elvis Presley.* With Chuck Crisafulli. New York, Gotham, 2006.

Stanley, David. *Raised on Rock, Growing Up at Graceland.* With Mark Bego. London, UK: Trafalgar, 1997.

Stanley, David, and Frank Coffey. *The Elvis Encyclopedia.* North Dighton, MA: JG Press, 2007.

Stanley, Rick. *Caught in a Trap: Elvis Presley's Tragic Lifelong Search for Love.* With Paul Harold. Dallas, TX: Word Publishing Group, 1992.

Thompson, Charles C., II, and James P. Cole. *The Death of Elvis: What Really Happened.* London, UK: Orion, 1993.

West, Red, Sonny West, and Dave Hebler. *Elvis: What Happened?* As told to Steve Dunleavy. New York: Vintage, 1991.

West, Sonny. *Elvis: Still Taking Care of Business.* With Marshall Terrill. Chicago, IL: Triumph Books, 2007.

5. JOHN LENNON

Bresler, Fenton. *Who Killed John Lennon?* New York: St. Martin's, 1989.

Coleman, Ray. *Lennon: The Definitive Biography.* New York: McGraw Hill, 1985.

Fawcett, Anthony. *John Lennon: One Day at a Time.* New York: Stein & Day, 1983.

Giuliano, Geoffrey. *Lennon in America: 1971–1980, Based in Part on the Lost Lennon Diaries.* New York: Cooper Square Press, 2000.

Green, John. *Dakota Days.* New York: St. Martin's, 1983.

Grossman, Albert. *The Lives of John Lennon.* New York: William Morrow, 1988.

Harrison, George. *I, Me, Mine.* New York: Chronicle, 2002.

Henke, James. *Lennon Legend.* New York: Chronicle Books, 2003.

Hopkins, Jerry. *Yoko Ono.* New York: Macmillan, 1986.

Jones, Jack. *Let Me Take You Down: Inside the Mind of Mark David Chapman, the Man Who Killed John Lennon.* New York: Villard Books, 1992.

Lennon, Cynthia. *John.* New York: Crown, 2005.

Miles, Barry. *Paul McCartney: Many Years from Now.* Owl, 1998.

Norman, Phillip. *John Lennon: The Life.* New York: Ecco, 2008.

Pang, May, and Henry Edwards. *Loving John.* New York: Warner Books, 1983.

The Playboy Interviews with John Lennon and Yoko Ono. Edited by David Sheff. New York: Putnam, 1981.

Rolling Stone, eds. *The Ballad of John and Yoko.* New York: Doubleday Dolphin, 1982.

Rosen, Robert. *Nowhere Man: The Final Days of John Lennon.* Oakland, CA: Quick American Archives, 2002.

Salwicz, Chris. *McCartney: The Definitive Biography.* New York: St. Martin's, 1986.

Seaman, Fred. *The Last Days of John Lennon.* New York: Birch Lane, 1991.

Shapiro, Marc. *Behind Sad Eyes: The Life of George Harrison.* New York: St. Martin's, 2002.

Shevey, Sandra. *The Other Side of John Lennon.* London, UK: Pan Macmillan, 1990.

Shotton, Pete, and Nicholas Schaffner. *John Lennon: In My Life.* New York: Grove Press, 1976.

Spitz, Bob. *The Beatles.* New York: Little Brown, 2005.

Wiener, Anthony. *Come Together: John Lennon in His Time.* Champaign: University of Illinois Press, 1990.

6. KURT COBAIN

Azerrad, Michael. *Come as You Are: The Story of Nirvana.* New York: Main Street Books, 1993.

Black, Suzi. *Nirvana Tribute: The Life and Death of Kurt Cobain the Full Story.* Omnibus, 1995.

Brite. Poppy Z. *Courtney Love: The Real Story.* New York: Touchstone, 1997.

Cobain, Kurt. *Journals.* New York: Riverhead Books, 2002.

Cross, Charles R. *Heavier than Heaven: Biography of Kurt Cobain.* Hyperion, New York: 2001.

Harrison, Hank. *Kurt Cobain: Beyond Nirvana.* Arkives Press, San Francisco, 2002/2008.

Molanphy, Chris. *Kurt Cobain: Voice of a Generation.* New York: Barnes & Noble Books, 2003.

Rossi, Melissa. *Courtney Love: Queen Of Noise.* New York: Pocket Books, 1996.

Sandford, Christopher. *Kurt Cobain.* New York: Carroll & Graf, 1995.

Thompson, Dave. *Never Fade Away: The Kurt Cobain Story.* New York: St. Martin's, 1994.

Wallace, Max, and Ian Halperin. *Love & Death: The Murder of Kurt Cobain.* New York: Atria, 2004.

7. JERRY GARCIA

Brightman, Carol. *Sweet Chaos: The Grateful Dead's American Adventure.* New York: Clarkson Potter, 1998.

Gans, David. *Conversations with the Dead: The Grateful Dead Interview Book.* New York: Carol Publishing, 1991.

Greenfield, Robert. *Dark Star: An Oral History of Jerry Garcia.* New York: Broadway Books, 1997.

Harrison, Hank. *The Dead.* San Francisco, CA: Celestial Arts, 1980.

Jackson, Blair. *Garcia: An American Life.* New York: Penguin, 2000.

Lesh, Phil. *Searching for the Sound: My Life in the Grateful Dead.* New York: Little Brown, 2005.

McNally, Dennis. *A Long Strange Trip: The Inside History of the Grateful Dead.* New York: Broadway Books, 2002.

Scully, Rock. *Living with the Dead: Twenty Years on the Bus with Garcia and the Grateful Dead.* With David Dalton. New York: Little Brown, 1995.

Troy, Sandy. *Captain Trips: A Biography of Jerry Garcia.* New York: Thunder's Mouth, 1995.

Weir, Bob. *Home Before Daylight: My Life on the Road with the Grateful Dead.* With Steve Parish. New York: St. Martin's, 2003.

ANTHOLOGY SOURCES

Constantine, Alex. *The Covert War Against Rock: What You Don't Know About the Deaths of Jim Morrison, Tupac Shakur, Michael Hutchence, Brian Jones, Jimi Hendrix, Phil Ochs, Bob Marley, Peter Tosh, John Lennon.* Venice, CA: Feral House, 2000.

Des Barres, Pamela. *Rock Bottom: Dark Moments in Music Babylon.* New York: St. Martin's, 1996.

Driver, Jim, ed. *The Mammoth Book of Sex, Drugs, & Rock 'n' Roll.* Philadelphia, PA: Running Press, 2006.

Evans-Wentz, W. Y., ed. *The Tibetan Book of the Dead.* London, UK: Oxford University Press, 1960.

Herman, Gary. *Rock 'n' Roll Babylon.* London, UK: Plexus, 1982.

Huxley, Aldous. *The Doors of Perception.* New York: Harper & Brothers, 1954.

Katz, Gary L. *Death by Rock and Roll: The Untimely Deaths of Rock's Legends.* London, UK: Robson Books, 1995.

Kent, Nick. *The Dark Stuff: Selected Writings on Rock Music.* Cambridge, MA: Da Capo, 1994.

Kohut, Joe, and John J. Kohut, eds. *Rock Talk: The Great Rock and Roll Quote Book.* New York: Faber & Faber, 1994.

Leary, Timothy, Ralph Metzner, and Richard Alpert. *The Psychedelic Experience: A Manual Based on the Tibetan Book of the Dead.* University Books, 1972.

Lenson, David. *On Drugs.* Minneapolis: University of Minnesota Press, 1995.

Luerssen, John D. *Mouthing Off: A Book of Rock & Roll Quotes.* Pittsburgh, PA: Telegraph Company, 2002.

Mckenna, Terence. *Food of the Gods: The Search for the Original Tree of Knowledge.* Bantam Books, N.Y., 1992.

Obstfeld, Raymond. *Jabberrock!: The Ultimate Book of Rock 'n' roll Quotes.* Edited by Patricia Fitzgerald. New York: Henry Holt, 1997.

Patterson, R. Gary. *Take a Walk on the Dark Side: Rock and Roll Myths, Legends, and Curses.* New York: Fireside, 2004.

Pike, Jeff. *The Death of Rock 'n' Roll: Untimely Demises, Morbid Preoccupations, and Premature Forecasts of Doom in Pop Music.* New York: Faber & Faber, 1993.

Quisling, Erik, and Austin Williams. *Straight Whiskey: A Living History of Sex, Drugs and Rock 'n' Roll on the Sunset Strip.* New York: Bonus Books, 2003.

Stanton, Scott. *The Tombstone Tourist: Musicians.* New York: Pocket Books, 2003.

Thompson, Dave. *Better to Burn Out: The Cult of Death in Rock 'n' Roll.* Thunder's Mouth, 1998.

Walton, Stuart. *Out of It: A Cultural History of Intoxication*. New York: Harmony Books, 2001.

Wenner, Jann S., and Joe Levy, eds. *The Rolling Stone Interviews*. Boston, MA: Back Bay Books, 2007.

White, Timothy. *Rock Lives: Profiles and Interviews*. New York: Henry Holt, 1991.

OTHER SOURCES

Clapton, Eric. *Clapton: The Autobiography*. New York: Broadway Books, 2007.

Faithfull, Marianne. *Faithfull: An Autobiography*. With David Dalton. New York: Little Brown, 1994.

Heylin, Clinton. *Bob Dylan, Behind the Shades, Revisited*. New York: William Morrow 2001.

Schumacher, Michael. *Crossroads: The Life and Music of Eric Clapton*. New York: Hyperion, 1995.

Sounes, Howard. *Down the Highway: The Life of Bob Dylan*. New York: Grove, 2001.

Index